THE FOLLOWING PUBLICATIONS AND PRODUCTS MAY ALSO BE ORDERED FROM UNIFORMED SERVICES ALMANAC, INC.

DIVORCE AND THE MILITARY (230 pages $14.95)
This important book deals with the unique issues involved in a divorce when one of the spouses is a military member. Covers dependent benefits, Uniformed Services Former Spouse Protection Act, coverage under the 20/20/20 and 20/20/15 rules, income vs. property issues, legal citations, residence requirements, how to select counsel and many more vital subjects.

AMERICAN GUIDANCE FOR SENIORS (540 pages $19.95)
Award winning book providing vital information for seniors and their caregivers. Covers Social Security, Medicare, health care, assisted living, listings of organizations for seniors, taxes, financial planning and much, much more.

1996 FEDERAL PERSONNEL GUIDE (192 pages $9.95 including postage)
A comprehensive digest of important information on federal compensation, organization, promotions, retirement (CSRS/FERS), insurance, health care, and other benefits for civil service, other federal government employees and supervisors.

MILITARY PAY CALCULATOR PRO™ 96 (Ver 1.1 $15.95)
The ultimate Windows pay program for Active Duty, Reserve (IDT & ADT) and Retired pay. Calculates federal taxes and FICA taxes, SBP, SGLI, BAS, BAQ, VHA, etc., and prints out pay tables and six types of reports. Great tool for "what if" analysis for promotions, retirements and pay raises. Extensive on-line help.

Title	Price	Quantity	Total
DIVORCE AND THE MILITARY	$14.95	x _____	= _____
AMERICAN GUIDANCE FOR SENIORS	$19.95	x _____	= _____
FEDERAL PERSONNEL GUIDE	$9.95	x _____	= _____
MILITARY PAY CALCULATOR PRO™	$15.95	x _____	= _____

(Virginia residents add 4.5% for sales tax)   Subtotal
                                               Shipping & Handling _____
(Excluding Federal Personnel Guide,
add $3.00 for one item, $1.00 for each additional item)
                                               Total _____
Enclosed is my check or money order made payable to USA, Inc.
Please send my order to: (use address label or print clearly)

NAME: _____

ADDRESS: _____

CITY: _____ STATE: _____ ZIP: _____

Mail to USA, Inc., P.O. Box 4144, Falls Church, VA 22044
(For credit card orders, please call, (703) 532-1631. Please allow 4 to 6 weeks for delivery.)

S0-FPI-245

THE FOLLOWING TITLES ARE PUBLISHED ANNUALLY BY UNIFORMED SERVICES ALMANAC, INC.

Title/Publication Date	Price	Quantity	Total
UNIFORMED SERVICES ALMANAC/Jan.	$6.25	x _____ =	_____
RESERVE FORCES ALMANAC/Feb.	$6.25	x _____ =	_____
NATIONAL GUARD ALMANAC/Feb.	$6.25	x _____ =	_____
RETIRED MILITARY ALMANAC/Mar.	$6.25	x _____ =	_____

(Virginia residents add 4.5% for sales tax)   **Subtotal**
                                       Shipping & Handling _____
(Add $1.25 per book for 4th class book mail or $2.25 per book for first class mail.)
                                       Total _____

Enclosed is my check or money order made payable to USA, Inc.
Please send my order to: (use address label or print clearly)

NAME: _____

ADDRESS: _____

CITY: _____ STATE: _____ ZIP: _____

Mail to USA, Inc., P.O. Box 4144, Falls Church, VA 22044
(For credit card orders or multiple copy rates, please call, (703) 532-1631.
Please allow 4 to 6 weeks for delivery.)

The **UNIFORMED SERVICES ALMANAC,** for active duty personnel, provides accurate, timely information on pay, allowances, taxes, health care and CHAMPUS benefits, SBP, retirement, travel and transportation, Space-A, Veterans and Social Security Benefits and many more subjects of vital concern to active duty personnel and their families. The Almanac also contains detailed installation listings and important statistical data.

The **RESERVE FORCES ALMANAC** is specifically prepared for members of the Army, Air Force, Navy, Marine Corps and Coast Guard Reserves. This annual 252 page edition contains detailed drill pay tables for daily, weekend and annual drill periods, plus information on military retirement, tax information and tips, Federal benefits, Reserve Component SBP, VA and Social Security coverage, promotion information and many more subjects of importance for all reservists and their families.

The **NATIONAL GUARD ALMANAC** is published for members of the Army and Air National Guard and their families. This 252 page edition contains detailed drill and annual pay tables, retirement point and pay computation tables, and other important information relative to State and Federal benefits available to Guard members. This is the most comprehensive book on Guard related material available.

The **RETIRED MILITARY ALMANAC** is published, not only for the already retired members, but for all military personnel considering retirement. This 252 page edition contains information on benefits, entitlements, privileges and restrictions as well as detailed coverage of retired pay, military health care, CHAMPUS, VA and Social Security, SBP, legislation, installation listings and many other subjects. Also included is information on Federal and State taxes

★ ★ ★ 1996 ★ ★ ★
UNIFORMED SERVICES ALMANAC

Publisher—Lt. Col. Sol Gordon, USAF (Ret)
Editors— Ronald S. Hunter
MSG Gary L. Smith, USA (Ret)
Debra M. Gordon

PRICE—$6.25

(Plus $1.25 P & H = $7.50 via Book Mail)
($8.50 via 1st Class Mail)
(See inside front cover for multiple copy rates)
Call for special government prices.

Published Annually by:
UNIFORMED SERVICES ALMANAC, INC.
P.O. BOX 4144, Falls Church, VA 22004
Telephone: (703) 532-1631 Fax: (703) 532-1635
E-mail address: MILITARYALMANAC@MSN.COM

Publishers of:
UNIFORMED SERVICES ALMANAC—for active duty personnel
RESERVE FORCES ALMANAC—for members of the Reserve Forces
NATIONAL GUARD ALMANAC—for members of the National Guard
RETIRED MILITARY ALMANAC—for retired personnel

Copyright 1996
By UNIFORMED SERVICES ALMANAC, INC.
Lt. Col. Sol Gordon, USAF (Ret), President
All Rights Reserved
Printed in the U.S.A.
(The publisher bears no responsibility to any person with respect to loss or damage caused directly or indirectly by the information presented.)

UNIFORMED SERVICES ALMANAC
FOREWORD

Although we have occasionally had to delay publication of the UNIFORMED SERVICES ALMANAC in some years due to the delay in passage of vital legislation, this is the first time in our almost forty years of publication that we must go to press before a Defense Authorization Act has been passed. The Authorization Act, although generally paralleling the Appropriations Act, which has already passed, is significant because it includes policy changes that cannot otherwise be implemented. It also is the authority for the DoD to implement the pay raise for military members for their basic pay and allowances, including BAS, BAQ, VHA, etc. Without the Authorization Act, the Uniformed Services will receive an across-the-board increase of 2 percent in pay and allowances effective January 1, 1996 instead of the 2.4 percent increase in basic pay and BAS and a 5.2 percent increase in BAQ and VHA contained in the Authorization Act. Other personnel provisions, including the retired military COLA adjustment, health care, and SGLI are also uncertain without passage of the Authorization Act or other enabling legislation.

Since both the Congress and the Administration have indicated that the amount of the proposed increases for the members are not in contention, and because of the likelihood that a compromise bill will be passed early in 1996 authorizing the increases, we have provided pay and allowance tables and other information based on the assumption that the 2.4 percent basic pay and BAS and the 5.2 percent for BAQ and VHA will, in fact, be the correct figures for 1996.

In addition to the impasse on the Defense Authorization Act, the Congress and Administration have also not been able to get together on other vital legislation which has resulted in a partial shutdown of the government and failure to pass other important legislation including bills affecting the Department of Veterans Affairs. Once again, we have prepared the tables in the almanac based on what we expect the final bills to include for veteran's compensation and pensions.

The **UNIFORMED SERVICES ALMANAC** is not an official publication of the DoD or the United States Government. We do, however, rely to a large extent on many DoD and other government agencies and offices to insure that the information we provide is as accurate and up-to-date as possible. Without the cooperation and assistance of these offices and the personnel who man the desks, our task would be much more difficult. We therefore express our sincere appreciation to everyone who has worked with us, and to particularly acknowledge the cooperation of the Assistant Secretary of Defense (ASD)—Public Affairs; ASD-Health Affairs; Deputy ASD-Military Personnel and Force Management; the Defense Manpower Data Center and the Office of the Actuary; the Defense Accounting and Finance Center; the Department of Veterans Affairs; the Social Security Administration; OCHAMPUS; the Department of Labor; HUD; and several other offices of the military services which have been most generous and cooperative.

The publisher bears no responsibility or liability to any person with respect to loss or damage caused directly or indirectly by the information presented herein.

Sol Gordon, Lt. Col USAF (Ret)
Publisher

UNIFORMED SERVICES ALMANAC
INSIGNIA OF THE UNITED STATES ARMED FORCES
OFFICERS

	WARRANT			COMMISSIONED										
	W-1	W-2	W-3	O-1	O-2	O-3	O-4	O-5	O-6	O-7	O-8	O-9	O-10	
NAVY–COAST GUARD	Warrant Officer W1	Chief Warrant Officer W2	Chief Warrant Officer W3	Ensign	Lieutenant Junior Grade	Lieutenant	Lieutenant Commander	Commander	Captain	Rear Admiral Lower	Rear Admiral Upper	Vice Admiral	Admiral	Fleet Admiral
MARINES	Warrant Officer W1	Chief Warrant Officer W2	Chief Warrant Officer W3	Chief Warrant Officer W4	Second Lieutenant	First Lieutenant	Captain	Major	Lieutenant Colonel	Colonel	Brigadier General	Major General	Lieutenant General	General
ARMY	Warrant Officer W1	Chief Warrant Officer W2	Chief Warrant Officer W3	Chief Warrant Officer W-4/W-5	Second Lieutenant	First Lieutenant	Captain	Major	Lieutenant Colonel	Colonel	Brigadier General	Major General	Lieutenant General	General	General of the Army
AIR FORCE				Second Lieutenant	First Lieutenant	Captain	Major	Lieutenant Colonel	Colonel	Brigadier General	Major General	Lieutenant General	General	General of the Air Force

ENLISTED

	E-1	E-2	E-3	E-4	E-5	E-6	E-7	E-8	E-9
NAVY*	Seaman Recruit	Seaman Apprentice	Seaman	Petty Officer Third Class	Petty Officer Second Class	Petty Officer First Class	Chief Petty Officer	Senior Chief Petty Officer	Master Chief Petty Officer
MARINES	Private	Private First Class	Lance Corporal	Corporal	Sergeant	Staff Sergeant	Gunnery Sergeant	1st Sgt / MSgt	Sgt Major / MGy Sgt
ARMY	Private	Private	Private First Class	Corporal / Specialist 4	Sergeant	Staff Sergeant	Sergeant First Class / Platoon Sgt	First Sergeant / Master Sergeant 8	Cmd. Sergeant Major / Sergeant Major 9
AIR FORCE	Airman Basic ‡	Airman ‡	Airman First Class	Senior Airman	Staff Sergeant	Technical Sergeant	Master Sergeant	Senior Master Sergeant	Chief Master Sergeant

*Includes NAVY and COAST GUARD.
‡Blue Stars on blue background.

3

UNIFORMED SERVICES ALMANAC

ARMED FORCES COMPARABLE RANKS AND ABBREVIATIONS

	ARMY		AIR FORCE		MARINE CORPS		NAVY & COAST GUARD	
COMMISSIONED OFFICERS
O-10	General	(GEN)	General	(Gen)	General	(Gen)	Admiral	(ADM)
O-9	Lieutenant General	(LTG)	Lieutenant General	(LtGen)	Lieutenant General	(LtGen)	Vice Admiral	(VADM)
O-8	Major General	(MG)	Major General	(MajGen)	Major General	(MajGen)	Rear Admiral Upper	(RADMU)
O-7	Brigadier General	(BG)	Brigadier General	(BrigGen)	Brigadier General	(BrigGen)	Rear Admiral Lower	(RADML)
O-6	Colonel	(COL)	Colonel	(Col)	Colonel	(Col)	Captain	(CAPT)
O-5	Lieutenant Colonel	(LTC)	Lieutenant Colonel	(LtCol)	Lieutenant Colonel	(LtCol)	Commander	(CDR)
O-4	Major	(MAJ)	Major	(Maj)	Major	(Maj)	Lieutenant Commander	(LCDR)
O-3	Captain	(CPT)	Captain	(Capt)	Captain	(Capt)	Lieutenant	(LT)
O-2	First Lieutenant	(1LT)	First Lieutenant	(1Lt)	First Lieutenant	(1stLt)	Lieutenant Junior Grade	(LTJG)
O-1	Second Lieutenant	(2LT)	Second Lieutenant	(2Lt)	Second Lieutenant	(2ndLt)	Ensign	(ENS)
WARRANT OFFICERS
W-5	Chief Warrant Officer	(CW5)						
W-4	Chief Warrant Officer	(CW4)			Chief Warrant Officer	(CWO-4)	Chief Warrant Officer	(CWO-4)
W-3	Chief Warrant Officer	(CW3)			Chief Warrant Officer	(CWO3)	Chief Warrant Officer	(CWO-3)
W-2	Chief Warrant Officer	(CW2)			Chief Warrant Officer	(CWO2)	Chief Warrant Officer	(CWO-2)
W-1	Warrant Officer	(WO1)			Warrant Officer	(WO1)	Warrant Officer	(WO-1)
ENLISTED PERSONNEL
E-9	Command Sergeant Major	(CSM)	Chief Master Sergeant	(CMSgt)	Sergeant Major	(SgtMaj)	Master Chief Petty Officer	(MCPO)
E-9	Sergeant Major	(SGM)			Master Gunnery Sgt.	(MGySgt)		
E-8	First Sergeant	(1SG)	Senior Master Sergeant	(SMSgt)	First Sergeant	(1stSgt)	Senior Chief Petty Officer	(SCPO)
E-8	Master Sergeant	(MSG)			Master Sergeant	(MSgt)		
E-7	Sergeant First Class	(SFC)	Master Sergeant	(MSgt)	Gunnery Sergeant	(GySgt)	Chief Petty Officer	(CPO)
E-6	Staff Sergeant	(SSG)	Technical Sergeant	(TSgt)	Staff Sergeant	(SSgt)	Petty Officer First Class	(PO1)
E-5	Sergeant	(SGT)	Staff Sergeant	(SSgt)	Sergeant	(Sgt)	Petty Officer Second Class	(PO2)
E-4	Corporal	(CPL)			Corporal	(Cpl)	Petty Officer Third Class	(PO3)
E-4	Specialist	(SPC)	Senior Airman	(SrA)				
E-3	Private First Class	(PFC)	Airman First Class	(A1C)	Lance Corporal	(LCpl)	Seaman	(SA)
E-2	Private	(PV2)	Airman	(Amn)	Private First Class	(PFC)	Seaman Apprentice	(SA)
E-1	Private	(PV1)	Airman Basic	(AB)	Private	(Pvt)	Seaman Recruit	(SR)

4

UNIFORMED SERVICES ALMANAC

TABLE OF CONTENTS
PUBLICATION DATE -- JANUARY 20, 1996

Foreword 2
Insignia--Officers/Enlisted 3
Table of Comparable Ranks and Abbreviations 4
Table of Contents 5
Selected Legislation of Interest to Military Personnel 8

PART I PAY, ALLOWANCES, BENEFITS, MILITARY RETIREMENT

Military Pay 11
Officers' Pay 12
Officers' BAQ Table 13
Officers' Basic Pay Table 14
Officers' Basic Military Compensation Table 15
Officers' "Take-Home" Pay Tables 16
Officers' Special and Incentive Pay 22
Enlisted Pay 30
Enlisted BAQ and BAS Tables 30
Enlisted Special and Incentive Pay 31
Enlisted Basic Pay and BMC Tables 34
Enlisted "Take-Home Pay" Tables 35
Uniform Allowances 38
Bonuses 40
Miscellaneous Type Payments 41
   Family Separation Allowance 41
   Separation, Readjustment and Disability Severance Pay 42
   Voluntary Separation Incentives 43
   Authorized Leave/Accrued Leave 45
   Overseas Housing and Station Allowances 46
   Educational Benefits for Servicemembers 47
Basic Allowance for Quarters 48
Garnishment 52
CONUS COLA 53
Variable Housing Allowance 56
VHA Tables 57
Travel and Transportation Allowances 63
   Do-It-Yourself Moving 67
   Table of PCS HHG Weight Allowances 68
Space Available Travel 69
DoD Overseas Dependent Schools 72
Military Retirement 75
   Types of Retirement 76
   Retired Pay Computation 78
   Retirement Income Tax Provisions 80
   Former Spouse Protection Act 81
   Active Duty and Retired Pay Increase Table 82
   Retired Pay Table 83
   Identification Cards 88
   Privileges of Base Facilities 89
Guide to Military Installation Facilities 89

UNIFORMED SERVICES ALMANAC

PART II HEALTH CARE, INSURANCE, SBP & SOCIAL SECURITY

Uniformed Services Health Benefits 96
   Health Care Benefits Table 97
   DoD TRICARE Managed Care Program 98
   Medical Care for Dependents 102
   Continued Health Care Benefit Program 106
   TRICARE Active Duty Family Member Dental Plan 106
   CHAMPUS 107
   Program for Persons with Disabilities 120
   DEERS 122
   Health Benefits for Retirees 123
   Satellite Primary Health Care 123
   CHAMPUS Claims Processors 125
Survivor Benefit Plan 129
   Coverages Available 129
   Cost (Premiums) 132
   Social Security and DIC Offset 135
   COLA Adjustments 136
   Tax Treatment 137
Survivor Benefits Table 137
Social Security 138
   Payments to Social Security 138
   Social Security Benefits 140
   Social Security Credits 141
   Disability Benefits 142
   How Credit is Earned 143
   Amounts of Social Security Benefits 145
   Reduced Retirement Benefits by Age 62 147
   Benefits by Additional Work 147
   Lump Sum Death Payment 148
   Earned Income After Social Security Start 149
   Social Security Financing Schedule 150

PART III VETERANS' BENEFITS & PROGRAMS

Veterans Benefits 151
Service Connected Disability 151
Educational Assistance 154
Montgomery GI Bill 154
Vocational Rehabilitation Program 156
Home Loans 158
Hospitalization 161
Persian Gulf, Agent Orange and Radiation Treatment 163
Nursing Home Care 164
Outpatient Treatment 165
CHAMPVA 168
Appeals 169
Dependency and Indemnity Compensation 170
Burial 172
Death Gratuity 177
Veterans and Military Insurance Programs 178
VMLI, SGLI, VGLI 181

UNIFORMED SERVICES ALMANAC

Veterans Preference in Government Employment 183
Uniformed Services Employment and Reemployment Rights 185
Employment of Retired Military Personnel 186
Unemployment Compensation for Ex-Servicemembers 190
Veterans Employment and Training Programs 193
Soldiers and Sailors Civil Relief Act 196
Selective Service System 198

PART IV FEDERAL & STATE TAXES
Federal Income Tax Information 200
   Monthly Tax Computation 200
   Gross Income 202
   Combat Zone Exclusion 203
   Community Property 204
   Adjustments to Income 205
   Earned Income Credit 205
   Miscellaneous Itemized Deductions 207
   Moving Expenses 209
   Sale of Home 211
   Extensions 213
State Income Taxes 215
   State Income Tax Tables 217
   State Tax Authorities 223

PART V THE RESERVE FORCES
The Reserve Forces 225
   Total Force Policy 226
   Total Resere Strength 227
   Categories of the Reserve Forces 228
   Call to Active Duty 228
   Longevity and Retirement Credit 229
   Reserve Officers on EAD 230
   The National Guard 231
   Reserve Forces 232
   Reserve Personnel Statistics 234

PART VI DoD STATISTICS & OTHER INFO
National Military and Veterans Organizations 235
U.S. Military Service Academies 238
Armed Forces Retirement Homes 239
Home Buying for Service Members 243
Selected Personnel Statistics 246
   Active Duty Military Personnel by Grade and Service 246
   Average Time in Service for Promotions 246
   Female Military Personnel by Grade and Service 247
   Active Duty Military Personnel and Dependents 247
   Retirees by State 248
   Locations of Military Dependents 248
   Where They Serve 249
   Educational Levels 250
   Active Duty Military Personnel by Ethnic Group 250
   Total Lifetime Military Retirement Pay 251
   Senior Officials/Congressional Committees 252

UNIFORMED SERVICES ALMANAC
SELECTED LEGISLATION OF INTEREST TO MILITARY PERSONNEL
(104TH Congress - 1st Session)

Following is a partial listing of legislation of interest and significance to military personnel. The listing is not all inclusive, but is representative of some of the key legislation considered by the last Congress. Many of the bills which were not acted upon during the 1st session of the 104th Congress will be reintroduced during the 2nd Session of the 104th Congress convened in January 1996. Except for those bills enacted into law, the bill number is reflected.

VETERANS LEGISLATION

P.L. 104-57, November 22, 1995. Increases, effective December 1, 1995, the rates of compensation for veterans with service-connected disabilities and the rates for dependency and indemnity compensation (DIC) for the survivors of certain disabled veterans and additional DIC for surviving spouses with minor children by the same percentage (2.6 percent) as the increase in benefits provided under the OASDI provisions of the Social Security Act. Further provides that resulting amounts that are not even dollars to be rounded down to the next lower whole dollar.

The following bills were not acted upon or were vetoed by the President and will be reintroduced and considered during the 2nd session of the 104th Congress:

H.R. 109. Would provide that the effective date for discontinuance of compensation and pension shall be the date on which the recipient dies, rather than the last day of the predeeding month, in the case of a veteran with a surviving spouse.

H.R. 1385. Veterans Health Care Reform Act. Would provide for expansion of the VA's capacity to provide outpatient care to eligible veterans; to allocate resources to provide access to health care to: (a) veterans with a compensable service-connected disability; (b) veterans discharged or released from active duty due to a disability incurred in line of duty; (c) certain veterans in receipt of veteran's disability compensation and for other purposes.

H.R. 1482. Would improve and expand various veterans programs and benefits including the acceptance of a private physician's statements with respect to the filing of disability compensation claims; expands the effective date of discontinuance of compensation to the last day of the month in which the death occured if the surviving spouse of the veteran is not eligible for DIC; increases the automobile allowance from $5,500 to $6,000; extends vocational rehabilitation for pension recipients from Dec. 31, 1995 to Dec. 31, 1997 and for other purposes.

H.R. 1534. To extend certain expiring authorities of the VA, to authorize medical construction projects for the VA for FY 1996, and for other purposes.

H.R. 2099. Department of Veterans Affairs Appropriations Act. Makes appropriations for FY 1996 to the Department of Veterans Affairs. (Vetoed)

H.R. 2156. Veterans' Insurance Reform Act. Would merge Retired Reservists SGLI into the VGLI program and would extend VGLI coverage to members of the Ready Reserve who retire with less than 20 years of service, would permit an insured to convert a VGLI policy to a commercial insurance policy at any time, and permit conversion of SGLI to a commercial policy upon separation from service.

UNIFORMED SERVICES ALMANAC

H.R. 2353. To extend certain expiring authorities of the VA relating to the delivery of health and medical care, and for other purposes.

DEFENSE APPROPRIATIONS LEGISLATION

P.L. 104-32, October 3, 1995. FY 1996 Defense Construction Appropriations Act. Appropriates funds for FY 1996 for military construction, family housing, and base realignment and closure functions.

P.L. 104-61, December 1, 1995. FY 1996 Defense Appropriations Act. Provides funds for FY 1996 for military operations including pay, allowances, clothing, and other purposes for military personnel: Army, $19.9 million; Navy, $17 million; Marine Corps, $5.8 million; Air Force, $17.2 million. For Reserve Personnel: Army, $2.1 million; Navy, $1.3 million; Marine Corps, $378 thousand; Air Force, $784.5 thousand. For National Guard Personnel: Army, $3.2 million; Air Force, $1.2 million.

Provides for a 2.4 percent increase in basic pay and basic allowance for subsistence (BAS) and for a 5.2 percent increase in basic allowance for quarters (BAQ) and variable housing allowance (VHA). Appropriates funds for payments to the DoD Military Retirement Fund.

Provides for Active End Strength for FY 96 of: Army, 495,000; Navy, 428,340; Marine Corps, 174,000; Air Force, 388,200.

Provides for Selected Reserve End Strength for FY 96 of: Army Reserve, 230,000; Navy Reserve, 98,877; Marine Corps Reserve, 42,000; Air Force Reserve, 74,007; Army National Guard, 373,000; Air National Guard, 112,458.

DEFENSE AUTHORIZATION LEGISLATION

The FY 96 Authorization Act was vetoed by the President on December 21, 1995. The Authorization bill parallels the appropriations bill in most respects but is significant because it includes policy changes that cannot be implemented without its passage. The bill will be reintroduced when the Congress reconvenes in January and it is expected that the military pay raise of 2.4 percent for basic pay and BAS and 5.2 percent for BAQ and VHA, will be approved and made retroactive to January 1, 1996 when the compromise legislation is passed. Until the Authorization Act or other enabling legislation is approved, members will receive an across-the-board increase of 2 percent.

Other personnel provisions of the Authorization Act include:

-A limitation of no more than 12 percent of the service members without dependents who reside in government quarters to receive BAS.

-Authorization for payment of BAQ and VHA (and OHA if assigned overseas) to single members in the grade of E-6 and above who have been assigned to quarters that do not meet minimum adequacy standards or are assigned to shipboard sea duty.

-A provision that would prevent reduction of the amount of VHA as long as the member retains uninterrupted eligibility to receive VHA in the housing area and the member's housing costs are not reduced.

-Authorization for Family Separation Allowance to members aboard a ship or are away on TDY/TAD, even though the member elected to remain unaccompanied by dependents at the permanent duty station.

-Extends certain bonus authorities until September 30, 1997 for reserve reenlistment bonus; reserve enlistment bonus; selected reserve affiliation bonus; and other reserve bonuses; for nurse officer candidates; registered nurses, and nurse anesthetists; for various other special and incentive pays including pays for: nuclear qualified officers; aviation officers retention bonus; rentlisment bonus for active members; enlistment bonus for critical skills, and certain others.

-Authorization for hazardous duty incentive pay for warrant officers and enlisted members serving as air weapons controllers aboard AWAC systems.

-Would reduce the initial operational flying requirement for ACIP from 9 of the first 12 years to 8 of the first 12 years of aviation service.

-Would increase the maximum monthly rate of special duty assignment pay for recuiters to $375 per month.

- Would authorize payment of a dislocation allowance for members directed to move as a result of the closure or realignment of an installation.

Other provisions of the Act:

-Would establish the COLA payment date for military retirees to conform with the payment date established for Federal civilian retirees by making the military retired pay COLA for FY 96 and FY 97 effective the first day of March 1996, and the first day of December, 1996, respectively, and that the effective date for the FY 98 COLA conform to the date prescribed for Federal civilian retirees.

-Would require a report on the payment of annuities for certain military surviving spouses ("Forgotten Widows") who were widowed before the provisions of the Survivor Benefit Plan were applicable to them.

The Act would also:

-Provide for payment to survivors of deceased members for all leave accrued even beyond the 60 day limit.

-Provide that the burden for payment of administrative costs, incurred during garnishment actions, be shifted from the employer to the creditor.

-Provide for automatic enrollment of service members at the maximum SGLI insurance level of $200,000 instead of the $100,000 level (effective April 1, 1996).

-Provide for termination of SGLI for members of the ready reserve who fail to make premium payments for 120 days (effective April 1, 1996).

Additionally the Authorization Act would:

-Expand "well-baby visits" and immunizations to dependents under the age of six, and add coverage of health promotion and disease prevention visits associated with immunizations, pap smears, and mammograms.

-Would authorize reservists the same death and disability benefits as active duty members, during off-duty periods between successive inactive duty training periods performed at locations outside the reasonable commuting distance from the members residence.

-Would provide for medical care of surviving dependents of "gray area" retired reservists who die before age 60 as if the sponsor had attained age 60 and was receiving retirement benefits.

-Would provide for medical and dental care for members of the Selected Reserve assigned to early deploying units of the Army Selected Reserve and dental insurance for members of the Selected Reserve (for implementation in FY 97 after testing the plan in FY 96).

The Act also contained a number of other provisions regarding health care services including provisions for TRICARE implementation and CHAMPUS reform. (See the Health Care Benefits Section for details.)

UNIFORMED SERVICES ALMANAC

PART I

MILITARY PAY

Military compensation is comprised of several elements which include not only basic pay and allowances for quarters (BAQ) and subsistence (BAS), but a number of special and incentive pays such as flight pay, sea pay, hazardous duty pay, proficiency pay, bonuses and other non-quantifiable factors such as the tax advantage resulting from the tax-free status of the BAQ and BAS; the use of commissary and exchange stores; medical care for members and dependents; the potential for receipt of retired pay; death gratuity payments; dependency and indemnity compensation; survivor benefits; life insurance plans; and other similar considerations. Other factors in military compensation include such items as professional education and training, Veterans education assistance, and reimbursable items including clothing issues and maintenance, family separation and overseas allowances, travel and transportation allowances, dislocation allowances, a CONUS COLA and Variable Housing Allowance (VHA). These elements and others are discussed in detail throughout the Uniformed Services Almanac.

The FY 96 Defense Appropriations Act, P.L. 104-61 provides funds for a 2.4 percent increase in basic pay and Basic Allowance for Subsistence (BAS). It also appropriates funds for a 5.2 percent increase in Basic Allowance for Quarters (BAQ) and Variable Housing Allowance (VHA). The FY 96 Authorization Act which would actually authorize the pay raises was not signed at the time this edition went to press, but it is anticipated that the pay increase contained in the Authorization Act will be approved, and that the increases will be made retroactive to January 1, 1996. The pay tables shown in this edition all reflect the proposed pay increase although it is possible that members will see only a 2 percent across-the-board increase in the initial pay checks for 1996.

The actual amount of the basic pay increase is not exactly 2.4 percent since the method for computing the raise requires the following steps: First the DoD takes the prior year's monthly pay rate and adds the percentage of the authorized increase. That number is divided by 30 to get a daily rate. The daily rate is rounded down to the nearest penny and then multiplied by 30 to bring it back to a monthly rate. This result is ordinarily several cents less per month than the full percentage increase authorized. Because the figures are not rounded up, no one gets more than the authorized increase.

The detailed pay tables on the following pages are designed to provide complete pay data—after deductions for federal income taxes and Social Security. They apply to officers and enlisted members of the Uniformed Services including the Army, Navy, Air Force, Marine Corps, Coast Guard, and commissioned officers of the National Oceanic and Atmospheric Administration and Public Health Service. Since all members do not receive all elements of compensation, these tables do not include special or incentive pays nor do they include such things as voluntary allotments or withholding for state income taxes. Since income taxes are withheld from special and incentive pays, it is necessary that any one receiving such compensation adjust the tables by adding the value of these payments after calculating the amount of taxes withheld. For those who wish to make these calculations, we have provided the procedures for computing monthly tax withholding in the Tax Section of the Almanac.

UNIFORMED SERVICES ALMANAC

Social Security taxes or Federal Insurance Contributions Act (FICA) deductions are withheld from all military members basic pay and are based on the rates established by the Social Security Amendment Act of 1977 and subsequent legislation. Under the Social Security Amendments of 1983, the withholding rates have been increased to the current rate of 7.65 percent which includes 6.20 percent for Old Age, Survivors and Disability Insurance (OASDI) and 1.45 percent for Hospital Insurance (HI). FICA is withheld on a base which is increased annually based on average wage levels.

The withholding rate for 1996 remains at 7.65 percent. The base, however increased from $61,200 in 1995 to $62,700 in 1996. In 1996, the 1.45 percent for HI will be applied to an unlimited base.

During 1995, FICA taxes applied to the first $61,200 of basic pay up to a maximum of $4,681.80. In 1996, FICA taxes (7.65%) will be applied to the first $62,700 of basic pay with a maximum of $4,796.55 and 1.45 percent for HI applied to all wages above the base of $62,700.

BAS, BAQ and other allowances are not subject to FICA withholding nor are special and incentive pays.

In the event that more than $4,681.80 was withheld by more than one employer in 1995, the taxpayer can claim any excess withholding as a credit against the income tax liability as provided for on IRS form 1040. Since the law required that FICA taxes be withheld on the first $61,200 earned from each employer in 1995, a person with a part-time job may find that more than $4,681.80 of the combined total wages was withheld for Social Security. The member would then claim the excess as a credit when filing the federal income tax return.

On January 15, 1991, the military departments' finance centers became part of the new Defense Finance and Accounting Service (DFAS) which replaced the Services' individual finance centers. DFAS has converted Air Force and Army active duty, guard and reserve pay accounts to the new standard Defense Joint Military Pay System "DJMS". In November, 1995, the Navy began incrementally converting accounts. Marine Corps accounts have been converted to the new joint DFAS-Marine Corps fully integrated pay and personnel system, the Marine Corps Total Force System (MCTFS). The new systems provide monthly leave and earning statements (LESs). The LES gives soldiers, airmen, marines and sailors an account of their pay and contains pay related remarks.

All federal income tax withholding is predicated on the monthly pay rate. Compensation for military personnel on active duty may be subject to withholding for State income taxes, if requested by the state. However, the obligation of filing and paying State income taxes directly to the State taxing authority which have not requested withholding, rests with the member. Pay information (a copy of the form W-2, withholding statement) will be sent to the State of legal residence. Tax reporting occurs only if there is an agreement to withhold and only to the state of legal residence claimed by member.

OFFICERS PAY

Officers' pay shown in Table 1 reflects basic pay and allowances without the addition of any special or incentive pay categories. For those drawing special or incentive pay such as flight or submarine duty pay, the "take home" pay will have to be adjusted individually. These special pays are not covered in the Officers' Pay Tables, but the appropriate amounts are furnished in this pay section. When additional taxable income is involved, "take-home" pay can be computed by referring to income tax rate tables shown in the Tax Section.

UNIFORMED SERVICES ALMANAC

OFFICERS' MONTHLY BASIC ALLOWANCE FOR QUARTERS BAQ RATES (January 1, 1996)

Pay Grade	Without Dependents Full Rate*	Without Dependents Partial Rate**	With Dependents
Commissioned Officers			
O-10	788.40	50.70	970.50
O-9	788.40	50.70	970.50
O-8	788.40	50.70	970.50
O-7	788.40	50.70	970.50
O-6	723.30	39.60	873.90
O-5	696.60	33.00	842.40
O-4	645.60	26.70	742.50
O-3	517.50	22.20	614.40
O-2	410.40	17.70	524.70
O-1	345.60	13.20	468.90
O-3E	558.60	22.20	660.30
O-2E	474.90	17.70	595.80
O-1E	408.30	13.20	550.50
Warrant Officers			
W-5	655.80	25.20	716.70
W-4	582.60	25.20	657.00
W-3	489.60	20.70	602.10
W-2	434.70	15.90	553.80
W-1	363.90	13.80	479.10

*Full rate is authorized for members without dependents who are not occupying government quarters.
**Payment of the partial rate of BAQ at these rates to members of the uniformed services without dependents who, under Title 37 U.S.C. 403(b) or (c) are not entitled to the full rate of BAQ, is authorized by Title 37 U.S.C. 1009(c)(2) and Part IV of Executive Order 11157, as amended.

NET BAQ "DECREASE" FOR "TAKE HOME" PAY TABLES ON PAGES 16-21 FOR OFFICERS WITHOUT DEPENDENTS

Grade	Monthly Amount Full Rate	Monthly Amount Partial Rate	Grade	Monthly Amount Full Rate	Monthly Amount Partial Rate
O-10	182.10	919.80	O-1	123.30	455.70
O-9	182.10	919.80	O3E	101.70	638.10
O-8	182.10	919.80	O2E	120.90	578.10
O-7	182.10	919.80	O1E	142.20	537.30
O-6	150.60	834.30	W-5	60.90	691.50
O-5	145.80	809.40	W-4	74.40	631.80
O-4	96.90	715.80	W-3	112.50	581.40
O-3	96.90	592.20	W-2	119.10	537.90
O-2	114.30	507.00	W-1	115.20	465.30

UNIFORMED SERVICES ALMANAC

ARMED FORCES OFFICERS' PAY
Basic Pay Rates, Effective January 1, 1996

YEARS OF SERVICE

Pay Grade	Under 2	Over 2	Over 3	Over 4	Over 6	Over 8	Over 10	Over 12	Over 14	Over 16	Over 18	Over 20	Over 22	Over 24	Over 26
O-10	7145.70	7397.10	7397.10	7397.10	7397.10	7681.20	7681.20	8106.60	8106.60	8686.50	8686.50	9268.20	9268.20	9268.20	9845.40
O-9	6333.00	6498.90	6637.50	6637.50	6637.50	6806.10	6806.10	7089.30	7089.30	7681.20	7681.20	8106.60	8106.60	8106.60	8686.50
O-8	5736.00	5908.20	6048.30	6048.30	6048.30	6498.90	6498.90	6806.10	6806.10	7089.30	7397.10	7681.20	7870.50	7870.50	7870.50
O-7	4766.10	5090.40	5090.40	5090.40	5318.70	5318.70	6498.90	5626.80	5908.20	6498.90	6945.90	6945.90	6945.90	6945.90	6945.90
O-6	3532.50	3881.10	4135.50	4135.50	4135.50	4135.50	4135.50	4135.50	4276.20	4952.40	5205.00	5318.70	5626.80	5817.00	6102.60
O-5	2825.40	3317.40	3546.90	3546.90	3546.90	3546.90	3654.00	3851.10	4109.10	4416.60	4669.50	4811.40	4979.40	4979.40	4979.40
O-4	2381.40	2900.10	3093.60	3093.60	3150.90	3289.80	3514.50	3711.90	3881.10	4051.80	4163.10	4163.10	4163.10	4163.10	4163.10
O-3	2213.10	2474.40	2645.40	2926.80	3066.90	3176.70	3348.90	3514.50	3600.60	3600.60	3600.60	3600.60	3600.60	3600.60	3600.60
O-2	1929.90	2107.50	2532.30	2617.20	2671.50	2671.50	2671.50	2671.50	2671.50	2671.50	2671.50	2671.50	2671.50	2671.50	2671.50
O-1	1675.50	1743.90	2107.50	2107.50	2107.50	2107.50	2107.50	2107.50	2107.50	2107.50	2107.50	2107.50	2107.50	2107.50	2107.50

COMMISSIONED OFFICERS WITH OVER 4 YEARS OF ACTIVE SERVICE AS AN ENLISTED MEMBER OR WARRANT OFFICER

Pay Grade	Under 2	Over 2	Over 3	Over 4	Over 6	Over 8	Over 10	Over 12	Over 14	Over 16	Over 18	Over 20	Over 22	Over 24	Over 26
O-3E	0.00	0.00	0.00	2926.80	3066.90	3176.70	3348.90	3514.50	3654.00	3654.00	3654.00	3654.00	3654.00	3654.00	3654.00
O-2E	0.00	0.00	0.00	2617.20	2671.50	2756.10	2900.10	3011.10	3093.60	3093.60	3093.60	3093.60	3093.60	3093.60	3093.60
O-1E	0.00	0.00	0.00	2107.50	2251.80	2334.60	2419.20	2503.20	2617.20	2617.20	2617.20	2617.20	2617.20	2617.20	2617.20

WARRANT OFFICERS

Pay Grade	Under 2	Over 2	Over 3	Over 4	Over 6	Over 8	Over 10	Over 12	Over 14	Over 16	Over 18	Over 20	Over 22	Over 24	Over 26
W-5	0.00	0.00	0.00	0.00	0.00	0.00	0.00	0.00	0.00	0.00	0.00	3848.10	3993.90	4109.40	4282.50
W-4	2254.80	2419.20	2419.20	2474.40	2586.90	2700.90	2814.30	3011.10	3150.90	3261.60	3348.90	3456.90	3572.70	3684.00	3851.10
W-3	2049.30	2223.00	2223.00	2251.80	2277.90	2444.70	2586.90	2671.50	2756.10	2838.60	2926.80	3041.10	3150.90	3150.90	3261.60
W-2	1794.90	1941.90	1941.90	1998.30	2107.50	2223.00	2307.30	2391.90	2474.40	2561.40	2645.40	2728.50	2838.60	2838.60	2838.60
W-1	1495.20	1714.50	1714.50	1857.60	1941.90	2025.00	2107.50	2194.50	2277.90	2362.80	2444.70	2532.30	2532.30	2532.30	2532.30

Note: Statutory limitation allows a maximum of $9,016.80 per month regardless of years of service.
Cadet and Midshipmen pay is $558.04

UNIFORMED SERVICES ALMANAC

BASIC MILITARY COMPENSATION*
Average Annual Basic Military Compensation (BMC) (Amounts rounded down to nearest dollar)

YEARS OF SERVICE

Pay Grade	Under 2	Over 2	Over 3	Over 4	Over 6	Over 8	Over 10	Over 12	Over 14	Over 16	Over 18	Over 20	Over 22	Over 24	Over 26/30
O-10	0	0	0	0	0	0	0	0	0	0	0	0	0	0	127,556
O-9	0	0	0	0	0	0	0	0	0	0	0	0	0	0	123,363
O-8	0	0	0	0	0	0	0	0	0	96,656	107,434	110,843	113,116	116,159	110,067
O-7	0	0	0	0	0	0	0	0	0	76,346	101,951	102,020	101,939	113,196	101,950
O-6	0	0	0	65,538	65,369	65,413	65,410	65,405	67,366	68,682	79,405	80,776	84,475	101,926	90,184
O-5	47,926	53,814	56,688	56,757	56,747	56,751	58,154	60,824	64,402	62,064	72,112	73,963	76,073	86,757	0
O-4	41,211	47,481	49,809	49,809	50,496	52,168	54,947	57,463	59,730	0	63,597	0	0	0	0
O-3	37,237	40,528	42,622	45,999	47,681	48,998	51,065	53,101	54,182	0	0	0	0	0	0
O-2	31,956	34,270	39,805	40,838	41,490	0	0	0	0	0	0	0	0	0	0
O-1	27,721	28,528	33,094	0	0	0	0	0	0	0	0	0	0	0	0

COMMISSIONED OFFICERS WITH OVER 4 YEARS OF ACTIVE SERVICE AS AN ENLISTED MEMBER OR WARRANT OFFICER

O-3E	0	0	0	41,930	48,322	49,653	51,723	53,790	55,568	0	0	0	0	0	0
O-2E	0	0	0	34,163	42,528	43,543	45,271	46,602	47,592	0	0	0	0	0	0
O-1E	0	0	0	34,163	36,112	37,222	38,354	39,482	40,911	0	0	0	0	0	0

WARRANT OFFICERS

W-5	0	0	0	0	0	0	0	47,521	49,242	50,565	51,615	59,017	60,952	62,733	64,983
W-4	0	0	0	0	0	0	41,657	42,673	43,688	44,678	45,736	52,937	54,360	55,772	57,944
W-3	0	0	0	0	0	39,939	37,529	38,567	39,580	40,643	41,651	47,108	48,426	48,426	49,754
W-2	0	0	33,043	33,736	35,076	36,494	37,529	38,567	39,580	40,643	41,651	42,648	43,969	0	0
W-1	26,624	29,179	29,184	30,873	31,888	32,918	33,936	35,017	36,050	37,100	38,112	39,187	0	0	0

*Basic Military Compensation (BMC) combines basic pay, basic allowance for quarters and basic allowance for subsistence and the federal tax advantage on the tax free allowances. The formula for calculating BMC is the same as was previously used for Regular Military Compensation (RMC) but does not include an average amount for the Variable Housing Allowance (VHA) which is paid to about 1/3 of all active duty members living off base in the CONUS. The BMC is at best, a guide to income for any member in a given grade and year of service. Members drawing VHA can add the amount to the BMC figures above to compute a rough estimate of their RMC. (As of January 1, 1996 based on 2.4% increase in Basic Pay and BAS, and 5.2% increase in BAQ and VHA)

UNIFORMED SERVICES ALMANAC

COMMISSIONED OFFICERS—MONTHLY PAY

Table 1

(Adjust "Net Take-Home Pay" for SPECIAL PAY, VHA, State Taxes and any voluntary allotments) (See footnotes at end of pay table.)

G R A D E	Yrs of Svc Over	Annual Total Basic Pay BAQ & BAS[1]	BASIC PAY Monthly	BASIC PAY Daily[2]	Non-Taxable Cash Allowances BAQ[3]	Non-Taxable Cash Allowances BAS	MONTHLY Net Before Taxes	Soc. Sec. 7.65% FICA Ded.*	\multicolumn{5}{c	}{Net Take Home Pay Each Month After Federal Taxes and Social Security Deductions — Number of Withholding Exemptions Claimed† — MARRIED}	\multicolumn{3}{c	}{SINGLE}
									0	1	2	3	4	5	0[3]	1[3]	2
No.	(1)	(2)	(3)	(4)	(5)	(6)	(7)	(8)	(9)	(10)	(11)	(12)	(13)	(14)	(15)	(16)	(17)
O-10	8	107816	7681.20	256.04	970.50	149.67	8984.70	587.61	6799.80	6865.55	6925.05	6984.55	7044.05	7103.55	6458.81	6524.68	6590.56
O-10	12	112921	8106.60	270.22	970.50	149.67	9410.10	620.15	7060.78	7126.66	7192.53	7258.29	7317.79	7377.29	6719.79	6785.67	6851.54
O-10	16	119880	8686.50	289.55	970.50	149.67	9990.00	664.25	7416.55	7482.43	7548.30	7614.18	7680.05	7745.93	7075.56	7141.44	7207.31
O-10	20	126860	9268.20	308.94	970.50	149.67	10571.70	709.02	7773.42	7839.30	7905.17	7971.05	8036.92	8102.80	7432.43	7498.31	7564.18
O-10	26	133787	9845.40	328.18	970.50	149.67	11148.90	753.17	8127.54	8193.41	8259.29	8325.16	8391.04	8456.91	7786.55	7852.42	7918.30
O-10	M	123844	9016.80	300.56	970.50	149.67	10320.30	689.79	7619.19	7685.07	7750.94	7816.82	7882.69	7948.57	7278.20	7344.08	7409.95
COLUMNS 2, 7, AND 9 THROUGH 17 INCLUDE $183.33 MONTHLY PERSONAL MONEY ALLOWANCE																	
O-9	8	95615	6806.10	226.87	970.50	149.67	7967.94	520.67	6101.25	6160.75	6220.25	6279.75	6339.25	6398.75	5780.27	5846.14	5912.02
O-9	12	99014	7089.30	236.31	970.50	149.67	8251.14	542.33	6283.49	6342.99	6402.49	6461.99	6521.49	6580.99	5954.01	6019.89	6085.76
O-9	16	106116	7681.20	256.04	970.50	149.67	8843.04	587.61	6658.13	6723.88	6783.38	6842.88	6902.38	6961.88	6317.14	6383.02	6448.89
O-9	20	111221	8106.60	270.22	970.50	149.67	9268.44	620.15	6919.12	6984.99	7050.87	7116.62	7176.12	7235.62	6578.13	6644.00	6709.88
O-9	26	118180	8686.50	289.55	970.50	149.67	9848.34	664.52	7274.88	7340.76	7406.63	7472.51	7538.38	7604.26	6933.89	6999.77	7065.64
COLUMNS 2, 7, AND 9 THROUGH 17 INCLUDE $41.67 MONTHLY PERSONAL MONEY ALLOWANCE																	
O-8	8	91429	6498.90	216.63	970.50	149.67	7619.07	497.17	5861.90	5921.40	5980.90	6040.40	6099.90	6159.40	5550.14	5616.01	5681.89
O-8	12	95115	6806.10	226.87	970.50	149.67	7926.27	520.67	6059.59	6119.09	6178.59	6238.09	6297.59	6357.09	5738.60	5804.48	5870.35
O-8	16	98514	7089.30	236.31	970.50	149.67	8209.47	542.33	6241.82	6301.32	6360.82	6420.32	6479.82	6539.32	5912.35	5978.22	6044.10
O-8	18	102207	7397.10	246.57	970.50	149.67	8517.27	565.88	6439.89	6499.39	6558.89	6618.39	6677.89	6737.39	6101.18	6167.06	6232.93
O-8	20	105616	7681.20	256.04	970.50	149.67	8801.37	587.61	6616.47	6682.21	6741.71	6801.21	6860.71	6920.21	6275.48	6341.35	6407.23
O-8	22	107888	7870.50	262.35	970.50	149.67	8990.67	602.09	6732.60	6798.48	6863.53	6923.03	6982.53	7042.03	6391.61	6457.49	6523.36
O-7	6	77266	5318.70	177.29	970.50	149.67	6438.87	406.88	5102.44	5161.94	5221.44	5280.94	5340.44	5399.94	4826.08	4891.96	4957.83
O-7	10	80964	5626.80	187.56	970.50	149.67	6746.97	430.45	5300.71	5360.21	5419.71	5479.21	5538.71	5598.21	5015.10	5080.98	5146.85
O-7	14	84340	5908.20	196.94	970.50	149.67	7028.37	451.98	5481.79	5541.29	5600.79	5660.29	5719.79	5779.29	5187.74	5253.62	5319.49
O-7	16	91429	6498.90	216.63	970.50	149.67	7619.07	497.17	5861.90	5921.40	5980.90	6040.40	6099.90	6159.40	5550.14	5616.01	5681.89
O-7	18	96793	6945.90	231.53	970.50	149.67	8066.07	531.36	6149.55	6209.05	6268.55	6328.05	6387.55	6447.05	5824.37	5890.24	5956.12

16

UNIFORMED SERVICES ALMANAC

COMMISSIONED OFFICERS — MONTHLY PAY
Table 1

(Adjust "Net Take-Home Pay" for SPECIAL PAY, VHA, State Taxes and any voluntary allotments) (See footnotes at end of pay table.)

G R A D E	Yrs of Svc Over	Annual Total Basic Pay BAQ & BAS[1]	BASIC PAY Monthly	BASIC PAY Daily[2]	MONTHLY Non-Taxable Cash Allowances BAQ[3]	MONTHLY Non-Taxable Cash Allowances BAS	MONTHLY Net Before Taxes	MONTHLY Soc. Sec. 7.65% FICA Ded.*	Net Take Home Pay Each Month After Federal Taxes and Social Security Deductions — Number of Withholding Exemptions Claimed† MARRIED 0	1	2	3	4	5	SINGLE 0[3]	1[3]	2
(1)		(2)	(3)	(4)	(5)	(6)	(7)	(8)	(9)	(10)	(11)	(12)	(13)	(14)	(15)	(16)	(17)
O-6	3	61909	4135.50	137.85	873.90	149.67	5159.07	316.37	4244.45	4303.95	4363.45	4398.25	4430.13	4462.00	3993.34	4052.84	4112.34
O-6	14	63597	4276.20	142.54	873.90	149.67	5299.77	327.13	4334.99	4394.49	4453.99	4507.09	4538.96	4570.84	4083.88	4143.38	4202.88
O-6	16	71712	4952.40	165.08	873.90	149.67	5975.97	378.86	4770.13	4829.63	4889.13	4948.63	5008.13	5067.63	4504.76	4570.63	4636.51
O-6	18	74743	5205.00	173.50	873.90	149.67	6228.57	398.18	4932.68	4992.18	5051.68	5111.18	5170.68	5230.18	4659.73	4725.60	4791.48
O-6	20	76107	5318.70	177.29	873.90	149.67	6342.27	406.88	5005.84	5065.34	5124.84	5184.34	5243.84	5303.34	4729.48	4795.36	4861.23
O-6	22	79804	5626.80	187.56	873.90	149.67	6650.37	430.45	5204.11	5263.61	5323.11	5382.61	5442.11	5501.61	4918.50	4984.38	5050.25
O-6	26	85514	6102.60	203.42	873.90	149.67	7126.17	466.85	5510.28	5569.78	5629.28	5688.78	5748.28	5807.78	5210.41	5276.28	5342.16
O-5	3	54468	3546.90	118.23	842.40	149.67	4538.97	271.34	3815.85	3847.72	3879.60	3911.47	3943.35	3975.22	3583.08	3642.58	3702.08
O-5	10	55753	3654.00	121.80	842.40	149.67	4646.07	279.53	3898.69	3930.56	3962.44	3994.31	4026.19	4058.06	3652.00	3711.50	3771.00
O-5	12	58118	3851.10	128.37	842.40	149.67	4843.17	294.61	4029.94	4083.02	4114.90	4146.77	4178.65	4210.52	3778.83	3838.33	3897.83
O-5	14	61214	4109.10	136.97	842.40	149.67	5101.17	314.35	4195.97	4255.47	4314.46	4336.33	4378.21	4410.08	3944.86	4004.36	4063.86
O-5	16	64904	4416.60	147.22	842.40	149.67	5408.67	337.87	4393.84	4453.34	4512.84	4572.34	4616.06	4647.94	4142.73	4202.23	4261.73
O-5	18	67939	4669.50	155.65	842.40	149.67	5661.57	357.22	4556.58	4616.08	4675.58	4735.08	4794.58	4843.55	4299.70	4364.97	4424.47
O-5	20	69642	4811.40	160.38	842.40	149.67	5803.47	368.07	4647.90	4707.40	4766.90	4826.40	4885.90	4945.40	4386.75	4452.63	4515.79
O-5	22	71658	4979.40	165.98	842.40	149.67	5971.47	380.92	4756.00	4815.50	4875.00	4934.50	4994.00	5053.50	4489.82	4555.70	4621.57
O-4	3	47829	3093.60	103.12	742.50	149.67	3985.77	236.66	3365.32	3397.19	3429.07	3460.94	3492.82	3524.69	3191.48	3250.98	3310.48
O-4	6	48517	3150.90	105.03	742.50	149.67	4043.07	241.04	3409.64	3441.52	3473.39	3505.27	3537.14	3569.02	3228.35	3287.85	3347.35
O-4	8	50184	3289.80	109.66	742.50	149.67	4181.97	251.67	3517.08	3548.96	3580.83	3612.71	3644.58	3676.46	3317.74	3377.24	3436.74
O-4	10	52880	3514.50	117.15	742.50	149.67	4406.67	268.86	3690.89	3722.76	3754.64	3786.51	3818.39	3850.26	3462.33	3521.83	3581.33
O-4	12	55249	3711.90	123.73	742.50	149.67	4604.07	283.96	3840.47	3875.45	3907.32	3939.20	3971.07	4002.95	3589.36	3648.86	3708.36
O-4	14	57279	3881.10	129.37	742.50	149.67	4773.27	296.90	3949.35	4006.33	4038.20	4070.08	4101.95	4133.83	3698.24	3757.74	3817.24
O-4	16	59328	4051.80	135.06	742.50	149.67	4943.97	309.96	4059.19	4118.69	4170.24	4202.11	4233.99	4265.86	3808.08	3867.58	3927.08
O-4	18	60663	4163.10	138.77	742.50	149.67	5055.27	318.48	4130.81	4190.31	4249.81	4288.20	4320.08	4351.95	3879.70	3939.20	3998.70

17

UNIFORMED SERVICES ALMANAC

Table 1
COMMISSIONED OFFICERS — MONTHLY PAY

(Adjust "Net Take-Home Pay" for SPECIAL PAY, VHA, State Taxes and any voluntary allotments) (See footnotes at end of pay table.)

G R A D E	Yrs of Svc Over	Annual Total Basic Pay BAQ & BAS[1]	BASIC PAY Monthly	BASIC PAY Daily[2]	Non-Taxable Cash Allowances BAQ[3]	Non-Taxable Cash Allowances BAS	MONTHLY Net Before Taxes	Soc. Sec. 7.65% FICA Ded.*	\multicolumn{6}{c	}{Net Take Home Pay Each Month After Federal Taxes and Social Security Deductions — Number of Withholding Exemptions Claimed† MARRIED}	\multicolumn{3}{c	}{SINGLE}
									0	1	2	3	4	5	0[3]	1[3]	2
(1)		(2)	(3)	(4)	(5)	(6)	(7)	(8)	(9)	(10)	(11)	(12)	(13)	(14)	(15)	(16)	(17)
O-3	2	38862	2474.40	82.48	614.40	149.67	3238.47	189.29	2758.27	2790.14	2822.02	2853.89	2885.77	2917.64	2664.93	2724.43	2774.62
O-3	3	40914	2645.40	88.18	614.40	149.67	3409.47	202.37	2890.54	2922.41	2954.29	2986.16	3018.04	3049.91	2774.96	2834.46	2893.96
O-3	4	44290	2926.80	97.56	614.40	149.67	3690.87	223.90	3108.20	3140.07	3171.95	3203.82	3235.70	3267.57	2956.05	3015.55	3075.05
O-3	6	45972	3066.90	102.23	614.40	149.67	3830.97	234.62	3216.57	3248.44	3280.32	3312.19	3344.07	3375.94	3046.20	3105.70	3165.20
O-3	8	47289	3176.70	105.89	614.40	149.67	3940.77	243.02	3301.50	3333.37	3365.25	3397.12	3429.00	3460.87	3116.86	3176.36	3235.86
O-3	10	49356	3348.90	111.63	614.40	149.67	4112.97	256.19	3434.69	3466.57	3498.44	3530.32	3562.19	3594.07	3227.67	3287.17	3346.67
O-3	12	51343	3514.50	117.15	614.40	149.67	4278.57	268.86	3562.79	3594.66	3626.54	3658.41	3690.29	3722.16	3334.23	3393.73	3453.23
O-3	14	52376	3600.60	120.02	614.40	149.67	4364.67	275.45	3629.38	3661.26	3693.13	3725.01	3756.88	3788.76	3389.64	3449.14	3508.64
O-2	<2	31251	1929.90	64.33	524.70	149.67	2604.27	147.64	2247.40	2279.27	2311.15	2343.02	2374.90	2406.77	2200.00	2231.87	2263.75
O-2	2	33382	2107.20	70.25	524.70	149.67	2781.87	161.22	2384.77	2416.65	2448.52	2480.40	2512.27	2544.15	2337.37	2369.25	2401.12
O-2	3	38480	2532.30	84.41	524.70	149.67	3206.67	193.72	2713.35	2745.23	2777.10	2808.98	2840.85	2872.73	2612.49	2671.99	2729.70
O-2	4	39499	2617.20	87.24	524.70	149.67	3291.57	200.22	2779.02	2810.90	2842.77	2874.65	2906.52	2938.40	2667.12	2726.62	2786.12
O-2	6	40150	2671.50	89.05	524.70	149.67	3345.87	204.37	2821.03	2852.90	2884.78	2916.65	2948.53	2980.40	2702.06	2761.56	2821.06
O-1	<2	27529	1675.50	55.85	468.90	149.67	2294.07	128.18	1994.82	2026.69	2058.57	2090.44	2122.32	2154.19	1947.42	1979.29	2011.17
O-1	2	28350	1743.90	58.13	468.90	149.67	2362.47	133.41	2047.73	2079.60	2111.48	2143.35	2175.23	2207.10	2000.33	2032.20	2064.08
O-1	3	32713	2107.50	70.25	468.90	149.67	2726.07	161.22	2328.97	2360.85	2392.72	2424.60	2456.47	2488.35	2281.57	2313.45	2345.32
O-3E	4	44290	2926.80	97.56	614.40	149.67	3690.87	223.90	3108.20	3140.07	3171.95	3203.82	3235.70	3267.57	2956.05	3015.55	3075.05
O-3E	6	45972	3066.90	102.23	614.40	149.67	3830.97	234.62	3216.57	3248.44	3280.32	3312.19	3344.07	3375.94	3046.20	3105.70	3165.20
O-3E	8	47289	3176.70	105.89	614.40	149.67	3940.77	243.02	3301.50	3333.37	3365.25	3397.12	3429.00	3460.87	3116.86	3176.36	3235.86
O-3E	10	49356	3348.90	111.63	614.40	149.67	4112.97	256.19	3434.69	3466.57	3498.44	3530.32	3562.19	3594.07	3227.67	3287.17	3346.67
O-3E	12	51343	3514.50	117.15	614.40	149.67	4278.57	268.86	3562.79	3594.66	3626.54	3658.41	3690.29	3722.16	3334.23	3393.73	3453.23
O-3E	14	53017	3654.00	121.80	614.40	149.67	4418.07	279.53	3670.69	3702.56	3734.44	3766.31	3798.19	3830.06	3424.00	3483.50	3543.00

UNIFORMED SERVICES ALMANAC

Table 1
COMMISSIONED OFFICERS — MONTHLY PAY

(Adjust "Net Take-Home Pay" for SPECIAL PAY, VHA, State Taxes and any voluntary allotments) (See footnotes at end of pay table.)

G R A D E	Yrs of Svc Over	Annual Total Basic Pay BAQ & BAS[1]	BASIC PAY Monthly	BASIC PAY Daily[2]	Non-Taxable Cash Allowances BAQ[3]	Non-Taxable Cash Allowances BAS	MONTHLY Net Before Taxes	Soc. Sec. 7.65% FICA Ded.*	\multicolumn{9}{c	}{Net Take Home Pay Each Month After Federal Taxes and Social Security Deductions — Number of Withholding Exemptions Claimed†}
									0	MARRIED 1	2	3	4	5	0[3]	SINGLE 1[3]	2
No.	(1)	(2)	(3)	(4)	(5)	(6)	(7)	(8)	(9)	(10)	(11)	(12)	(13)	(14)	(15)	(16)	(17)
O-2E	4	39499	2617.20	87.24	524.70	149.67	3291.57	200.22	2779.02	2810.90	2842.77	2874.65	2906.52	2938.40	2667.12	2726.62	2786.12
O-2E	6	40150	2671.50	89.05	524.70	149.67	3345.87	204.37	2821.03	2852.90	2884.78	2916.65	2948.53	2980.40	2702.06	2761.56	2821.06
O-2E	8	41166	2756.10	91.87	524.70	149.67	3430.47	210.84	2886.46	2918.34	2950.21	2982.09	3013.96	3045.84	2756.50	2816.00	2875.50
O-2E	10	42894	2900.10	96.67	524.70	149.67	3574.47	221.86	2997.85	3029.72	3061.60	3093.47	3125.35	3157.22	2849.16	2908.66	2968.16
O-2E	12	44226	3011.10	100.37	524.70	149.67	3685.47	230.35	3083.71	3115.58	3147.46	3179.33	3211.21	3243.08	2920.59	2980.09	3039.59
O-2E	14	45216	3093.60	103.12	524.70	149.67	3767.97	236.66	3147.52	3179.39	3211.27	3243.14	3275.02	3306.89	2973.68	3033.18	3092.68
O-1E	4	32713	2107.50	70.25	468.90	149.67	2726.07	161.22	2328.97	2360.85	2392.72	2424.60	2456.47	2488.35	2281.57	2313.45	2345.32
O-1E	6	34444	2251.80	75.06	468.90	149.67	2870.37	172.26	2440.59	2472.46	2504.34	2536.21	2568.09	2599.96	2376.18	2425.06	2456.94
O-1E	8	35438	2334.60	77.82	468.90	149.67	2953.17	178.60	2504.63	2536.51	2568.38	2600.26	2632.13	2664.01	2429.47	2488.97	2520.98
O-1E	10	36453	2419.20	80.64	468.90	149.67	3037.77	185.07	2570.07	2601.95	2633.82	2665.70	2697.57	2729.45	2483.91	2543.41	2586.42
O-1E	12	37461	2503.20	83.44	468.90	149.67	3121.77	191.49	2635.05	2666.92	2698.80	2730.67	2762.55	2794.42	2537.96	2597.46	2651.40
O-1E	14	38829	2617.20	87.24	468.90	149.67	3235.77	200.22	2723.22	2755.10	2786.97	2818.85	2850.72	2882.60	2611.32	2670.82	2730.32
\multicolumn{18}{	c	}{WARRANT OFFICERS}
W-5	20	56574	3848.10	128.27	716.70	149.67	4564.80	294.38	3902.31	3955.00	3986.88	4018.75	4050.63	4082.50	3651.20	3710.70	3770.20
W-5	22	58323	3993.90	133.13	716.70	149.67	4710.60	305.53	3996.13	4055.63	4099.65	4131.53	4163.40	4195.28	3745.02	3804.52	3864.02
W-5	24	59709	4109.40	136.98	716.70	149.67	4826.10	314.37	4070.46	4129.96	4188.99	4220.87	4252.74	4284.62	3819.35	3878.85	3938.35
W-5	26	61786	4282.50	142.75	716.70	149.67	4999.20	327.61	4181.85	4241.35	4300.85	4354.76	4386.63	4418.51	3930.74	3990.24	4049.74
W-4	4	39373	2474.40	82.48	657.00	149.67	3131.40	189.29	2800.87	2832.74	2864.62	2896.49	2928.37	2960.24	2707.53	2767.03	2817.22
W-4	6	40723	2586.90	86.23	657.00	149.67	3243.90	197.90	2887.89	2919.76	2951.64	2983.51	3015.39	3047.26	2779.92	2839.42	2898.92
W-4	8	42091	2700.90	90.03	657.00	149.67	3357.90	206.62	2976.07	3007.94	3039.82	3071.69	3103.57	3135.44	2853.28	2912.78	2972.28
W-4	10	43452	2814.30	93.81	657.00	149.67	3471.30	215.29	3063.78	3095.66	3127.53	3159.41	3191.28	3223.16	2926.25	2985.75	3045.25
W-4	12	45813	3011.10	100.37	657.00	149.67	3668.10	230.35	3216.01	3247.88	3279.76	3311.63	3343.51	3375.38	3052.89	3112.39	3171.89
W-4	14	47491	3150.90	105.03	657.00	149.67	3807.90	241.04	3324.14	3356.02	3387.89	3419.77	3451.64	3483.52	3142.85	3202.35	3261.85
W-4	16	48819	3261.60	108.72	657.00	149.67	3918.60	249.51	3409.77	3441.64	3473.52	3505.39	3537.27	3569.14	3214.09	3273.59	3333.09
W-4	18	49867	3348.90	111.63	657.00	149.67	4005.90	256.19	3477.29	3509.17	3541.04	3572.92	3604.79	3636.67	3270.27	3329.77	3389.27
W-4	20	51163	3456.90	115.23	657.00	149.67	4113.90	264.45	3560.83	3592.71	3624.58	3656.46	3688.33	3720.21	3339.77	3399.27	3458.77
W-4	22	52552	3572.70	119.09	657.00	149.67	4229.70	273.31	3650.40	3682.28	3714.15	3746.03	3777.90	3809.78	3414.28	3473.78	3533.28
W-4	26	55893	3851.10	128.37	657.00	149.67	4508.10	294.61	3844.54	3897.62	3929.50	3961.37	3993.25	4025.12	3593.43	3652.93	3712.43

19

UNIFORMED SERVICES ALMANAC

Table 1
COMMISSIONED OFFICERS—MONTHLY PAY

(Adjust "Net Take-Home Pay" for SPECIAL PAY, VHA, State Taxes and any voluntary allotments) (See footnotes at end of pay table.)

G R A D E	Yrs of Svc Over	Annual Total Basic Pay BAQ & BAS[1]	BASIC PAY Monthly	BASIC PAY Daily[2]	Non-Taxable Cash Allowances BAQ[3]	Non-Taxable Cash Allowances BAS	MONTHLY Net Before Taxes	Soc. Sec. 7.65% FICA Ded.*	Net Take Home Pay Each Month After Federal Taxes and Social Security Deductions — Number of Withholding Exemptions Claimed† MARRIED 0	1	2	3	4	5	SINGLE 0[3]	1[3]	2
(1)	(2)		(3)	(4)	(5)	(6)	(7)	(8)	(9)	(10)	(11)	(12)	(13)	(14)	(15)	(16)	(17)
W-3	2	35697	2223.00	74.10	602.10	149.67	2825.10	170.06	2551.51	2583.39	2615.26	2647.14	2679.01	2710.89	2490.85	2535.99	2567.86
W-3	4	36043	2251.80	75.06	602.10	149.67	2853.90	172.26	2573.79	2605.66	2637.54	2669.41	2701.29	2733.16	2509.38	2558.26	2590.14
W-3	6	36356	2277.90	75.93	602.10	149.67	2880.00	174.26	2593.98	2625.85	2657.73	2689.60	2721.48	2753.35	2526.18	2578.45	2610.33
W-3	8	38358	2444.70	81.49	602.10	149.67	3046.80	187.02	2723.00	2754.87	2786.75	2818.62	2850.50	2882.37	2633.51	2693.01	2739.35
W-3	10	40064	2586.90	86.23	602.10	149.67	3189.00	197.90	2832.99	2864.86	2896.74	2928.61	2960.49	2992.36	2725.02	2784.52	2844.02
W-3	12	41079	2671.50	89.05	602.10	149.67	3273.60	204.37	2898.43	2930.30	2962.18	2994.05	3025.93	3057.80	2779.46	2838.96	2898.46
W-3	14	42094	2756.10	91.87	602.10	149.67	3358.20	210.84	2963.86	2995.74	3027.61	3059.49	3091.36	3123.24	2833.90	2893.40	2952.90
W-3	16	43088	2838.60	94.62	602.10	149.67	3440.70	217.15	3027.68	3059.55	3091.43	3123.30	3155.18	3187.05	2886.99	2946.49	3005.99
W-3	18	44143	2926.80	97.56	602.10	149.67	3528.90	223.90	3095.90	3127.77	3159.65	3191.52	3223.40	3255.27	2943.75	3003.25	3062.75
W-3	20	45514	3041.10	101.37	602.10	149.67	3643.20	232.64	3184.31	3216.19	3248.06	3279.94	3311.81	3343.69	3017.30	3076.80	3136.30
W-3	22	46832	3150.90	105.03	602.10	149.67	3753.00	241.04	3269.24	3301.12	3332.99	3364.87	3396.74	3428.62	3087.95	3147.45	3206.95
W-3	26	48160	3261.60	108.72	602.10	149.67	3863.70	249.51	3354.87	3386.74	3418.62	3450.49	3482.37	3514.24	3159.19	3218.69	3278.19
W-2	<2	29980	1794.90	59.83	553.80	149.67	2348.70	137.31	2172.08	2203.95	2235.83	2267.70	2299.58	2331.45	2124.68	2156.55	2188.43
W-2	2	31744	1941.90	64.73	553.80	149.67	2495.70	148.56	2285.78	2317.65	2349.53	2381.40	2413.28	2445.15	2238.38	2270.25	2302.13
W-2	4	32421	1998.30	66.61	553.80	149.67	2552.10	152.87	2329.41	2361.28	2393.16	2425.03	2456.91	2488.78	2282.01	2313.88	2345.76
W-2	6	33732	2107.50	70.25	553.80	149.67	2661.30	161.22	2413.87	2445.75	2477.62	2509.50	2541.37	2573.25	2366.47	2398.35	2430.22
W-2	8	35118	2223.00	74.10	553.80	149.67	2776.80	170.06	2503.21	2535.09	2566.96	2598.84	2630.71	2662.59	2442.55	2487.69	2519.56
W-2	10	36129	2307.30	76.91	553.80	149.67	2861.10	176.51	2568.42	2600.29	2632.17	2664.04	2695.92	2727.79	2496.80	2552.89	2584.77
W-2	12	37144	2391.90	79.73	553.80	149.67	2945.70	182.98	2633.85	2665.73	2697.60	2729.48	2761.35	2793.23	2551.24	2610.74	2650.20
W-2	14	38134	2474.40	82.48	553.80	149.67	3028.20	189.29	2697.67	2729.54	2761.42	2793.29	2825.17	2857.04	2604.33	2663.83	2714.02
W-2	16	39178	2561.40	85.38	553.80	149.67	3115.20	195.95	2764.96	2796.84	2828.71	2860.59	2892.46	2924.34	2660.31	2719.81	2779.31
W-2	18	40186	2645.40	88.18	553.80	149.67	3199.20	202.37	2829.94	2861.81	2893.69	2925.56	2957.44	2989.31	2714.36	2773.86	2833.36
W-2	20	41184	2728.50	90.95	553.80	149.67	3282.30	208.73	2894.21	2926.09	2957.96	2989.84	3021.71	3053.59	2767.84	2827.34	2886.84
W-2	22	42505	2838.60	94.62	553.80	149.67	3392.40	217.15	2979.38	3011.25	3043.13	3075.00	3106.88	3138.75	2838.69	2898.19	2957.69

20

UNIFORMED SERVICES ALMANAC

Table 1
COMMISSIONED OFFICERS — MONTHLY PAY

(Adjust "Net Take-Home Pay" for SPECIAL PAY, VHA, State Taxes and any voluntary allotments) (See footnotes at end of pay table.)

G R A D E	Yrs of Svc Over	Annual Total Basic Pay BAQ & BAS[1]	BASIC PAY Monthly	BASIC PAY Daily[2]	Non-Taxable Cash Allowances BAQ[3]	Non-Taxable Cash Allowances BAS	MONTHLY Net Before Taxes	Soc. Sec. 7.65% FICA Ded.*	Net Take Home Pay Each Month After Federal Taxes and Social Security Deductions — Number of Withholding Exemptions Claimed† MARRIED 0	1	2	3	4	5	SINGLE 0[3]	1[3]	2
No.	(1)	(2)	(3)	(4)	(5)	(6)	(7)	(8)	(9)	(10)	(11)	(12)	(13)	(14)	(15)	(16)	(17)
W-1	<2	25488	1495.20	49.84	479.10	149.67	1974.30	114.38	1865.56	1897.43	1929.31	1961.18	1993.06	2009.59	1818.16	1850.03	1881.91
W-1	2	28119	1714.50	57.15	479.10	149.67	2193.60	131.16	2035.19	2067.06	2098.94	2130.81	2162.69	2194.56	1987.79	2019.66	2051.54
W-1	4	29836	1857.60	61.92	479.10	149.67	2336.70	142.11	2145.87	2177.75	2209.62	2241.50	2273.37	2305.25	2098.47	2130.35	2162.22
W-1	6	30848	1941.90	64.73	479.10	149.67	2421.00	148.56	2211.08	2242.95	2274.83	2306.70	2338.58	2370.45	2163.68	2195.55	2227.43
W-1	8	31845	2025.00	67.50	479.10	149.67	2504.10	154.91	2275.36	2307.23	2339.11	2370.98	2402.86	2434.73	2227.96	2259.83	2291.71
W-1	10	32835	2107.50	70.25	479.10	149.67	2586.60	161.22	2339.17	2371.05	2402.92	2434.80	2466.67	2498.55	2291.77	2323.65	2355.52
W-1	12	33879	2194.50	73.15	479.10	149.67	2673.60	167.88	2406.47	2438.34	2470.22	2502.09	2533.97	2565.84	2349.51	2390.94	2422.82
W-1	14	34880	2277.90	75.93	479.10	149.67	2757.00	174.26	2470.98	2502.85	2534.73	2566.60	2598.48	2630.35	2403.18	2455.45	2487.33
W-1	16	35899	2362.80	78.76	479.10	149.67	2841.90	180.75	2536.65	2568.52	2600.40	2632.27	2664.15	2696.02	2457.81	2517.31	2553.00
W-1	18	36882	2444.70	81.49	479.10	149.67	2923.80	187.02	2600.00	2631.87	2663.75	2695.62	2727.50	2759.37	2510.51	2570.01	2616.35
W-1	20	37933	2532.30	84.41	479.10	149.67	3011.40	193.72	2667.75	2699.63	2731.50	2763.38	2795.25	2827.13	2566.89	2626.39	2684.10

"M" — Maximum pay permitted under statutory limitation of $9,016.80 per month.
[1]Includes basic pay and non-taxable allowances shown in columns (5) and (6) for information only.
[2]Single day rate-for special purposes including drill pay rate for reserves. Monthly base pay divided by 30.
[3]Monthly quarters allowances with dependents. Must be adjusted if quarters allowances without dependents—Adjust take-home pay columns (2), (7), (15)-(17).
* Social Security Deduction applies to first $62,700 basic pay and an additional 1.45% on an unlimited basis. After $62,700 and FICA deductions to "Net Take-Home Pay" unless salary is greater than $62,700.
† Percentage method of computation of witholding tax.

21

Allotments for savings bonds, insurance premiums, mortgage payments, etc., must also be deducted from the "take-home" pay amounts in the tables. For example, an officer with a $48.00 allotment for a commercial life insurance policy; $50.00 for US Government savings bonds and $950.00 for a mortgage payment, would reduce the "take-home" pay amount by a total of $1,048.00. Adjustments must also be made for any state tax withholding.

Included in the pay tables are annual amounts of total gross pay and cash allowances. These are for informational and comparative purposes. Daily pay amounts are for special purposes and drill period pay of Reserves, and reflect basic pay monthly rates divided by thirty.

Under nontaxable cash allowances, the amount for subsistence is a constant amount of $149.67 for all officers. Amounts paid for monthly quarters vary depending on whether the officer is with or without dependents, the grade of the officer and whether the officer is occupying government quarters. Members *without dependents* who occupy government quarters and those on sea or field duty receive a partial quarters allowance. This partial allowance or "rebate," which ranges from $13.20 for an O-1 to $50.70 for O-7 and above, is paid to single personnel to compensate for the amount that base pay would have been increased, had the President not reallocated a portion of the FY 77 basic pay increase and transferred it to BAQ. Since the majority of officers are entitled to quarters "with dependents," these amounts were used in the tables. The applicable adjustment or decrease must be made in the "Net take-home" pay columns of the pay tables, as well as appropriate adjustments in columns (2) and (5) of the pay table, for those who draw BAQ at the "without dependents" rate.

Officers drawing Variable Housing Allowance, overseas Cost-of-Living allowances, Housing Allowances, CONUS COLA or Family Separation Pay must increase the "take-home" pay shown in the tables accordingly.

Officers with dependents who are furnished government quarters for themselves and their families do not draw an allowance for quarters. Officers without dependents who do not occupy government quarters are entitled to draw BAQ at the "full" rate, while those who are on sea or field duty or who are either required or chose to occupy government quarters draw "partial" BAQ rate. Since the "Take Home" pay tables have been formulated using the BAQ rate "with dependents," officers in any of the above categories must adjust the amounts in columns 2, 7, and 9-17 in Table I accordingly.

OFFICERS' SPECIAL AND INCENTIVE PAY

(The following Special and Incentive pays are extended or changed as indicated based on the assumption that the FY 96 Defense Authorization Act will be passed.)

Special Pay for Navy Nuclear-Qualified Officers. There are three categories: (1) Nuclear Officer Accession Bonus not to exceed $8,000; (2) Continuation Pay for a 3, 4 or 5 year period of obligated active service in an amount not to exceed $12,000 per year not to be paid simultaneously with Nuclear Career Annual Incentive Bonus; (3) Nuclear Career Annual Incentive Bonus, if not serving under Continuation Pay obligated service, is payable in an amount not to exceed $10,000 for unrestricted line officers and $4,500 for limited duty officers and warrant officers. Authorization for this special pay was extended to 30 September 1997.

Hostile Fire or Imminent Danger Pay. Special pay of $150.00 per month is payable to members assigned to or associated with a unit subject to hostile

UNIFORMED SERVICES ALMANAC

fire or explosion of hostile mines or imminent danger in places or situations as may be designated by the Secretary of Defense. Some of the currently designated areas include, but are not limited to: Vietnam; Cambodia; Lebanon; Sudan; Kuwait; Iraq; Persian Gulf; Saudi Arabia; Turkey; Somalia; Haiti; and the former country of Yugoslavia, including Slovenia, Croatia, and Boznia-Herzogovina. This pay is not payable in time of war declared by the United States Congress.

Special Pay for Diving Duty. Officers assigned to diving duty are entitled to special pay at a rate not to exceed $200 per month. Entitlement to this special pay requires that members be assigned by orders to diving duty; maintain proficiency by frequent and regular dives; and are actually performing diving duty.

Incentive Pay for Hazardous Duty. Flying duty as a noncrew member, parachute jumping, demolitions, toxic fuel handlers, flight deck duty, experimental stress duty, etc., $110.00 per month.

Members meeting the performance requirements for more than one type of hazardous duty pay during the same period are entitled to receive payment for a maximum of two types of incentive pay provided they were assigned to a unit whose mission requires the performance of both types of hazardous duty involved.

Air Weapons Controller Pay. Hazardous duty incentive pay for officers participating in frequent and regular aerial flights as airborne warning and control system (AWACS) air weapons controllers is authorized as shown on the following table. Payments are based on the total years of weapons controller experience (gained in ground duties or as an air weapons controller crew member). An officer entitled to ACIP is not entitled to this pay.

AIR WEAPONS CONTROLLER PAY

Pay Grade	2 or less	Over 2	Over 3	Over 4	Over 6	Over 8	Over 10	Over 12	Over 14	Over 16	Over 18	Over 20	Over 22	Over 24	Over 25
O-7	200	200	200	200	200	200	200	200	200	200	200	200	200	200	110
O-6	225	250	300	325	350	350	350	350	350	350	350	300	250	250	225
O-5	200	250	300	325	350	350	350	350	350	350	350	300	250	250	225
O-4	175	225	275	300	350	350	350	350	350	350	350	300	250	250	225
O-3	125	156	188	206	350	350	350	350	350	350	300	275	250	225	200
O-2	125	156	188	206	250	300	300	300	300	300	275	245	210	200	180
O-1	125	156	188	206	250	250	250	250	250	250	245	210	200	180	150

Aviation Career Incentive Pay. The flight pay system was significantly revamped in June 1974 by enactment of Public Law 93-294. The current system was designed to improve aviator retention and concentrate the highest rates of pay in the most flight-intensive period of an aviator's career. The *establishment of performance standards* or "gates" for receipt of continuous Aviation Career Incentive Pay (ACIP) is a major feature of the system. These standards are: (a) performance of at least 6 years of operational flying duty in the first 12 years of aviation service to qualify for 18 years of continuous pay; (b) performance of at least 11 years of operational flying duty in the first 18 years of aviation service to qualify for continuous pay for as long as an officer qualifies for flight pay; or (c) performance of at least 9 but less than 11 years of operational flying duty in the first 18 years of aviation service to qualify for 22 years of continuous pay.

UNIFORMED SERVICES ALMANAC

Revised Criteria Effective 1 October 1991.
Continuous through 12 years aviation service, if qualified   *No change*
Continuous through 18 years, if 9 of first 12 years of aviation service involve operational flying
Continuous through 22 years, if 10 of first 18 years of aviation service involve operational flying
Continuous through 25 years, if 12 of first 18 years of aviation service involve operational flying

Transition Provisions

• Those with fewer than 6 years of aviation service as of October 1, 1991 will be managed under the "new gate" criteria throughout their careers.

• Those with 6 or more years of aviation service who *have met* the "old gates" as of October 1, 1991 will be managed under the "old gate" criterion for their next gate; thereafter, the "new gates" would control the entitlement to continuous ACIP.

• Those with 6-12 years of aviation service as of October 1, 1991 *who have not met* the "old gate" criterion (6 years of flight duty) must make *both the "old gate"* (6 years of flight duty by the 12th year of aviation service) *and a transition gate* (9 years of flight duty by the 15th year of aviation service) in order to draw continuous ACIP through the 18th year. Beyond the 18th year of service, the "new gate" criteria would control the entitlement to continuous ACIP.

• Those with more than 12 years of aviation service as of October 1, 1991 will continue to be managed throughout their careers under the "old gate" criteria *whether or not they have met* the "old gate" criteria as of October 1, 1991.

• Secretaries of Military Departments may permit aviators who would disqualify for continuous ACIP under these new provisions to draw continuous ACIP, on a case-by-case basis, when merited by individual circumstances.

AVIATION CAREER INCENTIVE PAY

PHASE I	
Monthly Rate	Years of Aviation Service as an Officer*
$125	2 or less
$156	over 2
$188	over 3
$206	over 4
$650	over 6
PHASE II	
$585	over 18
$495	over 20
$385	over 22
$250	over 25
WARRANT OFFICERS**	
$125	2 or less
$156	over 2
$188	over 3
$206	over 4
$650	over 6

*ACIP for officers in the grade of O-7 is limited to $200 per month, and to $206 per month for officers in grade O-8 or above.
**ACIP does not end at 25 years officer service, but may be paid during entire career.

UNIFORMED SERVICES ALMANAC

Special Pay for Aviation Career Officers. The FY 1990 DoD Authorization Act authorized payment of a retention bonus to qualified aviation career officers serving in critical aviation specialties. Upon acceptance of a written agreement by the Secretary concerned, aviators may be paid up to $12,000 per year to remain on active duty to complete 14 years of service (long term contract); those who agree to serve shorter terms (additional 1 or 2 years) may be paid up to $6000 per year for each additional year of service (short term contract). Eligibility for this bonus is limited to aviation career officers who have completed at least 6 but less than 13 years of active duty and meet all other eligibility criteria as defined in Title 37, Sec 301b. Authority for payment of this bonus has been extended to September 30, 1996.

Officer Career Sea Pay. Career Sea Pay is based on accrued years of sea duty — defined as assignment to a ship, ship-based staff or ship-based aviation unit and while serving on a ship which primary mission is accomplished while underway. Members who have served 36 *consecutive* months of sea duty are entitled to a career sea pay premium of $100 per month for the 37th consecutive month and each subsequent consecutive month of sea duty.

Submarine Duty Incentive Pay. Officers assigned to submarine or self-propelled submersible vehicle duty on a career basis are entitled to incentive pay at the rates shown in the Officer Submarine Duty Pay Table.

OFFICER CAREER SEA PAY

Pay Grade	1 or less	Over 1	Over 2	Over 3	Over 4	Over 5	Over 6	Over 7	Over 8	Over 9	Over 10	Over 11	Over 12	Over 14	Over 16	Over 18	Over 20
COMMISSIONED OFFICERS																
O-6	–	–	–	225	230	240	255	265	280	290	300	310	325	340	355	380
O-5	–	–	–	225	225	225	225	230	245	250	260	265	265	285	300	315	340
O-4	–	–	–	185	190	200	205	215	220	220	225	225	240	270	280	290	300
O-3	–	–	–	150	160	185	190	195	205	215	225	225	240	260	270	280	290
O-2	–	–	–	150	160	185	190	195	205	215	225	225	240	250	260	270	280
O-1	–	–	–	150	160	185	190	195	205	215	225	225	240	250	260	270	280
WARRANT OFFICERS																
W-4	150	150	150	150	170	290	310	310	310	310	350	375	400	450	450	500	500
W-3	150	150	150	150	170	270	280	285	290	310	350	375	400	425	425	450	450
W-2	150	150	150	150	170	260	265	265	270	310	340	340	375	400	400	400	400
W-1	130	135	140	150	170	175	200	250	270	300	325	325	340	360	375	375	375

OFFICER SUBMARINE DUTY PAY

Pay Grade	2 or less	Over 2	Over 3	Over 4	Over 6	Over 8	Over 10	Over 12	Over 14	Over 16	Over 18	Over 20	Over 22	Over 26
COMMISSIONED OFFICERS Years of service													
O-10	355	355	355	355	355	355	355	355	355	355	355	355	355	355
O-9	355	355	355	355	355	355	355	355	355	355	355	355	355	355
O-8	355	355	355	355	355	355	355	355	355	355	355	355	355	355
O-7	355	355	355	355	355	355	355	355	355	540	535	535	410	355
O-6	595	595	595	595	595	595	595	595	595	595	595	595	595	595
O-5	595	595	595	595	595	595	595	595	595	595	595	595	595	595
O-4	365	365	365	405	595	595	595	595	595	595	595	595	595	595
O-3	355	355	355	390	595	595	595	595	595	595	595	595	595	595
O-2	235	235	235	235	235	235	355	355	355	355	355	355	355	355
O-1	175	175	175	175	175	175	355	355	355	355	355	355	355	355
WARRANT OFFICERS Years of service													
W-4	310	355	355	355	355	355	355	355	355	355	355	355	355	355
W-3	310	355	355	355	355	355	355	355	355	355	355	355	355	355
W-2	310	355	355	355	355	355	355	355	355	355	355	355	355	355
W-1	310	355	355	355	355	355	355	355	355	355	355	355	355	355

UNIFORMED SERVICES ALMANAC

Continuation Pay for Scientific and Engineering Officers. Officers who have been certified as having the technical qualifications for detail to engineering or scientific duty, *may* be paid a continuation bonus of an amount not to exceed $3,000 multiplied by the number of years, or monthly fraction thereof, of obligated service to which the officer and the concerned service Secretary agrees. To qualify, the officer must have at least 3 but less than 19 years of engineering or scientific duty; and serve in a skill designated as critical by the SECDEF. The period of obligated service must be at least one year, but not more than four years.

Foreign Language Proficiency Pay. Provides a special incentive up to $100 per month for officers of the armed forces to become proficient, or to increase their proficiency, in foreign languages, in order to enhance the foreign language capabilities of members of the armed forces.

Civilian Clothing Allowance. In high risk areas, officers assigned to locations outside the United States may be entitled to a civilian clothing allowance in amounts that the SECDEF shall determine, in that the officer is required to wear civilian clothes all or a substantial part of the time, in the performance of official duties.

Medical Officers. Four types of special pay are authorized for Medical officers.

1. *Variable Special Pay.* Medical officers who are undergoing internship training (first year of graduate professional education) are entitled to variable special pay of $1,200 per year. Medical officers who are serving in pay grade O-7 or above are entitled to variable special pay of $7,000 per year. All other medical officers are entitled to variable special pay as indicated in the following table. Payments are made monthly.

2. *Additional Special Pay.* A medical officer who is not undergoing internship or initial residency training is entitled to additional special pay in the amount of $15,000 per year. The officer must execute a written agreement to remain on active duty for a period of not less than one year. Payments are made annually at the beginning of the 12-month period.

3. *Board Certified Pay.* Medical officers are entitled to a board certified pay from $2,500 to $6,000 depending on years of creditable service (1) as indicated in the following table. Payments are made monthly.

4. *Incentive Special Pay.* In addition to all other special pays, a medical officer who is not undergoing internship or initial residency training may be authorized incentive special pay in an amount not to exceed $36,000 for any 12-month period beginning in FY 96. Payments are made annually at the beginning of the 12-month period.

Incentive Special Pay

Specialty	Annual Amounts (In Dollars)
Orthopedic Surgery	36,000
Surgical Subspecialities	36,000
Anesthesiology	33,000
Radiology/Nuclear Medicine	29,000
OB/GYN	29,000
Otolaryngology	27,000
Ophthalmology	27,000
Urology	24,000
General Surgery	22,000

UNIFORMED SERVICES ALMANAC

Critical Care[1]/Gastroenterology	20,000
Emergency Medicine	18,000
Other Internal Medicine and Pediatric Subspecialities	15,000
Pathology	15,000
Neurology	13,000
Dermatology	14,000
Internal Medicine	9,000
Pediatrics	8,000
Psychiatry	7,000
Prev/Occup/Phys/Aerospace Med (3 yr trained)	7,000
Family Practice	6,000

[1]Critical Care includes Cardiology, Pulmonary Medicine, Neonatology, and any fellowship trained critical care or intensive medicine specialties.

MEDICAL OFFICERS SPECIAL PAYS

Creditable Service	Variable Special Pay	Additional* Special Pay	Board Certified Pay	Maximum	Incentive Special Pay $
O-6 and below					
0-6 Years	$5,000	15,000	2,500	22,500	Up to 36,000
6-8 Years	12,000	15,000	2,500	29,500	Up to 36,000
8-10 Years	11,500	15,000	2,500	29,000	Up to 36,000
10-12 Years	11,000	15,000	3,500	30,000	Up to 36,000
12-14 Years	10,000	15,000	4,000	29,000	Up to 36,000
14-18 Years	9,000	15,000	5,000	29,000	Up to 36,000
18-22 Years	8,000	15,000	6,000	29,000	Up to 36,000
Over 22 Years	7,000	15,000	6,000	28,000	Up to 36,000
O-7 and above					
Over 18 Years	7,000	15,000	6,000	28,000	N/A

Variable Special Pay. Payable to all military physicians depending on years of creditable service. Payable to affected personnel monthly.
Additional Special Pay. * Paid to all military physicians not in initial internship or residency. Officers must execute a written agreement to remain on active duty for one year.
Board Certification. Payable to all military physicians who have achieved board certification in a medical specialty. Rates depend on years of creditable services. Payable monthly
Incentive Special Pay. Paid to physicians in designated specialties. Maximum allowance is $36,000 for one year written agreement.
(1) Creditable Service is computed by adding all periods which the officer spent in medical internship or residency training while not on active duty to all periods of active duty as a physician or dentist.

Multiyear Special Pay. In addition to all other special pays, a medical officer who has completed at least eight years of creditable service or has completed any active duty service commitment incurred for medical education and training, and; has completed specialty qualification, and; executes a written agreement to remain on active duty for two, three or four years, that is accepted by the Secretary of the Military Department concerned is eligible for Multiyear Special Pay as indicated in the following table. Payments are made annually.

UNIFORMED SERVICES ALMANAC

Multiyear Special Pay

Specialty	Annual Amounts by Contract Length		
	2 Year	3 Year	4 Year
Category One	$4,000	$8,000	$14,000
Family Practice			
Emergency Medicine			
Urology			
Orthopedic Surgery			
General Internal Medicine			
Category Two	$3,000	$6,000	$10,000
Neurology			
General Surgery			
Critical Care[1]/			
Gastroenterology			
Otolaryngology			
Radiology/Nuclear Medicine			
Psychiatry			
OB/GYN			
Category Three	$2,000	$4,000	$8,000
Dermatology			
Preventive/Occup/Phys Med			
Opthalmology			
Surgical Subspecialities			
Aerospace Medicine			
(3 yr residency trained only)			
Pediatrics			
Pathology			

[1]Critical Care includes Cardiology, Pulmonary Medicine, Neonatology, and any fellowship trained critical care or intensive medicine specialties.

The following specialties are not eligible for MSP: Other Internal Medicine, Pediatric Subspecialities, and Anesthesiology.

Dental Officers.
Three types of special pay are authorized for Dental officers.
1. *Variable Special Pay.* Dental officers who are undergoing internship training (first year of graduate professional education) are entitled to variable special pay of $1,200 per year. Dental officers who are serving in pay grade O-7 or above are entitled to variable special pay of $1,000 per year. All other Dental officers are entitled to variable special pay as indicated in the following table. Payments are made monthly.
2. *Additional Special Pay.* A Dental officer who is not undergoing internship or residency training is entitled to additional special pay provided he or she first executes a written agreement to remain on active duty for a period of not less than one year. Dental officers are entitled to additional special pay from $6,000 to $10,000 per year based on years of creditable service (1) as indicated in the preceding table. Payments are made annually at the beginning of the 12-month period.
3. *Board Certified Pay.* Dental officers are entitled to board certified pay from $2,000 to $4,000 per year based on years of creditable service as indicated in the preceding table. Payments are made monthly.

UNIFORMED SERVICES ALMANAC

A "Save Pay" provision is included in the dental special pay legislation to ensure that no Dental officer receives special pay less than the amount he or she was entitled to under the previous dental continuation/special pay program.

DENTAL OFFICER SPECIAL PAYS

Creditable Service	Variable Special Pay	Additional Special Pay	Board Certified Pay
O-6 and below			
Interns	1,200	—	—
0-3 Years	1,200	—	—
3-6 Years	2,000	6,000	2,000
6-10 Years	4,000	6,000	2,000
10-12 Years	6,000	6,000	2,000
12-14 Years	6,000	6,000	3,000
14-18 Years	4,000	8,000	4,000
Over 18 Years	3,000	10,000	4,000
O-7 and above			
Over 18 Years	1,000	10,000	4,000

Variable Special Pay. Payable to all military dentists depending on years of creditable service. Payable monthly.

Additional Special Pay. Payable to all military dentists not in internship or residency. Officers must execute a written agreement to remain on active duty for one year. Payable in a lump sum.

Board Certified Pay. Paid to all dental officers who have achieved board certification in a dental specialty. Rates depend on years of creditable service. Payable monthly.

Nurse Corps Officers

Accession Bonus. A registered nurse who agrees to serve on active duty for at least four years may be paid an accession bonus up to $5,000. This authority has been extended to September 30, 1997.

Incentive Special Pay for Certified Registered Nurse Anesthetists. Qualified Certified Registered Nurse Anesthetists (CRNA) may be paid incentive special pay (ISP) of up to $15,000 for a minimum one year written agreement. The ISP rate shall be $6,000 per year during any period for which the officer is obligated for training as a CRNA. The ISP rate shall be $15,000 per year for any contract for which the officer is not obligated for training as a CRNA at the beginning of the contract year. This authority extends to September 30, 1996.

Other Health Professionals. Veterinary and Optometry officers are authorized Special Pay at the rate of $100 per month. (Note: Air Force veterinarians assigned as Environmental Health officers are not entitled to this special pay.)

Diplomate Pay for Psychologists and Nonphysician Board Certified Pay. Optometrists, podiatrists, audiologists, dieticians, occupational therapists, pharmacists, physical therapists, social workers, and clinical psychologists may receive diplomate or board certified pay from $2,000 to $5,000 per year based on creditable services as indicated in the following table.

Less than 10 years	$2,000
10-12	$2,500
12-14	$3,000
14-18	$4,000
18 or more	$5,000

UNIFORMED SERVICES ALMANAC
ENLISTED PAY

Enlisted pay is presented in detail in Table II. This table reflects basic pay and Basic Allowance for Quarters (BAQ) at the *With Dependents* rate. Adjustments must be made for single members and those claiming not more than one exemption for tax purposes. Due to the various rates for Basic Allowance for Subsistence (BAS), CONUS COLA, Variable Housing Allowance (VHA), and for Clothing Allowances, these factors must be included on an individual basis. Personnel drawing Overseas or Sea Pay and those entitled to special or incentive pay such as Flight or Submarine Pay, or family separation allowance, must also compute these items on an individual basis. Tables for determining these amounts can be found on pages following the "take-home" pay tables. BAS, BAQ, and clothing allowances are nontaxable and therefore, in computing "take-home" pay after adding any other payments, caution should be exercised to allow for increased income tax withholding.

BASIC ALLOWANCE FOR QUARTERS (BAQ)
ENLISTED MEMBERS: (January 1, 1996)

Pay Grade	Without Dependents Full Rate*	Without Dependents Partial Rate**	With Dependents
E-9	478.50	18.60	630.60
E-8	439.20	15.30	581.40
E-7	375.00	12.00	539.70
E-6	339.60	9.90	498.90
E-5	313.20	8.70	448.50
E-4	272.40	8.10	390.00
E-3	267.30	7.80	363.00
E-2	217.20	7.20	345.60
E-1>4	193.50	6.90	345.60
E-1<4	193.50	6.90	345.60

*Full Rate is authorized for members without dependents who are not occupying government quarters.
**Partial rate is authorized for members without dependents who live in government quarters or are on field or sea duty.

NET "TAKE HOME PAY" DECREASE
"SINGLE" — WITHOUT DEPENDENTS

Pay Grade	Monthly Amount Full Rate $	Monthly Amount Partial Rate $
E-9	152.10	612.00
E-8	142.20	566.10
E-7	164.70	527.70
E-6	159.30	489.00
E-5	135.30	439.80
E-4	117.60	381.90
E-3	95.70	355.20
E-2	128.40	338.40
E-1	152.10	338.70

Members *without dependents* who occupy government quarters and those on sea or field duty receive a partial quarters allowance. This partial allowance or BAQ "rebate", which ranges from $6.90 for an E-1 to $18.60 for an E-9, is paid to single personnel to compensate for the amount that base pay would have been increased had the President not reallocated a portion of the FY 77 basic pay increase, and transferred it to BAQ.

UNIFORMED SERVICES ALMANAC

New annual clothing maintenance allowances were established effective October 1, 1995 for enlisted personnel of the Armed Forces. These new rates are shown in detail on the following pages. Therefore, the "take-home" pay tables must be adjusted accordingly based on branch of service and sex. For example, a Marine Corps sergeant (E-5), male, would draw the standard clothing allowance of $25.80 (one-twelfth the annual rate), which would be added to the appropriate column in Table II.

Almost all service members have a monthly deduction of $18.00 for a $200,000 SGLI insurance policy. Another deduction for Army and Air Force enlisted personnel is the contribution for the Soldiers' and Airmens' Home which is currently $1.00. There are any number of other voluntary allotments which may be initiated which will further decrease the "net take-home" pay. Allotments for mortgage payments, life insurance, savings, etc., must all be considered for adjustments to pay Table II.

Enlisted personnel serving an overseas tour unaccompanied by their families will find it necessary to make an adjustment for family separation allowance to determine their correct "take-home" pay. If accompanied, adjustment must be made for Cost-of-Living and/or Housing Allowances.

Basic Allowance for Subsistence (BAS) — Enlisted Members: (January 1, 1996)
When on leave or authorized to mess separately. .... $7.15 per day
When rations in-kind are not available. .... $8.06 per day
When assigned to duty under emergency conditions where no
  messing facilities of the United States are available. ...... $10.67 per day

Note: For members who have been enlisted 4 months or less see page 37 for BAS amounts.

ENLISTED PERSONNEL — SPECIAL AND INCENTIVE PAY

(The following Special and Incentive pays are extended or changed as indicated based on the assumption that the FY 96 Defense Authorization Act will be passed.)

Flight Pay (Crew Member). Hazardous duty pay as an enlisted flight crew member ranges from $110.00 per month for an E-1 to $200.00 per month for an E-9. Entitlement to flight pay requires duty as a flight crew member involving frequent and regular participation in aerial flight. (See Enlisted Flight Pay Table.)

ENLISTED MEMBERS FLYING PAY

Pay Grade	Under 2	Over 2	Over 3	Over 4	Over 6	Over 8	Over 10	Over 12	Over 14
E-9	$200	$200	$200	$200	$200	$200	$200	$200	$200
E-8	200	200	200	200	200	200	200	200	200
E-7	200	200	200	200	200	200	200	200	200
E-6	175	175	175	175	175	175	175	175	175
E-5	150	150	150	150	150	150	150	150	150
E-4	125	125	125	125	125	125	125	125	125
E-3	110	110	110	110	110	110	110	110	110
E-2	110	110	110	110	110	110	110	110	110
E-1	110	110	110	110	110	110	110	110	110

Submarine Duty Pay. Hazardous duty pay as an enlisted submarine crew member ranges from $75.00 per month as an E-1 to $355.00 per month as an E-9. Entitlement requires assignment to submarine duty. (See Submarine Duty Pay Table.)

UNIFORMED SERVICES ALMANAC

ENLISTED MEMBERS SUBMARINE DUTY PAY

Pay Grade	2 or less	Over 2	Over 3	Over 4	Over 6	Over 8	Over 10	Over 12	Over 14	Over 16	Over 18	Over 20	Over 22	Over 25
E-9	225	225	225	270	295	310	315	330	345	355	355	355	355	355
E-8	225	225	225	250	270	295	310	315	330	330	345	345	345	345
E-7	225	225	225	250	255	265	275	295	310	310	310	310	310	310
E-6	155	170	175	215	230	245	255	265	265	265	265	265	265	265
E-5	140	155	155	175	190	195	195	195	195	195	195	195	195	195
E-4	80	95	100	170	175	175	175	175	175	175	175	175	175	175
E-3	80	90	100	170	175	175	90	90	90	90	90	90	90	90
E-2	75	90	90	90	90	90	90	90	90	90	90	90	90	90
E-1	75	75	75	75	75	75	75	75	75	75	75	75	75	75

Other Hazardous Duty Incentive Pay. Enlisted personnel engaged in: aerial flight as a noncrew member; parachute jumping; explosive demolitions duty; operation or duty as crew member on submersible or research vehicles; experimental stress duty including working inside a high or low-pressure chamber; duty involving flight deck operations on the deck of an aircraft carrier or any ship from which aircraft are launched; and certain other hazardous duties including toxic fuel handlers and personnel exposed to viruses or bacteria in laboratory situations, are entitled to incentive pay of $110.00 per month. One exception to the $110.00 per month for parachute jumping, is authority to pay, $165.00 per month for parachute jumping at high altitudes with a low altitude opening.

Diving Pay. Enlisted members who are assigned by orders to diving duty and who are required to maintain proficiency as a diver by frequent and regular dives, are entitled to special pay from $110.00 for a diver 2nd class up to a maximum of $300.00 per month for Master Divers, for periods during which diving duty is actually performed.

Special Pay for Hostile Fire and Imminent Danger. Special pay of $150.00 per month is payable to members assigned to duties subject to hostile fire or explosion of hostile mines or imminent danger in places or situations as prescribed by the Secretary of Defense. Some of the currently designated areas include but are not limited to: Vietnam; Cambodia; Lebanon; Sudan; Kuwait; Iraq; Persian Gulf; Saudi Arabia; Turkey; Somalia; Haiti; and the former country of Yugoslavia, including Slovenia, Croatia, and Boznia-Herzogovina.

Foreign Language Proficiency Pay. Provides a special incentive up to $100 per month for members of the armed forces to become proficient, or to increase their proficiency, in foreign languages, in order to enhance the foreign language capabilities of the armed forces.

Special Duty Assignment Pay. This is a special pay designed to provide an additional monthly amount to enlisted members who are required to perform extremely demanding duties or duties demanding an unusual degree of responsibility. Special Duty Assignment Pay is authorized for enlisted members in designated specialties. The maximum payable is $275.00 per month. A member may not be paid both the proficiency pay and the special duty assignment pay.

Certain Places Pay. Also known as Foreign Duty Pay, this special pay is authorized for enlisted members while on duty at a designated place outside the 48 contiguous states and the District of Columbia at the following rates: E-7, E-8, E-9 - $22.50; E-6 - $20.00; E-5 - $16.00; E-4 - $13.00; E-3 - $9.00; E-1, E-2 - $8.00.

UNIFORMED SERVICES ALMANAC

Career Sea Pay. Career sea pay is authorized for enlisted members based on accrued years of sea duty, defined as assignment to a ship, ship-based staff or ship-based aviation unit and while serving on a ship whose primary mission is accomplished while underway. The rates in the following tables are for enlisted members with less than five years of sea duty who reported for sea duty after May 1, 1988. Slightly different rates are authorized for members with sea duty prior to May 1, 1988. Members who have served 36 months of consecutive sea duty are entitled to a career sea pay premium of $100 per month for the 37th month and each subsequent consecutive month of sea duty.

ENLISTED MEMBERS CAREER SEA PAY

Pay Grade	1 or less	Over 1	Over 2	Over 3	Over 4	Over 5	Over 6	Over 7	Over 8	Over 9	Over 10	Over 11	Over 12	Over 13	Over 14	Over 16	Over 18
E-4	50	60	120	150	160	160	160	160	160	160	160	160	160	160	160	160	160
E-5	50	60	120	150	170	315	325	350	350	350	350	350	350	350	350	350	350
E-6	100	100	120	150	170	315	325	350	350	365	365	365	380	395	410	425	450
E-7	100	100	120	175	190	350	350	375	390	400	400	410	420	450	475	500	500
E-8	100	100	120	175	190	350	350	375	390	400	400	410	420	450	475	500	520
E-9	100	100	120	175	190	350	350	375	390	400	400	410	420	450	475	520	520

Special Pay for Nuclear Qualified Enlisted Members. An enlisted member of the naval service who is currently qualified for duty in connection with the supervision, operation and maintenance of naval nuclear propulsion plants may be paid a bonus not to exceed six months of basic pay times the number of years of additional obligated service not to exceed six years or $15,000 whichever is less. Members must have completed at least six, but not more than ten, years of active duty and executed a reenlistment agreement for not less than two years.

UNIFORMED SERVICES ALMANAC

ARMED FORCES ENLISTED PAY
Basic Pay Rates, Effective January 1, 1996

Pay Grade	Under 2	Over 2	Over 3	Over 4	Over 6	Over 8	Over 10	Over 12	Over 14	Over 16	Over 18	Over 20	Over 22	Over 24	Over 26
E-9	0.00	0.00	0.00	0.00	0.00	0.00	2623.20	2682.00	2742.60	2805.60	2868.60	2924.10	3077.40	3197.40	3377.10
E-8	0.00	0.00	0.00	0.00	0.00	2199.60	2262.90	2322.30	2382.60	2445.60	2501.40	2562.90	2713.50	2834.40	3015.90
E-7	1535.70	1658.10	1719.00	1779.60	1840.20	1898.70	1959.60	2020.80	2112.00	2172.00	2232.00	2261.40	2413.20	2533.20	2713.50
E-6	1321.20	1440.30	1500.00	1563.90	1622.70	1680.90	1742.70	1832.40	1890.00	1950.90	1980.60	1980.60	1980.60	1980.60	1980.60
E-5	1159.50	1262.10	1323.30	1380.90	1471.80	1531.80	1592.10	1650.90	1680.90	1680.90	1680.90	1680.90	1680.90	1680.90	1680.90
E-4	1081.20	1142.10	1209.30	1302.60	1354.20	1354.20	1354.20	1354.20	1354.20	1354.20	1354.20	1354.20	1354.20	1354.20	1354.20
E-3	1019.10	1074.90	1117.50	1161.90	1161.90	1161.90	1161.90	1161.90	1161.90	1161.90	1161.90	1161.90	1161.90	1161.90	1161.90
E-2	980.70	980.70	980.70	980.70	980.70	980.70	980.70	980.70	980.70	980.70	980.70	980.70	980.70	980.70	980.70
E-1	874.80	874.80	874.80	874.80	874.80	874.80	874.80	874.80	874.80	874.80	874.80	874.80	874.80	874.80	874.80

Note: While serving as the senior member of the Service, basic pay is $4104.90 regardless of years of service.

ENLISTED PERSONNEL*
Average Annual Basic Military Compensation (BMC) (Amounts rounded down to nearest dollar)

Pay Grade	Under 2	Over 2	Over 3	Over 4	Over 6	Over 8	Over 10	Over 12	Over 14	Over 16	Over 18	Over 20	Over 22	Over 24	Over 26
E-9	0	0	0	0	0	0	0	0	44,884	45,622	46,377	47,043	48,882	50,322	52,495
E-8	0	0	0	0	0	0	38,433	39,099	39,828	40,591	41,268	42,012	43,819	45,270	47,449
E-7	0	0	0	0	0	33,299	34,038	34,783	35,893	36,623	37,354	37,711	39,559	41,020	43,189
E-6	25,639	27,220	27,977	28,704	32,569	30,001	30,750	31,839	32,530	33,276	33,640	0	0	0	0
E-5	22,774	24,117	24,886	25,601	29,348	27,455	28,164	28,823	29,156	0	0	0	0	0	0
E-4	20,654	21,427	22,274	23,422	26,716	0	0	0	0	0	0	0	0	0	0
E-3	19,411	20,096	20,620	21,166	24,055	0	0	0	0	0	0	0	0	0	0
E-2	18,184	0	0	0	0	0	0	0	0	0	0	0	0	0	0
E-1	16,571	0	0	0	0	0	0	0	0	0	0	0	0	0	0

*Basic Military Compensation (BMC) combines basic pay, basic allowance for quarters pay, basic allowance for subsistence and the federal tax advantage on the tax free allowances. The formula for calculating BMC is the same as was previously used for Regular Military Compensation (RMC) but does not include an average amount for the Variable Housing Allowance (VHA) which is paid to about 1/3 of all active duty members living off base in the CONUS. The BMC is at best, a guide to income for any member in a given grade and year of service. Members drawing VHA can add the amount to the BMC figures above to compute a rough estimate of their RMC. (As of January 1, 1996 based on 2.4% increase in Basic Pay and BAS, and 5.2% increase in BAQ and VHA)

UNIFORMED SERVICES ALMANAC

ENLISTED PERSONNEL—MONTHLY PAY

Table II

(Adjust "Net Take-Home Pay" for SPECIAL PAY, VHA, State Taxes and any voluntary allotments) (See footnotes at end of pay table.)

G R A D E	Yrs of Svc Over	Annual Total Basic Pay & BAQ[1]	BASIC PAY Monthly	BASIC PAY Daily[2]	Basic Allow- ance for Qtrs With Dep.	Monthly Basic Pay and BAQ[3]	Soc. Sec. 7.65% FICA Dec.	\multicolumn{7}{c	}{Net Take Home Pay Each Month After Federal Taxes and Social Security Deductions** Number of Withholding Exemptions Claimed†}							
								0 MARRIED	1	2	3	4	5	0[3] SINGLE	1[3]	2
(1)		(2)	(3)	(4)	(5)	(6)	(7)	(8)	(9)	(10)	(11)	(12)	(13)	(14)	(15)	(16)
E-9	10	39046	2623.20	87.44	630.60	3253.80	200.67	2739.90	2771.77	2803.65	2835.52	2867.40	2899.27	2627.21	2686.71	2746.21
E-9	12	39751	2682.00	89.40	630.60	3312.60	205.17	2785.38	2817.25	2849.13	2881.00	2912.88	2944.75	2665.05	2724.55	2784.05
E-9	14	40478	2742.60	91.42	630.60	3373.20	209.81	2832.25	2864.13	2896.00	2927.88	2959.75	2991.63	2704.04	2763.54	2823.04
E-9	16	41234	2805.60	93.52	630.60	3436.20	214.63	2880.98	2912.86	2944.73	2976.61	3008.48	3040.36	2744.58	2804.08	2863.58
E-9	18	41990	2868.60	95.62	630.60	3499.20	219.45	2929.71	2961.59	2993.46	3025.34	3057.21	3089.09	2785.12	2844.62	2904.12
E-9	20	42656	2924.10	97.47	630.60	3554.70	223.69	2972.64	3004.52	3036.39	3068.27	3100.14	3132.02	2820.84	2880.34	2939.84
E-9	22	44496	3077.40	102.58	630.60	3708.00	230.65	3091.22	3123.09	3154.97	3186.84	3218.72	3250.59	2919.49	2978.99	3038.49
E-9	26	48092	3377.10	112.57	630.60	4007.70	258.35	3323.04	3354.91	3386.79	3418.66	3450.54	3482.41	3112.34	3171.84	3231.34
E-8	8	33372	2199.60	73.32	581.40	2781.00	168.27	2363.04	2394.92	2426.79	2458.67	2490.54	2522.42	2305.42	2347.52	2379.39
E-8	10	34132	2262.90	75.43	581.40	2844.30	173.11	2412.00	2443.88	2475.75	2507.63	2539.50	2571.38	2346.16	2396.48	2428.35
E-8	12	34844	2322.30	77.41	581.40	2903.70	177.66	2457.95	2489.82	2521.70	2553.57	2585.45	2617.32	2384.38	2442.42	2474.30
E-8	14	35568	2382.60	79.42	581.40	2964.00	182.27	2504.59	2536.47	2568.34	2600.22	2632.09	2663.97	2423.18	2482.68	2520.94
E-8	16	36324	2445.60	81.52	581.40	3027.00	187.09	2553.32	2585.20	2617.07	2648.95	2680.82	2712.70	2463.72	2523.22	2569.67
E-8	18	36994	2501.40	83.38	581.40	3082.80	191.36	2596.48	2628.36	2660.23	2692.11	2723.98	2755.86	2499.63	2559.13	2612.83
E-8	20	37732	2562.90	85.43	581.40	3144.30	196.06	2644.05	2675.93	2707.80	2739.68	2771.55	2803.43	2539.21	2598.71	2658.21
E-8	22	39539	2713.50	90.45	581.40	3294.90	207.58	2760.54	2792.42	2824.29	2856.17	2888.04	2919.92	2636.12	2695.62	2755.12
E-8	26	43168	3015.90	100.53	581.40	3597.30	230.72	2994.45	3026.32	3058.20	3090.07	3121.95	3153.82	2830.71	2890.21	2949.71
E-7	8	29261	1898.70	63.29	539.70	2438.40	145.25	2088.59	2120.47	2152.34	2184.22	2216.09	2247.97	2041.19	2073.07	2104.94
E-7	10	29992	1959.60	65.32	539.70	2499.30	149.91	2135.70	2167.58	2199.45	2231.33	2263.20	2295.08	2088.30	2120.18	2152.05
E-7	12	30726	2020.80	67.36	539.70	2560.50	154.59	2183.04	2214.91	2246.79	2278.66	2310.54	2342.41	2135.64	2167.51	2199.39
E-7	14	31820	2112.00	70.40	539.70	2651.70	161.57	2253.58	2285.46	2317.33	2349.21	2381.08	2412.96	2206.18	2238.06	2269.93
E-7	16	32540	2172.00	72.40	539.70	2711.70	166.16	2299.99	2331.87	2363.74	2395.62	2427.49	2459.37	2245.96	2284.47	2316.34
E-7	18	33260	2232.00	74.40	539.70	2771.70	170.75	2346.40	2378.28	2410.15	2442.03	2473.90	2505.78	2284.57	2330.88	2362.75
E-7	20	33613	2261.40	75.38	539.70	2801.10	173.00	2369.14	2401.02	2432.89	2464.77	2496.64	2528.52	2303.49	2353.62	2385.49
E-7	22	35435	2413.20	80.44	539.70	2952.90	184.61	2486.56	2518.44	2550.31	2582.19	2614.06	2645.94	2401.17	2460.67	2502.91
E-7	26	39038	2713.50	90.45	539.70	3253.20	207.58	2718.84	2750.72	2782.59	2814.47	2846.34	2878.22	2594.42	2653.92	2713.42

35

UNIFORMED SERVICES ALMANAC

ENLISTED PERSONNEL—MONTHLY PAY
Table II

(Adjust "Net Take-Home Pay" for SPECIAL PAY, VHA, State Taxes and any voluntary allotments) (See footnotes at end of pay table.)

G R A D E	Yrs of Svc Over	Annual Total Basic Pay & BAQ[1]	BASIC PAY Monthly	BASIC PAY Daily[2]	Basic Allowance for Qtrs With Dep.	Monthly Basic Pay and BAQ[3]	Soc. Sec. 7.65% FICA Dec.	Net Take Home Pay Each Month After Federal Taxes and Social Security Deductions** — Number of Withholding Exemptions Claimed† MARRIED 0	1	2	3	4	5	SINGLE 0[3]	1[3]	2
No.	(1)	(2)	(3)	(4)	(5)	(6)	(7)	(8)	(9)	(10)	(11)	(12)	(13)	(14)	(15)	(16)
E-6	2	23270	1440.30	48.01	498.90	1939.20	110.18	1693.22	1725.10	1756.97	1788.85	1820.72	1829.02	1645.82	1677.70	1709.57
E-6	3	23987	1500.00	50.00	498.90	1998.90	114.75	1739.40	1771.28	1803.15	1835.03	1866.90	1884.15	1692.00	1723.88	1755.75
E-6	4	24754	1563.90	52.13	498.90	2062.80	119.64	1788.83	1820.70	1852.58	1884.45	1916.33	1943.16	1741.43	1773.30	1805.18
E-6	6	25459	1622.70	54.09	498.90	2121.60	124.14	1834.31	1866.18	1898.06	1929.93	1961.81	1993.68	1786.91	1818.78	1850.66
E-6	8	26158	1680.90	56.03	498.90	2179.80	128.55	1879.33	1911.20	1943.08	1974.95	2006.83	2038.70	1831.93	1863.80	1895.68
E-6	10	26899	1742.70	58.09	498.90	2241.60	133.32	1927.13	1959.00	1990.88	2022.75	2054.63	2086.50	1879.73	1911.60	1943.48
E-6	12	27976	1832.40	61.08	498.90	2331.30	140.18	1996.51	2028.39	2060.26	2092.14	2124.01	2155.89	1949.11	1980.99	2012.86
E-6	14	28667	1890.00	63.00	498.90	2388.90	144.59	2041.07	2072.94	2104.82	2136.69	2168.57	2200.44	1993.67	2025.54	2057.42
E-6	16	29398	1950.90	65.03	498.90	2449.80	149.24	2088.17	2120.05	2151.92	2183.80	2215.67	2247.55	2040.77	2072.65	2104.52
E-6	18	29754	1980.60	66.02	498.90	2479.50	151.52	2111.14	2143.02	2174.89	2206.77	2238.64	2270.52	2063.74	2095.62	2127.49
E-5	2	20527	1262.10	42.07	448.50	1710.60	96.55	1504.98	1536.86	1568.73	1600.61	1614.05	1614.05	1457.58	1489.46	1521.33
E-5	3	21262	1323.30	44.11	448.50	1771.80	101.23	1552.32	1584.20	1616.07	1647.95	1670.57	1670.57	1504.92	1536.80	1568.67
E-5	4	21953	1380.90	46.03	448.50	1829.40	105.64	1596.88	1628.75	1660.63	1692.50	1723.76	1723.76	1549.48	1581.35	1613.23
E-5	6	23044	1471.80	49.06	448.50	1920.30	112.59	1667.19	1699.06	1730.94	1762.81	1794.69	1807.71	1619.79	1651.66	1683.54
E-5	8	23764	1531.80	51.06	448.50	1980.30	117.18	1713.60	1745.47	1777.35	1809.22	1841.10	1863.12	1666.20	1698.07	1729.95
E-5	10	24487	1592.10	53.07	448.50	2040.60	121.80	1760.24	1792.11	1823.99	1855.86	1887.74	1918.80	1712.84	1744.71	1776.59
E-5	12	25193	1650.90	55.03	448.50	2099.40	126.29	1805.72	1837.60	1869.47	1901.35	1933.22	1965.10	1758.32	1790.20	1822.07
E-5	14	25553	1680.90	56.03	448.50	2129.40	128.59	1828.93	1860.80	1892.68	1924.55	1956.43	1988.30	1781.53	1813.40	1845.28
E-4	<2	17654	1081.20	36.04	390.00	1471.20	82.71	1306.56	1338.43	1370.31	1388.49	1388.49	1388.49	1259.16	1291.03	1322.91
E-4	2	18385	1142.10	38.07	390.00	1532.10	87.37	1353.66	1385.54	1417.41	1444.73	1444.73	1444.73	1306.26	1338.14	1370.01
E-4	3	19192	1209.30	40.31	390.00	1599.30	92.51	1405.64	1437.52	1469.39	1501.27	1506.79	1506.79	1358.24	1390.12	1421.99
E-4	4	20311	1302.60	43.42	390.00	1692.60	99.65	1477.81	1509.69	1541.56	1573.44	1592.95	1592.95	1430.41	1462.29	1494.16
E-4	6	20930	1354.20	45.14	390.00	1744.20	103.60	1517.72	1549.60	1581.47	1613.35	1640.60	1640.60	1470.32	1502.20	1534.07

36

UNIFORMED SERVICES ALMANAC

ENLISTED PERSONNEL—MONTHLY PAY

Table II

(Adjust "Net Take-Home Pay" for SPECIAL PAY, VHA, State Taxes and any voluntary allotments) (See footnotes at end of pay table.)

G R A D E (1)	Yrs of Svc Over (1)	Annual Total Basic Pay & BAQ[1] (2)	BASIC PAY Monthly (3)	BASIC PAY Daily[2] (4)	Basic Allowance for Qtrs With Dep. (5)	Monthly Basic Pay and BAQ[3] (6)	Soc. Sec. 7.65% FICA Dec. (7)	Net Take Home Pay Each Month After Federal Taxes and Social Security Deductions** Number of Withholding Exemptions Claimed†								
								MARRIED						SINGLE		
								0 (8)	1 (9)	2 (10)	3 (11)	4 (12)	5 (13)	0[3] (14)	1[3] (15)	2 (16)
No.																
E-3	<2	16585	1019.10	33.97	363.00	1382.10	77.96	1231.52	1263.40	1295.27	1304.14	1304.14	1304.14	1184.12	1216.00	1247.87
E-3	2	17255	1074.90	35.83	363.00	1437.90	82.23	1274.69	1306.56	1338.44	1355.67	1355.67	1355.67	1227.29	1259.16	1291.04
E-3	3	17766	1117.50	37.25	363.00	1480.50	85.49	1307.64	1339.51	1371.39	1395.01	1395.01	1395.01	1260.24	1292.11	1323.99
E-3	4	18299	1161.90	38.73	363.00	1524.90	88.89	1341.98	1373.85	1405.73	1436.01	1436.01	1436.01	1294.58	1326.45	1358.33
E-2	<2	15916	980.70	32.69	345.60	1326.30	75.02	1184.42	1216.30	1248.17	1251.28	1251.28	1251.28	1137.02	1168.90	1200.77

** If paid twice a month, use 1/2 these monthly amounts.
[1] Includes basic pay amounts plus BAQ With Dependents cash allowances—for information only.
[2] Single day rate for special purposes including drill pay for reserves. (Monthly base pay divided by 30).
[3] Add clothing allowance which varies by length of service and sex—see Uniform Allowance section. Also add BAS as applicable. Pertains to columns (8) through (16).
(See below.)
† Percentage method of computation of witholding tax.

BASIC ALLOWANCE FOR SUBSISTENCE (BAS)

Basic Allowance for Subsistence (BAS)—Enlisted Members (January 1, 1996)

	< 4 MONTHS	OTHERS
When on leave or authorized to mess separately	$6.59	$7.15 per day.
When rations in-kind are not available	$7.43	$8.06 per day.
When assigned to duty under emergency conditions where no messing facilities of the United States are available	$9.86	$10.67 per day.

37

UNIFORMED SERVICES ALMANAC
UNIFORM ALLOWANCES

CLOTHING MONETARY ALLOWANCES FOR ENLISTED PERSONNEL OF THE ARMED FORCES

DoD Instruction 1338.18 authorizes the Secretary of Defense to prescribe the quantity and kind of clothing which shall be furnished to enlisted personnel of the Armed Forces, or the cash allowances in lieu thereof. This authority is exercised through implementing instructions issued by the individual Service Secretaries and applies to enlisted personnel of the Army, the Navy, the Marine Corps, the Air Force, the Naval Reserve, the Marine Corps Reserve, the National Guard of the United States, the Air National Guard of the United States, the Army Reserve, and the Air Force Reserve.

Officers receive a onetime payment after commissioning to buy clothing. They do not receive any allowances to maintain their uniforms.

Enlisted members are issued the standard wardrobe when they enter active duty. They get a clothing-replacement allowance on their anniversary date.

The replacement allowance is paid at the "basic" rate for members with less than three years of service, and at the "standard" rate for members with three or more years of service.

There are three types of clothing allowances which cover both initial allowances and replacement requirements, as follows:

1. Initial Clothing Allowances
2. Cash Clothing Replacement Allowances
3. Supplementary Clothing Allowances (as authorized by individual services)

Military Clothing Allowance Rates Effective October 1, 1995*

1. *Initial Clothing Allowances*

	Enlisted Male	Enlisted Female
Army	$958.00	$1171.16
Navy	894.08	1269.67
Air Force	829.61	1017.93
Marine Corps	923.30	1147.07

2. *Cash Clothing Replacement Allowance (Annual Rates)*

	Basic Enlisted Male	Basic Enlisted Female	Standard Enlisted Male	Standard Enlisted Female
Army	$194.40	$234.00	$277.20	$334.80
Navy	205.20	259.20	291.60	370.80
Air Force	172.80	219.60	248.40	313.20
Marine Corps	216.00	198.00	309.60	284.40

UNIFORMED SERVICES ALMANAC

3. *Extra Clothing Allowances*

    A. **Special Initial and Replacement Allowances**

		Special Initial Allowance	Annual Special Replacement Allowance
(1) Naval enlisted personnel eligible to wear Chief Petty Officer type uniforms:			
— Male		$720.35	$396.00
— Female		853.05	540.00
(2) Naval Officer Candidates.	(M)	1017.40	
& Naval Aviation Cadets	(F)	1330.10	
(3) Members of Navy Unit Bands below E-7.	(M)	$720.35	$396.00
	(F)	853.05	540.00
(4) Partial initial allowance for Naval Reservists (E-1 - E-6) entering active duty.	(M)	$162.65	
	(F)	282.06	

    B. **Civilian Clothing Allowances....**

	Up to 12 mo	12-24 mo	over 24 mo
(1) Where both winter and summer clothing are required.	$721.00	$962.00	$1217.00
(2) Where either winter or summer clothing is required.	$482.00	$632.00	$787.00

   (3) Where civilian clothing is required in connection with authorized TDY in excess of 15 days.

Less than 30 days	Over 30 days
$240.00	$449.00

*Note: There will be some minor corrections to these rates but they were not available at press time.

    C. **Special Continuing Civilian Clothing Allowance**

A special continuing civilian clothing allowance is authorized under the following conditions: Service members who voluntarily extend their tours or are directed to remain in the assignment requiring the wearing of civilian clothing for at least an additional 6 months are authorized 20 percent of the initial allowance at the current fiscal year rate. Members who voluntarily extend their tours or who are directed to remain in the assignment requiring the wearing of civilian clothing for at least an additional 12 months are authorized 30 percent of the initial allowance at the current fiscal year rate. Officers who have received an initial civilian clothing allowance for duties performed at an overseas permanent duty station and who are ordered to a consecutive permanent overseas assignment requiring the wearing of civilian clothing are authorized 50 percent of the allowance for the latter tour assignment. Enlisted members who have received an initial civilian clothing allowance for duties performed at a permanent duty station and who are ordered to a consecutive permanent assignment requiring the wearing of civilian clothing are authorized 50 percent of the allowance for the latter tour assignment. Service members who received a lesser allowance in the past 12 months than that proposed above and who are still assigned to duty requiring the wearing of civilian clothing are authorized an amount that equals the new rate.

D. Supplementary Clothing Allowances

(1) The Secretaries of the Military Departments or the Commandant of the Marine Corps may prescribe supplementary allowances for personnel assigned to special organizations or details where the nature of the duties to be performed, are such as to clearly require additional items of individual uniform clothing. Any allowance in excess of these amounts must be given prior approval by the Secretary of Defense.
(2) Categories of personnel for whom such allowances may be prescribed include, but are not limited to, military police, recruiters, special units or detachments, such as those regularly assigned as escorts for the bodies of deceased members of the Armed Forces, ceremonial detachments permanently assigned to national cemeteries, and those assigned to locations where climatic conditions require special articles of clothing.

ENLISTMENT AND REENLISTMENT BONUSES
ENLISTMENT BONUS

Currently, there are two provisions in law governing award of the enlistment bonus to certain individuals who enlist in the Armed Forces.

One provision authorizes the award of an enlistment bonus to an enlisted member as an inducement to enlist or extend his or her initial period of active duty in a designated skill of an armed force to a total of at least four years. Bonus amounts are prescribed by the Secretary of Defense but may not exceed $12,000. Payments will be in lump sum or in periodic installments as determined by the Secretary. However, the first installment may not exceed $7,000 and the remainder shall be paid in equal installments which may not be paid less frequently than once every three months. A more restrictive enlistment bonus provision applies to an individual who enlists in the Army for a period of at least three years in a skill designated as critical. These members may be paid a bonus in an amount prescribed by the Secretary of the Army not to exceed $4,000. The authorizing legislation contains a safeguard provision to insure that recipients of the bonus fulfill the obligation to serve. Failure to do so results in recoupment of the bonus for the unserved portion of the enlistment.

The provisions of the law governing enlistment bonuses have been extended to September 30, 1997.

UNIFORMED SERVICES ALMANAC
SELECTIVE REENLISTMENT BONUS*

This is an additional payment awarded to enlisted members serving in a designated critical military skill* upon their reenlistment or extension for a period of at least three years. The payment is designed to provide additional financial incentive for the retention of enlisted personnel on active duty who are in shortage skills which require long and costly training.

The Selective Reenlistment Bonus is:
- Used to assist in attaining and sustaining career manning levels in critical military specialties with inadequate retention rates.
- Can be paid for any problem reenlistment point up to 16 years of service.
- Based upon multiples of basic pay multiplied by years (not to exceed six years).
- Restricted to a maximum of $45,000 per reenlistment. However, no more than 10 percent of the bonuses awarded during any fiscal year can exceed $20,000.
- Paid in a combination of lump sum and installment payments.

The authorizing legislation contains a safeguard provision to insure that recipients of the bonus fulfill the obligation to serve. Failure to do so can result in recoupment of the bonus for the unserved portion of the reenlistment. Legislative provisions for this bonus have been extended to September 30, 1996. Members should consult with their personnel offices or career counselors for specific details concerning reenlistment bonuses.

*Consult individual Service Regulations for qualifying critical skills.

MISCELLANEOUS TYPE PAYMENTS
FAMILY SEPARATION ALLOWANCE

There are two types of allowance payable to members serving under conditions requiring separation of the member from his or her dependents. Family separation allowance is payable in addition to any other allowance or per diem to which the member may be entitled. In view of the varied circumstances and conditions that may be involved, a member should contact his or her personnel or finance officer to ascertain extent of entitlement, if any, when assigned to permanent duty, or temporary duty away from all or part of his or her family even though the dependents may not have been residing in the same household with the member prior to such assignment.

TYPE I. A family separation allowance at the rate equal to the quarters allowance for a member in the same grade without dependents is payable to a member with dependents assigned to permanent duty outside the United States or in Alaska when Government quarters, or quarters under the jurisdiction of a uniformed service, are not available to the member. Further, the member's dependents must not be residing at or near his or her permanent duty station and are not authorized to move to or near the permanent duty station at Government expense.

TYPE II. A family separation allowance of $75.00 per month, in addition to any per diem or other allowance (including Type I family separation allowance), is payable to members with dependents when:

1. Dependents do not reside at or near the member's permanent duty station and the member did not elect to serve an unaccompanied overseas tour;

2. The member is assigned to duty on board a ship away from the ship's home port for a continuous period of more than thirty days; or

3. The member is away from his or her permanent duty station on temporary duty for a continuous period in excess of thirty days and his or her dependents do not reside at or near the temporary duty station.

SEPARATION, READJUSTMENT AND DISABILITY SEVERANCE PAY

Congress has enacted statutes throughout the years to provide funds to members who are involuntarily separated for the purpose of aiding such members to readjust to civilian life. Among these statutes are those authorizing payment for Separation Pay, Readjustment Pay, Severance Pay and Disability Severance Pay. Following is a brief outline of the conditions under which each is payable.

Separation Pay. This pay was authorized by the Defense Officer Personnel Management Act (DOPMA) and went into effect September 15, 1981. Regular officers and reserve officers serving on active duty on or before September 14, 1981, who become eligible, *may elect* to receive either Separation Pay or Readjustment or Severance Pay whichever is more favorable. The 1991 Defense Authorization Act, P.L. 101-510 extended authority for payment of separation pay to regular enlisted members, imposed a requirement that a member must serve 6 years of active duty and complete the initial enlistment or service obligation, eliminated the $30,000 cap on amount of separation pay, and established a requirement for service in the Ready Reserves. Separation Pay is now payable to eligible officers and enlisted who are involuntarily separated as a result of strength management policies and who have completed at least six but less than twenty years of active service. The FY 1994 Defense Authorization Act, P.L. 103-160, November 30, 1993, provides that officers selected for involuntary separation must have six years of continuous service to qualify for involuntary separation pay. An exception is made for those with five years, but not six years of service on the date of enactment. The law requires that officers of the Reserve Components serve 6 *continuous* years of active duty prior to separation and complete his or her initial service obligation to be eligible for separation pay. Generally, officers involuntarily separated for failure of selection for promotion or reduction-in-force and reserve members who are denied continuance of active duty are entitled to Separation Pay. Separation pay is calculated based on ten percent of the product of the member's years of active duty service and twelve times the monthly basic pay with no cap. Members who qualify for and accept separation pay will be required to serve in the Ready Reserves for a period of not less than three years.

Additional benefits for those involuntarily separated include:

Medical Transition Assistance: Those involuntarily separated who have served less than 6 years are eligible for military health care to include CHAMPUS for 60 days, as are their dependents. Those who have served 6 or more years are eligible for 120 days. They are also eligible for enrollment in the Continued Health Care Benefit Program (CHCBP) for health care.

Government Housing: Those involuntarily separated may remain in government housing for 180 days, providing it does not displace active duty personnel. There may be a small rental charge for these quarters, but this can be waived if there is hardship.

Household Goods: Authorization is granted for storage of household goods for one year on a non-temporary basis, if involuntarily separated.

UNIFORMED SERVICES ALMANAC

DoD Education Activity Schools: Involuntarily separated personnel authorized use of Department of Defense Schools, or who have tuition paid by DoD, may continue their children in such education in order to complete graduation, if they are in the 11th Grade.

Commissary and Exchange Privileges: Involuntarily separated personnel are authorized continued Commissary and Exchange privileges for 2 years after separation.

Travel and Transportation Allowances: Involuntarily separated personnel will be provided travel and transportation allowances to their *home of choice* within the United States. If selecting an overseas destination, they will be reimbursed as if the home of selection was in the CONUS, unless the overseas destination was their entry point to active duty.

Transition Counseling and Job Certification/Verification: Involuntarily separated personnel will be counseled on benefits such as educational opportunities, job search and placement, and financial planning assistance among many others. In addition, they will be helped in obtaining verification and certification of job skills acquired during military service, to use in finding a job. This assistance will also be provided to overseas personnel.

Education Benefits: This permits involuntarily separated personnel to participate, i.e., buy into the Montgomery G.I. Bill.

VOLUNTARY SEPARATION INCENTIVES

The 1992 Defense Authorization Act, P.L. 102-190 contained two important programs to help the Department reduce and reshape the active military force. These programs are the Voluntary Separation Incentive (VSI) and the Special Separation Benefit (SSB).

P.L. 102-484, the FY 93 Defense Authorization Act gave the Military Departments the authority to **permit** early retirement for **selected** military members with more than 15 but less than 20 years of service. Retired pay is calculated by the following formula: Monthly Base Pay x Years x 2.5% (standard retired pay formula). The only difference is that the retirement pay rate is reduced by a factor of 1 percent for each year of service less than 20 years. An early retirement entitles the service member to all of the normal retirement benefits of a person retiring with 20 or more years. Early retirees are also eligible for transition benefits and services.

P.L. 103-160, the Defense Authorization Act for FY 94, extended the provisions for SSB, VSI and early retirement authority to October 1, 1999.

These separation incentives are being offered to military members most affected by the drawdown. The incentives will minimize involuntary separations, ease the transition of servicemembers into the civilian sector, and help bring personnel numbers in line with the Department's new, smaller force structure requirements.

Servicemembers in selected job specialties with more than six but less than 20 years of active service are being offered the VSI and SSB incentives. These individuals must volunteer for release from active duty and serve in a Reserve component. They will also be required to choose either the VSI or the SSB. The Service Secretary will then approve or disapprove the request based upon the needs of the Service.

The Voluntary Separation Incentive (VSI) program provides annual payments to the separating member equal to 2.5% of annual basic pay multiplied by the member's years of service. The payments will be made in equal installments for a period equal to twice the number of years of service of the member. In the event of the member's death, the remaining VSI installments may be bequeathed to designated survivors.

The Special Separation Benefit (SSB) incentive program provides a lump-sum payment of 15% of annual basic pay multiplied by the member's years of active service.

In order to shape the future force, the incentives were offered to members in duty skills, grades, and length of service where existing personnel inventories exceed future requirements. Members in critical or shortage skills were not offered these incentives.

The Department of Defense reduced the size of the active military force to 1.59 million in 1995. Over 95% of the drawdown was achieved through reduced accessions, denied first-term reenlistments, increased early retirements, and voluntary release programs. The VSI, SSB and early retirement programs helped minimize involuntary separations and assisted the Department in achieving two key goals during the drawdown; maintaining readiness and treating people fairly.

In addition to the above, those who chose voluntary separation or will in the future, will have the same privileges granted to involuntarily separated personnel shown previously. This authority is contained in P.L. 102-484, the 1993 Defense Authorization Act.

The FY 95 Defense Appropriations Act directed two changes affecting VSI and SSB separated personnel. Participants receiving bonus payments during the same year in which separated are subject to a bonus offset, and participants forfeit VSI/SSB payments if appointed to DoD civilian positions within 180 days of separation.

Active duty or full-time members of the National Guard who separate from military service programs after November 11, 1993, and receive any bonus payments during the same calendar year in which they are separated, shall have the bonus payments received in that year reduced by an amount equal to any such bonus, and the members will not be paid any future bonus payments.

This offset procedure will not apply to members who separate during the last year of certain special and incentive bonuses authorized by Chapter 5, Title 37 USC.

Active duty or full-time members of the National Guard who separate from military service under the VSI or SSB programs after September 30, 1994, and are rehired in a civilian position of the DoD within 180 days of separation from the military, shall have the VSI or SSB separation payments recouped. All employment by the DoD in any capacity, including temporary positions, nonappropriated fund positions, and employment under personal service contracts, is covered.

VSI and SSB separation payments are taxed as income in the year in which received. Under current tax law, members who receive VSI or SSB pay that is later recouped may not be able to fully recover taxes resulting from the VSI or SSB payment. Members are eligible for and entitled to receive all transition benefits associated with VSI or SSB separation through the prescribed expiration date for those benefits.

Severance/Readjustment Pays: In 1980, Congress, in the Defense Officer Personnel Management Act unified the separation pay authority into one provision of Title 10 — namely Section 1174. Under special saving procedures, personnel who meet established eligibility criteria and were on active duty on

UNIFORMED SERVICES ALMANAC

or before September 14, 1981, are entitled to either separation pay or the old "severance" or "readjustment" pay, whichever is more advantageous.

Disability Severance Pay: A member of the Armed Forces on active duty who is found physically unfit for military service as the result of a disability which:
    1. was incurred or aggravated while the member was entitled to basic pay;
    2. was incurred in line of duty while on active duty;
    3. is rated at less than 30 percent under the VA Schedule for rating disabilities; and
    4. is, or may be permanent,
is entitled to disability severance pay when discharged. The severance pay is computed by multiplying the monthly basic pay of the member's grade at the time of discharge or the monthly basic pay of any higher grade in which he or she served satisfactorily by twice the number of years of active service. The maximum payment is 2 years basic pay.

Disability severance pay is also payable to a member who had originally been placed on the Temporary Disability Retired List who, on reexamination is found to have recovered to the extent that although still physically unfit for service, the disability rating is less than 30 percent.

AUTHORIZED LEAVE

All Service members on active duty for 30 consecutive days or more are entitled to accrue leave under applicable Service leave directives. While on authorized leave they are generally entitled to full pay and allowances. This includes: basic pay; special pay; incentive pay for hazardous duty; BAS; BAQ; clothing maintenance allowances; family separation allowances; and station allowances.

Members may elect to carry all or part of an advance leave balance over to a new term of service when discharged for the purpose of reenlisting within 24 hours of discharge or extending an enlistment; or, when accepting an appointment as a warrant or commissioned officer of the armed forces. The carryover leave may not exceed 30 days. Applicable service leave directives are: Army - AR 630-5; Navy - MILPERSMAN; Marine Corps - MCO P1050.3; Air Force - AFR 35-9.

ACCRUED LEAVE

Members are entitled to payment of unused accrued leave unless the member continues on active duty under conditions which require accrued leave to be carried forward. Also, an enlisted member who voluntarily extends enlistment for the first time is entitled to payment for unused accrued leave. A military member can be paid for no more than 60 days of accrued leave during a military career. A member eligible for an accrued leave settlement may elect to receive payment for a portion of the accrued leave, not to exceed a career total of 60 days, and have the remaining accrued leave carried forward to a new or extended enlistment. The combination of elections may exceed 60 days.

Settlement for leave accrued after September 1, 1976 includes basic pay only. The last leave earned is considered the first leave used.

UNIFORMED SERVICES ALMANAC
OVERSEAS HOUSING AND STATION ALLOWANCES

Station Allowance Overseas. There are several types of Station Allowances authorized for members and dependents on permanent duty in certain specified areas outside the United States. **Because these allowances are based on many factors such as the cost-of-living in a particular country or the applicable per diem rates in the area of assignment, the member should check with the Finance or Disbursing Office regarding rates and limits:**

Overseas Housing Allowance (OHA). A member on duty outside of the United States may receive a housing allowance consisting of the difference between basic allowance for quarters and the applicable housing cost (including utilities and occupancy expenses) in that area. To apply for OHA, you must complete DD Form 2367 and bring a copy of your lease to the local housing office or your commander. OHA may not cover all housing and utility costs if your rent is higher than the established rate ceiling or if utility and occupancy costs also affect the amount of OHA received.

Move-In Housing Allowance (MIHA). Move-In Housing Allowance, a component of the Overseas Housing Allowance, is authorized for personnel assigned overseas. The Move-In Housing Allowance addresses most of the costs currently covered by the Initial/Terminal Occupancy Allowance in Overseas Housing Allowance. However, the method of payment will differ. Where Initial/Terminal Occupancy Allowance is paid in monthly installments, Move-In Housing Allowance is paid in lump-sum supplemental payments when the member initially becomes eligible for Overseas Housing Allowance and incurs occupancy related expenses. Move-In Housing Allowance consists of three (3) supplemental payment components:

1. Move-In Housing Allowance/Miscellaneous: Rates are published in the Joint Federal Travel Regulation and reflect average expenditures made by members to purchase household necessities for their residence. This entitlement is paid in a lump-sum and no receipts are required. Examples of such necessities are sinks, toilets, light fixtures, kitchen cabinets, and a refrigerator and stove (which sometimes are not provided in overseas dwellings).

2. Move-In Housing Allowance/Rent: This covers all rent related expenses; receipts are required. These expenses are fixed, one time, nonrefundable charges levied by the landlord, the landlord(s) agent or a foreign government which the member must pay before occupying a dwelling. Examples are real estate agent fees, redecoration fees, and onetime lease taxes.

3. Move-In Housing Allowance/Security: These security related expenses are for members assigned to designated areas where dwellings must be modified to minimize exposure to a terrorist threat. Receipts are required. Qualifying areas and allowable items are published in the Joint Federal Travel Regulation. Expenditures which are not related to the physical dwelling, such as personal security guards or dogs, are not allowed under Move-In Housing Allowance. Move-In Housing Allowance security payments must be approved by the senior officer in the country.

All members eligible for Overseas Housing Allowance, even those who are eligible for Initial/Terminal Occupancy Allowance, are covered by Move-In Housing Allowance/Security provided expenses are incurred on or after September 1, 1990.

Cost of Living Allowance (COLA). This allowance is authorized for the purpose of defraying the average excess costs experienced by members in certain high-cost areas overseas (including Alaska and Hawaii), where the average costs of living exceed the comparative costs for a member's quarters living expenses for similar members in the United States. The amount of the COLA is determined by reviewing the results of two surveys which are conducted annually: a living-pattern survey and a market basket survey. Foreign exchange rates also may affect the amount of the COLA received.

Temporary Lodging Allowance (TLA). This allowance is authorized to partially reimburse members upon initial arrival or just prior to departing overseas duty stations for expenses incurred while occupying temporary quarters. Payable for specific periods, generally not to exceed 60 days, while awaiting assignment of Government Quarters or other permanent living accommodations.

Interim Housing Allowance. This is designed to reimburse a member for expenses incurred for renting non-government family housing before the arrival of his or her dependents at a new permanent duty station.

Evacuation Allowance. This is a per diem allowance payable for command sponsored dependents whenever they are evacuated from the vicinity of the sponsor's duty station to an authorized safe haven.

EDUCATIONAL BENEFITS FOR SERVICEMEMBERS

An educational benefit program (the New GI Bill) is available to those individuals who became members of the Armed Forces on or after July 1, 1985. In addition to active duty benefits, it provides benefits for service in the Selected Reserve.

The Veterans' Educational Assistance Act of 1984 as amended (the Montgomery GI Bill) provides a basic benefit of $400 per month for 36 months for a total of $14,400 effective April 1, 1993. For personnel who entered service prior to January 1, 1990, an additional $700 per month may be provided at the discretion of the Secretary of Defense, for those serving in selected shortage skills. The program is voluntary; however, all service members are assumed to be enrolled unless they elect not to participate upon entry into the Service. Participating active duty members will have their pay reduced by $100 per month for their initial 12 months of Service. This reduction in pay is nonrefundable.

Eligibility

Active duty personnel must agree to serve for:

1. Three years to be eligible for the basic benefit of $400 per month for 36 months for a total of $14,400, effective April 1, 1993, or

2. Two years on active duty and four years in the Selected Reserve. A benefit of $325 per month for 36 months for a total of $11,700 effective April 1, 1993, is offered to those who enter with a two-year obligation.

Selected Reserve personnel who obligate themselves for 6 years after June 30, 1985 are eligible for up to $190 a month for 36 months, effective April 1, 1993, for a total benefit of $6,840. There is no reduction in pay for Reserve members. Before September 30, 1990, a reservist with a bachelor's degree was not eligible for benefits. However, a reservist with a bachelor's degree can become eligible beginning October 1, 1990, by signing a new contract that will result in a six year reserve obligation after the date he or she signs it. Members are eligible for the educational benefits as soon as they have completed initial active duty training and 180 days service in the Selected Reserve. Selected Reserve members currently participating in the educational assistance program shall continue in that program in accordance with their agreements.

UNIFORMED SERVICES ALMANAC

Vietnam-Era GI Bill participants whose benefits ended December 31, 1989 can:
1. Serve 3 years beyond July 1, 1985 and qualify for the new basic benefit ($14,400), effective April 1, 1993, and
2. Also receive half of their Vietnam-era stipend.

Servicemembers must have a high school diploma or a high school equivalency certificate to qualify.

BASIC ALLOWANCE FOR QUARTERS (BAQ)

BAQ is payable to members on active duty according to the pay grade in which they are serving. In the past, BAQ rates have been linked to the annual percentage increase in basic pay. Under a program initiated by the DoD effective in 1985, BAQ rates (and VHA rates) are tied to median rental costs nationwide. Under this plan, BAQ will continue to rise according to increases in basic pay, but will be adjusted periodically to reflect changes in rental costs and return BAQ rates to a level set at 65 percent of national median rental costs.

See Officers' and Enlisted Pay Sections for current BAQ rates for officers and enlisted personnel.

ENTITLEMENTS

Members with Dependents. A member with dependents is entitled to BAQ when:
1. Adequate Government quarters are not furnished for the member and dependents.
2. Adequate Government quarters are not furnished for the member's dependents or if the dependents are prevented from occupying such quarters, even if quarters are furnished for the member.
3. Dependents are not enroute or do not accompany the member to the PCS station or vicinity.

Members without Dependents. A member without dependents is generally entitled to BAQ unless assigned to or occupying Government quarters which are suitable and adequate for the member's grade. Members without dependents, in pay grades above E-6, may elect not to occupy assigned government quarters at the permanent duty station, and draw BAQ unless a determination is made that such an option would adversely affect training, discipline, or readiness.

A member, without dependents, who is assigned to single type quarters or is on field or sea duty, and is not entitled to receive BAQ is generally entitled to a partial BAQ.

Members Married to a Member. When both husband and wife are members of the Uniformed Services, and stationed at the same or adjacent military installations, both members are authorized the BAQ prescribed for a member without dependents when Government family quarters are not assigned, notwithstanding the availability of adequate single quarters for either or both. However, such members assigned to family type quarters are not entitled to a BAQ. In the case of a member married to another member with an eligible dependent child, one parent may claim the child for BAQ entitlement, and the other parent receives BAQ at the "without dependent" rate. *When otherwise entitled,* either parent may claim the child for Family Separation Allowance (FSA). FSA may alternate between parents based on the same dependent child,

UNIFORMED SERVICES ALMANAC

however, FSA may not be paid simultaneously to both members on behalf of the same child.

A dual-service couple with no children living off base: each member gets housing allowance at the single or without dependent rate for their pay grades. A couple with children living off base: One member gets the housing allowance at the single rate, the other at the with dependent rate. A couple living on base: neither member gets BAQ.

Each of the Service Secretaries have designated authorities for determining dependency or relationship for BAQ entitlements. Consult your personnel or housing office for specific guidance as to if and when full or partial BAQ is authorized.

RELATIONSHIP AND DEPENDENCY

A member's lawful spouse and legitimate, unmarried, minor children are at all times considered dependents for BAQ purposes, except under certain unusual circumstances. A determination of relationship is required, but usually a determination of dependency is not.

When two members, with no other dependents, are married to each other, they may elect which member will receive BAQ on behalf of any adopted or natural born children of the marriage. If there is no agreement, entitlement will be assigned to the senior member. Entitlement can be transferred in the event of promotion or other change of circumstances, but these elections can only be applied to BAQ entitlement for current and future months and cannot be applied retroactively.

Validity of Marriage. In order to be entitled to BAQ for a spouse, the marriage must be valid. Any instance where the validity of a member's marriage is questioned is considered a case of doubtful relationship. Such cases include:

1. Remarriage Within a Prohibited Period Following Divorce. Under the laws of some states, a marriage is not dissolved until a specific period has elapsed after granting of a divorce decree. Remarriage is prohibited within the specified period. In all states which grant an interlocutory decree before they grant a final divorce decree, remarriage may not be contracted before the final decree is granted.

2. Marriage by Proxy. Proxy marriages are considered valid if performed in a jurisdiction which recognizes common-law marriages and has no statute or other prohibition regarding proxy marriages.

3. Marriage by Telephone. A marriage by telephone will be recognized only if a statute or court decision authorizes or recognizes such marriages in the jurisdiction where the marriage was performed.

4. Common-law Marriages. Under laws of certain states an informal or "common-law" marriage may be entered into by persons who do not obtain a license to marry or go through certain other formalities.

5. Foreign Nation Divorce. A foreign nation divorce may or may not be recognized as valid, depending on factors such as the place of residence of the parties, whether they appeared in person to obtain the divorce and applicable state laws.

6. Annulled Marriage. If a member's marriage is annulled by court decree, no BAQ payments may be made. The same applies if the marriage is considered void for reasons such as a preexisting marriage of the spouse.

UNIFORMED SERVICES ALMANAC

Determination and Validation. Requests for determination of validity of a marriage or for validation of payments should be sent to:

Army:	Defense Finance and Accounting Service Indianapolis Center Attn: FJFCD Indianapolis, IN 46249-0001 (317) 542-2800 (collect)
Navy:	Defense Finance and Accounting Service Cleveland Center P. O. Box 998002 Code LF Cleveland, OH 44199-8002 1-800-321-1080, (216) 522-5955 (collect)
Air Force:	DFAS — Denver Center/FJPD 6760 E. Irvington Pl. Denver, CO 80279-3000 1-800-433-0461, (303) 676-7818
Marine Corps:	Commandant of the Marine Corps Attn: Code MHP-20 Washington, DC 20380 (703) 696-2055

SUPPORT OF DEPENDENTS

Proof of support of a lawful spouse or unmarried, minor, legitimate child of a member is generally not required. The term child includes a stepchild of the member (except when the member is divorced from the child's parent by blood, or when another military member is the natural parent and claims the child as a dependent) and an adopted child of the member, including a child placed in the home by a placement agency as part of the formal adoption process, or a child placed in the legal custody of the member. However, if a complaint of nonsupport or inadequate support is received from or on behalf of a dependent, proof of support may be required. Failure to support a dependent, on whose behalf BAQ is being received, can result in nonentitlement to BAQ and recoupment for periods of nonsupport. Proof of support may be required in cases such as:

1. Unmarried, legitimate child over 21 years of age, if because of a mental or physical condition, the child is unable to support himself or herself and is dependent on the member for over one-half of his or her support.

2. An unmarried child under 23 years of age who is enrolled in a full-time course of study in an institution of higher education and who is dependent on the member for over one-half of his or her support.

3. An unmarried, minor, illegitimate child whose alleged member-father has been judicially decreed as the father or judicially ordered to contribute to the child's support, or whose parentage has been admitted in writing under oath by the father or mother, may be claimed as a dependent under certain conditions, for purposes of entitlement to BAQ at the with-dependents rate. For the complete details for this involved category of dependent, please consult your personnel office.

UNIFORMED SERVICES ALMANAC

4. A member may be entitled to BAQ on behalf of parents, but not on the basis of relationship alone. The additional factor of dependency must also be met. The parents must be dependent upon the member for over one-half of their support and this dependency must be determined on the basis of an affidavit submitted by the parent and any other evidence that the Secretary concerned may require. In determining dependency of a parent, the total income and expenses of the parent must be considered. Among others, the following factors are included:

   a. Charity. Contributions made to parents by charitable organizations are not considered income.

   b. Parents in a Charitable Institution. Residence of a parent in a charitable institution, public or private, is not a bar to entitlement.

   c. Social Security, Unemployment Compensation, and Pensions. These elements are considered income and are considered in determining whether the member contributes more than one-half of the parents support.

   d. Capital Assets. Unliquidated capital assets such as a home are not considered income, and parents are not required to deplete their capital assets in order to establish dependency on a member for BAQ purposes.

Members who have questions regarding any category of dependency of relationship should consult the personnel office for guidance.

INELIGIBLE DEPENDENTS

The following persons are not considered dependents for purposes of entitlement to basic allowance for quarters for dependents even though they may be dependent upon the member for support:

1. A former spouse - regardless of whether spouse was awarded alimony in the divorce decree.
2. Stepchild, when the service member has been divorced from the child's natural parent.
3. A member's child who has been adopted.
4. Mother-in-law or father-in-law.
5. Grandparents.
6. Brothers and sisters.
7. Stepparent, after the divorce from a blood parent.
8. Any person being claimed as a dependent by another service member.
9. Dependents, who because of their employment or training, are given living accommodations at the expense of the Government.
10. A veteran receiving full-time training and a subsistence allowance under the GI Bill.
11. A child entering Active Duty in any of the uniformed services, or into any of the Service Academies.

CHANGES THAT MAY INCREASE OR DECREASE BAQ

Increases:
1. Marriage, thereby adding a spouse as a dependent.
2. Promotion of the member to a higher grade.

Decreases:
1. Death of an only dependent.
2. Demotion of the service member.
3. Divorce if the member has no other dependents.

UNIFORMED SERVICES ALMANAC

4. A change in circumstances where the parent no longer needs support from the member: for example, the parent returned to gainful employment, Social Security payment, pension or unemployment compensation are now being paid, contributions from other members of the household commenced or were increased in an amount sufficient for support, or the parent remarried.

Discontinuance of BAQ
 1. Death of the member.
 2. Discharge of the member from service. (Except for those voluntarily or involuntarily discharged — BAQ may continue for a set period of time when government quarters are authorized.)
 3. When adequate Government family quarters are furnished.
 4. When a Military court-martial sentence states that the member forfeit all pay and allowances.
 5. When a member is absent without leave. However, under certain conditions BAQ payments may be continued for dependents for a period up to 2 months after the member absented himself or herself without authority.

GARNISHMENT

Public Law 93-647, January 4, 1975, authorized the garnishment of active duty and retired military personnel salaries and annuities to enforce obligations of alimony and child support. Public Law 95-30, May 23, 1977, set maximum limitations on the percentage of the payment which would be subject to garnishment. The limits are based on the individuals' aggregate disposable earnings, which would include all pay, pensions, disability compensation, Social Security benefits, etc., received from any agency of the federal government. The limits allow garnishment of government earnings of no more than:

 a. Fifty percent of disposable earnings if the individual is supporting a second family.
 b. Sixty percent of disposable earnings if the individual is not supporting a second family.
 c. An additional five percent in each of the above if the individual is in arrears for more than 12 weeks.

A valid court order or similar legal process must be issued prior to the garnishment of active duty or retired pay. The order should name the agency as the garnishee and state on its face that it is to enforce an obligation to provide child support or to make alimony payments. Court costs and attorney's fees can also be deducted if the court order directs such action. An individual attempting to have such a court order reversed must assume any costs involved in such an action.

Garnishment orders involving military personnel, either active or retired, should be sent by certified or registered mail, return receipt requested, to the finance service center of the particular military service concerned.

Effective January 1, 1995 the law permits creditors to garnish the wages of active duty members delinquent on paying bills.

Creditors are requried to submit completed DD Form 2653 along with a court judgement to DFAS-Cleveland Center for processing. DFAS-Cleveland Center will notify the member and the members commanding officer of the court judgement. Action is required by both the member and the members commanding officer prior to deduction of the members pay.

JAG and financial counseling offices may assist members who receive notices of wage garnishment, but military lawyers cannot represent, in court, a member seeking to have a court-ordered debt modified or reversed.

Under the law, garnishment will be limited to 25 percent of a members pay. BAS and BAQ are excluded from deductions.

CONUS COLA

Members of the uniformed services move about the country as a requirement of their service - often with no choice. Over a career, a member is likely to be assigned to a variety of low-cost, moderate-cost, and high-cost locations. Private sector pay scales tend to reflect local living costs in US cities or regions, but military pay tables do not. Until recently, the Variable Housing Allowance (VHA) introduced in the early 1980s, was the only pay element that was adjusted for regional cost differences. Congress in the FY 95 National Defense Authorization Act, enacted the CONUS Cost-of-Living Allowance (COLA) to provide compensation for variations in non-housing costs in the continental United States.

The Seventh quadrennial Review of Military Compensation (QRMC) in a 1991 study found non-housing costs vary from 5 percent below to 19 percent above the national average. A follow-up study using December 1994 data found non-housing costs vary from 5 percent below to 20 percent above. Given these results, it is possible for a member to move to a high-cost area and suffer a more severe loss of non-housing purchasing power than that resulting from a reduction in grade.

Disparities between high-cost and low-cost cities had to be addressed both to prevent a substantial degradation in the military member's standard of living in high-cost areas and to avoid situations wherein members systematically avoid assignment to high-cost areas. Given cost-of-living differences, it is unlikely that members assigned to the highest-cost areas would ever regain purchasing power lost as a result of their location over the course of their career. For these reasons the Department of Defense sought, and the Congress approved, a cost-of-living allowance for members assigned to the highest-cost areas in the 48 contiguous States (CONUS COLA).

The DoD has established a "with" and "without dependent" rate for CONUS COLA. The without dependent rate would equal the spendable income by grade for zero dependents, while the with dependent rate would be set at 2.5 dependents (the average number of dependents in military households).

A total of 87 Military Housing Areas (MHAs) where expenses are at least 9 percent higher than the national average will be receiving the CONUS COLA. Most of the 31,900 service members stationed in these areas will receive the modest allowance with the majority assigned to the following 20 MHAs: CALIFORNIA - San Francisco (1); San Bernadino (3); Los Angeles (1); Bridgeport (1); CONNECTICUT - New Haven (8); ILLINOIS - Chicago (3); MASSACHUSETTS - Boston (3); Nantucket (1); Worcester (2); S. Weymouth (5); Essex County (4); Hampden (1); NEW JERSEY - Atlantic City (3); Perth Amboy (1); Northern NJ (2); NEW YORK - Buffalo (1); Long Island (6); New York (6), Griffiss AFB (1); Westchester (11). The MHA factor is in parentheses ( ). The remaining sites located in California, Connecticut, Massachusetts, Michigan, New York, and New Jersey account for just over 250 members. See note on CONUS COLA Tables for instructions on figuring your pay.

UNIFORMED SERVICES ALMANAC

CONUS COLA BASE AMOUNT (with dependents)

YEARS OF SERVICE

Pay Grade	Under 2	Over 2	Over 3	Over 4	Over 6	Over 8	Over 10	Over 12	Over 14	Over 16	Over 18	Over 20	Over 22	Over 24	Over 26
O-10	42	42	42	42	42	43	43	44	44	45	45	45	45	45	45
O-9	40	40	41	41	41	41	41	42	42	43	43	44	44	44	45
O-8	39	39	39	39	39	40	40	41	41	42	42	43	43	43	43
O-7	35	36	36	36	37	37	37	37	39	40	41	41	41	41	41
O-6	29	31	33	33	33	33	33	33	35	35	36	36	37	37	39
O-5	26	29	29	29	29	29	29	31	33	34	34	35	35	35	35
O-4	24	26	28	28	28	28	29	29	29	31	31	31	31	31	31
O-3	22	23	24	25	26	26	28	28	29	29	29	29	29	29	29
O-2	21	22	23	23	24	24	24	24	24	24	24	24	24	24	24
O-1	20	20	21	21	21	21	21	21	21	21	21	21	21	21	21

COMMISSIONED OFFICERS WITH OVER 4 YEARS OF ACTIVE SERVICE AS AN ENLISTED MEMBER OR WARRANT OFFICER

O-3E	0	0	0	26	26	28	28	29	29	29	29	29	29	29	29
O-2E	0	0	0	24	24	24	25	25	26	26	26	26	26	26	26
O-1E	0	0	0	22	22	23	23	23	24	24	24	24	24	24	24

WARRANT OFFICERS

W-5	0	0	0	0	0	0	0	0	0	0	0	29	31	31	33
W-4	23	24	24	24	24	25	25	26	26	28	28	28	29	29	29
W-3	22	22	22	23	23	23	24	24	25	25	25	26	26	26	28
W-2	20	21	21	21	22	22	22	23	23	23	24	24	25	25	25
W-1	19	20	20	20	21	21	22	23	22	22	23	23	23	23	23

ENLISTED MEMBERS

E-9	0	0	0	0	0	0	25	25	25	25	25	26	26	28	28
E-8	0	0	0	0	0	23	23	23	23	24	24	24	25	25	26
E-7	20	20	20	21	21	21	21	21	21	22	22	23	23	24	24
E-6	18	19	19	20	20	20	20	21	21	21	21	21	21	21	21
E-5	17	17	18	18	19	19	19	20	20	20	20	20	20	20	20
E-4	16	16	17	17	17	17	17	17	17	17	17	17	17	17	17
E-3	16	16	16	16	16	16	16	16	16	16	16	16	16	16	16
E-2	16	16	16	16	16	16	16	16	16	16	16	16	16	16	16
E-1	14	14	14	14	14	14	14	14	14	14	14	14	14	14	14

NOTE: To figure your CONUS COLA payment, multiply the Military Housing Areas (MHAs) factor - located in the CONUS COLA text on page 53 - for your area by the base amount on the CONUS COLA Tables. For example, an O-3 with dependents and 14 years of service (base amount = $29), living in New York (Factor = 6) would receive $174.00 [Multiply $29 x 6 = $174].

UNIFORMED SERVICES ALMANAC

CONUS COLA BASE AMOUNT (without dependents)

YEARS OF SERVICE

Pay Grade	Under 2	Over 2	Over 3	Over 4	Over 6	Over 8	Over 10	Over 12	Over 14	Over 16	Over 18	Over 20	Over 22	Over 24	Over 26/30
O-10	32	33	33	33	33	33	33	33	34	34	34	35	35	35	35
O-9	30	31	31	31	31	31	31	32	32	33	33	33	33	33	34
O-8	29	29	30	30	30	31	31	31	31	32	33	33	33	33	33
O-7	27	27	27	27	28	28	29	29	29	31	32	32	32	32	32
O-6	24	24	24	24	24	24	24	24	25	27	27	28	28	29	30
O-5	21	23	23	22	22	23	23	24	24	25	26	26	27	27	27
O-4	19	21	22	22	22	22	23	24	24	24	24	24	24	24	24
O-3	17	19	19	20	21	21	22	22	23	24	23	23	23	23	23
O-2	16	16	18	18	19	19	19	19	19	19	19	19	19	19	19
O-1	14	15	16	16	16	16	16	16	16	16	16	16	16	16	16

COMMISSIONED OFFICERS WITH OVER 4 YEARS OF ACTIVE SERVICE AS AN ENLISTED MEMBER OR WARRANT OFFICER

Pay Grade	Under 2	Over 2	Over 3	Over 4	Over 6	Over 8	Over 10	Over 12	Over 14	Over 16	Over 18	Over 20	Over 22	Over 24	Over 26/30
O-3E	0	0	0	21	21	22	22	23	23	23	23	23	23	23	23
O-2E	0	0	0	19	19	19	20	20	21	21	21	21	21	21	21
O-1E	0	0	0	16	17	17	18	18	18	18	18	18	18	18	18

WARRANT OFFICERS

Pay Grade	Under 2	Over 2	Over 3	Over 4	Over 6	Over 8	Over 10	Over 12	Over 14	Over 16	Over 18	Over 20	Over 22	Over 24	Over 26/30
W-5	0	0	0	0	0	0	0	0	0	0	0	24	24	24	24
W-4	18	19	19	19	19	20	20	21	22	22	22	23	23	23	24
W-3	16	17	17	17	17	18	19	19	20	20	20	21	21	21	21
W-2	16	16	16	16	16	17	17	18	18	18	19	19	19	19	19
W-1	14	15	15	16	16	16	16	16	17	17	17	18	18	18	18

ENLISTED MEMBERS

Pay Grade	Under 2	Over 2	Over 3	Over 4	Over 6	Over 8	Over 10	Over 12	Over 14	Over 16	Over 18	Over 20	Over 22	Over 24	Over 26/30
E-9	0	0	0	0	0	0	19	20	20	20	20	20	21	22	22
E-8	0	0	0	0	0	17	17	18	18	18	19	19	19	20	21
E-7	14	15	15	16	16	16	16	16	16	17	17	17	18	18	19
E-6	14	14	14	14	15	15	15	16	16	16	16	16	16	16	16
E-5	13	13	14	14	14	14	14	14	15	15	15	15	15	15	15
E-4	12	12	13	13	13	13	13	13	13	13	13	13	13	13	13
E-3	12	12	12	12	12	12	12	12	12	12	12	12	12	12	12
E-2	12	12	12	12	12	12	12	12	12	12	12	12	12	12	12
E-1	11	11	11	11	11	11	11	11	11	11	11	11	11	11	11

NOTE: To figure your CONUS COLA payment, multiply the CONUS COLA base amount by the Military Housing Areas (MHAs) factor - located in the CONUS COLA text on page 53 - for your area by the base amount on the CONUS COLA Tables. For example, an O-3 without dependents and 14 years of service (base amount = $23), living in New York (Factor = 6) would receive $138.00 [Multiply $23 x 6 = $138].

In order for the COLA payments to be meaningful to the military member, the DoD will set the minimum COLA payment at 1 percent. Any member assigned to an area that has a CONUS COLA index greater than the threshold would get 1 percent of spendable income as the base COLA payment. Members assigned to locations that have a CONUS COLA index of 110 or greater will be rounded to the nearest 1 percent. Thus an area would need a COLA index of at least 110.5 to receive a COLA payment of 2 percent (110.5 - 109 = 1.5 = 2).

VARIABLE HOUSING ALLOWANCE (VHA)

(NOTE: The VHA rates on the following pages may change subject to approval by the Congress and the Administration. As of the time we go to press, the VHA rates and the VHA ZIPCODE-MHA table for 1996 have been produced on the assumption that BAQ will increase by 5.2 percent. Due to the uncertainty of the budget, there is a possibility that the BAQ increase will be a different amount. If so, this would require a recomputation of the VHA rates. Final VHA rates will not be known until enactment of the FY96 Defense Authorization Act).

Section 403a (Title 37USC), as amended, and subsection (d) provide for the annual establishment of the VHA rates. This allowance was established because the Congress determined that personnel assigned to high housing cost areas for the convenience of the government should not have to bear the entire burden of such higher costs. The initial allowance provided VHA for members drawing BAQ whenever a member was assigned to a high housing cost area where the average monthly cost of housing in the area for members serving in the same pay grade exceeded 115 percent of the members BAQ entitlement.

The FY 85 DoD Appropriations Act eliminated payment of VHA for Reservists and Guard members called to active duty for less than 140 days.

This was waived for those members of the Reserve Forces called to active duty in connection with Operation Desert Shield/Storm.

VHA is based on median housing costs established by annual housing cost census of Uniformed Service members. The current census began in June and ended in September 1995. The 68 percent response rate (6 percentage points higher than last year) provides a firm statistical basis for accurate measurement of local and national median housing costs.

Subsection (d) limits VHA budget growth based on the Military Housing Cost Index (MHCI). The FY 96 MHCI is 2.3 percent, which will constrain overall annual VHA growth. Where applicable, VHA rates include adjustment pursuant to the Bateman Amendment which limits the decline in VHA.

No VHA will be paid to members who live in government quarters who are not entitled to BAQ or who receive BAQ at the "Partial" rate. Effective October 1, 1991, single servicemembers, who live in government barracks (including ships) and provide child support payments shall receive the difference between BAQ "with dependent" rate and BAQ at "without dependent" rate for the purpose of child support. If a member is paying child support and not living in government housing, he or she can receive BAQ at the "with dependent" rate.

P.L. 103-160, the FY 94 Defense Authorization Act provided that members in paygrades E-6 and above, who are assigned to sea duty and are entitled to BAQ with dependent rate, solely because of child support payments, will now be entitled to VHA at the without dependent rate.

UNIFORMED SERVICES ALMANAC

SELECTED MILITARY HOUSING AREAS AND VHA FOR PAY GRADES DRAWING BAQ AT "WITH DEPENDENTS" RATES (As of January 1, 1996)

MHA NAME	E-1	E-2	E-3	E-4	E-5	E-6	E-7	E-8	E-9	W-1	W-2	W-3	W-4	W-5	O-1	O-2	O-3	O-4	O-5	O-6	O-7+
Anchorage, AK	345.24	347.48	357.55	416.34	503.58	552.30	639.66	676.92	705.62	578.68	538.06	591.85	645.27	645.27	423.53	502.11	613.54	597.46	574.46	568.06	521.02
Fairbanks, AK	273.65	278.30	295.63	327.37	397.13	430.14	480.15	477.50	578.92	429.68	409.91	421.33	471.31	471.31	285.88	338.01	443.30	401.75	386.92	369.20	319.90
Anniston/Ft McClellan, AL	0.00	0.00	0.00	0.00	0.00	0.00	0.00	0.00	0.00	1.03	0.00	0.00	0.00	0.00	0.00	0.00	0.00	0.00	0.00	0.00	0.00
Ft Rucker, AL	0.00	0.00	0.00	0.00	0.00	0.00	0.00	0.00	0.00	0.00	0.00	0.00	0.00	0.00	0.00	0.00	0.00	0.00	0.00	0.00	0.00
Huntsville, AL	0.00	0.00	0.00	0.00	0.00	0.00	0.00	32.17	36.85	147.87	89.51	64.36	108.36	108.36	14.18	38.73	77.41	62.10	38.69	40.92	0.00
Montgomery, AL	61.66	61.66	56.39	52.57	48.55	48.62	65.99	49.16	51.01	70.57	48.88	60.28	88.61	88.61	42.07	39.98	60.79	19.00	0.00	0.00	0.00
Little Rock, AR	20.75	20.75	22.69	28.34	11.98	35.26	46.47	60.41	108.30	120.45	71.10	87.15	70.69	70.69	16.12	43.15	33.16	30.12	72.31	40.81	0.00
Ft Chaffee/Ft Smith, AR	0.00	0.00	0.00	0.00	0.00	0.00	0.00	2.59	36.54	50.26	8.21	0.00	14.42	14.42	0.00	0.00	0.00	0.00	0.00	0.00	0.00
Ft Huachuca, AZ	49.32	49.32	40.72	52.37	83.03	105.84	137.63	115.81	144.07	127.67	100.70	54.25	66.00	66.00	0.00	15.53	37.34	44.27	81.26	49.78	0.00
Davis-Monthan AFB, AZ	93.97	93.97	89.54	96.70	126.54	182.54	147.34	179.84	213.80	240.24	227.94	198.68	211.42	211.42	98.01	157.84	190.96	238.08	238.31	243.18	187.61
Yuma, AZ	122.46	122.46	127.49	120.82	143.08	145.64	206.10	213.05	212.05	242.24	191.08	187.59	221.63	221.63	165.72	116.63	183.53	142.32	134.47	147.09	69.73
Oakland, CA	323.16	323.16	316.78	345.86	361.36	404.07	421.59	430.02	467.93	572.64	565.41	517.11	598.92	598.92	422.72	437.35	525.07	584.54	554.03	554.58	454.89
San Francisco, CA	366.75	366.75	349.35	361.01	421.30	456.30	555.75	514.84	540.15	278.50	717.75	698.70	802.29	802.29	578.84	620.06	625.49	627.53	774.76	825.00	760.40
China Lake NAVWEPCEN, CA	11.25	5.43	0.00	0.00	64.43	33.93	75.33	130.27	210.21	134.68	88.33	78.68	151.79	151.79	18.01	42.38	67.53	83.22	130.72	141.90	88.34
Lemore NAS, CA	90.93	99.00	90.73	100.86	121.17	159.35	138.08	173.99	235.98	221.05	208.33	203.43	219.44	219.44	102.64	147.24	149.00	191.07	240.51	213.14	137.02
Camp Pendleton, CA	189.63	203.26	200.88	206.31	242.54	285.10	321.04	323.71	308.57	352.36	356.30	341.64	394.27	394.27	232.08	239.07	256.30	268.23	309.62	324.23	305.06
Vandenberg AFB, CA	202.86	202.86	196.33	199.68	240.84	262.75	287.04	327.91	380.02	287.63	222.56	240.25	266.93	266.93	141.88	155.58	195.74	215.82	240.98	209.47	133.29
Barstow/Ft Irwin, CA	70.36	70.36	73.20	74.18	77.47	119.75	114.93	191.73	263.69	134.60	59.90	47.55	83.94	83.94	22.60	30.08	13.13	4.43	39.03	47.23	0.00
Edwards AFB, CA	82.75	82.75	81.87	88.07	105.24	110.36	167.59	215.98	313.33	172.51	136.40	105.51	199.88	199.88	64.53	87.39	107.88	72.28	136.28	188.74	112.16
Twenty Nine Palms MCB CA	0.00	0.00	0.00	0.00	0.00	0.00	1.33	63.09	141.67	97.94	27.63	21.54	66.54	66.54	0.00	0.00	0.00	0.00	16.64	4.59	0.00
Beale AFB, CA	67.14	67.14	59.89	78.24	84.15	117.82	180.84	151.29	249.65	198.69	165.56	136.47	197.08	197.08	31.77	65.68	108.48	129.19	98.07	93.00	14.62
Vallejo/Travis AFB, CA	266.23	266.23	281.83	295.94	291.96	313.41	362.67	365.92	397.30	395.20	353.50	325.76	395.05	395.05	271.08	278.90	306.76	508.52	283.53	252.03	176.65
Los Angeles, CA	278.37	283.31	281.83	288.58	329.41	370.91	454.97	471.22	515.81	544.41	543.11	511.35	681.13	681.13	417.93	457.76	478.09	508.52	568.65	595.28	526.37
San Diego, CA	191.33	198.63	196.24	202.02	244.40	331.10	334.32	343.04	328.22	460.69	425.45	443.75	525.95	525.95	357.31	343.27	375.44	429.74	429.71	456.66	424.78
Monterey, CA	239.41	239.41	236.16	202.44	217.22	231.15	393.31	367.81	405.59	452.20	408.98	426.17	521.64	521.64	308.63	350.87	349.01	499.60	463.64	451.88	380.26
Denver, CO	121.68	121.91	118.77	137.20	175.84	215.03	208.63	235.51	213.92	278.86	204.16	187.76	172.94	172.94	171.76	206.25	190.30	234.98	180.08	194.20	117.72
Colorado Springs, CO	116.08	110.79	105.21	130.38	148.53	154.85	185.97	181.75	154.24	288.61	189.42	167.90	162.56	162.56	166.07	162.33	186.86	199.78	198.34	251.81	176.43
Ft Collins, CO	144.78	144.78	138.50	136.61	178.52	173.55	234.06	235.09	221.54	288.14	287.29	206.21	208.04	208.04	222.76	236.99	213.28	241.01	239.54	231.04	155.26
New London, CT	186.39	181.54	189.04	201.29	221.55	255.85	308.39	347.30	334.56	302.56	327.73	297.15	338.70	338.70	230.40	238.99	219.99	247.48	327.46	322.09	311.43
Washington, DC	300.00	300.00	298.08	313.87	339.28	393.79	438.81	482.32	465.24	525.24	563.61	477.97	535.04	535.04	440.55	426.44	478.80	496.21	477.34	454.45	375.89
Dover AFB, DE	147.36	150.33	154.49	130.66	152.23	136.15	224.57	249.16	276.85	244.06	215.74	185.29	182.92	182.92	156.03	113.66	151.52	136.72	131.21	110.88	32.83
Eglin AFB, FL	79.46	65.60	58.98	66.38	87.39	79.53	70.68	97.13	65.33	83.55	65.83	68.60	96.12	96.12	67.51	50.21	88.40	63.88	75.45	32.06	0.00
Jacksonville, FL	105.70	93.81	87.86	104.42	125.49	133.72	153.99	207.85	138.90	241.03	212.08	171.55	218.75	218.75	147.35	178.63	146.45	151.65	179.05	225.51	149.82
Patrick AFB, FL	112.23	112.23	111.56	97.85	106.04	124.24	118.15	164.00	180.20	201.32	190.74	178.43	194.93	194.93	84.63	113.26	151.84	171.55	177.44	150.35	78.78
Ft Lauderdale, FL	240.61	240.61	231.17	269.59	293.08	313.05	349.28	368.08	342.18	471.66	434.44	429.26	486.16	486.16	357.14	386.11	459.41	509.78	487.60	487.60	416.65
Pensacola, FL	35.63	35.63	23.12	21.10	47.90	39.34	35.85	61.97	25.03	65.27	62.14	66.27	107.91	107.91	30.79	23.35	68.67	74.46	111.69	93.53	15.16
Tampa, FL	121.35	121.35	124.90	129.88	125.41	138.93	178.44	228.73	225.40	265.10	245.05	243.10	259.00	259.00	146.70	200.05	189.12	252.32	283.11	278.22	218.90
Key West, FL	427.34	428.74	430.67	449.93	443.00	557.00	516.20	491.09	496.73	602.81	555.78	543.10	578.42	578.42	523.70	500.42	546.70	556.88	556.88	535.19	465.13
Atlanta, GA	127.33	127.33	112.38	148.25	148.19	182.55	163.29	170.61	98.08	283.22	252.62	204.32	201.29	201.29	140.63	192.39	214.02	190.35	97.70	150.58	73.28
Ft Gordon, GA	57.34	57.34	52.21	59.10	59.88	70.71	95.33	49.47	83.78	187.78	121.23	122.52	115.78	115.78	72.98	60.30	65.40	52.30	67.28	107.23	29.11

UNIFORMED SERVICES ALMANAC

SELECTED MILITARY HOUSING AREAS AND VHA FOR PAY GRADES DRAWING BAQ AT "WITH DEPENDENTS" RATES (As of January 1, 1996) (Continued)

MHA NAME	E-1	E-2	E-3	E-4	E-5	E-6	E-7	E-8	E-9	W-1	W-2	W-3	W-4	W-5	O-1	O-2	O-3	O-4	O-5	O-6	O-7+
Ft Benning, GA	34.76	34.76	33.58	33.21	29.89	32.46	83.09	81.88	48.15	80.48	78.62	63.22	91.16	91.18	59.92	59.14	56.50	0.00	0.00	0.00	0.00
Robins AFB, GA	56.23	56.23	50.59	56.83	48.33	55.44	83.41	78.32	54.00	142.49	112.34	55.52	97.24	97.24	47.04	48.74	31.40	35.24	20.45	5.50	0.00
Ft Stewart, GA	52.55	52.55	38.28	48.24	52.47	63.51	72.85	43.31	55.13	113.36	47.57	40.94	52.04	52.04	26.56	28.56	0.00	0.00	0.00	0.00	0.00
Moody AFB, GA	29.50	29.50	23.75	28.16	30.73	10.05	30.85	68.54	33.07	108.07	66.80	49.17	79.17	79.17	13.47	26.48	0.00	39.68	41.47	9.97	0.00
Honolulu County, HI	520.40	520.40	516.20	551.56	581.40	639.30	671.00	715.56	775.37	778.56	721.47	816.33	772.23	772.23	690.11	648.13	695.81	674.03	720.79	689.29	625.67
Mountain Home AFB, ID	0.00	0.00	0.00	0.27	11.80	60.68	42.13	61.76	0.00	107.06	39.60	50.75	55.39	55.39	0.00	0.00	0.00	3.83	17.72	13.26	0.00
Chanute AFB, IL	55.74	57.69	45.95	50.29	61.07	36.18	70.65	85.92	113.37	157.301	10.84	72.91	94.11	94.11	30.97	64.41	62.34	57.65	79.69	54.39	0.00
Great Lakes NAVTRACEN, IL	197.58	-197.58	195.73	205.48	228.43	257.68	254.09	281.74	171.41	44.26	372.83	389.66	368.91	368.91	301.58	333.60	317.47	449.41	439.45	419.05	346.81
Scott AFB, IL	79.49	78.49	57.25	67.72	68.39	101.78	132.25	154.01	125.58	139.16	116.99	117.95	124.30	124.30	50.25	42.16	149.53	119.16	148.60	159.80	82.67
Indianapolis/Ft Harrison, IN	54.58	54.58	47.85	46.38	66.75	76.68	95.43	90.33	142.86	193.49	145.39	143.29	163.65	163.65	74.87	100.45	141.18	102.62	150.43	118.93	44.84
Ft Riley, KS	20.98	6.53	0.00	0.00	0.00	0.00	0.00	80.35	11.12	49.92	58.43	74.31	45.78	45.78	13.49	2.20	39.13	81.93	0.00	0.00	0.00
Wichita/McConnell AFB, KS	71.00	71.00	66.73	63.29	72.33	93.78	84.28	80.35	121.67	85.74	106.01	110.51	106.84	106.84	34.59	60.08	99.53	81.93	81.11	56.10	0.00
Ft Leavenworth, KS	32.57	32.57	33.70	7.69	41.55	72.67	76.85	39.59	97.26	77.91	106.34	117.75	92.49	92.49	30.38	27.13	96.39	0.00	0.00	0.00	0.00
Ft Campbell, KY	41.69	29.48	24.72	28.17	19.10	15.89	33.69	5.33	12.91	87.66	36.72	94.98	85.66	85.66	14.18	28.47	0.00	0.00	10.16	0.00	0.00
Ft Knox, KY	0.00	0.00	0.00	0.00	0.00	0.00	0.00	3.99	25.69	7.29	0.00	0.00	0.00	0.00	0.00	0.00	0.00	0.00	0.00	0.00	0.00
England AFB, LA	0.00	0.00	0.00	0.00	0.00	0.00	0.00	0.00	0.00	0.00	0.00	0.00	26.00	0.00	0.00	0.00	0.00	0.00	0.00	0.00	0.00
Ft Polk, LA	0.00	0.00	0.00	0.00	0.00	0.00	0.00	0.00	0.00	25.29	1.06	0.00	0.00	0.00	0.00	0.00	4.98	0.00	0.00	0.00	0.00
New Orleans, LA	47.11	56.57	40.79	24.34	40.97	58.15	75.40	28.39	79.49	182.72	143.17	105.58	138.79	138.79	89.75	97.56	93.85	90.87	46.89	15.66	0.00
Shreveport/Barksdale AFB, LA	46.21	51.62	52.86	45.12	31.99	31.12	56.99	65.24	42.34	95.01	62.91	42.92	70.97	70.97	27.97	0.00	29.55	15.38	15.12	19.37	0.00
Boston, MA	309.34	312.90	302.03	311.11	317.59	380.19	446.89	430.20	462.10	556.12	556.68	549.15	606.00	606.00	428.16	424.07	530.08	624.18	614.11	589.26	620.80
Ft Devens/Ayer, MA	181.84	181.64	183.11	191.33	215.08	253.57	309.49	317.83	366.41	391.33	381.66	370.56	407.71	407.71	255.98	290.37	329.59	360.19	441.99	410.49	415.17
Hanscom Field, MA	264.88	267.31	268.14	285.48	300.66	339.71	412.33	397.48	438.83	483.23	477.61	471.16	500.75	500.75	349.61	387.31	427.80	500.07	486.85	506.80	496.84
Aberdeen Proving Grounds, MD	80.55	80.55	63.15	59.69	102.33	153.85	165.75	219.82	263.07	220.71	171.82	172.07	189.53	189.50	109.23	134.07	166.58	195.02	158.04	142.27	64.82
Annapolis, MD	270.96	271.49	264.83	284.51	288.93	318.87	360.73	389.84	407.15	390.46	386.98	354.09	368.53	368.53	298.53	306.25	320.02	380.56	364.29	356.44	283.02
Ft G.G. Meade, MD	295.00	297.51	307.43	290.28	322.59	363.15	397.16	371.68	397.78	441.69	446.48	398.18	394.21	394.21	364.47	370.62	390.14	375.85	367.03	358.75	285.38
Patuxent River, MD	197.49	198.98	197.42	210.48	235.35	253.81	315.56	285.62	297.95	360.53	323.55	323.26	290.14	290.14	260.62	262.73	271.44	317.41	302.27	270.77	195.74
KI Sawyer AFB, MI	0.00	0.00	0.00	0.00	0.00	8.12	28.88	78.90	122.19	99.76	63.29	60.46	73.30	73.30	0.00	0.00	10.68	38.81	33.16	1.65	0.00
Whiteman AFB, MO	0.00	0.00	0.00	0.00	0.00	1.92	26.75	50.17	52.11	78.82	43.97	46.12	50.21	50.21	0.00	0.00	21.02	0.00	24.77	0.00	0.00
Ft Leonard Wood, MO	0.00	0.00	0.00	0.00	0.00	0.00	0.00	15.17	8.54	0.00	72.28	41.50	0.000	0.00	0.00	0.00	0.00	0.00	0.00	0.00	0.00
Gulfport, MS	70.28	78.81	67.10	57.45	51.67	39.11	29.78	47.55	86.95	104.86	9.37	2.21	49.23	49.23	33.62	4.71	21.02	21.63	0.00	0.00	0.00
Malmstrom AFB/Great Fls, MT	0.00	0.00	0.00	0.00	0.00	0.00	12.39	31.34	79.44	43.87	9.37	3.88	9.90	9.90	0.00	0.00	19.30	0.00	0.00	0.00	0.00
Morehead/Cherry Pt MCAS, NC	36.75	36.75	34.80	18.90	32.15	25.65	49.72	43.81	77.11	53.23	10.81	42.26	9.68	9.68	54.60	0.00	34.56	21.07	36.14	48.66	0.00
Camp Lejeune, NC	33.49	22.38	16.49	17.59	17.89	1.49	12.16	59.76	17.78	127.92	65.03	28.30	48.97	28.56	103.31	51.33	17.47	0.00	0.00	0.00	0.00
Ft Bragg/Pope AFB, NC	89.67	79.09	73.20	78.41	76.71	64.42	78.35	55.87	55.74	124.77	23.73	83.48	9.96	8.29	145.39	43.13	57.57	43.19	58.75	47.33	0.00
Seymore Johnson AFB, NC	49.21	49.21	43.98	61.86	48.66	84.66	58.35	49.01	28.78	172.05	66.52	73.58	69.37	64.37	88.38	106.63	71.03	32.01	52.09	37.57	0.00
Grand Forks, ND	0.00	0.00	0.00	0.00	0.00	0.00	0.00	0.00	66.07	159.24	60.04	62.93	63.03	40.44	0.00	76.47	13.08	13.48	60.50	47.89	0.00
Minot AFB, ND	0.00	0.00	0.00	0.00	0.00	0.00	0.00	23.72	51.01	9.22	2.02	0.00	78.90	37.38	0.00	0.00	0.00	0.00	0.00	0.00	0.00
Omaha/Offutt AFB, NE	53.37	53.37	46.74	50.03	51.67	0.00	0.00	51.01	1.92	1.00	60.00	128.60	124.03	0.00	51.18	0.00	0.00	0.00	41.21	0.00	0.00
Ft Monmouth/Earle NWS, NJ	232.03	232.03	233.22	250.88	311.81	277.20	340.49	115.34	184.74	183.37	128.60	124.03	119.86	70.92	51.18	75.96	92.27	74.52	41.21	0.00	0.00
	232.03	232.03	233.22	250.88	311.81	277.20	340.49	357.57	387.72	426.68	437.18	462.74	507.64	481.35	355.17	380.88	441.98	474.77	477.24	482.05	439.35

58

UNIFORMED SERVICES ALMANAC

SELECTED MILITARY HOUSING AREAS AND VHA FOR PAY GRADES DRAWING BAQ AT "WITH DEPENDENTS" RATES (As of January 1, 1996) (Continued)

MHA NAME	E-1	E-2	E-3	E-4	E-5	E-6	E-7	E-8	E-9	W-1	W-2	W-3	W-4	W-5	O-1	O-2	O-3	O-4	O-5	O-6	O-7+
Ft Dix/McGuire/Lakehurst, NJ	247.83	248.42	260.06	265.36	297.88	320.14	368.51	412.63	390.15	341.25	318.56	342.16	368.40	332.10	248.85	284.80	314.42	341.78	327.01	318.54	260.48
Holloman AFB, Alamogordo, NM	137.44	137.44	131.85	141.13	161.79	0.00	15.09	8.60	12.34	62.48	0.00	0.00	33.83	33.83	0.00	0.00	22.54	0.00	0.00	0.00	0.00
Albuquerque/Kirtland AFB, NM	137.44	137.44	131.85	141.13	161.79	234.89	218.82	229.38	332.96	287.65	226.20	230.97	224.00	224.00	158.68	154.89	189.81	232.08	168.98	126.30	124.68
Cannon AFB/Clovis, NM	0.00	0.00	0.00	0.00	0.00	0.00	1.93	34.47	44.99	79.07	44.18	37.58	55.49	55.49	0.00	0.00	0.00	21.67	21.78	18.59	0.00
Nellis AFB/Las Vegas, NV	226.98	230.42	233.31	247.01	257.60	285.18	326.28	307.75	293.86	311.80	297.48	286.08	311.62	311.62	219.48	226.04	264.25	293.09	268.16	236.66	160.99
Rome/Griffiss AFB, NY	60.77	60.77	50.67	46.12	73.45	93.12	124.02	128.98	194.06	102.65	102.81	129.87	149.70	149.70	52.57	52.60	64.94	131.07	119.49	126.24	48.49
Ft Drum/Watertown, NY	49.91	49.91	41.90	51.79	95.81	105.37	109.73	115.24	173.66	101.57	81.12	117.58	124.68	124.68	40.82	6.14	24.43	66.45	115.11	104.53	26.38
Wright-Patterson, OH	67.51	67.51	68.55	75.04	56.48	88.85	128.98	115.84	182.00	183.14	124.38	130.25	165.17	165.17	82.79	87.85	117.50	115.01	85.81	83.51	4.95
Altus AFB, OK	0.00	0.00	0.00	0.00	0.00	0.00	0.00	0.00	18.00	44.88	65.55	23.99	17.00	17.00	0.00	0.00	31.60	0.00	0.00	0.00	0.00
Vance AFB/Enid, OK	0.00	0.00	0.00	0.00	0.00	0.00	0.00	0.00	25.69	0.00	0.00	0.00	0.00	0.00	0.00	0.00	0.00	0.00	0.00	0.00	0.00
Ft Sill/Lawton, OK	0.00	0.00	0.00	0.00	0.00	0.00	0.00	0.00	6.96	53.83	32.02	0.00	0.00	0.00	0.00	0.00	0.00	0.00	0.00	0.00	0.00
Portland, OR	132.75	134.04	128.18	125.72	143.54	199.19	174.26	178.00	257.97	236.26	208.23	197.12	240.00	240.00	148.83	135.59	183.11	191.42	202.49	170.99	108.59
Carlisle Barracks, PA	43.77	43.77	28.43	22.67	32.24	62.77	125.37	98.20	172.52	150.50	127.10	104.12	97.32	97.32	50.81	41.61	53.25	60.62	11.32	18.12	0.00
Philadelphia, PA/Camden, NJ	177.72	177.72	176.83	209.50	177.21	232.90	307.40	374.24	326.97	403.09	377.97	377.89	397.91	397.91	285.98	309.28	340.22	411.81	366.69	408.09	335.65
NAS Willow Grove, PA	262.41	262.41	261.45	265.18	316.75	311.34	362.19	388.75	381.99	452.38	427.69	425.73	455.36	455.36	344.41	348.39	382.45	411.81	408.57	408.09	336.12
Newport, RI	187.56	189.77	172.37	178.93	213.42	276.46	304.75	317.47	363.83	340.45	336.47	333.68	381.89	381.89	200.33	258.36	281.94	322.71	390.85	363.37	372.44
Beaufort/Parris Island, SC	95.63	95.63	85.77	91.19	76.07	93.03	64.71	67.58	94.22	164.76	90.06	100.82	101.39	101.39	100.70	87.38	104.38	89.68	81.93	75.66	0.00
Charleston, SC	53.54	53.54	42.85	36.85	39.41	59.27	60.69	85.41	117.10	208.34	158.07	128.98	115.78	115.78	111.97	93.98	134.61	150.65	130.16	110.60	32.55
Columbia/Ft Jackson, SC	71.74	71.74	68.59	76.17	81.03	93.68	106.70	99.91	64.52	182.66	122.35	114.04	111.87	111.87	74.18	72.04	77.04	69.22	23.09	65.24	0.00
Myrtle Beach AFB, SC	11.06	11.06	1.63	0.00	0.00	0.00	1.73	11.30	15.48	128.16	53.35	54.20	33.64	33.64	23.31	26.64	15.40	28.13	20.52	12.20	0.00
Sumter/Shaw AFB, SC	48.43	46.43	42.54	48.27	32.44	40.11	59.00	50.42	81.66	94.53	19.83	6.33	0.00	0.00	0.00	0.00	0.00	0.00	0.00	0.00	0.00
Rapid City/Ellsworth AFB, SD	19.63	19.63	6.17	22.10	33.39	8.22	50.55	100.43	132.51	124.49	80.21	80.46	76.47	76.47	29.22	52.44	45.73	50.90	48.84	47.47	0.00
Abilene/Dyess AFB, TX	7.35	7.35	7.04	12.83	21.59	23.91	68.62	91.24	87.39	117.13	77.97	75.01	117.45	117.45	0.00	30.84	68.78	66.65	84.42	67.42	0.00
Austin/Bergstrom AFB, TX	115.15	115.15	102.88	110.80	151.14	153.89	183.36	180.95	184.20	250.55	192.53	186.63	178.88	178.88	171.53	161.30	179.00	177.53	163.58	132.07	54.43
Corpus Christi, TX	80.97	80.97	69.04	87.52	95.60	121.24	148.89	147.47	149.52	188.04	154.49	156.07	185.39	185.39	65.28	79.29	147.17	113.42	158.58	154.84	77.81
Laughlin AFB/Del Rio, TX	0.00	0.00	0.00	0.00	0.00	0.00	47.84	48.34	48.11	0.00	0.00	0.00	0.00	0.00	0.00	0.00	0.00	0.00	0.00	0.00	0.00
Lubbock/Reese AFB, TX	40.32	40.32	33.65	40.74	60.21	36.91	68.08	88.55	99.28	127.20	87.25	78.81	88.12	88.12	32.07	30.82	22.94	50.45	54.78	35.99	0.00
Goodfellow AFB, TX	5.30	5.30	0.38	13.56	32.92	22.61	32.32	65.82	77.66	73.23	43.00	25.89	66.53	66.53	0.00	0.00	3.89	0.16	0.00	0.00	0.00
San Antonio, TX	109.21	91.80	86.19	59.85	116.54	130.68	154.49	128.59	108.78	208.55	187.89	129.63	162.57	162.57	93.80	111.50	130.94	102.35	90.77	57.25	0.00
Wichita Fls/Sheppard AFB, TX	0.30	5.58	4.90	44.37	47.31	75.01	78.47	61.44	55.05	148.58	131.11	111.44	112.08	112.08	53.59	63.46	106.51	67.71	109.86	79.75	1.12
Ogden/Hill AFB, UT	85.27	85.27	84.00	98.41	76.65	88.48	96.28	137.72	160.85	132.73	93.84	69.27	106.28	106.28	22.64	36.90	49.24	18.22	34.02	41.15	0.00
Quantico/Woodbridge, VA	206.10	206.10	194.77	219.21	254.83	273.29	321.85	314.93	365.84	403.71	431.18	316.78	348.78	348.78	313.51	294.52	331.42	335.18	319.64	318.38	244.24
Hampton/Newport News, VA	97.52	90.99	93.18	101.25	128.57	149.04	172.00	190.94	180.44	294.23	276.14	249.24	219.98	219.98	158.40	202.29	189.74	252.61	208.70	221.14	145.18
Norfolk/Portsmouth, VA	114.24	109.37	112.19	131.46	150.38	175.93	193.62	193.62	191.36	320.54	315.53	263.37	206.69	206.69	197.76	196.76	213.49	252.81	250.15	248.47	170.97
Petersberg/Ft Lee, VA	49.33	49.33	48.17	59.85	54.27	96.79	110.89	128.73	171.97	155.27	137.72	104.78	74.08	74.08	38.07	51.18	31.67	72.69	51.76	20.28	0.00
Bremerton, WA	165.31	150.72	156.95	167.67	188.11	229.99	254.46	284.08	241.55	293.40	261.25	260.38	205.46	205.46	181.08	207.14	192.73	184.94	182.78	151.28	74.00
Seattle, WA	197.26	197.26	196.93	200.92	232.70	309.45	297.83	312.71	321.81	356.81	327.61	338.36	288.85	288.85	187.16	280.82	280.17	292.88	321.40	289.90	215.23
Spokane, WA	81.93	82.65	89.83	92.49	123.18	144.84	172.20	171.32	191.41	196.34	189.18	164.35	183.87	183.87	101.30	129.92	136.08	168.81	182.72	151.22	73.93
Whidbey Island, WA	158.37	158.37	159.69	188.69	221.11	269.17	308.35	272.13	284.28	312.71	285.10	271.88	226.02	226.02	193.97	236.05	211.45	217.11	158.29	159.11	81.97
Sparta/Ft McCoy, WI	0.00	0.00	0.00	0.00	0.00	0.00	20.42	31.44	80.69	101.32	51.60	62.15	79.80	79.80	0.00	0.00	18.69	28.21	36.81	17.58	0.00

UNIFORMED SERVICES ALMANAC

SELECTED MILITARY HOUSING AREAS AND VHA FOR PAY GRADES DRAWING BAQ AT "WITHOUT DEPENDENTS" RATES (As of January 1, 1996)

MHA NAME	E-1	E-2	E-3	E-4	E-5	E-6	E-7	E-8	E-9	W-1	W-2	W-3	W-4	W-5	O-1	O-2	O-3	O-4	O-5	O-6	O-7+
Anchorage, AK	193.30	218.38	263.29	290.80	351.65	375.95	444.46	511.36	535.42	439.54	422.34	481.26	572.20	572.20	312.16	392.73	516.78	519.49	475.03	470.17	423.26
Fairbanks, AK	153.22	175.53	217.69	228.65	277.33	292.79	333.63	360.71	439.28	326.36	321.75	342.60	417.93	417.93	210.69	264.38	373.38	349.32	319.96	305.57	259.94
Anniston/Ft McClellan, AL	0.00	0.00	0.00	0.00	0.00	0.00	0.00	0.00	0.00	0.78	0.00	0.00	0.00	0.00	0.00	0.00	0.00	0.00	0.00	0.00	0.00
Ft Rucker, AL	0.00	0.00	0.00	0.00	33.90	0.00	0.00	24.31	27.96	112.31	70.26	52.34	96.09	96.09	10.45	30.29	65.20	54.00	31.99	33.87	0.00
Huntsville, AL	0.00	0.00	0.00	0.00	0.00	33.10	45.85	37.14	38.71	53.60	38.35	49.02	78.58	78.58	31.01	31.27	51.21	16.52	0.00	0.00	0.00
Montgomery, AL	34.52	38.75	41.52	36.72	0.00	0.00	0.00	1.95	27.73	8.68	6.44	0.00	12.79	12.79	0.00	12.14	31.45	38.49	67.19	41.18	0.00
Ft Chaffee/Ft Smith, AR	27.61	31.00	29.98	36.58	57.98	72.04	95.63	87.33	109.32	96.97	79.04	44.11	58.53	58.53	54.52	123.46	160.84	207.01	221.87	201.26	136.16
Ft Huachuca, AZ	52.61	59.05	65.93	67.54	88.37	110.64	102.37	135.85	162.23	182.93	178.92	161.56	187.47	187.47	0.00	91.22	123.75	111.20	121.75	56.65	56.65
Davis-Monthan AFB, AZ	68.56	76.96	93.88	84.39	99.91	99.14	143.21	160.94	160.91	184.00	149.98	152.54	196.53	196.53	100.67	342.08	442.26	508.26	458.14	459.01	393.91
Yuma, AZ	180.93	203.10	233.26	241.57	252.35	275.05	292.93	324.85	355.07	434.95	443.81	420.49	529.32	529.32	311.56	484.99	526.84	633.51	640.67	682.82	617.72
Oakland, CA	205.34	230.49	257.25	252.15	294.21	310.60	386.15	388.92	409.86	553.33	563.39	568.15	711.44	711.44	426.63	33.15	72.36	108.13	117.45	176.41	71.77
San Francisco, CA	6.30	3.41	0.00	0.00	44.99	23.09	52.34	98.41	159.51	102.30	69.33	63.98	134.60	134.60	13.27	115.17	125.50	166.13	198.88	268.35	111.31
China Lake NAVWEPCEN, CA	50.91	62.22	66.81	70.45	84.61	108.47	95.94	131.43	179.06	267.64	279.67	165.42	194.59	194.59	75.65	186.99	215.88	250.62	256.04	173.38	247.82
Camp Pendleton, CA	106.18	127.81	147.92	144.10	169.37	194.07	223.07	244.53	234.14	203.51	277.80	195.36	236.70	236.70	171.05	268.50	164.87	187.66	198.88	377.96	108.28
Vandenberg AFB, CA	113.58	127.49	144.57	139.47	168.19	178.85	199.44	247.71	288.36	174.69	47.02	85.79	236.70	236.70	104.57	23.52	316.22	373.66	355.34	156.61	0.00
Barstow/Ft Irwin, CA	39.40	44.22	53.90	51.81	54.10	81.51	79.86	144.83	200.09	122.23	107.07	17.52	74.43	74.43	16.66	68.36	11.06	62.85	32.27	39.09	91.12
Edwards AFB, CA	46.33	52.01	60.29	61.51	73.49	75.12	116.45	163.14	237.76	131.03	21.69	110.97	177.24	177.24	47.56	51.37	90.87	112.33	112.70	13.76	3.80
Twenty Nine Palms MCB, CA	37.59	42.20	44.10	54.65	58.77	80.20	125.65	114.28	107.50	74.39	129.95	300.17	59.01	59.01	23.42	218.15	91.37	250.43	81.10	76.97	11.87
Beale AFB, CA	149.06	167.32	190.22	206.70	203.89	213.34	251.99	276.42	189.44	150.91	277.47	264.89	174.76	174.76	199.80	308.03	258.38	250.43	234.46	208.60	143.50
Vallejo/Travis AFB, CA	155.86	178.05	207.53	201.57	230.04	252.48	316.13	355.97	301.47	391.40	426.31	415.80	350.32	350.32	308.03	268.50	402.69	470.23	470.23	492.70	427.60
Los Angeles, CA	107.13	142.83	144.51	141.10	170.67	194.50	232.29	259.14	249.05	349.92	333.95	360.84	603.99	603.99	263.35	274.28	316.22	373.66	355.34	377.96	345.06
San Diego, CA	134.05	150.46	173.90	141.39	151.69	225.38	273.28	277.85	307.76	343.47	321.02	345.54	466.39	466.39	227.48	161.32	293.97	434.40	383.39	374.01	308.91
Monterey, CA	68.13	76.62	87.46	95.83	122.79	146.37	144.96	177.91	167.04	211.81	160.26	136.42	462.57	462.57	122.40	126.97	160.73	173.71	148.91	160.73	95.63
Denver, CO	64.99	69.63	77.47	91.06	103.73	105.41	129.22	130.30	117.04	219.21	148.68	85.87	153.35	153.35	126.20	172.37	157.39	209.56	164.01	208.42	143.32
Colorado Springs, CO	81.06	90.99	100.51	95.41	124.67	118.14	162.63	177.59	168.11	226.48	177.53	167.68	144.15	144.15	164.18	172.37	179.64	217.57	198.08	191.23	126.13
Ft Collins, CO	104.36	114.09	139.20	140.59	154.72	174.16	214.28	262.36	253.86	229.81	257.25	241.63	300.35	300.35	169.82	172.37	203.28	209.56	270.78	266.59	253.00
Washington, DC	167.97	188.54	218.03	219.23	236.93	268.05	304.90	364.35	353.03	398.95	442.40	388.66	474.45	474.45	324.70	333.55	403.28	431.45	394.72	376.14	305.36
Dover AFB, DE	82.51	94.48	113.76	91.26	106.30	92.68	156.04	188.22	210.08	185.38	169.35	150.67	162.20	162.20	115.00	88.90	127.63	118.88	108.50	91.77	26.67
Eglin AFB, FL	44.49	41.23	43.43	46.36	61.03	54.14	49.09	73.38	49.57	63.46	51.67	55.79	85.23	85.23	49.76	39.27	72.78	55.29	62.39	26.54	0.00
Jacksonville, FL	59.18	58.95	64.69	72.94	87.64	91.02	107.00	157.01	105.39	183.07	166.47	139.50	193.98	193.98	108.60	139.72	123.36	131.86	148.06	186.65	121.55
Patrick AFB, FL	62.84	70.53	82.15	68.35	74.05	84.57	82.09	123.89	136.74	152.91	149.32	145.09	172.85	172.85	62.37	88.59	127.89	149.16	141.77	124.44	62.35
Ft Lauderdale, FL	134.72	151.22	170.29	188.30	204.65	213.09	242.68	278.06	258.25	358.25	341.01	349.05	431.11	431.11	285.34	302.00	302.85	399.46	421.55	403.57	338.47
Pensacola, FL	19.95	22.39	17.02	14.74	33.45	26.78	24.91	46.81	18.99	49.57	48.77	53.89	95.69	95.69	22.70	18.27	57.84	64.74	92.36	77.41	12.31
Tampa, FL	67.94	76.27	91.97	90.71	87.58	94.57	122.59	172.79	171.44	201.36	192.35	197.59	229.67	229.67	108.13	156.47	159.30	199.39	234.11	230.28	177.82
Atlanta, GA	71.29	80.03	82.76	103.55	103.48	124.26	113.46	128.88	77.42	199.93	198.29	166.15	178.49	178.49	108.35	50.88	72.89	165.51	80.79	124.63	59.53
Ft Gordon, GA	32.10	36.04	38.45	63.46	41.82	48.13	66.24	37.37	63.57	142.63	95.16	99.63	102.67	102.67	53.79	47.17	55.09	45.48	55.64	88.75	23.65
Ft Benning, GA	19.46	21.84	24.73	23.19	20.87	22.09	57.73	61.86	36.54	61.13	61.71	51.41	80.84	80.84	44.16	46.26	47.59	0.00	0.00	0.00	0.00

UNIFORMED SERVICES ALMANAC

SELECTED MILITARY HOUSING AREAS AND VHA FOR PAY GRADES DRAWING BAQ AT "WITHOUT DEPENDENTS" RATES (As of January 1, 1996) (Continued)

MHA NAME	E-1	E-2	E-3	E-4	E-5	E-6	E-7	E-8	E-9	W-1	W-2	W-3	W-4	W-5	O-1	O-2	O-3	O-4	O-5	O-6	O-7+
Robins AFB, GA	31.48	35.34	37.25	39.70	33.75	37.74	57.96	59.16	40.98	108.23	88.18	61.41	86.23	86.23	34.67	38.13	26.44	30.64	16.91	4.55	0.00
Ft Stewart, GA	29.42	33.03	28.19	33.70	36.64	43.23	50.62	32.72	41.83	86.10	37.34	33.29	46.15	46.15	19.57	20.71	0.00	34.50	0.00	0.00	0.00
Moody AFB, GA	16.52	18.54	17.49	19.67	21.46	6.84	21.44	51.77	25.09	82.08	52.43	39.99	70.20	70.20	9.93	0.00	0.00	34.50	34.29	8.25	0.00
Honolulu County, HI	291.37	327.06	380.11	385.24	406.01	435.17	466.23	540.55	588.35	591.35	566.31	663.80	684.78	684.78	508.64	506.94	588.07	586.06	596.04	570.50	508.27
Mountain Home AFB, ID	0.00	0.00	0.00	0.19	8.24	41.30	29.27	46.65	82.00	81.32	31.09	41.27	49.11	49.11	0.00	0.00	0.00	3.23	32.10	14.65	0.00
Chanute, IL	31.21	36.26	33.84	35.13	42.65	24.62	49.09	64.90	86.02	119.48	87.00	59.29	83.45	83.45	22.83	50.38	52.51	65.77	65.90	45.02	0.00
Great Lakes NAVTRACEN, IL	110.62	124.17	144.13	143.52	159.52	175.40	176.55	212.83	240.85	314.65	292.65	316.85	327.14	327.14	222.28	260.93	267.40	390.76	363.39	346.84	281.73
Scott AFB, IL	44.51	49.96	42.16	47.30	47.76	69.28	91.89	116.34	95.29	105.70	91.83	95.91	110.22	110.22	37.03	32.98	125.04	130.61	122.88	132.26	67.16
Indianapolis/Ft Harrison, IN	30.56	34.30	35.23	32.40	46.61	52.19	66.31	68.24	108.40	146.97	114.13	116.52	145.11	145.11	55.19	78.57	118.92	89.23	124.39	98.43	36.42
Ft Riley, KS	11.75	4.10	0.00	0.00	0.00	0.83	0.00	0.00	8.44	37.92	45.86	60.42	40.58	40.58	9.94	1.72	32.96	0.00	0.00	0.00	0.00
Wichita/McConnell AFB, KS	39.75	44.62	49.14	44.20	50.51	63.83	58.56	60.70	92.33	72.72	83.21	89.86	94.74	94.74	25.48	46.99	83.83	71.24	67.07	46.43	0.00
Ft Leavenworth, KS	18.23	20.47	24.82	5.37	29.02	49.47	53.40	29.91	73.80	59.17	83.47	95.75	82.01	82.01	22.39	21.22	81.19	0.00	0.00	0.00	0.00
Ft Campbell, KY	23.34	18.53	18.20	19.68	13.34	10.82	23.41	4.02	9.79	66.58	28.82	77.22	75.96	75.96	10.43	23.05	0.00	0.00	8.40	0.00	0.00
Ft Knox, KY	0.00	0.00	0.00	0.00	0.00	0.00	0.00	3.02	19.49	5.54	0.00	0.00	0.00	0.00	0.00	0.00	0.00	0.00	0.00	10.97	0.00
England AFB, LA	0.00	0.00	0.00	0.00	0.00	0.00	0.00	0.00	0.00	0.00	0.00	0.00	0.00	0.00	0.00	0.00	0.00	0.00	0.00	0.00	0.00
Ft Polk, LA	0.00	0.00	0.00	0.00	0.00	0.00	0.00	0.00	0.00	19.21	0.83	0.00	0.00	0.00	0.00	0.00	4.20	0.00	0.00	0.00	0.00
New Orleans, LA	28.37	35.55	30.04	17.00	28.61	38.22	52.39	21.45	60.31	138.79	112.38	85.85	121.30	121.30	66.15	76.31	78.88	79.01	38.77	12.96	0.00
Shreveport/Barksdale AFB, LA	25.87	32.44	38.92	31.51	22.34	21.18	39.60	49.29	32.13	72.16	49.38	34.90	62.93	62.93	20.62	0.00	24.89	13.37	12.50	16.04	0.00
Boston, MA	173.20	196.65	222.40	217.30	221.78	258.79	310.38	324.98	350.64	422.53	436.86	446.54	537.37	537.37	315.57	331.69	446.48	542.72	507.82	487.71	504.32
Ft Devens/Ayer, MA	101.70	114.16	134.83	133.64	150.19	172.61	215.04	240.09	278.03	297.23	299.58	301.32	361.54	361.54	188.67	227.12	277.61	313.19	365.49	339.75	337.27
Hanscom Field, MA	148.31	168.00	197.45	199.39	209.78	231.24	286.50	300.26	332.99	367.04	374.89	383.13	444.04	444.04	257.88	287.29	360.33	434.81	402.59	419.46	403.61
Aberdeen Proving Grounds, MD	45.10	50.62	46.50	41.69	71.46	104.72	115.18	166.00	199.62	167.64	165.58	139.92	150.54	150.54	80.51	104.87	140.31	169.57	130.68	117.75	52.66
Annapolis, MD	151.71	170.63	195.01	198.72	208.75	217.05	250.65	294.34	308.95	296.57	287.93	325.00	325.02	325.02	220.03	239.54	269.55	313.50	301.24	295.01	229.91
Ft G. G. Meade, MD	165.17	186.98	226.38	202.75	225.27	247.19	275.96	280.92	301.82	335.48	350.46	323.78	349.57	349.57	268.63	289.89	328.61	326.80	303.50	296.93	231.83
Patuxent River, MD	110.57	125.06	145.37	147.01	164.35	172.76	219.26	215.77	226.09	273.84	276.42	263.10	268.81	268.81	192.09	205.50	228.63	275.99	249.95	224.11	159.01
KI Sawyer AFB, MI	0.00	0.00	0.00	0.00	0.00	1.31	18.59	37.90	39.54	49.68	49.68	49.16	65.00	65.00	0.00	6.43	9.00	33.75	27.42	1.37	0.00
Whiteman AFB, MO	0.00	0.00	0.00	0.00	0.00	5.53	20.07	59.60	92.71	75.77	34.51	37.50	44.52	44.52	0.00	0.00	17.71	0.00	20.48	0.00	0.00
Ft Leonard Wood, MO	39.34	49.53	49.41	40.12	36.08	26.62	20.69	35.92	65.98	59.87	56.73	33.74	43.65	43.65	24.78	3.68	16.26	18.81	0.00	0.00	0.00
Gulfport, MS	0.00	0.00	0.00	0.00	0.00	0.00	8.61	23.68	60.28	6.49	7.36	1.80	8.78	8.78	0.00	0.00	0.00	0.00	0.00	0.00	0.00
Columbus AFB, MS	0.00	0.00	0.00	0.00	0.00	0.00	9.45	32.84	58.51	33.17	8.33	3.18	8.59	8.59	0.00	0.00	0.00	0.00	0.00	0.00	0.00
Malmstrom AFB/Great Fls, MT	20.58	23.10	25.63	13.20	22.45	17.46	34.55	45.14	13.49	40.43	51.04	34.37	43.43	43.43	40.24	40.15	29.11	18.32	29.88	38.62	0.00
Morehead/Cherry Pt MCAS, NC	18.75	14.06	12.14	12.28	12.49	1.02	8.45	0.00	0.00	94.77	18.63	23.01	8.83	8.83	76.15	33.73	14.71	0.00	0.00	0.00	0.00
Camp Lejeune, NC	50.20	49.70	53.90	54.76	53.57	43.85	53.05	42.20	42.29	130.68	52.21	67.88	61.52	61.52	107.16	83.40	56.91	37.55	48.58	39.17	0.00
Ft Bragg/Pope AFB, NC	27.55	30.93	32.38	43.21	33.98	44.01	40.54	37.02	21.84	120.95	66.36	59.83	55.89	55.89	65.14	59.81	59.83	27.83	43.08	31.09	0.00
Seymour Johnson AFB, NC	0.00	0.00	0.00	0.00	0.00	0.00	0.00	37.19	50.13	69.89	47.13	51.17	69.96	69.96	0.00	0.00	11.02	11.72	50.03	39.64	0.00
Grand Forks, ND	0.00	0.00	0.00	0.00	0.00	0.00	0.00	17.91	0.00	1.21	0.00	0.00	0.00	0.00	0.00	0.00	0.00	0.00	0.00	0.00	0.00
Minot AFB, ND	29.88	33.54	34.42	34.95	64.16	63.55	67.38	87.13	125.01	143.08	100.94	100.85	106.28	106.28	37.72	59.41	77.72	64.80	34.08	0.00	0.00
Omaha/Offutt AFB, NE	129.91	145.83	171.74	175.23	217.61	188.69	236.58	270.11	279.03	324.07	343.14	376.28	450.16	450.16	261.78	297.91	372.27	412.81	394.64	398.98	356.91
Ft Monmouth/Earls NWS, NJ	138.64	156.12	191.50	185.34	208.00	217.92	268.56	311.71	296.05	259.20	250.05	278.22	324.90	324.90	183.41	222.76	264.83	297.18	270.41	281.99	211.61
Ft Dix/McGuire/Lakehurst, NJ																					

61

UNIFORMED SERVICES ALMANAC

SELECTED MILITARY HOUSING AREAS AND VHA FOR PAY GRADES DRAWING BAQ AT "WITHOUT DEPENDENTS" RATES (As of January 1, 1996) (Continued)

MHA NAME	E-1	E-2	E-3	E-4	E-5	E-6	E-7	E-8	E-9	W-1	W-2	W-3	W-4	W-5	O-1	O-2	O-3	O-4	O-5	O-6	O-7+
Holloman AFB/Alamogordo, NM	0.00	0.00	0.00	0.00	0.00	0.00	10.48	6.50	9.36	47.48	0.00	0.00	29.82	29.82	0.00	0.00	18.99	0.00	0.00	0.00	0.00
Albuquerque/Kirtland AFB, NM	76.95	86.38	97.09	98.57	112.98	159.75	151.91	173.28	252.85	218.49	177.55	187.82	198.64	198.64	115.81	121.15	159.87	201.78	139.72	104.54	101.27
Cannon AFB/Clovis, NM	0.00	0.00	0.00	0.00	0.00	0.00	1.34	26.04	34.14	60.05	34.88	30.58	49.21	49.21	0.00	0.00	0.00	18.84	18.01	15.38	0.00
Nellis AFB/Las Vegas, NV	127.08	144.81	171.80	172.53	179.89	194.11	226.71	232.48	222.98	236.83	233.51	232.62	276.33	276.33	161.77	176.80	222.58	254.84	221.75	195.88	130.78
West Point, NY	106.31	119.33	135.13	130.02	137.64	144.45	196.03	217.33	257.64	345.70	374.19	426.18	483.02	483.02	286.67	328.12	374.58	481.53	493.04	478.25	446.78
Rome/Griffiss AFB, NY	34.03	38.19	37.31	32.21	51.29	63.39	86.17	97.44	147.25	77.97	80.70	105.61	132.75	132.75	38.75	41.14	54.89	113.97	98.81	104.49	39.39
Ft Drum/Watertown, NY	27.94	31.37	30.85	38.17	86.91	71.73	78.24	87.05	131.77	77.15	63.87	95.61	110.58	110.58	30.09	20.58	57.77	57.77	95.18	86.51	21.41
Wright-Patterson AFB, OH	37.80	42.43	50.48	62.42	39.44	60.48	89.62	87.51	138.10	139.10	97.63	105.92	146.47	146.47	61.02	68.71	98.97	100.00	70.80	69.12	4.02
Altus AFB, OK	0.00	0.00	0.00	0.00	0.00	0.00	0.00	0.00	19.49	49.79	35.23	19.51	15.07	15.07	0.00	0.00	20.58	0.00	0.00	0.00	0.00
Vance/Enid AFB, OK	0.00	0.00	0.00	0.00	0.00	0.00	0.00	0.00	0.00	0.00	0.00	0.00	0.00	0.00	0.00	0.00	26.82	0.00	0.00	0.00	0.00
Ft Sill/Lawton, OK	0.00	0.00	0.00	0.00	0.00	0.00	0.00	0.00	5.28	40.88	25.13	0.00	0.00	0.00	0.00	0.00	0.00	0.00	0.00	0.00	0.00
Portland, OR	74.33	84.24	92.91	87.81	100.24	135.59	121.08	134.46	195.91	179.45	164.23	160.29	212.82	212.82	89.20	106.05	154.23	166.44	167.44	141.52	88.21
Carlisle Barracks, PA	24.58	27.51	20.94	15.84	22.51	42.73	87.11	72.67	130.91	114.31	99.78	84.67	86.30	86.30	37.45	32.55	44.85	52.71	9.36	13.34	0.00
Philadelphia, PA/Camden, NJ	99.50	111.68	130.21	146.33	123.75	158.53	251.66	293.67	248.10	306.16	296.69	307.36	352.85	352.85	210.78	241.91	286.56	358.06	303.22	337.77	272.67
NAS Willow Grove, PA	146.92	164.92	185.22	124.97	123.75	211.93	251.68	293.67	289.68	343.60	335.71	346.18	403.79	403.79	253.84	272.50	322.13	356.85	363.84	338.16	273.05
Newport, RI	105.01	119.26	126.92	124.97	149.04	188.18	211.75	280.81	276.08	258.59	264.11	271.33	338.64	338.64	147.65	202.08	237.48	280.59	280.59	330.23	302.58
Beaufort/Parris Island, SC	53.54	60.10	63.16	63.70	53.12	63.33	44.98	51.05	71.49	125.15	70.70	90.11	89.91	89.91	74.22	68.34	87.92	77.98	67.75	62.62	0.00
Charleston, SC	29.98	33.65	31.55	25.74	27.52	40.34	42.17	64.52	88.86	158.24	122.51	104.88	102.67	102.67	82.53	73.51	113.38	130.99	107.63	91.54	26.44
Columbia/Ft Jackson, SC	40.17	45.09	50.51	53.20	56.59	63.77	74.14	75.48	48.96	138.74	96.03	92.73	99.21	99.21	54.87	56.35	66.51	80.59	19.09	53.99	0.00
Myrtle Beach, SC	6.18	6.95	1.20	0.00	0.00	0.00	1.20	8.54	11.75	97.26	41.87	44.07	29.83	29.83	17.18	20.84	12.97	24.48	18.97	10.10	0.00
Sumter/Shaw AFB, SC	26.00	29.18	31.32	33.72	22.85	27.30	40.99	38.09	61.97	77.00	15.57	5.15	0.00	0.00	21.54	41.02	38.52	44.28	10.89	53.99	0.00
Rapid City/Ellsworth AFB, SD	10.99	12.33	4.55	15.43	23.31	5.60	35.12	75.86	100.55	94.56	82.96	65.43	87.81	87.81	0.00	24.12	57.92	57.95	40.39	39.29	0.00
Abilene/Dyess AFB, TX	4.12	4.62	5.18	8.96	20.09	16.28	47.68	68.93	66.32	88.96	71.59	63.84	104.15	104.15	21.54	24.12	57.92	57.95	89.81	55.80	0.00
Austin/Bergstrom AFB, TX	64.47	72.37	75.76	77.39	105.55	104.61	127.40	136.70	124.59	146.59	151.12	151.78	158.62	158.62	128.42	128.17	150.77	154.36	135.27	128.15	44.21
Corpus Christi, TX	45.33	50.89	50.84	61.13	66.76	82.53	103.45	111.40	113.45	142.83	121.26	126.91	164.39	164.39	48.11	62.02	123.98	98.62	131.12	128.15	63.05
Laughlin AFB/Del Rio, TX	0.00	0.00	0.00	0.00	0.00	0.00	3.32	36.52	66.86	100.81	0.00	0.00	0.00	0.00	0.00	0.00	0.00	0.00	0.00	0.00	0.00
Lubbock/Reese AFB, TX	22.58	25.34	24.78	28.46	42.04	25.13	47.30	65.38	75.32	96.62	68.48	62.46	78.14	78.14	23.84	23.95	19.32	43.86	45.30	29.79	0.00
Goodfellow AFB, TX	2.97	3.33	0.28	9.47	22.99	15.39	22.48	49.57	58.93	55.62	33.75	20.89	50.13	50.13	0.00	0.00	3.28	0.14	0.00	0.00	0.00
San Antonio, TX	61.15	57.69	63.47	67.20	81.39	88.95	107.35	97.14	82.55	158.41	131.78	105.41	144.16	144.16	69.13	87.21	110.29	89.00	75.06	47.38	60.12
Ft Hood, TX	41.52	38.94	41.24	41.85	59.84	69.77	77.70	77.79	43.74	146.59	98.45	104.36	133.64	133.64	66.81	101.50	98.46	103.18	111.85	85.88	174.84
Wichita Fls/Sheppard AFB, TX	0.17	3.50	3.61	30.99	33.04	51.06	54.52	46.41	41.77	112.86	102.92	90.62	99.39	99.39	39.50	49.84	88.71	58.87	93.08	0.00	0.91
Ogden/Hill AFB, UT	47.74	53.59	61.86	88.73	53.53	60.23	66.90	104.03	122.00	100.81	73.66	56.33	94.23	94.23	16.69	28.88	41.47	15.84	28.13	34.06	0.00
Quantico/Woodbridge, VA	115.39	129.53	143.43	153.11	177.96	186.03	223.63	237.90	277.60	306.64	333.43	257.59	309.28	309.28	231.07	230.36	279.15	291.44	284.32	263.51	198.41
Hampton/Newport News, VA	54.80	57.18	68.62	70.72	90.48	101.45	119.51	144.24	136.92	223.48	218.75	202.67	195.07	195.07	117.48	158.23	159.81	192.65	172.58	183.03	117.94
Norfolk/Portsmouth, VA	63.98	68.73	82.61	91.82	105.02	119.75	144.06	145.21	145.21	243.46	247.67	214.16	183.29	183.29	145.76	153.90	179.82	219.64	206.88	203.99	138.89
Petersburg/Ft Lee, VA	27.62	31.00	35.47	41.80	37.50	69.34	77.05	97.24	130.49	117.93	108.11	85.20	66.69	66.69	28.06	40.03	26.88	63.20	42.80	16.77	0.00
Bremerton, WA	92.58	94.72	115.58	117.11	131.36	158.56	176.81	199.49	183.28	222.85	205.07	211.71	182.00	182.00	133.46	162.01	162.88	160.81	151.15	125.21	60.12
Seattle, WA	118.44	123.87	145.01	140.33	162.50	210.64	208.94	238.22	244.19	270.86	257.18	275.14	256.14	256.14	80.81	219.65	235.98	254.66	285.77	239.94	174.84
Spokane, WA	46.87	51.05	66.15	64.80	58.02	98.54	119.65	128.42	145.24	149.13	132.78	133.64	163.05	163.05	74.86	101.62	114.62	146.87	151.09	125.18	60.06
Whidbey Island, WA	88.87	99.53	117.59	131.79	154.41	183.22	214.25	205.57	215.71	237.52	223.78	221.08	200.43	200.43	142.98	184.63	178.10	180.87	130.89	131.69	66.59
Sparta/Ft McCoy, WI	0.00	0.00	0.00	0.00	0.00	13.90	16.11	23.75	61.38	76.96	40.50	50.54	70.58	70.58	0.00	0.00	14.06	24.53	30.27	14.63	0.00

62

UNIFORMED SERVICES ALMANAC

Assuming enactment of the FY 96 Defense Authorization Act, FY96 VHA rates are based on reported housing costs. The census of uniformed service members shows an overall housing cost growth of 2.4 percent over the last year.

These rates are effective January 1996 and go to the estimated 850,000 members eligible for the allowance.

The 1996 VHA increases limit the median member's monthly out-of-pocket costs to about 21.2 percent of the national median housing cost.

VHA rates are established according to geographical areas which are grouped into Military Housing Areas (MHAs). MHAs generally include an area where members both live and work. Most military installations or detachments are included in one of the approximately 350 established MHAs.

VHA rates are based on local housing costs including utilities and maintenance. *A member's VHA rate depends on his or her pay grade and the MHA as determined by the member's permanent authorized duty station within the USA (including Alaska and Hawaii). The MHA for a member overseas in an unaccompanied status is determined by the location of his or her dependents within the USA.*

The preceeding tables provide a partial listing of MHAs and the VHA rates for selected pay grades drawing BAQ at both the "With and Without Dependents" rates. Additional information regarding VHA and rates can be obtained from installation Personnel offices and Finance offices.

TRAVEL AND TRANSPORTATION ALLOWANCES

GENERAL

When travel is required of a member of the Uniformed Services in compliance with valid orders, the Government either furnishes the transportation or reimburses the member in accordance with rate schedules set by law for the particular situation. The Joint Federal Travel Regulations (JFTR), Volume 1, published by the Per Diem, Travel and Transportation Allowance Committee, is the statutory directive for payment of travel and transportation allowances. For details concerning these allowances, consult the local Transportation or Finance office.

Local Travel and Transportation. If you are required to travel within and around your duty station, generally you will do so during duty hours and be furnished Government transportation and your meal times will be undisturbed. In the event that the Government is unable to furnish you transportation, you may be authorized a monetary allowance in lieu of transportation, for the use of your own car and any toll charges incurred may be reimbursed. The current mileage rate is 30 cents per mile for travel by privately owned conveyance. Members may also be reimbursed on an actual expense basis for any meals procured (not to exceed two meals) not to exceed the rate for that meal in the Meal and Incidental Expense (M&IE) portion of the per diem allowance for the locality concerned (JFTR Volume 1 — Appendices B or D) when on TDY for a round trip of 10 hours or less, when on a PCS with TDY enroute at a location near but outside the limits of the permanent station or when on TDY near the permanent station and the member commutes from his or her permanent quarters to and from the TDY location.

UNIFORMED SERVICES ALMANAC
DEPENDENT STUDENT TRAVEL

The FY 84 DoD Authorization Act (P.L. 98-94) authorized annual funded roundtrip travel for dependent students of servicemembers assigned overseas. To be eligible, students must have been eligible to have accompanied their sponsor overseas; must be enrolled in undergraduate degree programs in a college or university, and must be unmarried and less than 23 years of age and dependent on his/her sponsor for more than 1/2 his or her support and receive prior approval by DFAS. Travel benefits are also authorized for students attending secondary schools in the CONUS, Alaska or Hawaii, if appropriate DoD-run schools are not available in the overseas area of assignment. Only one trip per year door to door is authorized between the U.S. and the overseas location and return.

TEMPORARY DUTY ALLOWANCES

Subsistence Allowances. TDY involves travel away from your duty station with the Government furnishing you the required tickets for rail, bus, or air carriers and a per diem allowance to cover your food, lodging, and incidental expenses at your TDY location. This per diem is intended to cover the actual expenses of lodging (not to exceed the maximum specified in the per diem rate for the locality concerned as provided in JFTR Volume 1 Appendices B or D). In addition, the per diem allows a predetermined amount to the traveler for meals and incidental expenses, regardless of the amount the traveler spends for these items. This per diem system became effective on January 1, 1988 for both CONUS and overseas travel and is known as the "Lodgings Plus Per Diem System." In the CONUS, there are over 600 localities with a specified per diem rate including about 140 with two rates to account for seasonal price changes. For travel in all other areas in CONUS, a per diem rate of $66 is currently prescribed ($40 for lodging and $26 for meals). Rates are set using an annual cost survey of hotels and restaurants nationwide. The finance and accounting office can provide the member with details.

Officers receive both per diem and BAS while on TDY/TAD as do enlisted personnel with some exceptions. Enlisted members are not due BAS during field duty, sea duty or mandatory unit messing.

Monetary Allowance in Lieu of Transportation (MALT). If the Government doesn't furnish you a ticket and your orders permit you to seek your own transportation, you may be paid a monetary allowance in place of that transportation at the rate of 24.5/30/88.5 cents per mile depending on mode of transportation (motorcycle, car, privately owned airplane). If you travel by privately owned vehicle (POV) and your orders authorize that way of traveling as being advantageous to the Government, per diem will be payable for the time spent traveling by POV. If your orders have no such statement, per diem will be paid only for air travel time generally and the excess time will be considered as leave. In addition, MALT and per diem will be limited to the cost, to the Government, had an airline ticket been used.

Reimbursement for Cost of Transportation. If the Government was unable to give you tickets, you may be reimbursed the full costs paid for the mode of transportation authorized and actually used. Be ready to prove what you paid and explain why the Government was unable to furnish you transportation requests (TRs) or tickets. You must submit a request to your Transportation Officer for Government procured transportation for transoceanic travel. A word of warning - do not use foreign carriers unless you are absolutely sure that no United States carrier is available.

UNIFORMED SERVICES ALMANAC

Actual Expense Allowances. When your duty is of an unusual nature and the per diem allowance payable is insufficient, there is a procedure whereby you can petition, through channels, for actual expense allowance within CONUS up to 150 percent of the applicable per diem rate (up to 300 percent for Presidentially declared disaster areas or any other area designated by GSA) and outside CONUS up to 300% of the applicable per diem rate. (In excess of 300% of the rate may be authorized overseas in advance only), or the applicable per diem plus $50, whichever is greater. If you have a good case, relief is provided, if possible, under law. See Chapter 4, Part C, Volume 1 JFTR.

Miscellaneous Reimbursements. There are a variety of reimbursements available in proper cases. Taxi fares or limousine costs, parking, ferry fares, bridge, road and tunnel tolls to and from common carrier terminals are allowable generally. Fees for travelers checks within limits, passport costs, baggage handling, and official telephone or telegraph costs are usually reimbursable. Have receipts for costs of $25 or more to prove your expenses.

PERMANENT CHANGE OF STATION ALLOWANCES

Personal Travel Allowances. A monetary allowance of 15 cents per mile plus a flat rate per diem is payable for land travel by privately owned conveyance (POC) of members traveling alone on PCS. Per diem per travel day for member is $50 per day. You must submit a request to your Transportation Officer for Government procured transportation for transoceanic travel.

Dependent Travel Allowances. For dependent travel, the Government will pay a member an allowance if one dependent accompanies the member, a total rate of 17 cents per mile; two dependents, 19 cents per mile; if more than two dependents, the rate is 20 cents per mile. In addition a flat rate of $37.50 per day for dependents 12 and over and a flat rate of $25.00 for those under 12, per travel day is authorized. Government transportation and Government procured transportation is normally permitted for these dependents for transoceanic travel. The limit is the distance between permanent duty stations.

When land travel is performed partly by transportation request (TR) and partly at personal expense for a separate leg of a journey or by other mixed modes, a monetary allowance in lieu of transportation plus a flat per diem will be payable for the ordered travel, or what it would have cost the government had a TR been used, whichever is greater; plus a per diem. If a TR was used, the cost of that request will be deducted from the entitlement.

Separation and retirement are considered *permanent* changes of station.

Dislocation Allowances. A dislocation allowance is provided to partially reimburse a member for expenses associated with relocating the household including movement or shipment of a mobile home. If the member has dependents, any relocation of their household caused by the change of station will generally be the basis of payment. If a member does not move dependents or if the member is single, the allowance is payable whenever the member is not assigned Government quarters at the new permanent station. The amount is equivalent to two times the monthly rate of BAQ prescribed for the member's pay grade and at the with or without dependents rate based on the member's dependency status on the effective date of the permanent change of station orders. Dislocation allowances are not payable on separation or on retirement.

Temporary Lodging Expenses (TLE). Temporary lodging expense reimbursement is authorized, not to exceed $110 per day, when a member is ordered to or from a station in CONUS. If the new duty station is in CONUS,

UNIFORMED SERVICES ALMANAC

the member may be reimbursed up to 10 days of TLE (effective April, 1994). If the member's old station is in CONUS and the new station overseas, the member may be reimbursed up to 5 days of TLE.

Travel to Ports for Shipment or Pickup of POV. A member entitled to the shipment of a privately-owned vehicle to or from an overseas location is entitled to a monetary allowance (depending on number of passengers in the car *and if the travel is performed concurrently with the PCS travel)* for one-way transportation of the POV: (a) from the old permanent duty station to the port of *embarkation,* and/or (b) from the port of *debarkation* to the new permanent duty station. See your transportation office for details.

Mobile Home Allowances. Mobile Home Allowances may be authorized for movement of house trailers for members incident to permanent change of station orders. These allowances are in lieu of the transportation of baggage and household goods and are authorized only for mobile home shipments between points within the 48 contiguous States, between the CONUS and Alaska, and between points within Alaska. The transportation of a mobile home is subject to an overall cost limitation of the total amount of the cost of transporting the member's maximum authorized weight allowance of household goods from the old permanent station to the new permanent station. Members may also arrange to personally transport the mobile home, subject to the same cost limitations.

FUNDED EMERGENCY LEAVE TRAVEL

The biggest limitation governing this type of travel is that commercial travel may be used only when Government transportation is not available.

Funded emergency leave travel from points outside CONUS provides for commercial transportation for service members and/or their command sponsored dependents from their overseas duty stations *or their location when notification of the emergency is received* to the nearest international airport in CONUS or an airport in Hawaii, Alaska, Puerto Rico, Guam, or U.S. possessions or an airport at any other overseas location as determined by appropriate authority and return.

Funded emergency leave travel also provides for commercial transportation for service members who are on temporary duty or who are on ships operating away from homeport.

For a member stationed in the CONUS whose domicile is outside CONUS, the cost of commercial transportation authorized or approved will not exceed the cost of government procured commercial air travel from the international airport nearest the member's permanent duty station or the location of the member when notified of the personal emergency. (The term domicile means the member's home of record, place from which called, or ordered, to active duty, place of first enlistment, or place of permanent legal residence.)

For more information and details, see JFTR, Volume 1, paragraphs U7205 *(for the member's travel) and U5244 (for dependent travel).* Your personnel or transportation office can provide additional guidance.

TRAVEL ALLOWANCE — SEPARATION AND RETIREMENT

Upon separation from the service under honorable conditions, a service member is entitled to per diem and transportation at the rate of 15¢ per mile, when traveling by POV, from the place from where separated to their home of record (or place from which called or ordered to active duty). This travel must be completed within 180 days of separation. Upon retirement from active duty for either length of service (following at least 8 years of continuous service), or when retired for disability, or involuntary separation under certain conditions, and upon separation under the VSI or SSB program, a member may select a home any place in the United States, and receive per diem and a transportation allowance of 15¢ per mile from the place from where retired. This travel must generally be completed within one year after termination of active duty. Allowances for dependent travel, shipment of household goods, and storage of HHG (for one year) may also be provided.

TRANSPORTATION OF HOUSEHOLD GOODS AND AUTOMOBILE

You are entitled to the packing, crating, draying, shipping, storage, unpacking, or uncrating of your household goods, in connection with your permanent change of station orders. You may be permitted to ship certain items on TDY orders. The maximum net weight allowances which can be shipped on PCS and TDY orders are listed in the table of weight allowances in the JFTR, and in part, the PCS allowances are on the chart which follows. The amount allowed to be shipped to certain overseas areas may be restricted. Check with your transportation officer (TO).

In addition to the shipment of your household goods and personal baggage, personnel with permanent change of station orders to, from, and between most overseas stations or with units undergoing changes of homeport *may ship one privately owned or leased vehicle at Government expense.* (Motor vehicles which are your personal property or for which you have a lease for 12 months or more and are designed to carry passengers or property, such as automobiles, jeeps, motorcycles, motor scooters, and motor bikes, including mopeds, are considered as privately owned vehicles. Each military service has its own rules on the types of mopeds, minibikes and similar vehicles that can be shipped. Consult the installation TO for details.) When you receive a PCS, in nearly all instances you are responsible for delivery of your vehicle to the point of embarkation for shipment. **Note:** There may also be certain restrictions governing the shipment of privately owned vehicles to certain overseas areas; there are also certain restrictions regarding the reentry of vehicles into the United States after they have been operated on leaded fuel overseas. Consult the TO before shipping privately owned vehicles to or from overseas areas.

DO-IT-YOURSELF MOVING

The do-it-yourself (DITY) moving program, offers a monetary incentive to members who do their own packing, crating and moving of personal property. However, the amount of the allowance for DITY moving must provide a savings to the US Government when the total cost of this method of transportation is compared to that which a professional mover would charge.

Under this program, there are two ways to move yourself and qualify for an incentive. First, you may use your own, a borrowed or rental vehicle, the primary design of which must be for other than moving passengers. You must have the prior written approval of the installation TO, except in the rare instance where the DITY is approved at a higher level for you after you make the move. The monetary incentive paid the member performing a DITY move

UNIFORMED SERVICES ALMANAC

is equal to 80 percent of what it would have cost the Government to commercially move the authorized or actual household goods weight. An advance operating allowance may be paid under certain circumstances when rental equipment is used, however, that amount will be deducted from the incentive payment at final settlement.

Any service member who is otherwise eligible to move personal property at Government expense is eligible to use this program. This includes those making a PCS, TDY, TAD or separating, retiring and moving to or from Government quarters under orders. The program is voluntary and may be used in whole or in part. A member, for example, may ship some household goods on a Government bill of lading and the balance, up to the allowed weight allowance, under the do-it-yourself program.

A service member arranges for a do-it-yourself move by applying at the Personal Property TO just as he or she would for any other type move. There are several key elements involved in a do-it-yourself move:

1. The **interview** with the Personal Property Transportation representative where all factors of the program will be covered in detail. All forms and instructions will be provided to the member by the Transportation representative.

2. **Packing** will probably take more time than it would a professional. Packing materials can be purchased from commercial suppliers.

3. **Arranging for the rental equipment** (if desired) is the next step and must be done by the member directly with the rental company. The member will have to get weight tickets before and after loading the vehicle to support a claim at the time of final settlement.

4. **Making the trip** is perhaps the most important element in the program for this is where both the government and the member achieve the benefits from the program. The benefits to the member take the form of a "Monetary Incentive Payment" which, in addition to travel allowances for the member and his or her family, if authorized, is paid using a formula which takes into consideration the estimated cost of having the move made by professionals and the actual cost of the do-it-yourself move.

5. **Arriving at the destination** completes the process and it is at this time that the member submits the necessary "weight tickets", other forms and, if necessary submits a claim for damages and or losses.

More specific details and information can be obtained from the Personal Property Transportation office at your installation.

PCS HHG WEIGHT ALLOWANCES (Pounds)

PayGrade OFFICERS:	Without Dependents	With Dependents
O-10	18,000	18,000
O-9	18,000	18,000
O-8	18,000	18,000
O-7	18,000	18,000
O-6	18,000	18,000
O-5	16,000	17,500
O-4	14,000	17,000
O-3	13,000	14,500
O-2	12,500	13,500
O-1	10,000	12,000
W-5	16,000	17,500
W-4	14,000	17,000
W-3	13,000	14,500
W-2	12,500	13,500
W-1	10,000	12,000

UNIFORMED SERVICES ALMANAC

ENLISTED:

E-9	12,000	14,500
E-8	11,000	13,500
E-7	10,500	12,500
E-6	8,000	11,000
E-5	7,000	9,000
E-4[1]	7,000	8,000
E-4[2]	3,500	7,000
E-3	2,000	5,000
E-2	1,500	5,000
E-1	1,500	5,000
Cadets and Midshipmen	350	

[1]Member with more than two years of service.
[2]Member with less than two years of service.

SPACE AVAILABLE TRAVEL

Military personnel, their spouses and bona fide dependents who travel with them, are eligible for Space Available (Space-A) travel on DoD owned or controlled aircraft on flights to, from and between overseas areas. Dependents are permitted to travel on DoD owned or controlled aircraft to or from an overseas location when a CONUS leg segment (enroute stop) is involved. For example: Dependents may travel on a mission which operates from Hickam AFB, Hawaii, to Offutt AFB, Nebraska, even though an enroute stop is made in California. Conversely, dependents may travel on a mission which operates from Andrews AFB, Maryland, to Howard AFB, Panama, even though an enroute stop is made in Florida. Dependent travel beyond the first CONUS point is contingent on the aircraft's mission.

Members may personally report to the Space-A counter at the passenger terminal to register for Space-A flights or may mail or fax their travel request to the locations from which they plan to depart. The fax should provide the first names of dependent family members traveling with them, a statement that required border clearance documents are current and a list of up to five country destinations. Travelers remain on the Space-A list up to 45 days or until their leave expires, whichever is first, and retirees may remain on the list up to 60 days. A valid ID card is required for all passengers. Passports, visas, immunization records are also required for overseas travel along with leave orders or other travel authorizations. Once registered, the traveller must wait for notification that their travel category and date/time of sign up has been reached. When selected for a flight, the traveller must be ready to process. Space-A travellers are not required to be present for all scheduled departures.

In addition to frequent long waiting periods, it should be noted that the Government is not obligated to provide return or continuing transportation to Space-A passengers. Adequate funds should be available to procure commercial transportation for return flights or lengthy stays awaiting Space-A flights. Successful Space-A journeys require patience and flexibility.

There may be some charges involved. Transportation officers and terminal personnel can provide the traveler with more specific information regarding these charges, e.g., Federal Inspection fees and commercial gateway head tax.

General Space Available Information

Space-A air travel seats are normally available after all official duty passengers have been accommodated. Passengers are permitted to sign up for a maximum of five destinations with the last destination being "All" to qualify for any opportune missions to a destination not normally served by the departure terminal. Those traveling in categories I, II, III, IV, or V are permitted to revalidate for forty-five days on the Space-A register. Passengers in category VI may revalidate for sixty days.

Space available passengers are removed from the Space-A register when they:
  a. Are selected for a flight.
  b. Fail to revalidate on their proper date.
  c. Have not moved by their leave expiration date.

Space-A travelers may reregister after they are removed from the list, however, they will be given a new date/time of sign up and drop to the bottom of the list in their respective category.

The Space-A passenger should be prepared to spend time awaiting travel, and always be ready to travel at his/her expense. As long as seats are available on an aircraft, every attempt will be made to utilize them for Space-A passengers.

Passengers will be offered air transportation on a first come, first served basis, based upon established space available categories:

  a. **Categories**. There are six categories of space-available travel. Space-available travelers are placed in one of the six categories based on their status (e.g., active duty, Uniformed Services member, DoDEA teacher, etc.) and their situation (e.g., emergency leave, ordinary leave, etc.). Once accepted for movement, a space-available passenger may not be "bumped" by another space-available passenger, regardless of category.

  b. **Priority of Movement**. The numerical order of space-available categories indicates the precedence of movement between categories; e.g., travelers in Cat III move before travelers in Cat IV. The order in which travelers are listed in a particular category does not indicate priority of movement in that category. In each category, transportation is furnished on a first-in, first-out basis.

  c. **Changes to Movement Priorities**. Wherever the issue may arise, the local installation commander may change the priority of movement of any space-available traveler for emergency or extreme humanitarian reasons when the facts provided fully support such an exception. The installation commander may delegate the authority to make such changes to no lower than the Chief of the Passenger Service Center or its equivalent. When a movement priority is changed, the passenger shall be moved no higher than the bottom of the Cat I space-available list. Where AMC units are tenants, the senior local AMC authority shall advise the installation commander of this authority and offer technical assistance, as needed.

  Categories. Following are the general categories for Space-available travel:

  Category I. Emergency Leave Unfunded Travel. This category includes transportation for bona fide immediate family emergencies, Uniformed Services members with emergency status, dependents of Uniformed Services members and certain others.

  Category II. Environmental and Morale Leave (EML). Includes sponsors in an EML status and their dependents traveling with them, also in an EML status. "Sponsors" includes: Uniformed Services members; U.S. civilian employees eligible for Government-funded transportation to the U.S. at tour completion; American Red Cross, USO professional staff and DoDEA teachers during the school year.

  Category III. Ordinary Leave. Close blood or affinitive relatives, house hunting permissive TDY, Medal of Honor Holders and certain others.

  Category IV. Unaccompanied dependents on EML and DoDEA teachers on EML during summer.

UNIFORMED SERVICES ALMANAC

Category V. Permissive TDY (non-house hunting), Foreign Military, students, dependents, and others.
Category VI. Retired Uniformed Service members, dependents, Reserve, ROTC, NUPOC and CEC.

All passengers when reregistering for overseas travel are required to have in their possession a current ID card, valid leave orders, passports/visas, and a current immunization record (when applicable).

Individuals traveling in a leave or pass status cannot be signed up prior to the effective date on the leave order and must remain in a leave or pass status while awaiting travel and during the entire period of travel.

Individuals traveling in a pass status (without leave orders) can sign up for a maximum of three days.

All services require military members, including ROTC personnel, to wear the appropriate military uniform when traveling on DoD owned aircraft.

Air Mobility Command travelers are now authorized to wear appropriate civilian clothing, whether flying in a duty or space-available status on military-arranged charter flights. While no longer requiring uniforms, AMC does require that civilian attire be neat, clean and suitable for the occasion. Passengers must wear shoes. Sandals, shorts, tank tops, halters, and clothing with obscene or offensive phrases or designs are not permitted. Clothing that discredits the military is also unacceptable. The new policy applies only to AMC charter flights.

Passengers will insure all their baggage is properly tagged with the name and address of the owner. Baggage identification tags are available at the Passenger Service Counter. There is no storage of baggage permitted in the terminal. Normal baggage allowances for Space-A passengers is two pieces not to exceed 70 pounds each, however, on smaller aircraft such as T-39s, C-21s, and C-12s, 30 pounds is the maximum.

All Space-A travelers, except those traveling on official business, and flying Space-A *from* overseas air terminals, may be charged a user's fee by the U.S. Customs Service.

Military personnel planning to use Space-A transportation, should check with the Space-A counter at the nearest Aerial Port to obtain specific information regarding eligibility, attire, priorities, baggage, etc. prior to proceeding.

Following is a list of military and commercial gateways from which Space-A travelers may attempt to travel and overseas areas they serve. Commercial phone and fax numbers are also provided.

Andrews AFB, MD (301) 981-1854, FAX (301) 984-4241
—Europe, Caribbean, and South America
Charleston AFB, SC (803) 566-3082, FAX (803) 566-3060
—Caribbean and South America
Charleston IAP, SC (803) 767-0588, FAX (803) 566-3845
—Panama and Europe
Dover AFB, DE (302) 677-2854/4088, FAX (302) 677-2953
— Europe
Elmendorf AFB, AK (907) 552-2912, FAX (907) 552-3996
— Pacific
Hickam AFB, HI (808) 479-7494, FAX (808) 448-1503
— Pacific
McGuire AFB, NJ (609) 724-3078, FAX (609) 724-5026
—Europe, Lajes Field, Greenland and Iceland
McChord AFB, WA (206) 984-1110, FAX (206) 984-5659
—Alaska and the Pacific

UNIFORMED SERVICES ALMANAC

Norfolk NAS, VA (804) 444-4148, FAX (804) 445-8513
— Europe, Caribbean, Iceland
Los Angeles IAP (310) 363-0715/6, FAX (310) 363-2790
— Pacific
St. Louis IAP (314) 263-6269/6260, FAX (314) 263-6247
— Europe/Pacific
Scott AFB, IL (618) 256-4042, FAX (618) 256-1958
— Europe/Pacific
Philadelphia IAP (215) 897-5642, FAX (215) 897-5627
— Europe (Spain and Italy), and Iceland

DEPENDENTS' OVERSEAS SCHOOLS OPERATED BY THE DEPT. OF DEFENSE

The Department of Defense (DoD) has the responsibility for providing a quality education for minor dependents of all U.S. active duty military and DoD civilian personnel stationed abroad.

Where the number of children justify a DoD dependents' school, one is established, staffed by highly qualified teachers and administrators. In some locations students attend private schools where the tuition cost is paid by DoD, but the costs of uniforms and optional extracurricular activities are borne by the sponsor. Sponsors who have assignments to areas where there are no Department of Defense Education Activity (DODEA) schools, must gain approval from the appropriate DoDEA area superintendent prior to paying tuition or enrolling a dependent in a non-DoD school. There are no provisions for reimbursing funds which have been paid for by individuals for education in a private school or for correspondence courses. Where neither a DoD dependents' school nor a private school is available, accredited correspondence courses are provided at no expense to the family, however, application for such education *must* be made through appropriate channels.

IF YOU HAVE QUESTIONS CONTACT:

DoDEA headquarters or area offices.
Department of Defense Education Activity
4040 North Fairfax Drive
Arlington, VA 22203-1635
(703) 696-4235 x100 Commercial
426-4235 DSN

PANAMA/ISLANDS AREA
Area Superintendent
Pacific/Islands Area
Department of Defense Education Activity
4040 North Fairfax Drive
Arlington, Virginia 22203-1635
This area includes the countries of Bermuda, Canada, Cuba and Panama.

PACIFIC AREA
Area Superintendent
Pacific Area
Department of Defense
PSC 556, Box 796
FPO AP 96372-0796
This area includes the countries of Okinawa, Japan, and Korea.

EUPOPE AREA
Area Superintendent
Europe Area
Unit 29649, Box 285
APO AE 09096
This area encompasses all of Bahrain, Belgium, Germany, Great Britain, Iceland, Italy, Netherlands, Portugal, Spain, and Turkey.

UNIFORMED SERVICES ALMANAC

Minor dependents living in an area where there are no DoDEA schools have the option of attending one of the DoDEA two dormitory schools offering classes for grades 9 through 12. There is no tuition charge for students of service personnel or DoD employees who are paid from appropriated funds.

There are two locations where five-to-seven day schools are operated: London and Lakenheath, England. Students attending the seven-day schools get at least two free air trips home a year. Five-day school students are provided transportation by DoD to go home on the weekends.

DoD Schools usually are not provided in such places as China, Africa, Central and South America, although Americans, such as Marine guards for embassies, may be stationed there. In some areas where there are no DoDEA schools, there are State Department operated schools that dependents of military personnel may attend. DoD pays the tuition for its dependents to attend private American-sponsored schools. These are the same schools that State Department dependents attend. Dependents may take correspondence courses offered through major educational institutions and administered by DoDEA officials.

For more information about other, non-DoD overseas American-sponsored elementary and secondary schools assisted by the U.S. Department of State, call (202) 875-6220.

Grades are shown in parentheses. Military Base: A-Army, N-Navy, F-Air Force, M-Marine Corps

1995-1996 SCHOOL YEAR
PACIFIC AREA

JAPAN
- Cummings (K-6)F
- Edgren (7-12)F
- Ernest J. King (K-12)N
- Jack N. Darby (K-6)N
- John Oliver Arnn (K-6)A
- Matthew C. Perry (K-12)M
- Nile C. Kinnick (7-12)N
- Richard Byrd (K-6)N
- Shirley Lanham (K-6)N
- Sollars (K-6)F
- Sullivans (K-6)N
- Yokota (K-12)F
- Zama (7-12)A

KOREA
- C. Turner Joy (K-6)N
- Osan (K-8)F
- Pusan (K-12)A
- Seoul (K-12)A
- Taegu (K-12)A

OKINAWA
- Amelia Earhart (4-6)F
- Bob Hope Primary (K-3)F
- Kadena (K-12)F
- Edward C. Killin (K-5)M
- Kinser (K-5)M
- Kubasaki (9-12)M
- Lester (6-8)N
- Stearley Heights (K-5)F
- William C. Bechtel (K-6)M
- Zukeran (K-6)M

Total Schools = 35 Total Enrollment = 25,672

UNIFORMED SERVICES ALMANAC
EUROPE AREA

BAHRAIN
- Bahrain (K-12)N

BELGIUM
- Brussels (K-12)A
- Kleine Brogel (K-6)F
- SHAPE (K-12)A

GERMANY
- Amberg (K-6)A
- Ansbach (1-12)A
- Argonner (K-5)A
- Augsburg (K-12)A
- Aukamm (K-5)A
- Babenhausen (K-6)A
- Bad Aibling (K-12)A
- Bad Kissingen (K-5)A
- Bad Kreuznach (K-12)A
- Bad Nauheim (K-6)A
- Bamberg (K-12)A
- Baumholder (7-12)A
- Bitburg (K-12)F
- Boeblingen (K-8)A
- Bonn (K-12)A
- Buechel (K-5)F
- Butzbach (K-6)A
- Darmstadt (K-8)A
- Dexheim (K-6)A
- Garmisch (K-8)A
- Geilenkirchen (K-6)A
- Gelnhausen (K-5)A
- Giessen (K-12)A
- Graenwoehr (K-6)A
- H.H. Arnold (9-12)A
- Hahn (K-8)F
- Hainerberg (K-5)A
- Halvorsen-Turne (K-8)F
- Hanau (6-12)A
- Heidelberg (6-12)A
- Hohenfels (K-8)A
- Idar Oberstein (K-6)A
- Illesheim (K-8)A
- Kaiserslautern (K-12)F
- Kalkar (K-6)F
- Kitzingen (K-4)A
- Landstuhl (K-8)F
- Mannheim (K-12)A
- Mark Twain (K-5)A
- Memmingen (K-8)F
- Moenchengladbach (K-6)F
- Neubruecke (K-6)A
- Noervenich (K-5)F
- Patch (K-12)A
- Patrick Henry (K-5)A
- Pirmasens (K-6)A
- Rainbow (K-6)A
- Ramstein (K-12)F
- Regensburg (K-8)
- Robinson Barracks (K-6)A
- Schweinfurt (K-8)A
- Sembach (K-8)F
- Smith (K-6)A
- Spangdahlem (K-8)F
- Sportfield (K-5)A
- Vilseck (K-12)A
- Vogelweh (K-5)F
- Wetzel (K-6)A
- Wiesbaden (6-8)A
- Worms (K-5)A
- Wuerzburg (K-12)A

GREAT BRITAIN
- Alconbury (K-12)F
- Chicksands (K-8)F
- Croughton (K-12)F
- Feltwell (K-5)F
- Lakenheath (K-12)F
- London Central (7-12)F
- Menwith (K-9)A
- Upwood (K-6)F
- West Ruislip (K-6)F
- William F. Halsey (K-8)F

ICELAND
- Alfred T. Mahan (K-12)N

ITALY
- Aviano (K-12)F
- Gaeta (K-8)N
- La Maddalena (K-8)N
- Livorno (K-12)A
- Naples (K-12)N
- Pordenone (K-6)A
- Sigonella (K-12)N
- Vajont (K-6)A
- Verona (K-8)A
- Vicenza (K-12)A

NETHERLANDS
- AFCENT (K-12)A
- Coevorden (K-6)N
- Volkel (K-6)F

PORTUGAL
- Lajes (K-12)F

SPAIN
- Rota (K-12)N
- Sevilla (K-8)F

TURKEY
- Ankara (K-12)F
- Incirlik (K-12)F
- Izmir (K-12)F

Total Schools = 128 Total Enrollment = 51,795

UNIFORMED SERVICES ALMANAC

PANAMA/ISLANDS AREA

PANAMA
- Balboa (K-12)A
- Curundu (K-8)A
- Ft. Clayton (K-6)A
- Ft. Kobbe (K-6)A
- Howard (K-6)F

Total Schools = 7 Total Enrollment = 3,910
Grand Total = 170   Schools Total Enrollment = 81,377*

*Figures are student enrollment for the September 1995 school year.

MILITARY RETIREMENT

One of the most attractive incentives of a military career has been a retirement system which provides monthly retirement income for those who serve a minimum of twenty years, for non-disability retirement, and entitles the retiree to retain many of the benefits of the services such as exchange and commissary privileges, medical care in uniformed services facilities on a space available basis, or through CHAMPUS, and many other desirable benefits, including provisions to provide income for survivors if desired (See the Survivor Benefit Plan section for details.) Members make no direct contributions towards military retirement. The Congress makes annual appropriations to meet current benefit payments for the military retirement system and for the Coast Guard, NOAA, and the USPHS which have similar systems.

Years of active service and retirement pay percent equivalents for members who entered active service prior to August 1, 1986 are as follows:

Years of Service	Percent	Years of Service	Percent
20	50	26	65
21	52 ½	27	67 ½
22	55	28	70
23	57 ½	29	72 ½
24	60	30 or more	75
25	62 ½		

For members entering service on or after September 8, 1980, a "high-three" average of basic pay is used in the computation. P.L. 98-94, September 24, 1983, contained several important provisions dealing with retired and retainer pay including the following:

- Repeal of the one year "look-back" provision. Any member who first became eligible to retire after September 24, 1983 could no longer use the one year "look-back" in computing retired pay which allowed retirees to base their annuities on the basic pay scales in effect when they retired or those in effect the previous year plus any CPI adjustments. (NOTE: This repeal did not affect the provisions of the "Tower" amendment which provided that a member's retired pay will not be less than it would have been if he or she retired on an earlier eligible date.)

- Required that monthly retired or retainer pay be rounded down to the next lower full dollar. This same rounding down applied to survivor annuities.
- Six month rounding rule. This provision considered any full month of service as one-twelfth of a year, whether or not the member has more or less than six full months for retired pay computation.

The 98th Congress also passed several other measures which impacted on military retired pay. P.L. 98-270 changed the basis for COLA adjustments and delayed the FY 1984 increase from May to December. P.L. 98-525 authorized service secretaries to enter into agreements with states to withhold state income taxes from military retirees when such action is requested by the retiree. (Many states have entered into such agreements. See Federal Tax Section for details.) It eliminated the Social Security offset from SBP annuities when the surviving spouse has earned benefits based on her or his own earnings. The Act expanded former spouse provisions regarding medical, exchange, and commissary privileges.

P.L. 99-145 repealed certain provisions of P.L. 98-525, which in effect, eliminated the Social Security offset and established a two-tier system.

The FY 1986 Defense Authorization Act provided for a number of changes in the Survivor Benefit Plan which are detailed in Part II.

The Military Retirement Reform Act, P.L. 99-348, July 1, 1986, significantly changed the computation for retirement from military service. All members who first entered the service on or after August 1, 1986 are affected. Members who entered the service prior to the effective date, including service academy cadets and midshipmen, delayed entry program members, ROTC scholarship students, and retirees are not affected. The Survivor Benefit Plan (SBP) for current members and retirees who became members prior to August 1, 1986 is also not affected.

Disability retirement and retirement for members of the Reserve Forces is calculated under the provisions governing pre-August 1986 members.

Under the new rules, the retired pay formula is the product of 2.5 times the years of creditable service minus one percentage point for each year less than 30 years. At age 62, the amount of retired pay is recalculated on the 2.5 percent times years of service formula, and that amount is restored to the member. The new retired pay multipliers are as follows:

20 years (2.5 x 20) - 10 = 40%   26 years (2.5 x 26) - 4 = 61%
21 years (2.5 x 21) - 9 = 43.5%   27 years (2.5 x 27) - 3 = 64.5%
22 years (2.5 x 22) - 8 = 47%   28 years (2.5 x 28) - 2 = 68%
23 years (2.5 x 23) - 7 = 50.5%   29 years (2.5 x 29) - 1 = 71.5%
24 years (2.5 x 24) - 6 = 54%   30 years (2.5 x 30) - 0 = 75%
25 years (2.5 x 25) - 5 = 57.5%

After age 62, the COLA increases will revert to the CPI-1 %, but the retired pay multiplier is restored to 2.5 times the years of creditable service. For example, a member who retired at 20 years with 40 percent of basic pay would have the retired pay multiplier increased to 50 percent upon reaching age 62.

TYPES OF RETIREMENT AND RETIRED PAY

Retirement for Length of Service

Generally, Regular and Reserve commissioned officers, warrant officers, and enlisted members may be retired after completing 20 and not more than 30 years of active service. For retirement as commissioned officers, at least 10 years (may be waived to 8 years during FY92-FY95 by the Service Secretaries if authorized by the Secretary of Defense) must be commissioned service. Within the period of 20 to 30 years' service, tenure is established based on grade. Ordinarily, a maximum of 30 years can be served prior to mandatory retirement, however, certain members are allowed to serve longer.

Enlisted members are credited for all years of active service. Officers are also credited with all active service and may also be credited for inactive service or constructive service for physicians and dentists if they entered on active duty prior to September 15, 1981, according to the branch of service. Active and inactive Reserve service may also be included, if applicable. However, inactive Reserve time is creditable on a retirement point basis only.

The retired grade of the member is generally the grade, (whether temporary or permanent), in which he or she is serving on the date of retirement. Officers in pay grades O-5 through O-8 must serve in that pay grade for at least three years (Secretary of Defense may authorize Secretary of military departments to reduce to 2 years during FY92-FY95) in order to retire in that pay grade. Officers in grade O-4 must have at least 6 months time in that grade.

An enlisted member or warrant officer retiring with less than 30 years of service who held a temporary higher grade than the grade in which he or she retired, receives retired pay in the grade held at time of retirement until his or her total active and retired service reaches 30 years. At that time, he or she is advanced to the higher grade and his or her retired pay is then based on the higher grade. (In the Navy and Marine Corps, the higher grade must have been held as a commissioned officer.)

EM and WOs holding Reserve Commissions who complete 20 years of active service, of which 10 years (may be waived to 8 years during FY92-FY95 by Service Secretary if authorized by SECDEF) is commissioned, may retire and receive pay on the basis of the commissioned rank.

Retirement for Disability

A member with at least 8 years of service unfit to perform the duties of his or her office or grade because of a permanent physical or mental disability may be retired if the disability is not the result of intentional misconduct or willful neglect and was not incurred during a period of unauthorized absence; and, the disability is rated at 30 percent or more or the member has at least 20 years of service. The disability rating is determined by applying the standard schedule of rating disabilities in use by the Department of Veterans Affairs at the time of the determination. A member with less than 8 years of service is eligible only if the disability was the result of performing active duty or incurred in line of duty. If it was not, the member is separated.

If the disability may not be permanent, the member is placed on the temporary disability retired list (TDRL) and is subject to physical examination no less than once every 18 months. After 5 years, he or she must be retired for permanent disability or, if the disability is less than 30 percent and he or she has less than 20 years of service, returned to active duty or separated.

The nature and amount of disability retirement pay benefits generally depend on the degree to which the disability keeps the member from performing his or her duties. Disability retirement pay is determined by multiplying the basic pay of the member's retired grade by the percentage of disability or by 2.5 percent times years of active service whichever is greater. Disability retired pay computed on the basis of years of service is, however, subject to taxation to the extent that it exceeds the pay the member would have received had his or her pay been computed on the basis of percentage of disability. For permanent disability retirement, the maximum benefit is 75 percent of basic pay with a minimum benefit of 30 percent. While on the TDRL, the minimum

UNIFORMED SERVICES ALMANAC

benefit is 50 percent of basic pay. For members entering service after September 1, 1980, a "high-three" average of basic pay is used in the computation. For members who entered the Uniformed Services after September 24, 1975, and who do not receive disability retired pay because of a combat-related injury or who are not eligible for disability compensation from the VA, amounts received as disability retired pay are fully subject to taxation.

Disability retired members are entitled to tax free veterans' disability compensation from the VA, but if they choose to accept it, they must forfeit, dollar for dollar, their military disability retired pay.

A service member becoming disabled while on active duty will be fully informed, before retirement, of the various rights and benefits to which he or she may be entitled.

Retirement for Age-Officers

Unless retired or separated earlier, all regular officers, with exceptions for certain officers assigned to positions at the military academies, shall be retired on the first day of the month following the month in which he or she becomes 62 years of age.

Officers serving in a position that carries a grade above major general or rear admiral may have his or her retirement deferred by the President up to the first day of the month following the month in which the officer becomes 64 years of age.

RETIRED PAY COMPUTATION

The amount of retired pay for members on active duty prior to August 1986 is equal to the basic pay of the retired grade of the member multiplied by 2.5 percent times the number of years of credited service. Twenty years of service provides retired pay at 50 percent of basic pay. The maximum benefit is 75 percent of basic pay regardless of the number of years served. For members entering on or after September 8, 1980, an average of the highest 36 months of basic pay is used in the computation of retired pay.

Personnel entering service on or after August 1, 1986 receive 40 percent of basic pay upon completion of 20 years of service (computed at 2.5 percent times years of service minus 1 percent for each year less than 30 years) but are entitled to 75 percent of basic pay if they serve for 30 years. The law does provide for adjustments to retired pay to reflect cost-of-living increases. These adjustments are based on increases to the Consumer Price Index (CPI) as determined by the Bureau of Labor and Statistics. Although active duty pay increases are also, to some degree, affected by cost-of-living, basic pay increases did not go up as frequently or by as much as did the retired pay increases in the early seventies. A retired pay "inversion" was created which resulted in certain retirement eligible members facing a possible loss of retirement income by remaining on active duty. Decisions in 1976 and 1977 to reallocate a portion of the active duty pay raises to Basic Allowance for Quarters (BAQ) further reduced the amount of potential retirement pay for some members.

P.L. 94-106, October 7, 1975 modified the computation of retired pay so that members initially entitled to receive retired pay on or after January 1, 1971 would not receive less pay than had they retired earlier in their career. The purpose of this legislation was to prevent retired pay inversions which can occur whenever retired pay increases exceed active duty pay increases. Each retirement eligible member will have his or her retired pay computed, on an individual comparative basis, using one of the following options:

- Pay at present grade and years of service at time of retirement.

UNIFORMED SERVICES ALMANAC

- One year "look-back" using prior pay scale at present grade and years of service at time of retirement *plus* cumulative CPI increases in retired pay from the prior year's pay scale.
- Any pay scale on or after July 1, 1971 at the grade and years of service a member would have had at that time, *if retirement eligible under those pay rates* plus cumulative CPI increase accruing from that earlier rate.

The FY 84 DoD Authorization Act, P.L. 98-94, 1983, repealed the one year "look-back" provision for members retiring after enactment. The repeal of the one year "look-back" provision does not affect the "Tower" amendment. Under the "Tower" amendment, a member initially entitled to receive retired pay on or after January 1, 1971, may not receive less pay than he or she would have received had he or she retired earlier in his or her career. The specific base pay to use in computing an individuals retired pay depends upon many particulars relating to the individual and recent retired and active pay increases.

Although the law protects the individual member from receiving less than he or she would get by serving on active duty for a longer period, there are still differences among members with similar grades. For example, an O-5 who retired in October 1972 with 20 years of service is receiving $428 more per month than an O-5 who retired in January 1996 with the same amount of service. Because of the options in computing retired pay, and the application of only partial CPI increases in some situations, depending on when the member retires, the Defense Finance and Accounting Service Center will make all calculations and automatically provide retirees with the benefit of the most advantageous retirement formula on an individual basis. Members who remain on active duty will, of course, continue to increase their retired pay potential through longevity increases, possible promotions, and application of the 2.5 percent multiplier for each year of continued service after twenty years for members on active duty prior to August 1, 1986.

RETIREMENT PAY EXAMPLES

The following basic examples for officers and enlisted personnel show the retirement amounts by years of service and basic pay for those with 20 years in service (pre August 1, 1986) who have become retirement eligible after December 31, 1995 as compared with disability retirements.

Example: **Retired pay based on years of service (YOS).**
Officer, grade O-5, 20 YOS, base pay = $4,811.40. Compute retired pay by multiplying base pay by 50% (2.5% x YOS). $4,811.40 x 50% = $2,405, monthly retired pay, subject to Federal income tax.

Example: **Retired pay based on percentage of disability.**
Enlisted member, grade E-7, 20 YOS, 60% disability rating. Compute disability retired pay by multiplying base pay of $2,261.40 by degree of disability (60%). $2,261.40 x 60% = $1,356, monthly disability retired pay, tax exempt, under certain conditions. (See Income Tax Section.)

Example: **Retired pay based on service with disability rating.**
Officer, grade O-5, 26 YOS, 60% disability, electing service retirement. Compute retired pay by multiplying base pay ($4,979.40) by 65% (2.5% x YOS) = $3,236.00. If computed on basis of disability, multiply base pay of $4,979.40 by 60% of disability to get $2,987.00. The difference between the two amounts ($3,236.00 minus $2,987.00) — $249.00 is taxable and the balance tax exempt. (See Income Tax Section.)

UNIFORMED SERVICES ALMANAC
RETIREMENT INCOME TAX PROVISIONS

Members of the Uniformed Services of the United States who are retired may be entitled to certain special benefits which can be termed as retirement income tax advantages. These are: (1) Disability retirement pay exclusion — in part or whole; (2) Application of disability income exclusion to includable portions of certain retirement pay; (3) Retirement income tax credits; and (4) Department of Veterans Affairs compensation or pension. The Tax Reform Act of 1976, P.L. 94-455, placed strict restrictions on these tax advantages, particularly in the Disability Retirement tax exemptions and the "sick pay" exclusions previously available.

(1) **Disability Retirement.** Effective January 1, 1976, the federal tax exemption for disability retirement pay was abolished, *except* for combat related disabilities and for those members who retired for disability prior to January 1, 1977 and those who were entitled to military disability retirement before that date. Also, no one who was on active duty or was a member of a Reserve component prior to September 25, 1975 will be affected by the law. Thus, if a member who began military service at any time before September 25, 1975 is retired for disability sometime in the future, part or all of his or her retired pay may be excluded from federal income taxation. The manner in which the retired pay is computed determines whether any of the pay is subject to federal income tax. If a member is receiving retired pay computed by multiplying the percentage of disability times basic pay, *all* retired pay will be exempt from federal taxation. If a member is retired for disability and chooses to have pay computed on the basis of length of service, then the amount of his or her retired pay which is in excess of the amount he or she would have received if he or she had elected to have pay computed on the basis of percentage of disability is not excluded.

(2) **Disability Income Exclusion.** The disability income exclusion has been repealed for tax years beginning after 1983. However, there is a tax credit for people who are permanently and totally disabled.

The Tax Reform Act of 1976 also did away with the sick-pay exclusion for all members retired for disability. Only retirees who are permanently and totally disabled and are under the age of 65 may still qualify. *Permanently and totally* for this purpose is defined as, "being unable to engage in any substantial gainful activity by reason of any medically determinable physical or mental impairment which can be expected to result in death or which has lasted or can be expected to last for a continuous period of not less than 12 months." Professional counsel from a legal assistance office or tax expert is recommended for those who feel they may qualify. Even for those who do qualify for the disability income exclusion, the maximum exclusion of $5,200 per year is reduced dollar for dollar on adjusted gross income in excess of $15,000. If the taxpayer is married, the exclusion is allowed only if a joint return is filed. Qualified retirees with adjusted gross income above $20,200 would not be eligible for any disability income exclusion.

(3) **VA Compensation or Pension.** Payment received from the Department of Veterans Affairs is tax exempt, but mere entitlement to the payment will not necessarily result in a tax saving unless a waiver of equivalent retired pay has been executed.

P.L. 99-514, the Tax Reform Act of 1986, October 22, 1986. Although not changing any of the tax provisions applicable to retired military pay, contained many provisions which impact on the financial management and/or financial planning of all military retirees.

UNIFORMED SERVICES ALMANAC
ADJUSTMENTS TO RETIRED PAY

Retirees are authorized an increase of 2.6 percent effective December 1, 1995. However, under the provisions of P.L. 104-61, the FY 96 Defense Appropriations Act, payment is prohibited for months before March, 1996 except for those members or former members retired for disability. The increase for non-disability retirees will appear in the April 1, 1996 payment. The Appropriations Act contains language that would pay the retiree COLA increase on April 1, 1996 and move it back to January 1 in 1997 and thereafter. However, the President must provide legislation offsetting the increased costs of moving the COLA increases forward in his budget submission or the provision for 1996 and beyond are not effective.

The delay in payment does not pertain to increases in survivor annuities (including SBP base amounts and associated annuities and premiums). Therefore, SBP costs will increase December 1, 1995 based on the COLA even though the COLA payment is delayed. If a retiree should die between December 1, 1995 and February 29, 1996, the survivor would receive an increased annuity as adjusted by the COLA increase.

Members who retired on or after the January 1, 1996 active duty pay raise will receive only a partial increase of 2.0 percent.

It should be noted that it is a percentage increase in the CPI which determines the amount of the raise for retirees and not the change in index points. Under the current procedures, the percentage adjustment is determined by the percentage increase in the average CPI for the same three month period of the preceding year. The average CPI index for the third quarter of 1995 was 150.2 (July 149.9, August 150.2, September 150.6). Subtracting the average third quarter CPI index for 1994, 146.4, results in a point difference of 3.8. Dividing 3.8 by the 1994 third quarter average of 146.4, results in the 2.6 percent increase effective December 1, 1995 (delayed until March as noted above).

Any questions regarding the amount of retired pay should be directed to the servicing Defense Finance and Accounting Service Center.

CPI-W SUMMARY JANUARY 1993 THROUGH NOVEMBER 1995

Month	CPI	Month	CPI	Month	CPI	Month	CPI
Jan 93	140.3	Oct 93	143.3	Jul 94	145.8	Apr 95	149.3
Feb 93	140.7	Nov 93	143.4	Aug 94	146.5	May 95	149.6
Mar 93	141.1	Dec 93	143.3	Sep 94	146.9	Jun 95	149.9
Apr 93	141.6	Jan 94	143.6	Oct 94	147.0	Jul 95	149.9
May 93	141.9	Feb 94	144.0	Nov 94	147.3	Aug 95	150.2
Jun 93	142.0	Mar 94	144.4	Dec 94	147.2	Sep 95	150.6
Jul 93	142.1	Apr 94	144.7	Jan 95	147.8	Oct 95	151.0
Aug 93	142.4	May 94	144.9	Feb 95	148.3	Nov 95	150.9
Sep 93	142.6	Jun 94	145.4	Mar 95	148.7		

UNIFORMED SERVICES FORMER SPOUSES PROTECTION ACT

Following is a general discussion of the legislative provisions of the USFSPA which is incorporated in Section 1408 of Title 10, U.S. Code. The points outlined are not designed to answer detailed questions concerning individual cases; rather, they serve as general information for use by Retirement Services Officers, Military Personnel Officers, active duty and retired servicemembers, spouses, and former spouses. It does not provide legal or judicial interpretation of enacted laws and does not deal with case law. Individuals seeking legal assistance are encouraged to contact military legal

UNIFORMED SERVICES ALMANAC
ACTIVE DUTY AND RETIRED PAY INCREASE TABLE

\multicolumn{4}{c	}{Active Duty Basic Pay Increases}	\multicolumn{4}{c}{Retired Pay Increases}
Year	Month	Actual %	Cumulative % (over base of 100)	Reverse Cumulative % Increase	Year	Month	Actual %	Cumulative % (over base of 100)	Reverse Cumulative % Increase

Year	Month	Actual %	Cumulative % (over base of 100)	Reverse Cumulative % Increase	Year	Month	Actual %	Cumulative % (over base of 100)	Reverse Cumulative % Increase
1958	Jun 1	8.3	8.3	703.8	1958	Jun 1	6.0*	6	467.2
1963	Oct 1	14.2	23.7	642.2	1963	Oct 1	5.0	11.3	435.1
1964	Sep 1	2.3	26.5	549.9	1965	Sep 1	4.4	16.2	409.6
1965	Sep 1	10.4	39.7	535.3	1966	Dec 1	3.7	20.5	388.1
1966	Jul 1	3.2	44.2	475.4	1968	Apr 1	3.9(2.9)	25.2	370.7
1967	Oct 1	5.6	52.2	457.6	1969	Feb 1	4.0(2.1)	30.2	353.1
1968	Jul 1	6.9	62.7	428.0	1969	Nov 1	5.3(0.9)	37.1	335.6
1969	Jul 1	12.6	83.2	393.9	1970	Aug 1	5.6(2.5)	44.8	313.7
1970	Jan 1	8.1	98.1	338.7	1971	Jun 1	4.5(0.6)	51.3	291.8
1971	Jan 1	7.9	113.7	305.8	1972	Jun 1	4.8(1.7)	58.6	274.9
1971	Nov 1	11.6	138.5	276.1	1973	Jul 1	6.1(3.6)	68.2	257.7
1972	Jan 1	7.2	155.7	237.0	1974	Jan 1	5.5(2.96)	77.5	237.2
1972	Oct 1	6.7	172.8	214.4	1974	Jul 1	6.3(6.3)	88.7	219.6
1973	Oct 1	6.2	189.7	194.6	1975	Jan 1	7.3(7.3)	102.4	200.6
1974	Oct 1	5.5	205.7	177.4	1975	Aug 1	5.1(5.0)	112.8	180.2
1975	Oct 1	5.0	220.9	163.0	1976	Mar 1	5.4(1.7)	124.3	166.6
1976	Oct 1	3.6	232.5	150.4	1977	Mar 1	4.8(1.0)	135.0	152.9
1977	Oct 1	6.2	253.1	141.7	1977	Sep 1	4.3(5.3)	145.1	141.3
1978	Oct 1	5.5	272.5	127.6	1978	Mar 1	2.4(1.1)	151.0	131.4
1979	Oct 1	7.0	298.6	115.8	1978	Sep 1	4.9(6.1)	163.3	126.0
1980	Oct 1	11.7	345.3	101.6	1979	Mar 1	3.9(1.9)	173.6	115.4
1981	Oct 1	14.3*	408.9	80.5	1979	Sep 1	6.9(8.8)	192.4	107.3
1982	Oct 1	4.0	429.3	57.9	1980	Mar 1	6.0(2.8)	210.0	94.0
1984	Jan 1	4.0†	450.5	51.9	1980	Sep 1	7.7(10.8)	233.9	83.0
1985	Jan 1	4.0†	472.5	46.0	1981	Mar 1	4.4(2.7)	248.6	69.9
1985	Oct 1	3.0	489.6	40.4	1982	Mar 1	8.7(1.0)	278.9	62.7
1987	Jan 1	3.0	507.3	36.3	1983	Apr 1	3.3‡(0.0)	291.4	49.7
1988	Jan 1	2.0	519.5	32.3	1984	Dec 1	3.5(2.8)	305.1***	44.9
1989	Jan 1	4.1	544.9	29.7	1986	Dec 1	1.3(1.3)	310.3	40.0
1990	Jan 1	3.6	568.1	24.6	1987	Dec 1	4.2(3.7)	327.6	38.2
1991	Jan 1	4.1	595.5	20.3	1988	Dec 1	4.0(3.2)	344.7	32.7
1992	Jan 1	4.2	624.7	15.6	1989	Dec 1	4.7(3.6)	365.6	27.6
1993	Jan 1	3.7	651.5	10.9	1990	Dec 1	5.4(4.4)	390.7	21.8
1994	Jan 1	2.2	668.0	7.0	1991	Dec 1	3.7(2.0)	408.9	15.6
1995	Jan 1	2.6	688.0	4.7	1992	Dec 1	3.0(2.3)	424.2	11.5
1996	Jan 1	2.4	706.9	2.4	1993	Dec 1	2.6(1.9)	437.8	8.2
					1994	Dec 1††	2.8(2.2)	452.8	5.5
					1995	Dec 1xx	2.6(2.0)	467.2	2.6

*Basic pay increases for enlisted personnel ranged from 10% for E-1; 10.7% for E-2, E-3; 13% for E-4; 16.5% for E-5, E-6; and 17% for E-7, E-8, E-9. For officers the hike was 14.3%.
†Except for E-1 with less than 4 months service.
‡For members under age 62 and not on disability retired pay.
***Cumulative increases subsequent to 1983 are based on the April 1983 3.3% increase.
††Delayed to March 1, 1995 by FY95 DoD Authorization Act.
xxDelayed to March 1, 1996.
NOTE: The Retired Pay Increase of 3.1% for December 1985 was cancelled. There was no active duty pay increase in 1983 and 1986.

UNIFORMED SERVICES ALMANAC

MONTHLY AMOUNT OF MILITARY NON-DISABILITY RETIREMENT PAY
(For individuals retiring after January 1, 1996)

Retirement amounts are rounded down to nearest whole dollar. Years of service are assumed to be equal to active service.

PAY GRADE	Over 15	Over 16	Over 17	Over 18	Over 19	Over 20	Over 21	Over 22	Over 23	Over 24	Over 25	Over 26	Over 27	Over 28	Over 29	Over 30
COMMISSIONED OFFICERS
O-10	2887	3335	3581	3830	4084	4508	4733	4959	5184	5410	5635	5860	6086	6311	6537	6762
O-9	2525	2949	3166	3387	3612	4053	4255	4458	4661	4863	5066	5646	5863	6080	6297	6514
O-8	2424	2722	2922	3262	3478	3840	4032	4328	4525	4722	4919	5115	5312	5509	5706	5902
O-7	2104	2495	2679	3063	3266	3472	3646	3820	3993	4167	4341	4514	4688	4862	5035	5209
O-6	1523	1901	2041	2295	2447	2659	2792	3094	3235	3490	3635	3966	4119	4271	4424	4576
O-5	1463	1695	1820	2059	2195	2405	2525	2738	2863	2987	3112	3236	3361	3485	3610	3734
O-4	1382	1555	1670	1835	1957	2081	2185	2289	2393	2497	2601	2706	2810	2914	3018	3122
O-3	1282	1382	1484	1587	1693	1800	1890	1980	2070	2160	2250	2340	2430	2520	2610	2700
O-2	951	1025	1101	1178	1256	1335	1402	1469	1536	1602	1669	1736	1803	1870	1936	2003
O-1	750	809	868	929	991	1053	1106	1159	1211	1264	1317	1369	1422	1475	1527	1580
COMMISSIONED OFFICERS WITH MORE THAN 4 YEARS ACTIVE SERVICE AS ENLISTED MEMBERS
O-3E	1301	1403	1506	1611	1718	1827	1918	2009	2101	2192	2283	2375	2466	2557	2649	2740
O-2E	1102	1187	1275	1364	1454	1546	1624	1701	1778	1856	1933	2010	2088	2165	2242	2320
O-1E	932	1005	1078	1154	1230	1308	1374	1439	1504	1570	1635	1701	1766	1832	1897	1962
WARRANT OFFICERS
W-5	1370	1477	1586	1697	1809	1924	2020	2196	2296	2465	2568	2783	2890	2997	3104	3211
W-4	1122	1252	1344	1476	1574	1728	1814	1964	2054	2210	2302	2503	2599	2695	2792	2888
W-3	981	1090	1170	1290	1376	1520	1596	1732	1811	1890	1969	2120	2201	2283	2364	2446
W-2	881	983	1055	1166	1244	1364	1432	1561	1632	1703	1774	1845	1916	1987	2057	2128
W-1	811	907	974	1078	1149	1266	1329	1392	1456	1519	1582	1645	1709	1772	1835	1899
ENLISTED MEMBERS
E-9	977	1077	1156	1265	1348	1462	1535	1692	1769	1918	1998	2195	2279	2363	2448	2532
E-8	848	939	1008	1103	1176	1281	1345	1492	1560	1700	1771	1960	2035	2111	2186	2261
E-7	752	834	895	984	1049	1130	1187	1327	1387	1519	1583	1763	1831	1899	1967	2035
E-6	673	749	804	873	931	990	1039	1089	1138	1188	1237	1287	1336	1386	1435	1485
E-5	598	645	692	741	790	840	882	924	966	1008	1050	1092	1134	1176	1218	1260
E-4	482	520	558	597	636	677	710	744	778	812	846	880	914	947	981	1015
E-3	413	446	478	512	546	580	610	639	668	697	726	755	784	813	842	871
E-2	349	376	404	432	461	490	514	539	563	588	612	637	661	686	711	735
E-1	311	335	360	385	411	437	459	481	503	524	546	568	590	612	634	656

NOTE: As a result of certain provisions for advancement on the retired list or under the "Tower Amendment", some individuals would receive amounts differing from those shown above. Figures shown assume that active service and pay service are equal. Military retired pay and pay cap increases prior to and including January 1, 1996. Active duty basic pay cap of $9016.80 per month levels out retired pay in upper grades. P.L. 102-484 granted DoD a Temporary Early Retirement Authority (TERA) for selected active duty members with as few as 15 years of service. Their retired pay is subject to reduction factors for service less than 20 years. The FY94 Defense Authorization Act Extended TERA through September 30, 1999.

assistance or retain civilian counsel. **This explanation is not a legal brief nor does it outline a legal position. Do not use it as evidence of intent, interpretation, or precedent in any legal action.**

For the most comprehensive and thorough explanation of the USFSPA, you should obtain a copy of DIVORCE AND THE MILITARY. See the insert in the front of this book for information on how to order this valuable book.

Background: Prior to the 1981 McCarty vs. McCarty case, state courts disagreed on whether they were authorized or constrained by federal legal precedent in dividing military retired pay in divorce-related property settlements. On June 26, 1981, the U.S. Supreme Court ruled in the McCarty vs. McCarty case that military retired pay could not be treated as community property in divorce cases. In response, Congress enacted the Uniformed Services Former Spouses Protection Act (USFSPA) which decreed that state courts **could** treat military retired pay as property in divorce cases if they so chose. The USFSPA was enacted by Public Law 97-252, September 8, 1982. It has subsequently been amended by Public Laws 98-94, September 24, 1983; 98-525, September 27, 1984; 99-145; November 8, 1985, 99-661, November 14, 1986; 100-180, December 4, 1987; 101-510, November 5, 1990; and 102-484, October 23, 1992.

Division of Retired Pay as Property. The USFSPA allows state courts to consider military retired pay as divisible property in divorce settlements after June 25, 1981. It also establishes procedures by which a former spouse could receive all or a portion of the court settlement as a direct payment from the finance service center. Some state courts continued to divide property in divorce cases adjudicated prior to the June 1981 date. The 101st Congress took action to correct this. P.L. 101-510, the 1991 DoD Authorization Act, November 5, 1990, permits cases so adjudicated to continue payments from November 1990 for two years and no longer. In addition, no other pre-June 25, 1981 cases can be reopened.

Understanding the distinction between the provision that authorizes a court to divide retired pay and the provision that allows direct payment of divided retired pay to a former spouse is essential. Specifically, the law *does not direct* state courts to divide retired pay; it *permits* them to. The law stipulates that only "disposable" pay may be divided. Disposable pay is defined as that pay (other than the percentage of pay based on Chapter 61 disability retirement) remaining after the following deductions:

- Debts owed the U.S. Government
- Federal, state, or local income taxes (for divorces prior to February 5, 1991, only)
- Amounts of retired pay waived for the receipt of Veterans Affairs disability compensation
  - National Service Life Insurance (NSLI) premiums
  - SBP costs for a former spouse receiving USFSPA payments

The law *does not* confer an entitlement to a portion of the retired pay to a former spouse as a result of length of marriage or number of years overlap in the marriage and service. However, once a court has awarded a former spouse a portion of retired pay as property, the former spouse may apply to the finance service center to receive that pay as a "direct payment." To qualify for a direct payment, the law requires a former spouse to have been married to the member during at least 10 years of the member's service creditable for retired pay.

The law further stipulates that Defense Finance and Accounting Service Centers may not send more than 50 percent of the member's disposable retired pay as a direct payment unless there are additional garnishments for alimony

UNIFORMED SERVICES ALMANAC

or child support under Title 42, U.S.C., section 659. In those cases, up to 65 percent of the disposable pay may be sent as a direct payment.

The law does not allow a court to consider military retired pay in a divorce-related property settlement unless the court has jurisdiction over the military servicemember or retiree by reason of:

- His/her residence other than by reason of military assignment in the territorial jurisdiction of the court; or
- His/her domicile in the territorial jurisdiction of the court; or
- His/her consent to the jurisdiction of the court.
- For active duty members, the law also requires compliance with the provisions of the Soldiers' and Sailors' Civil Relief Act of 1940.

When more than one former spouse has been awarded a division of a servicemember's retired pay, payments will be handled on a first-come, first-served basis. When conflicting court orders exist, the law instructs the service concerned to send the amount specified in the lower of the two conflicting orders (not to exceed 50% of disposable pay), and retain the difference until the matter is resolved.

The Defense Finance and Accounting Service Center must begin direct payment to the former spouse within 90 days of receipt of a valid court order. If a servicemember is not retired at the time of the court order, payments must begin no later than 90 days after the servicemember retires. The law does not authorize a court to order a member to apply for retirement or to retire at a specified time in order to start payment.

Remarriage of a former spouse does not stop the direct payment of retired pay as property unless the court so orders.

A former spouse can apply for direct payment by sending to the finance service center concerned a signed DD Form 2293 (Request for Former Spouse Payments From Retired Pay) or a statement that includes:

- Notice to make a direct payment to the former spouse from the servicemember's retired pay.
- A copy of the court order and other documents dividing retired pay as property. These must be certified by an official of the court that issued them.
- A statement from a lawyer that the court order has not been amended, superseded, or set aside.
- Sufficient identifying information about the member to enable processing of the application. The identification should give the member's full name, social security number, and uniformed service.
- An agreement by the former spouse that any future overpayments are recoverable and subject to involuntary collection from the former spouse or the estate of the former spouse.
- An agreement by the former spouse to promptly notify the service concerned if the court order upon which payment is based is vacated, modified, or set aside. This shall include notice of the former spouse's remarriage (if all or a part of the payment is for alimony), or notice of a change in eligibility for child support payment, (e.g., death, emancipation, adoption, or attainment of majority) of a child whose support is provided by a former spouse through direct payments from retired pay.

Request for direct payment is not accomplished until all required information is received by the finance service center.

Orders, garnishments, applications, or notifications dealing with the division of retired pay must be sent by certified mail, return receipt requested to the appropriate finance service center. (See list of addresses at the end of this section)

UNIFORMED SERVICES ALMANAC

Within 30 days of receiving the completed DD Form 2293, the service finance and accounting service center shall contact the servicemember with a notification which includes:
- A copy of the court order and accompanying documentation.
- An explanation of the limitations affecting direct payment to a former spouse from a servicemember's retired pay.
- A request that the servicemember submit notification to the designated agent if the court order has been amended, superseded, or set aside. The servicemember must provide an authenticated or certified copy of the operative court documents when there are conflicting court orders.
- The amount or percentage that will be deducted if the member fails to respond to the notification.
- The tentative effective date of direct payments to the former spouse.
- Notice to the servicemember that failure to respond within 30 days of the date the notice was mailed may result in the division of retired pay as provided in the notification.
- Notice that if the servicemember submits information in response to the notification, the servicemember thereby consents to the disclosure of such information to the former spouse or the former spouse's agent.

The service finance center shall not honor the court order if it is defective, modified, superseded, or set aside.

Payments to the former spouse shall begin within 90 days after the service finance center receives the completed paperwork. Payments shall conform with the normal pay and disbursement cycle of the servicemember's retired pay. Payments that are a percentage of retired pay as property will change in direct proportion to and on the effective date of future cost-of-living adjustments to retired pay, unless the court order directs otherwise. Payments will stop if the servicemember dies, the former spouse dies, or as stated in the court order, whichever occurs first.

Under the provisions of the FY 85 DoD Authorization Act, P.L. 98-525, October 19, 1984, medical, commissary, and base exchange privileges previously authorized by P.L. 97-252, have been expanded. Effective January 1, 1985, a former spouse married for 20 years to a person who had 20 years of service creditable toward retirement and who had 15 years overlap between the length of marriage and years of service (20/20/15 rule) will, under certain circumstances, be provided with military medical coverage. Being divorced after September 30, 1988—unremarried former spouses are eligible for medical for one year from date of divorce, followed by the right to convert to Continued Health Care Benefit Program (CHCBP). The program is intended to provide benefits similar to CHAMPUS for a specific period of time (18-36 months) to former service members and their family members, some unremarried former military spouses, and emancipated children, who enroll and pay quarterly premiums. Benefits are like those in the basic CHAMPUS program. If a former spouse is no longer eligible for an ID card, the retiree sponsor must notify the Defense Enrollment Eligibility Reporting System (DEERS) at 800-538-9552 (California residents at 800-334-4162; Alaska and Hawaii residents at 800-527-5602).

A retiree who fails to notify DEERS that a former spouse is no longer eligible for care may be liable for the former spouse's medical-care costs. Medical benefits for an unremarried former spouse whose marriage covered at least 20 years of military service will be granted regardless of the date of divorce, providing the spouse is not covered by employer-sponsored medical insurance. Commissary, exchange, and theatre privileges may be reinstated to a 20/20/20 former spouse whose remarriage ends in death, divorce, or annulment. Medical benefits are *not* restored. For further information, contact your nearest I.D. card issuing facility.

Retirees may also name a former spouse as beneficiary under the Survivor Benefit Plan (SBP) at the time of his or her retirement, even if he or she has remarried. Retirees who presently have SBP coverage for their spouse, and later divorce, have one year from the date of the divorce to elect former spouse coverage if they so desire. For divorces prior to November 14, 1986, coverage for a former spouse cannot be court ordered, but must be voluntary on the part of the member. However, former spouse coverage can be included as a part of the final divorce decree with the consent of the member. If the member fails to make that election, the former spouse has one year from the date of the court order to request a deemed SBP election. P.L. 99-661 permitted state courts to order a member to provide SBP to a former spouse (for divorces finalized after November 14, 1986). Note: Only one SBP coverage can be elected. Therefore, if a former spouse is covered by SBP, the current spouse cannot be covered.

The FY 90 Defense Authorization Act, P.L. 101-510, November 5, 1990, reemphasized that disability is *not* part of disposable retired pay. It also clarified payment of taxes on court divided retired pay and requires service finance and accounting centers to issue two 1099R forms, one to each recipient which requires both to pay taxes on their respective shares.

Servicemembers, regardless of whether still on active duty or retired, may also be required by a court to provide coverage for a former spouse under the Survivor Benefit Plan (SBP). There is no length-of-marriage service requirement as there is with the division of retired pay which must be satisfied before such a court order is enforceable. If a member becomes divorced while on active duty and is required by court order to elect former spouse SBP coverage upon retirement, the member must make the election (or be held in contempt of court). The court-ordered SBP election will be enforced only if the former spouse had requested that the election be deemed on the member's behalf, in writing, within one year of the date of the court order. See the section on SBP in this book for more details.

All correspondence between a former spouse and a finance and accounting service center must include the servicemember's social security number.

Section (h) of the USFSPA, added in 1992 by Section 653 of P.L. 102-484 provides that the spouse or former spouse is eligible to receive payments of the retired pay of a military member whose entitlement to retired pay is terminated as a result of misconduct involving abuse of a spouse or dependent child while a member. Payments are made by the government and continue so long as the former spouse remains unmarried. This means that, within the same Act, an apparent dichotomy exists in that payments (made by the government) to an abused spouse cease upon remarriage while payments (made by the military member) to an ex-spouse who was not abused survive remarriage.

DEFENSE FINANCE AND ACCOUNTING SERVICE CENTERS

Army, Air Force, Navy, and Marine Corps Defense Finance and Accounting Service, Cleveland Center, Retired Pay Department (Code RO), P.O. Box 99191, Cleveland, OH 44199-1126, 1-800-321-1080, (216) 522-5955 (Collect)

Coast Guard/ National Oceanic & Atmospheric Administration Commanding Officer (RPD), U.S. Coast Guard Pay and Personnel Center, 444 S.E. Quincy St., Topeka, KS 66683-3591, 1-800-772-8724, (913) 295-2657

UNIFORMED SERVICES ALMANAC

Public Health Services   USPHS, Compensation Branch, Parklawn Building, 5600 Fishers Lane, Room 4-50, Rockville, MD 20857, 1-800-638-8744, (301) 443-2475

IDENTIFICATION CARDS

Most military benefits for members and dependents such as exchange stores, commissaries, recreation facilities, theaters, and medical care facilities (including CHAMPUS and PRIMUS) require a valid identification card. Military members are issued ID cards (DD Form 2) upon entry on active duty and may obtain replacement or corrected cards at most service installations.

Since January 1994, DoD and the Coast Guard have been issuing new ID cards to active, reserve, retired and dependent personnel. Features of the new credit-card sized, tamper resistant ID card include a digital photograph image of the bearer, bar codes containing pertinent machine-readable data, and printed identification and entitlement information. The new ID card is less costly and is quick and easy to produce. The color of the cards will remain the same: active duty, green; reserve and their dependents, red; retirees, blue, and dependents, tan. The new ID cards will be fully implemented over a 4-year period. Meanwhile, the old ID cards will continue to be valid.

Dependent ID Cards. DD Forms 1172 (Application for Uniformed Services Identification and Privilege Card), are used to apply for issue or reissue of ID cards for dependents (DD Form 1173). DD Form 1172 can be obtained from most Armed Forces installations. Application forms must be verified from the sponsor's personnel records or from appropriate documentation as applicable, such as marriage certificates, birth certificates, certification of student status, adoption papers, or medical statements. Application forms must be completed and signed by the active duty sponsor. The services have agreed to assist each other in issuing ID cards to eligible dependents upon presentation of appropriate documentation and a completed application form.

DD Forms 1173 generally expire three years from date of issue or expiration of a sponsor's obligated service.

ID cards must be surrendered when they are replaced or expired or upon demand of a commissioned or noncommissioned officer or security or military police acting in the performance of duty or when the cardholder becomes ineligible.

Eligible dependents are generally defined as:
1. Lawful spouse.
2. Unremarried surviving spouse.
3. Unmarried children (including adopted or stepchildren) who are:
   a. Under 21 years of age.
   b. Over 21 but incapable of self-support. (Substantiating documentation is required.)
   c. Over 21 but under 23 who are attending an approved learning institution as a full time student. (Documentation is required.)
4. Parent or parent-in-law who is dependent for over one-half of his/her support on member. For medical care privileges, parent or parent-in-law must also reside in dwelling place provided or maintained by the member. Consult ID card issuing activity of sponsor's service for clarification or assistance in obtaining determination of eligibility.
5. Wards (as defined in appropriate instructions.)

UNIFORMED SERVICES ALMANAC

6. Unremarried former spouse. (One whose final decree of divorce is on or after February 1, 1983, and has been married to a military sponsor for a minimum of 20 years during which time the military member must have served 20 years of creditable service for retirement purposes.)

A remarried widow whose second marriage ends in divorce or death may receive commissary, theater, and exchange benefits but not medical benefits.

PRIVILEGES OF BASE FACILITIES

Active duty military personnel and their eligible dependents are authorized the use of many base facilities, subject to the availability and adequacy of these facilities as determined by the installation commander. (Exchange facilities are normally available regardless of store adequacy, and therefore are not listed under facilities.) The use of base facilities, for the most part, is a privilege which may be granted, rather than a right to which military personnel are automatically entitled. The presentation of proper identification cards (DD Form 2, green, or DD Form 1173 for dependents) is generally required for use of these base facilities.

The most common and frequently used facilities available are:

Officer, NCO, and Enlisted Clubs	Laundry and Dry Cleaning Stores
Commissaries	Consolidated Package Stores
Exchange stores	Libraries
Family Centers	Chapels and related services
Theaters	Transient Quarters
Clothing Sales Stores	Legal Assistance (limited)
Recreation Services	Casualty Assistance
Officer, NCO, and Enlisted Open Messes	

The use of Uniformed Services Health and Medical Care facilities is probably one of the most important rights extended to military personnel and their eligible dependents. Complete coverage of this important subject can be found in the Section on UNIFORMED SERVICES HEALTH BENEFITS.

GUIDE TO MILITARY INSTALLATION FACILITIES

The following listing is designed as a reference guide to facilities at most of the military installations in all 50 states. Facilities such as exchange stores and commissaries are generally available to all military personnel, while temporary living quarters, Family Campgrounds, recreation areas and/or lodges may be available only on a space available basis and some only at certain times of the year. Reservations are generally required for recreation areas and FAM CAMPS. It is advisable to call or write well in advance to determine if the facility you plan to use or visit will be available to you and your dependents. The area code and commercial telephone number for information is provided. Possession of a valid identification card is required to use these facilities. An asterisk (*) is placed at those installations which have Casualty Assistance Officers who are prepared to offer assistance when active duty personnel or their dependents die. In addition a dagger † is placed at those installations scheduled for base closure or realignment within the next few years.

The information contained in this guide is based on the latest information available at time of preparation. All facility listings are subject to change.

UNIFORMED SERVICES ALMANAC
ABBREVIATIONS

C — Commissary
F — Family Center
G — Golf Course
R — Recreation Area or Family Camp
T — Temporary Quarters
AD — Army Depot
AFB — Air Force Base
AFS — Air Force Station
ANGB — Air National Guard Base
CG — Coast Guard
Ctr — Center
IAP — International Airport
MC — Marine Corps

MCAS — Marine Corps Air Station
MCB — Marine Corps Base
NAB — Naval Amphibious Base
NAS — Naval Air Station
NB — Naval Base
NCBC — Naval Contruction Battalion Center
NETC — Naval Education Training Center
NH — Naval Hospital
NS — Naval Station
NSA — Naval Support Activity
NSC — Naval Supply Center
NWS — Naval Weapons Center

STATE INSTALLATION/LOCATION/ZIP	PHONE	FACILITIES
ALABAMA		
Fort McClellan, Anniston 36205*†	(205) 848-4611	F C T R G
Fort Rucker, Ozark 36362*	(205) 255-1030	F C T R G
Redstone Arsenal, Huntsville 35898	(205) 876-2151	F C T R G
CG Aviation Training Ctr, Mobile 36608	(334) 639-6117	F C T R
Maxwell AFB, Gunter Anx, Montgomery 36114*	(334) 953-1110	F C T R G
ALASKA		
NAF, Adak, FPO AP 96506*†	(907) 592-4201	F T
Elmendorf AFB, Anchorage 99506*	(907) 552-1110	F C T R G
Fort Richardson, Anchorage 99505	(907) 384-1110	F C T R G
Fort Greely, Delta Junction, APO AP 96508	(907) 873-1110	F C T R
Eielson AFB, Fairbanks 99702*	(907) 377-1110	F C T R
Fort Wainwright, Fairbanks 99703	(907) 353-7500	F C T R G
CG Spt Ctr Base, Kodiak 99619	(907) 487-5170	F C T R G
ARIZONA		
Luke AFB, Glendale 85309*	(602) 856-7411	F C T R
Fort Huachuca, Sierra Vista 85613*	(520) 538-7111	F C T R G
Davis-Monthan AFB, Tucson 85707*	(520) 750-4717	F C T R G
MCAS, Yuma 85369*	(520) 341-2011	F C T R
Proving Ground, Yuma 85365	(602) 328-3287	F C T R
ARKANSAS		
Little Rock AFB, Jacksonville 72099*	(501) 988-3131	F C T R G
Fort Chaffee 72905†	(501) 484-3130	T R G
Pine Bluff Arsenal 71602	(501) 543-3000	F T R G
CALIFORNIA		
NAS, Alameda 94501†	(510) 263-3012	F C T
MC Logistics Base, Barstow 92311*	(619) 577-6211	F C T R G
Naval Weapons Ctr, China Lake 93555*	(619) 939-9011	F C T G
Travis AFB, Fairfield 94535*	(707) 424-1110	F C T R G
Sierra Army Depot, Herlong 96113	(916) 827-2111	F C T R
Fort Hunter Liggett, Jolon 93928	(408) 386-2000	F C T R G
NAS Lemoore 93246*	(209) 998-0100	F C T
Vandenburg AFB, Lompoc 93437*	(805) 734-8232	F C T R G
Los Angeles AFB, El Segundo 90245*	(310) 363-1110	F C T
Beale AFB, Marysville 95903*	(916) 634-3000	F C T R G
NAS Miramar 92145*	(619) 537-1011	F C T R G
Edwards AFB, Rosamond 93524*	(805) 277-1110	F C T R G

UNIFORMED SERVICES ALMANAC

STATE
INSTALLATION/LOCATION/ZIP   **PHONE**   **FACILITIES**

Installation/Location/ZIP	Phone	Facilities
Army Base, Oakland 94626†	(415) 466-9111	F C T R
Camp Pendleton MCB, Oceanside 92055	(619) 725-4111	F C T R G
CG Spt Ctr, Alameda 94501	(510) 437-3985	F T R
NAVAir Wpns Sta, Point Mugu 93042	(805) 989-1110	F C T R G
NCBC, Point Hueneme 93043*	(805) 982-4711	F C T R G
March AFB, Riverside 92518*†	(909) 655-1110	F C T R G
McClellan AFB, Sacramento 95652*†	(916) 643-4113	F C T R G
MCAS, El Toro Santa Ana 92709*†	(714) 726-2100	F C T R G
NS San Diego 92136*	(619) 556-1246	F C T G
North Island NAS, Coronado 92135	(619) 545-8123	F C T R G
NTC, San Diego 92133†	(619) 524-4011	F C T G
Presidio of Monterey, Monterey 93944	(408) 242-5000	F C T R
Treasure Island NS, San Francisco 94130*†	(415) 395-1000	F C T
CG Tng Ctr, Petaluma 94952	(707) 765-7211	F T
MCB, Twenty-nine Palms 92278*	(619) 830-6000	F C T R G
Fort Irwin, Barstow 92310	(619) 380-4111	F C T R
Naval PG School, Monterey 93943	(408) 656-2441	F C T G
NAB Coronado 92155	(619) 437-2011	T R
Naval Wpns Sta, Concord 94520*	(510) 246-2000	F G
NAF El Centro 92243	(619) 339-2699	C T
COLORADO		
Air Force Academy, Colorado Springs 80840*	(719) 472-1818	F C T R G
Peterson AFB, Colorado Springs 80914*	(719) 556-7321	F C T G
Fort Carson, Colorado Springs 80913*	(719) 526-5811	F C T R G
Fitzsimons Army Med. Ctr., Aurora 80045†	(303) 361-8241	F C T R G
CONNECTICUT		
Naval Submarine Base, Groton 06349*	(860) 449-4636	F C T R G
Coast Guard Academy, New London 06320	(203) 444-8444	F C T R
DELAWARE		
Dover AFB, Dover 19902*	(302) 677-2113	F C T R G
DISTRICT OF COLUMBIA		
Fort McNair, Washington 20319*	(202) 475-1782	T
Walter Reed Army Med. Ctr, Washington 20307*	(202) 782-3501	F C T
Naval District, Washington 20374*	(703) 545-6700	F T R
Bolling AFB, Washington 20332*	(703) 545-6700	F C T
FLORIDA		
Patrick AFB, Cocoa Beach 32925*	(407) 494-1110	F C T R G
Eglin AFB, Ft. Walton Bch 32542*	(904) 882-1110	F C T R G
Hurlburt Field, Fort Walton Beach 32544*	(904) 884-1110	F C T R G
Homestead AFB, Homestead 33039*	(305) 257-8011	F C T R G
NAS Jacksonville 32212*	(904) 772-2345	F C T R G
Cecil Field NAS, Jacksonville 32215*†	(904) 778-5626	F C T R G
NAS Key West 33040*	(305) 293-2268	F C T R
Corry Sta, Pensacola, Fl 32511*	(904) 452-2000	F C T
NS Mayport 32228*	(904) 270-5011	F C T R G
Whiting Field NAS, Milton 32570*	(904) 623-7011	F C T R G
Naval Trng Ctr, Orlando 32815*†	(407) 646-4501	F C T R G
Tyndall AFB, Panama City 32403*	(904) 283-1113	F C T R G
NAS Pensacola 32508*	(904) 452-0111	F C T R G
Naval Hospital, Pensacola 32512*	(904) 452-6601	C R
MacDill AFB, Tampa 33621*	(813) 828-1110	F C T R G

UNIFORMED SERVICES ALMANAC

STATE
INSTALLATION/LOCATION/ZIP   **PHONE**   **FACILITIES**

GEORGIA
Installation	Phone	Facilities
Kings Bay NSB, St. Marys, FL 31547*	(912) 673-2001	F C T R G
Marine Corps Logistics Base, Albany 31704*	(912) 439-5000	F C T R G
Fort McPherson, Atlanta 30330*	(404) 752-3113	F C T R G
Fort Gillem, Forest Park 30050	(404) 363-5000	F C T
Fort Benning, Columbus 31905*	(706) 545-2011	F C T R G
Fort Gordon, Augusta 30905*	(706) 791-0110	F C T R G
Fort Stewart, Hinesville 31314*	(912) 767-1411	F C T R G
NAS Atlanta,Marietta 30060*	(404) 919-6392	F T R
Hunter Army Air Field, Savannah 31409	(912) 352-6521	F C T
Moody AFB, Valdosta 31699*	(912) 257-4211	F C T R G
Robins AFB, Warner Robins 31098*	(912) 926-1113	F C T R G

HAWAII
Installation	Phone	Facilities
NAS, Barbers Point, Kapolei 96862*†	(808) 684-6266	F C T R G
Fort Shafter, Honolulu 96858	(808) 471-7110	F C T G
Hickam AFB, Honolulu 96853*	(808) 471-7110	F C T R G
MCAS Kaneohe Bay 96863*	(808) 471-7110	F C T R G
Naval Base, Pearl Harbor 96860*	(808) 471-7110	F C T R G
Schofield Barracks, Wahiawa 96857*	(808) 471-7110	F C T G
Tripler Army Med. Ctr. Honolulu 96859	(808) 433-6661	T R
Hale Koa Hotel, Ft. DeRussy 96815	(800) 367-6027	T R

IDAHO
Installation	Phone	Facilities
Mountain Home AFB 83648*	(208) 828-1110	F C T R G

ILLINOIS
Installation	Phone	Facilities
Scott AFB, Belleville 62225*	(618) 256-1110	F C T R G
Chas. Melv Price Spt Ctr, Granite City 62040	(618) 452-4211	F C T G
Naval Trng. Ctr., Great Lakes 60088*	(708) 688-3500	F C T G

INDIANA
Installation	Phone	Facilities
NW Support Ctr., Crane 47522†	(812) 854-2511	C T G

KANSAS
Installation	Phone	Facilities
Fort Riley, Junction City 66442*	(913) 239-2672	F C T R G
Fort Leavenworth, Leavenworth 66027*	(913) 684-4021	F C T G
McConnell AFB, Wichita 67221*	(316) 652-6100	F C T R G

KENTUCKY
Installation	Phone	Facilities
Fort Campbell, Clarksville 42223*	(502) 798-2151	F C T R G
Fort Knox, Radcliffe 40121*	(502) 624-1181	F C T R G

LOUISIANA
Installation	Phone	Facilities
Fort Polk, Leesville 71459*	(318) 531-2911	F C T R G
Jackson Barracks, New Orleans 70146	(504) 271-6262	F T
NSA New Orleans 70142*	(504) 678-5011	F C T R
Barksdale AFB, Bossier City 71110*	(318) 456-2252	F C T R G
NAS New Orleans 70143	(504) 393-3011	F C T R G

MAINE
Installation	Phone	Facilities
NAS Brunswick 04011*	(207) 921-1110	F C T R G
Nav Sec. Gp Activity, Winter Harbor 04693	(207) 963-5534	C T R

MARYLAND
Installation	Phone	Facilities
Aberdeen Proving Ground, Aberdeen 21005	(410) 278-5201	F C T R G
USNA, Annapolis 21402/NS Annapolis	(410) 293-1000	F C T R
National Naval Med Ctr., Bethesda 20889	(301) 295-4611	T
Andrews AFB, Camp Springs 20331*	(301) 981-1110	F C T R G

UNIFORMED SERVICES ALMANAC

STATE
INSTALLATION/LOCATION/ZIP — **PHONE** — **FACILITIES**

Installation	Phone	Facilities
Fort Ritchie, Cascade 21719†	(301) 878-1300	F C T R
Coast Guard Yard, Curtis Bay 21226	(410) 789-1600	T R
Fort George G. Meade, Odenton 20755*	(301) 677-6261	F C T R G
NAS, Patuxent 20670*	(301) 342-3000	F C T R G
Fort Detrick, Frederick 21702	(301) 619-8000	F C T R
MASSACHUSETTS		
Fort Devens, Ayer 01433*†	(508) 796-2748	F C T G
Hanscom AFB, Bedford 01731*	(617) 377-4441	F C T R G
Cape Cod CG Air Station 02548	(508) 968-1000	F C T R G
NAS South Weymouth 02190*†	(617) 786-2933	F C T R
MICHIGAN		
Selfridge ANGB, Mt Clemens 48045	(810) 307-4011	F C T R G
MINNESOTA		
Minneapolis-St. Paul IAP 55450*	(612) 725-5011	T
MISSISSIPPI		
Keesler AFB, Biloxi 39534*	(601) 377-1110	F C T R G
Columbus AFB, Columbus 39710*	(601) 434-7322	F C T R G
NCBC, Gulfport 39501	(601) 871-2555	F C T R G
NAS Meridian 39309*	(601) 679-2211	F C T R G
NS Pascagoula 39567*	(601) 761-2002	F R
MISSOURI		
Whiteman AFB, Knob Noster 65305*	(816) 687-1110	F C T R G
Fort Leonard Wood, Rolla 65473*	(314) 596-0131	F C T G
MONTANA		
Malmstrom AFB, Great Falls 59402*	(406) 731-1110	F C T R
NEBRASKA		
Offutt AFB, Omaha 68113*	(402) 294-1110	F C T R G
NEVADA		
NAS Fallon 89496*	(702) 426-5161	F C T R
Nellis AFB, Las Vegas 89191*	(702) 652-1840	F C T R G
NEW HAMPSHIRE		
Portsmouth Naval Shipyard, 03804*	(207) 438-1000	F C T R
NEW JERSEY		
CG Training Center, Cape May 08204	(609) 898-6900	F T R
Naval Air Engr Sta., Lakehurst 08733*	(908) 323-2011	F C T R G
Earle Naval Wpns Sta, Colts Neck 07722*	(908) 866-2500	F R
Fort Monmouth, Eatontown 07703	(908) 532-9000	F C T R G
Fort Dix, Wrightstown 08640*†	(609) 562-1011	F C T G
McGuire AFB, Wrightstown 08641*	(609) 724-1100	F C T R G
NEW MEXICO		
Holloman AFB, Alamogordo 88330*	(505) 475-6511	F C T R G
Kirtland AFB, Albuquerque 87117*	(505) 846-0011	F C T R G
Cannon AFB, Clovis 88103*	(505) 784-3311	F C T R G
White Sands Missile Range, Las Cruces 88002	(505) 678-2121	F C T R G
NEW YORK		
Fort Hamilton, Brooklyn 11252*	(718) 630-4101	F C T
CG Base, Governors Island 10004	(212) 668-7324	F C T R G
Griffiss AFB, Rome 13441*	(315) 330-1110	F C T R G
Seneca Army Depot, Romulus 14541	(607) 869-1110	F C T R
Fort Drum, Watertown 13602*	(315) 772-6011	F C T R
US Military Academy, West Point 10996	(914) 938-4011	F C T R G

UNIFORMED SERVICES ALMANAC

STATE INSTALLATION/LOCATION/ZIP	PHONE	FACILITIES
NORTH CAROLINA		
MCAS, Cherry Point 28533*	(919) 466-2811	F C T R G
CG Spt Ctr, Elizabeth City 27909	(919) 335-6000	T R
Fort Bragg, Fayetteville 28307*	(919) 396-0011	F C T R G
Pope AFB, Fayetteville 28308*	(910) 394-0001	F C T R G
Seymour Johnson AFB, Goldsboro 27531*	(919) 736-5400	F C T R G
MCAS, New River, Jacksonville 28545*	(910) 451-1113	F C T R
Camp Lejeune, Jacksonville 28542*	(910) 451-1113	F C T R G
NORTH DAKOTA		
Grand Forks AFB, Grand Forks 58205*	(701) 747-3000	F C T R G
Minot AFB, Minot 58705*	(701) 723-1110	F C T R G
OHIO		
Rickenbacker ANB, Columbus 43217†	(614) 492-8211	T R
Wright-Patterson AFB, Dayton 45433*	(513) 257-1110	F C T R G
OKLAHOMA		
Altus AFB, Altus 73523*	(405) 482-8100	F C T R G
Vance AFB, Enid 73705*	(405) 237-2121	F C T R G
Fort Sill, Lawton 73503*	(405) 442-8111	F C T G
Tinker AFB, Oklahoma City 73145*	(405) 732-7321	F C T R G
McAlester Army Ammo Plant 74501*	(918) 451-2529	F C T R G
OREGON		
Coast Guard Gp, Astoria 97146		C
PENNSYLVANIA		
Carlisle Barracks, Carlisle 17013	(717) 245-3131	F C T R G
Chas. E. Kelly Spt Fac, Oakdale 15071	(412) 777-1173	C
Navship Pts Cont., Mechanicsburg 17055	(717) 790-2900	C T
Army Depot, New Cumberland 17070	(717) 770-6011	F C T R G
NB/NS Philadelphia 19112*†	(215) 897-5000	F C T R
NAS Willow Grove, Horsham 19090*	(215) 443-1000	F T
Letterkenny Army Dep., Chambersburg 17201†	(717) 267-8111	F T R
Fort Indiantown Gap, Annville 17003†	(717) 861-2000	F C T
Army Depot, Tobyhanna 18466	(717) 894-7000	F C T R
RHODE ISLAND		
NETC, Newport 02841*	(401) 841-3456	F C T R
SOUTH CAROLINA		
Charleston AFB, Charleston 29404*	(800) 438-2694	F C T R G
Fort Jackson, Columbia 29207*	(803) 751-7511	F C T G
MC Recruiting Depot, Parris Island 29905*	(803) 525-2111	F C T R G
Shaw AFB, Sumter 29152*	(803) 668-2778	F C T R G
MCAS Beaufort 29904*	(803) 522-7100	F T R G
SOUTH DAKOTA		
Ellsworth AFB, Rapid City 57706*	(605) 385-1000	F C T R G
TENNESSEE		
Memphis NAS, Millington 38054*	(901) 873-5509	F C T R G
Arnold AFB, Tullahoma 37389*	(615) 454-3000	C T R
TEXAS		
Dyess AFB, Abilene 79607*	(915) 696-0212	F C T R G
Chase Field NAS, Beeville 78103*	(512) 354-5119	F C T R G
NAS, Corpus Christi 78419*	(512) 939-2811	F C T R G
NAS, Dallas 75211*†	(214) 266-6111	F T R

UNIFORMED SERVICES ALMANAC

STATE INSTALLATION/LOCATION/ZIP	PHONE	FACILITIES
NS Ingleside, Corpus Christi 78362*	(512) 776-4774	F R
Laughlin AFB, Del Rio 78843*	(210) 298-3511	F C T R G
Fort Bliss, El Paso 79916*	(915) 568-2121	F C T G
Fort Worth NAS 76127*	(817) 782-5000	F C T
NAS, Kingsville 78363*	(512) 595-6136	F C T R
Fort Hood, Killeen 76544*	(817) 287-1110	F C T R G
Reese AFB, Lubbock 79489*	(806) 885-4511	F C T R G
Goodfellow AFB, San Angelo 76908*	(915) 654-3231	F C T R
Brooks AFB, San Antonio 78235*	(210) 536-1110	F C T R G
Fort Sam Houston, San Antonio 78234*	(210) 221-1211	F C T R G
Kelly AFB, San Antonio 78241*	(210) 925-1110	F C T R G
Lackland AFB, San Antonio 78236*	(210) 671-1110	F C T R G
Randolph AFB, San Antonio 78150*	(210) 652-1110	F C T R G
Sheppard AFB, Wichita Falls 76311*	(817) 676-2511	F C T R G
Army Depot Red River 75507	(214) 334-2141	F C T R G
UTAH		
Dugway Proving Ground 84022	(801) 831-3545	F C T R
Hill AFB, Ogden 84056*	(801) 777-7221	F C T R G
Tooele Army Depot 84074*	(801) 833-1110	F C T R
VIRGINIA		
Fort Belvoir, Alexandria 22060*	(703) 545-6700	F C T R G
Fort Myer, Arlington 22211	(703) 695-0441	F C T
Fort Pickett, Blackstone 23824	(804) 292-8621	T R
Fort A.P. Hill, Bowling Green 22427	(804) 633-5041	T R
Naval Surface Warfare Ctr, Dahlgren 22448*	(540) 663-8531	F C T R G
Fort Monroe, Hampton 23651	(804) 727-2111	F C T
Langley AFB, Hampton 23665*	(804) 764-9990	F C T R G
Fleet Combat Tng Ctr, Va Beach 23461	(804) 433-6234	T R
Naval Amphibious Base, Little Creek 23521*	(804) 464-7385	F C T R G
Fort Eustis, Newport News 23604*	(804) 878-1110	F C T R G
NB Norfolk 23511*	(804) 444-0000	F C T R G
NAS Oceana 23460*	(804) 433-2366	F C T R G
Fort Lee, Petersburg 23801*	(804) 765-3000	F C T G
NAV Wpns Sta, Yorktown 23691*	(804) 887-4545	F C R G
MC Devel. and Ed. Cmd, Quantico 22134*	(703) 784-2121	F C T R G
Fort Story, Virginia Beach 23459	(804) 422-7305	F C T
Vint Hill Farms, Warrenton 22186†	(703) 349-6000	F C T
CG Res Tng Ctr, Yorktown 23690	(804) 898-3500	F T R
WASHINGTON		
Bangor NSB, Silverdale 98315*	(360) 396-6111	F C T R
Puget Sound Nav Shipyard, Bremerton 98314*	(360) 476-3711	F C T R
Whidbey Island NAS, Oak Harbor 98278*	(360) 257-2211	F C T R G
Fairchild AFB, Spokane 99011*	(509) 247-1212	F C T R
Fort Lewis, Tacoma 98433*	(206) 967-1110	F C T R
McChord AFB, Tacoma 98438*	(206) 984-1910	F C T R G
CG Spt Ctr, Seattle 98134	(206) 217-6400	F T R
WISCONSIN		
Fort McCoy, Sparta 54656	(608) 388-2222	F C T R
WYOMING		
Francis E. Warren AFB, Cheyenne 82005*	(307) 775-1110	F C T R

PART II

UNIFORMED SERVICES HEALTH BENEFITS

This section presents a general guide to **Uniformed Services** health care in Uniformed Services medical facilities and under CHAMPUS. For more specific detail and information, contact the nearest medical facility or CHAMPUS representative or you can contact the CHAMPUS' Benefit Services Branch, by calling (303) 361-1126 (or DSN 943-1126) or writing to them at Benefit Services Branch, OCHAMPUS, Aurora, CO 80045-6900.

UNIFORMED SERVICES HEALTH BENEFITS PROGRAM

Public Law 89-614, September 30, 1966, "Military Medical Benefits Amendments of 1966," made major changes in the health benefits provided by the Government to dependents of members of the uniformed services who are serving on active duty, to retired members of the uniformed services, and to the dependents of retired and deceased members of the uniformed services, on a space available basis.

The uniformed services are the Army, Navy, Marine Corps, Air Force, Coast Guard, Commissioned Corps of the Public Health Service, and the Commissioned Corps of the National Oceanic & Atmospheric Administration.

The primary source of medical care under the medical program is the uniformed services medical facilities. If, however, care is not available at a military facility, certain categories of people may use the Civilian Health and Medical Program of the Uniformed Services (CHAMPUS), or in some areas, the PRIMUS and NAVCARE centers for Satellite Military Health Care.

Civilian health benefits fall into three broad beneficiary categories:

1. Civilian outpatient and inpatient care for the wives, children, and husbands of members of the uniformed services who are serving on active duty pursuant to a call or order that does not specify a period of 30 consecutive days or less.

2. Civilian inpatient and outpatient care for retired members and their wives, children, and husbands, and the wives, children, and husbands of members who died while on active duty or in a retired status. Care is also available for certain former spouses. See CHAMPUS eligibility section.

3. Civilian inpatient and outpatient care for certain voluntarily and involuntarily separated members who qualify for benefits under the Transition Assistance Management Program (TAMP) and their dependents.

Historically, health care services for DOD beneficiaries have been provided by military treatment facilities (MTFs) operated by the military departments. By definition, the first priority for MTF care is the active duty population. All other DOD beneficiaries may receive MTF care on a "space-available" basis. Since 1966, with the beginning of the Civilian Health and Medical Program of the Uniformed Services (CHAMPUS), non active duty beneficiaries (under age 65) have been able to receive health care from civilian sources (when not available at the MTF) and cost share the expense of that care with the DOD through the auspices of CHAMPUS.

UNIFORMED SERVICES ALMANAC

UNIFORMED SERVICES HEALTH BENEFITS

Eligible Patients	Uniformed Services Medical Facilities Inpatient	Outpatient	Civilian Health & Medical Program (CHAMPUS) Inpatient	Outpatient	Persons with Disabilities
Active Duty Member	Yes, First Priority		Not Eligible	Not Eligible	Not Eligible
Spouse or child of AD member, TAMP-eligible beneficiaries	Yes, if space available		Yes, may need nonavailable certificate	Yes, may need nonavailable certificate	Yes (needs prior approval)
Ret member, spouse or dep child or retiree, surviving spouse or dep child of AD member or retiree	Yes, if space available		Yes, unless eligible for MEDICARE (Part A) Certain Medicare eligibles now have CHAMPUS eligibility. See CHAMPUS Section.	Yes, unless eligible for MEDICARE (Part A) Certain Medicare eligibles now have CHAMPUS eligibility. May need NAV.	Not Eligible
Dependent parent or parents-in-law of AD, retired or deceased member, certain former spouses are authorized military hospital and CHAMPUS care if they do not have employer-sponsored health care.	Yes, if space available		Not Eligible	Not Eligible	Not Eligible
			New category of CHAMPUS eligibles for some former active duty members and families is outlined in section pertaining to CHAMPUS benefits.		
Costs	Inpatient	Outpatient	Inpatient	Outpatient	Persons with Disabilities
Active Duty Member	Daily Subsistence Charge	No Charge	Not Eligible	Not Eligible	Not Eligible
Spouse or child of AD member, TAMP eligible beneficiaries	$9.70 per day	No Charge	$9.70 per day or $25.00, not to exceed $1,000 per year whichever is greater	20% of allowed charges above deductible of $150 per person or $300 per family per FY for grades E-5 and above	Depends on grade. Government will pay up to $1000 a month for authorized care
Retired Enlisted	No Charge	No Charge	LESSER of 25% of billed hospital charges or $330 per day; not to exceed $7,500 per year also pay 25% of allowed physician charges	25% of allowed charges above deductible	Not Eligible
Retired Officer	Daily Subsistence Allowance	No charge	LESSER of 25% of billed hospital charges or $330 per day; not to exceed $7,500 per year also pay 25% of allowed physician charges	25% of allowed charges above deductible	Not Eligible
Spouse or dep child of retired or deceased member, certain former spouses	$9.70 per day	No Charge	LESSER of 25% of billed hospital charges or $330 per day; not to exceed $7,500 per year also pay 25% of allowed physician charges	25% of allowed charges above deductible	Not Eligible
Dependent parent or parents-in-law of AD, retired or deceased member	$9.70 per day	No Charge	Not Eligible	Not Eligible	Not Eligible

UNIFORMED SERVICES ALMANAC
DoD TRICARE MANAGED CARE PROGRAM

TRICARE is the DoD regional managed care program for members of the uniformed services and their families, and survivors and retired members and their families. TRICARE brings together the health care delivery systems of each of the military services, as well as the Civilian Health and Medical Program of the Uniformed Services (CHAMPUS), in a cooperative and supportive effort to better serve military patients and to better the resources available to military medicine.

Cooperation among the military services is inherent in the organization of TRICARE. Across the United States, twelve Regions have been identified, each administered by a Lead Agent. These Lead Agents are the commanders of one of the military medical centers located within the Region. With the designation of Lead Agent comes the responsibility to develop, in collaboration with all military treatment facility commanders in the Region, an integrated plan for the delivery of health care to beneficiaries residing within the Region.

TRICARE introduces to beneficiaries three choices for their health care delivery: TRICARE Standard, a fee-for-service option which is the same as standard CHAMPUS; TRICARE Extra, which offers a preferred provider option with discounts; and TRICARE Prime, an enrolled health maintenance organization (HMO) option. All active duty members will be enrolled in TRICARE Prime. All Medicare-eligible DoD beneficiaries, and those CHAMPUS-eligible beneficiaries who elect not to enroll in TRICARE Prime, will remain eligible for care in military medical facilities on a space-available basis.

TRICARE Standard - This option is the same as the standard CHAMPUS program.

TRICARE Extra - In the TRICARE Extra program, when CHAMPUS-eligible beneficiary uses a preferred network provider, he/she receives an out-of-pocket discount and usually does no have to file any claim forms. CHAMPUS beneficiaries do not enroll in TRICARE Extra, but may participate in Extra on a case-by-case basis just by using the network providers.

TRICARE Prime - This voluntary enrollment option offers patients the scope of coverage available today under CHAMPUS, plus additional preventive and primary care services. Prime includes features such as primary care managers, who are responsible for enrollee health care, to include referrals for specialty treatment. Another Prime feature is the health care finder, who assists patients in locating and making specialty appointments. TRICARE Prime cost sharing is, on average, significantly less than either Extra or Standard. Of particular note, CHAMPUS-eligible retirees who enroll in Prime pay only $11 per day for civilian inpatient care in comparison to the $323 per day plus 25% of professional fees charge faced by those retirees who use TRICARE Standard. Enrollees in TRICARE Prime usually have no claim forms to file and they obtain most of their care within the integrated military and civilian network of TRICARE providers. Additionally, under a new point of service option, Prime enrollees may retain freedom of choice to use non-network providers by at a significantly higher cost sharing than TRICARE Standard.

The cost sharing provisions for TRICARE Prime enrollment meet the statutory requirements of the National Defense Authorization Act for FY 1994. Instead of the usual standard CHAMPUS cost sharing requirements.

Prime enrollees will pay special per-service copayments, which vary by beneficiary category. Survivors, retirees and their family members, who enroll in TRICARE Prime will also pay an annual $230 individual enrollment fee or $460 family fee which is in lieu of the standard CHAMPUS deductible. There is no enrollment fee for active duty family members. These new Prime cost sharing provisions will be published soon in a proposed Federal rule, and the effects of the implementation of TRICARE Prime will be evaluated and documented each year. Based in part on the results of that evaluation, consideration should be given to introducing a fee beginning in fiscal year 1998, for care rendered in military facilities for some or all outpatient care and for some or all retirees, their family members, and survivors. Workable and desirable alternatives will be analyzed.

A major component of TRICARE is the series of managed care support contracts that supplement the capabilities of regional military health care delivery networks. There are to be seven fixed-price, at-risk contracts, supporting the twelve Regions, competitively awarded prior to the end of fiscal year 1996. The new TRICARE Prime cost sharing provisions will be phased in as each regional TRICARE contract begins operations. TRICARE Prime was first offered to beneficiaries living in Washington and Oregon when the new regional TRICARE contract began health care delivery services on March 1, 1995.

An important element of TRICARE, which is not visible to the patient population, is the new method of funding military medical facilities. The military departments receive resources based upon the population they serve. In turn, they allocate funds to their medical facilities on a similar basis. It is called a modified capitation methodology. By funding in this manner, the military medical managers are motivated to provide the best care possible for their patients in the most appropriate setting and in a timely way.

The downsizing of the Military Health Service System (MHSS) and various Base Realignment and Closure (BRAC) actions are requiring more beneficiaries to obtain their health care in the more expensive civilian sector. With health care costs escalating nationwide, fewer beneficiaries can afford to obtain health care under the old standard CHAMPUS rules. The Department of Defense has stated that they are committed to providing an equitable level of health services to their beneficiaries, regardless of whether they are adversely impacted by BRAC or other downsizing issues. TRICARE offers CHAMPUS eligible beneficiaries two options other than standard CHAMPUS. These options (TRICARE Prime and Extra) are designed to reduce their beneficiaries out-of-pocket costs, while also improving the cost effectiveness of the MHSS. The Managed Care Support contractor assists DoD in reducing the cost that beneficiaries bear, as well as, the government. TRICARE improves the efficiency of the remaining military treatment facilities (MTF) by reducing the amount of unnecessary care provided and replacing it with appropriate medical care. This allows the MTFs to recapture work, that would otherwise be provided under the more expensive Standard CHAMPUS program.

The only choice CHAMPUS eligible beneficiaries need to make is whether to enroll in TRICARE Prime or not. If they enroll, they agree to follow the rules on how to obtain their health care. With the exception of emergencies, Prime enrollees goes to their assigned Primary Care Manager (PCM) to obtain all their health care needs. If they decline to enroll, they retain their freedom of choice in choosing their civilian provider, but understand that this freedom comes at a higher out-of-pocket cost to them.

Non enrollees can still reduce their out-of-pocket costs when they choose to use the TRICARE Extra civilian provider network.

TRICARE addresses many concerns voiced over the years by beneficiaries. TRICARE addresses beneficiary concerns on access, patient convenience, and cost. TRICARE also ensures the quality of health care provided in the Military Health Service System (MHSS) remains high. In particular, TRICARE Prime guarantees enrollees appropriate health care in the MHSS within pre-established access standards. Regional Managed Care Support contracts augment the military treatment facilities capabilities, thereby providing beneficiaries with a greater variety of providers to seek care from. Health Care Finders also improve beneficiary convenience by assisting beneficiaries in obtaining their health services in a timely manner. The burden of filing claims is eliminated for the beneficiary when using the TRICARE Prime and Extra options. The uniform Health Maintenance Organization (HMO) benefit standardizes, by TRICARE option, the costs beneficiaries incur for their health care. More importantly, the TRICARE Prime option offers enhanced preventive medicine and wellness services to improve the health status of these beneficiaries. TRICARE was designed to provide beneficiaries with the best health service benefit within the Department of Defense's available health care resources.

Managed Care is designed to provide patients with the proper level of health care services, in a timely manner, at the right location, and with the appropriate type of provider. The Primary Care Manager (PCM) is the focal point to ensure enrolled beneficiaries obtain timely access to the appropriate level of medical care, whether it be primary care or specialty services.

There are different types of HMOs, but in general, all HMOs assume total responsibility for providing all the health care needs of their enrollees. They serve as an umbrella health care organization which either provides directly, or contracts for, a broad range of health services the enrollees require. In return, HMOs receive a prepaid capitated payment (enrollment fee and user fees) per enrollee. In terms of TRICARE Prime, the Government's military treatment facilities are considered staff model HMOs, which are also augmented by the Managed Care Support contractor's civilian provider network. The staff model HMO is considered the most effective type of HMO in controlling health care costs. HMOs focus on improving the overall health status of their enrollees. If successful in creating a healthier enrolled population, the HMO lowers the demand its enrollees require for health care services. HMOs attempt to provide their enrollees only with appropriate health services, consequently they strive to eliminate inappropriate services through their Utilization Management (UM) program.

A PPO is a type of managed care organization that enters contractual arrangements between a group of health care providers and a employer. In terms of TRICARE Extra, the Government contracts with a Managed Care Support Contractor, who in turn, contracts with civilian providers to establish the TRICARE Extra network. These health care providers agree to provide health services to beneficiaries at a discount from their customary fees. Where HMOs pay for health care on a prepaid basis, PPOs, use discounted fee schedules for services that are paid for at the time is rendered.

All active duty military personnel will be enrolled in TRICARE Prime automatically and assigned a primary care manager. When Prime is offered in their area, other categories of beneficiaries can enroll on a voluntary basis either by visiting or calling the local TRICARE Service Center.

Enrollment is for a 12-month period for TRICARE Prime. At the end of this initial 12 consecutive month enrollment period, you must choose to continue your enrollment in Prime or choose another option that best suits your situation. Under special circumstances, like when one is permanently reassigned to a new duty station, enrollees will be allowed to disenroll before the expiration of the twelve month enrollment period.

A primary care manager (PCM) is a provider either in a military hospital or clinic or in a civilian network that is selected by a TRICARE Prime beneficiary to assume primary responsibility for providing, arranging and coordinating your total health care. The PCM can be an individual or a practice site. A physician designated as a PCM could be one who practices in General or Family Practice, Internal Medicine, Pediatrics and OB/GYN. Nurse Practitioners and Physician's Assistants can also be PCMs.

Enrollees choosing a civilian primary care manager must obtain a referral in order to use the military treatment facility (MTF) or a PRIMUS/NAVCARE clinic.

Enrollees choosing a military treatment facility (MTF) as their primary care manager must obtain a referral to use a PRIMUS/NAVCARE clinic or civilian provider, unless the clinics are your PCM.

You may request to change your PCM at any time. Your request should be in writing and address the reasons for a PCM change. Contact you TRICARE Service Center to find out the specific local procedures for submitting a PCM change request. An attempt will be made to accommodate all enrollees valid requests for a new PCM. Keep in mind that PCM enrollment capacities may limit the ability to meet each individual's PCM request.

Any eligible beneficiary should access the nearest emergency room of any inpatient facility for true emergencies regardless of whether you join TRICARE Prime or remain in TRICARE Standard. If you are a TRICARE Prime enrollee, call your TRICARE Service Center no later than 24 hours after the emergency occurs. This will ensure that your medical claim is processed properly.

Your MTF Commander and lead agent wants to know your grievances with TRICARE. You may always use the local MTF Patient Assistance Representatives to file your grievance. Generally, the regional Managed Care Support Contractor is responsible for resolving grievances attributed to the civilian providers in the TRICARE civilian provider network. Contact the nearest TRICARE Service Center for specific local procedures for filing grievances.

Medicare beneficiaries are not eligible to enroll in TRICARE Prime at this time. This is due to laws that prohibit the transfer of Medicare funds to the TRICARE system. Although Congressional representatives have proposed a change in the law to allow "subvention" of funds from one system to the other, the change failed to pass the last Congress.

Until Medicare subvention is passed, military retirees who are Medicare eligible will continue to receive care in MTFs on a space available basis or may use the health care finder to access TRICARE providers who accept Medicare assignment. Most physicians who elect to join the contractor's network will be Medicare participating providers.

In base realignment and closure (BRAC) areas, Medicare eligible military retirees affected by base closure action may be authorized to participate in the mail order and retail pharmacy programs provided by the regional Managed Care Support Contractor. Contact your health benefits advisor

UNIFORMED SERVICES ALMANAC

in your local MTF or TRICARE Service Center to see if you qualify for these special pharmacy programs. Medicare eligible military beneficiaries may also choose to obtain their care form any Medicare at-risk HMO. Please see your health benefits advisor to locate the closest Medicare at-risk HMO in your area.

Additional test projects (called "Catchment Area Management", or "CAM" sites) are in operation in the service areas around the Luke Air Force Base Hospital in Arizona and the Charleston Naval Hospital, in South Carolina. If you are assigned to a new duty station, or just move to a new state or city, it's best to check with the Health Benefits Advisor at the nearest service hospital or clinic to see if there are any special programs or rules that you should know about before getting care.

NOTE: If you move away from a managed-care area, to a non-managed-care area, be sure to disenroll yourself and your family from the managed-care program before leaving your old place of residence. Check with your HBA.

UNIFORM HMO BENEFIT FEE and COPAYMENT SCHEDULE			
	Families of E4 and Below	Families of E5 and Above	Retirees, Survivors and Family Members
Annual Enrollment Fee or Premium (Individual/Family)	$0/$0	$0/$0	$230/$460
Copayments for Services outside Military Treatment Facilities			
Outpatient Visits, Including Separate Radiology or Lab Services and Home Health Visits	$6	$12	$12
Emergency Room Visits	$10	$30	$30
Mental Health Visits, Individual	$12	$25	$25
Ambulatory Surgery	$25	$25	$25
Ambulance Services	$10	$15	$20
Prescriptions	$5	$5	$9
Durable medical equipment, prosthesis, supplies	10 percent	15 percent	20 percent
Inpatient Per Diem, General	$11	$11	$11
Inpatient Per Diem, MH/Substance Use	$20	$20	$30

MEDICAL CARE FOR DEPENDENTS IN MEDICAL FACILITIES OF THE UNIFORMED SERVICES

Medical care is authorized in uniformed services medical facilities for dependents of active duty, retired, and deceased personnel, certain former spouses, and certain voluntarily and involuntarily separated members who qualify for benefits under TAMP and their dependents, when the commander of the medical facility or his or her designee, determines that space and facilities are available and the capabilities of the professional staff are sufficient for that purpose.

When the person in charge of the uniformed services facility does not have sufficient space, facilities, or professional staff to provide nonemergency care to all eligible persons, nonemergency care is furnished in the following order of priority:

1. Dependents of active duty members of the uniformed services, TAMP eligible individuals and dependents of members who died while serving on active duty.
2. Retired members and their dependents and the dependents of members who died while in a retired status.
3. Former Spouses. See CHAMPUS eligibility section for details.
4. All others, to include cabinet and secretarial designees.

Determinations made by the commander of the medical facility, or a designee, as to the availability of space and facilities and the capabilities of the professional staff shall be conclusive. A dependent will not be denied care on the basis of service affiliation or assignment of the sponsor or on the basis of location of the residence of the dependents.

Care Authorized Dependents in Uniformed Services Facilities

Dependents are eligible for the following types of care in uniformed services facilities, based on availability:

• Inpatient care, including services and supplies normally furnished by the hospital.
• Outpatient care and services.
• Drugs — prescriptions written by either Uniformed Services or civilian physicians are filled at Uniformed Services Facilities subject to availability of pharmaceuticals, consistent with control procedures and applicable laws.
• Treatment of medical and surgical conditions.
• Physical examinations, including eye examinations, and hearing evaluation, and all other tests and procedures necessary for a complete physical examination.
• Maternity (obstetrical) and infant care, routine care and examinations of newborn infant and well-baby care.
• Family planning services and supplies, including counseling and guidance. These services and supplies will be provided where available in accordance with sound medical practice to any dependent upon request.
• Diagnostic tests and services, including laboratory and X-ray examinations.
• Dental care may be provided outside the U.S. Within the U.S., routine dental care may be provided only at installations which have been specifically authorized to provide such care. At installations within the U.S. not authorized to provide dental care, dental care is limited to:
  a. Emergency dental or oral care.
  b. Dental care, deemed necessary as an adjunct to medical or surgical treatment of disease, condition, or injury.
  c. The taking of diagnostic x-rays.
  d. Consultant Services.
• Government ambulance service, surface or air, to transport dependents to, from, or between medical facilities when determined by the medical officer in charge to be medically necessary.
• Artificial limbs and artificial eyes, including initial issue, fitting, repair replacement, and adjustment.

UNIFORMED SERVICES ALMANAC

- Durable equipment, such as wheelchairs and hospital beds on a loan basis.
- Orthopedic braces (except orthopedic footwear), crutches, walking irons, elastic stockings, and similar orthopedic aids.
- Immunizations.

Care Not Authorized

Dependents shall not be provided the following types of care in uniformed services facilities:

- Domiciliary or custodial care.
- Prosthetic devices (other than artificial limbs and eyes), hearing aids, orthopedic footwear, spectacles or lenses, except that in overseas locations and in certain CONUS locations, the Secretary of Defense may authorize the sale of such items at government cost.

Supplemental Care

A Medical Treatment Facility (MTF) may use its supplemental care funds to purchase civilian care for any entitled beneficiary. When the care is beyond the capability of the MTF, the command may choose to disengage from care.

This means that the MTF is transferring the medical cognizance of the case to a civilian provider and the costs of this care may be borne by CHAMPUS, Medicare, or other third party insurance carriers. The selection of the alternate health care provider is ordinarily left to the patient but may be imposed on the patient, if the medical condition warrants special consideration.

Cooperative Care

When the patient requires services or equipment from civilian sources which are not available in the military facility, the facility Commander is authorized to refer CHAMPUS-eligible patients for civilian services or equipment, while retaining primary control of the patient under a plan called Cooperative Care. This is a plan which permits CHAMPUS to complement the uniformed services direct care system. CHAMPUS will share the cost of many services and equipment obtained from civilian sources by CHAMPUS eligible-patients who remain under the primary control of the military facility. The Cooperative Care Plan is designed to optimize the utilization of limited military facility capacity, while at the same time reducing cost to the patient. Formerly, when services or equipment which are currently included under Cooperative Care were required by a CHAMPUS-eligible patient, but not available in a military facility, the patient was transferred totally to the care of a civilian physician or facility, thus requiring the patient to share the cost of the needed service or equipment and physician's services. Cooperative Care reduces the cost to the patient by eliminating the cost of physicians' services.

The following types of care may be obtained from civilian sources on an inpatient or outpatient basis as part of Cooperative Care:

- Authorized nondiagnostic medical services such as physical therapy, occupational therapy (on an inpatient basis only), speech therapy, (limited) radiation therapy, and private duty (special) nursing care in the home.
- Pre-authorized adjunctive dental care, including orthodontia related to surgical correction of a cleft palate.
- Durable medical equipment if the equipment is not available on a loan basis from a uniformed service medical treatment facility.

UNIFORMED SERVICES ALMANAC

- Limited prosthetic devices, orthopedic braces and appliances.
- Covered optical devices, such as postsurgical cataract lenses.
- Civilian ambulance transportation to a uniformed service hospital, provided the transportation is ordered by someone other than personnel of the uniformed services' direct care system.
- All care under the CHAMPUS Program for the Handicapped (active duty families only).
- Psychotherapeutic/psychiatric care.

Cooperative Care claims are subject to the same rules and regulations as any other CHAMPUS claims. If a service/supply is not covered under CHAMPUS, the beneficiary is responsible for payment.

Services and Supplies *Not* Covered Under Cooperative Care

The Uniformed Services assume responsibility for the following types of medical care given by civilian sources to patients under the control of the uniformed services.

- Consultations
- Diagnostic testing, including CT Scans and genetic testing, required to arrive at a diagnosis or determine appropriate treatment.
- Prescription drugs.
- Medical supplies.
- Oxygen.
- Civilian ambulance service to a military hospital when the ambulance is ordered by authorized personnel at that hospital; and from a military hospital, regardless of who orders it.

Cross-Utilization of Medical Facilities

To provide effective cross-utilization of medical facilities of the uniformed services, dependents, regardless of the service affiliation of their sponsor, shall be given equal opportunity for care. Dependents may request and be furnished medical care at the medical facility of the uniformed service serving the area in which they reside or in the medical facility of the sponsor's own service depending upon the capability of the medical facilities concerned.

Charges

When health benefits are provided in facilities of the uniformed services, patients pay the following charges:

1. *Inpatient Care* —
   Active Duty Enlisted .... No Charge
   Active Duty Officer $4.75/day
   Active Duty Families and
   Retirees and their families $9.70/day

There is no charge for newborns when the mother is a patient.

2. *Outpatient Care* — No Charge.

Handicapped Dependents

Eligibility for benefits under the Program for the Handicapped terminates when the sponsor's active duty status ends with one exception. Surviving children and spouses of service members who die while eligible for receipt of hostile fire pay or from a disease or injury incurred while eligible for such pay, receiving benefits under the program at the time of the sponsor's death, continue to receive benefits until they pass their 21st birthday or their status as dependents terminates, whichever occurs first.

UNIFORMED SERVICES ALMANAC
TRANSPORTATION OF DEPENDENT PATIENTS

Transportation Authorized

If a dependent accompanying a member of the uniformed services requires medical attention which is not available in the locality, transportation of the dependent at the expense of the United States Government is authorized to the nearest appropriate facility in which adequate medical care is available. On his or her recovery or when it is administratively determined that the patient should be moved from the medical facility, the dependent may be transported at Government expense to the duty station of the member or to such other place determined to be appropriate under the circumstances. If a dependent is unable to travel unattended, roundtrip transportation and travel expenses may be furnished for necessary attendants. When Government transportation is not available, commercial transportation may be utilized for the transportation authorized.

Transportation is not authorized for elective surgery.

CONTINUED HEALTH CARE BENEFIT PROGRAM

NOTE: The U.S. V.I.P. program ended on Sept. 30, 1994 (policyholders got to keep their existing U.S. V.I.P. policies until expiration). On Oct. 1, 1994, the Defense Department replaced U.S. V.I.P. with the Continued Health Care Benefit Program (CHCBP).

CHCBP provides benefits similar to CHAMPUS for a specific period of time (18-36 months) to former servicemembers and their family members, unremarried former military spouses, emancipated children, and children placed with a member or former member for the purpose of adoption or legal custody. Benefits are like those in the basic CHAMPUS program.

Eligible persons must enroll in CHCBP within 60 days after separation from active duty or loss of eligibility for military health care. The Defense Department utilizes a civilian third party administrator (TPA) to provide administrative support for the program, including marketing, enrollment and DEERS updates. The TPA operates a toll free telephone line 24 hours daily for interested beneficiaries to call and direct questions and request an information package. They can be reached at 1-800-809-6119. Applications for enrollment into the CHCBP must be accompanied by a check for the first three months' coverage along with proof of eligibility. Upon acceptance, the TPA will send a letter of acceptance along with an ID card, which will serve as proof of enrollment when a person seeks care.

For more information about the CHCBP contact the TPA at the toll free number. Additionally, contact your Health Benefits Advisor for more specific benefit details, or for general information prior to separation, contact your military personnel and transition office.

TRICARE ACTIVE DUTY FAMILY MEMBER DENTAL PLAN

The Defense Department's TRICARE Active Duty Family Member Dental Plan is a voluntary program, which offers diagnostic, preventative, restorative, endodontic, periodontic, removable or fixed prosthodentic, orthodontia and oral surgery care to the enrolled families of **active-duty sponsors** in the seven uniformed services. Sponsors of enrolled families pay a small monthly premium by payroll deduction. The care is provided by civilian dentists. Claims are filed, either by the dentists or by the families who receive the dental care, with the civilian contractor who operates the dental plan for the services.

The TRICARE Active Duty Family Member Dental Plan is *not* a CHAMPUS program. It has nothing to do with any medical care-related dental treatment that may be provided to CHAMPUS-eligible persons under the CHAMPUS basic program. Nevertheless, active duty personnel and their dependents must be enrolled in DEERS to be eligible to participate in the TRICARE Active Duty Family Member Dental Plan.

It is a supplemental dental program for active duty dependents established by Congress.

The military family currently pays $6.77 for single coverage and $16.92 for family coverage. The government cost share of the premium is 60%.

For more information about the TRICARE Active Duty Family Member Dental Plan, contact your nearest military personnel office for questions about enrollment. For questions about benefits under the dental plan, contact your military personnel office, or your nearest Health Benefits Advisor. Or, call or write the following civilian contractor: United Concordia Companies, FMDP Customer Services, P.O. Box 898218, Camp Hill, PA 17089-8218. Telephone: 1-800-866-8499.

The TRICARE Active Duty Family Member Dental Plan is available throughout CONUS, Alaska, Hawaii, Canada, Puerto Rico, Virgin Islands and Guam.

To get claim forms, contact your Health Benefits Advisor or United Concordia.

United Concordia mails copies of its "Benefits booklet" to all enrolled families. Copies are mailed to the most recent sponsor address on file with DEERS. If active duty families did not receive a copy, it can be requested from United Concordia at the addresses listed above.

CIVILIAN HEALTH AND MEDICAL PROGRAM OF THE UNIFORMED SERVICES (CHAMPUS)

Department of Defense Instruction 6010.8-R, implemented June 1, 1977, and revised July 1, 1991 established uniform policy which provided appropriate criteria and established standards for the application of CHAMPUS.

Eligibility for Civilian Health Benefits

The following persons are entitled to civilian health benefits under CHAMPUS (Note: Active duty service members are not eligible for CHAMPUS benefits.):

1. Spouses and eligible children of:

   a. Members of the uniformed services, including reservists and guard personnel who are ordered to active duty for more than 30 days.

   b. Members of the uniformed services who died while serving on active duty.

   c. Retired members of the uniformed services entitled to retired, retainer, or equivalent pay or who died while in such a status. (This includes "Gray Area" reservists enrolled in RCSBP, who die prior to reaching age 60. Entitlement begins on date reservist would have reached age 60.)

   d. North Atlantic Treaty Organization (NATO) nation representatives who are in the U.S. on official business. (Outpatient benefits only.)

2. Retired members of the uniformed services who are entitled to retired, retainer, or equivalent pay.

UNIFORMED SERVICES ALMANAC

Retired members and their spouses and children and the spouses and children of deceased members who become eligible for hospital insurance benefits under Medicare Hospital Insurance benefits at any age lose eligibility for all types of civilian care under CHAMPUS. Individuals in this category retain eligibility for care in uniformed services facilities, even after age 65.

3. If you're eligible for Medicare because of disability and are under age 65, CHAMPUS-eligible persons retain eligibility for CHAMPUS if enrolled in Medicare Part B. CHAMPUS becomes second payor to Medicare.

4. *In addition to the categories of CHAMPUS-eligible persons listed above, Congress has granted eligibility for limited periods of CHAMPUS benefits to several categories of former active-duty service members and their eligible family members. Here's a list of the benefit periods and those who qualify for them:*

Up to 30 days, or until covered by any employer-sponsored health plan (whichever occurs earlier), following release from active duty for (1) Guard/Reserve members who were activated in connection with Operation Desert Storm, and their dependents; (2) Military members activated in connection with Operation Desert Storm who are subject to voluntary or involuntary "stop-loss" procedures, and their dependents. "Stop-loss" refers to the services' policy, begun during the Persian Gulf war, of keeping persons on active duty who would otherwise have been able to leave active service.

Sixty days for Department of Defense military members who were on active duty on or after Sept. 30, 1990, and who are involuntarily separated with fewer than six years of active service, and their dependents. The involuntary separation must occur during the seven-year period beginning Oct. 1, 1990.

One hundred-twenty days for Department of Defense military members who were on active duty on or after Sept. 30, 1990, and who are involuntarily separated with fewer than six years of active service, and their dependents. The involuntary separation must occur during the seven-year period beginning Oct. 1, 1990. One hundred twenty days for Department of Defense military members who are voluntarily separated under the Special Separation Benefit (SSB) and Voluntary Separation Incentive (VSI).

5. A former spouse of an active, retired, or deceased member may be eligible for health care in a uniformed service medical facility or under CHAMPUS if the former spouse falls into one of the following categories:

a. Must have been married to the service member for *at least 20 years, 20 of which* were while the member was on active duty (or active reserve status creditable toward retirement), and the divorce or annulment must have been final *on or after February 1, 1983*. Persons in this category are eligible for CHAMPUS benefits until age 65. This is the original category of eligibility that was established in 1983.

b. Must have been married to the service member for *at least 20 years, 20 of which* were spent on active duty (or active reserve status creditable toward retirement), and the divorce or annulment was final *before* February 1, 1983. Persons in this category are covered indefinitely, but only for care received *on or after January 1, 1985.*

c. Must have been married to the service member for *at least 20 years,* but *only 15 (but less than 20)* of those years must have been while the member was on active duty (or active reserve status creditable toward retirement). The divorce or annulment may have been made final at any time *before* April 1, 1985. Persons in this category are eligible for CHAMPUS benefits indefinitely, but only for care received *on or after January 1, 1985* or the date of the decree, whichever is later.

d. Must have been married to the service member for *at least 20 years,* but *only 15 (but less than 20)* of those years must have been spent on active duty (or active reserve status creditable toward retirement), and the divorce or annulment was made final *on or after April 1, 1985,* but before September 29, 1988. CHAMPUS eligibility for former spouses in this category will end on the last day of the two-year period beginning on the date of the final divorce decree. If the date of the final decree of divorce or annulment was on or after September 29, 1988, the former spouse is eligible only for care received for one year from the date of the decree.

The former spouse must also:

a. Not have been married since the divorce or annulment.

b. Have been married to the military member for at least 20 years on the date the divorce or annulment becomes final; and during the marriage, the member must have completed *20 years* of service which counts or will be counted toward retired pay eligibility.

c. Not be covered by an employer-sponsored health care plan. (If the former spouse cancels the employer-sponsored health coverage, eligibility for CHAMPUS and the rest of the Uniformed Services Health Benefits Program may be restored.)

Former spouses who meet all of the above requirements are eligible for all CHAMPUS benefits, except the Program for the Handicapped. They cannot count the annual deductible of their former military spouse toward their own CHAMPUS deductible. They pay CHAMPUS cost-share at the same rate as retired military family members — even if the former spouse was married to an active duty service member. For CHAMPUS to cost-share medical care, a former spouse must have a valid ID card issued by the nearest personnel office of their former spouse's service. The ID card must show the former spouse's eligibility for CHAMPUS. When the former spouses become eligible for Medicare (Part A) at age 65, they lose their CHAMPUS eligibility, but they are still eligible for medical care in military hospitals or clinics.

Non-Availability Statement Requirements

All users of CHAMPUS, except those with other primary coverage health care plans, who live within certain zip code zones located near a uniformed service military treatment facility (MTF) must first seek non-emergency inpatient care there before being eligible for care at a civilian facility. In many cases, the zip code zones extend further than the old 40-mile radius borders. If the uniformed service hospital does not have the proper facilities or professional capability to provide the type of medical care required, a Nonavailability Statement (NAS) is filed electronically which will entitle the user to apply for CHAMPUS benefits. **Families who live approximately 35 to 60 miles from an MTF, will have to check with the Health Benefits Advisor (HBA) at the nearest MTF to see if their homes fall within the zip code boundaries. Those persons with other primary coverage health care plans do not need to obtain an NAS, because CHAMPUS is, by law, second pay to all other types of health insurance except MEDICAID and CHAMPUS supplement plans. Members should always try to use an MTF or PRIMUS/ NAVCARE clinic before using CHAMPUS. This can save you money and paperwork.**

UNIFORMED SERVICES ALMANAC

CHAMPUS beneficiaries living in military treatment facility (MTF) and Uniform Service Treatment Facility (USTF) catchment areas (generally a 40-mile radius of the MTF) may be required to obtain an outpatient nonavailability statement from the MTF in order for claims to be paid (See page 124 for listing of USTF hospitals and centers). Certain outpatient procedures have been selected that require a nonavailability statement before claims may be paid. These procedures are generally for outpatient surgery or for certain high cost procedures which may be available in the MTF. These procedures include: certain hernia repairs; removal of tonsils or adenoids; breast mass or tumor removal; cataract removal; D&C; arthroscopy; and others. Beneficiaries who require outpatient surgery or other high cost outpatient procedures who live in MTF or USTF catchment area are strongly advised to contact the MTF prior to receiving the outpatient service to determine if an NAS is required.

The zip code restriction rule affects non-emergency inpatient hospital care and some outpatient procedures and does not affect users requiring emergency inpatient care, most outpatient care from a private doctor, or persons living outside the zip code limit. Outpatient nonavailability statements are generally not needed overseas. Outside the 50 states, a 40 mile radius is still used to determine if an NAS is required for inpatient care.

Health Benefits Authorized from Civilian Sources.

Authorized health benefits from civilian sources include but are not limited to the following:

- Hospitalization, including necessary services and supplies furnished by the hospital.
- Outpatient care.
- Drugs and medicines obtainable only by prescription and insulin for a known diabetic.
- Treatment of medical and surgical conditions including ambulatory surgery.
- Treatment of nervous, mental, and chronic conditions. CHAMPUS helps pay for psychotherapy, either in the hospital or on an outpatient basis. If your provider of health care believes you need more than five psychotherapy sessions a week in the hospital, or more than two psychotherapy sessions a week as an outpatient, a CHAMPUS contractor must review the medical necessity for the care. Also, if you need more than 23 outpatient psychotherapy sessions in a fiscal year (Oct 1 - Sept 30), approval is required. The sessions cannot simply be counseling sessions, such as for people who are undergoing marital or family difficulties. They must be for treatment of a mental disorder that has a medical diagnosis.

Before getting mental health care, be sure to check with your HBA because approval may be required. Also, certain reviews and paperwork must be completed at various points during mental health care for CHAMPUS to share the bills.

Inpatient care is limited to: (1) 30 days per fiscal year for patients aged 19 or older; (2) 45 days for patients under 19; (3) 150 days for inpatient care in residential treatment centers, unless CHAMPUS grants a waiver for extraordinary medical or psychological reasons. The limits do not apply to: (a) services provided under the Program for the Handicapped; or (b) mental health services provided as partial hospitalization, which is limited to 60 days of treatment per fiscal year, except for alcohol rehabilitation, which is limited to 21 days per 365-day period.

Some outpatient procedures for which NASs may be required are: certain hernia repairs; breast mass or tumor removal, nose repair (rhinoplasty — changing noseshape); removal of tonsils or adenoids; cataract removal; strabismus repair (surgery to lengthen or shorten muscles that help the eyes to function together); dilation and curettage (widening of the cervical canal and scraping the uterine cavity); gynecological laparoscopy (use of an instrument called a laproscope to examine female reproductive organs in the abdomen; upper GI endoscopy (visual exam of the interior of the upper gastrointestinal tract); myringoformy tympanostomy (incision of the tympanic membrane in the ear to relieve pressure and drain the middle ear. Includes placement of tubes in the ear to aid drainage); litigation or transaction of the fallopian tubes; arthroscopy (use of an instrument to visually examine the interior of a joint); cystoscopy (use of an instrument to examine interior of the bladder); neuroplasty (decompression or freeing of nerves from scar tissue).

Other health care benefits from civilian sources include: (Check with Health Benefits Advisor (HBA) for details and coverage limits.)

- Mammograms and pap smears with certain rules on frequency.
- Limited coverage for BIOFEEDBACK.
- Treatment of contagious diseases.
- Treatment of alcoholism. **Note:** Persons who have questions regarding CHAMPUS coverage of alcoholism treatment and admission standards for children with mental disorders who may require treatment at residential treatment centers should consult a health benefits advisor or with their CHAMPUS claims processor.
- Hospice care.
- Limited treatment for surgical implants.
- Treatment of morbid obesity.
- Cardiac Rehabilitation.
- Drug Abuse. See treatment of Mental Health Coverage.
- Plastic or reconstructive surgery.
- Well baby care for children up to two years of age.
- Speech therapy and treatment for hearing impaired. Under certain limited circumstances, CHAMPUS will help pay for speech therapy when the speech problem is caused by certain diseases or illness.
- Maternity (obstetrical) and infant care including prenatal care, delivery, postnatal care, treatment of complications of pregnancy, and inpatient care for the newborn infant.
- Private duty (special) nursing when the hospital does not have an intensive care unit.
- Family planning services including medical care, counseling and guidance. Also includes surgical procedures to produce sterilization provided such procedures are consistent with the medical and legal standards of practice in the applicable jurisdiction. Also genetic testing performed in certain high-risk situations.
- Diagnostic tests, including laboratory and X-ray examinations, when rendered in connection with a specific diagnosis or definitive set of symptoms. CT and MRI scans are authorized under certain diagnostic conditions.
- Dental care, required as a necessary adjunct to medical or surgical treatment of a primary condition other than dental. When hospitalized for non-adjunctive dental care, hospital charges and fees for professional services required because of hospitalization are also payable, but the fees of the

dentist are not payable. Adjunctive dental care must be preauthorized by the CHAMPUS Claims Processor for dental claims.
- Non-governmental local ambulance service to and from a hospital when medically necessary.
- Eye examinations, one per year, for active-duty family members only.
- Artificial limbs and eyes.
- Durable medical equipment, such as wheelchairs, and hospital beds on a rental or purchase basis. CHAMPUS can share the cost of equipment, such as wheelchairs or respirators, when it is cheaper than leasing or renting these items. Persons should check with their CHAMPUS claims processor before committing themselves to renting or buying durable medical equipment.
- Medical equipment and supplies ordered by the attending physician, or by other professional persons whose services were ordered by a physician, except those specifically excluded by law.
- Anesthetics and oxygen and their administration.
- Blood transfusions, including the cost of blood and blood plasma except when donated or replaced, and blood plasma expanders.
- Radiation therapy, physical therapy, occupational therapy (on an inpatient basis only), inhalation therapy, chemotherapy, shock therapy, and hemodialysis.
- Orthopedic braces (except orthopedic shoes) and crutches.
- Home calls when medically necessary.
- Funding for abortions is prohibited except where the life of the mother is endangered. For details regarding exceptions, contact the nearest Health Benefits Advisor.
- Organ transplants. Transplantation must be done at a CHAMPUS-approved organ transplant center. Transplants are approved for cornea, kidney, liver, liver-kidney, lung, heart-lung, and bone marrow for certain diagnoses. There are many limitations imposed on transplant approvals, so that one must check with the CHAMPUS claims processor for details.
- One screening for blood lead level in infants is allowed under CHAMPUS or in a military hospital.
- Home health care for active-duty servicemembers and deceased active duty members' families in the United States. This is part of a test program. Servicemembers desiring to take part in the program may direct their request to CHAMPUS Program Office of Home Health Care, Aurora, CO, 80045-6900.
- With respect to authorized services of a physician; doctor of optometry when practicing within the scope of his license; doctors of podiatry or surgical chiropody; qualified clinical psychologist; certified nurse midwives; and, when ordered and supervised by a physician as essential for the proper care and treatment of the patient, services of other professional personnel — which includes but not limited to physical therapists, nurse anesthetists, speech therapists, speech pathologists, audiologists, psychiatric and/or clinical social workers, occupational therapists, nurses, licensed midwives, and similar practitioners. Certified nurse midwives may provide services independent of a physician. CHAMPUS pays nurse practitioners directly as individual providers of care if they meet certain professional standards. CHAMPUS does not recognize "physician assistants or extenders" for payment under CHAMPUS as independent providers of care.

UNIFORMED SERVICES ALMANAC

Health Benefits Not Authorized from Civilian Sources

A number of services and treatments are not covered or authorized under CHAMPUS including some of the following. Consult your HBA before getting treatment if you have any questions.
- Abortions except in very limited circumstances.
- Acupuncture
- Artificial insemination, or any forms of artificial conception
- Autopsy or post mortem
- Aversion therapy in connection with alcoholism
- Bed-wetting correctional devices
- Birth control for which you do not need a doctor's prescription. But CHAMPUS will cost-share some kinds of birth control.
- Camps such as camps for diabetes or obese people
- Care or supplies furnished or prescribed by a person in the immediate family
- Chiropractors and naturopaths.
- Christian Science "absent treatment," also called "treatment through prayer and spiritual means," in which the patient is not physically present when the Christian Science service is rendered.
- Cosmetic, plastic or reconstructive surgery
- Custodial Care in an institution or at home. Custodial care is taking care of someone's daily needs such as eating, dressing or a place to sleep, as opposed to someone's medical needs. Some aspects of the care may be covered, such as limited specific skilled nursing services, prescription medicines and up to 12 physician visits per calendar year. Medically necessary care for an inpatient in a hospital is covered, even if the person's condition is considered "custodial." This can be a gray area, so check with your HBA if you have questions.
- Dental care and dental x-rays except as provided elsewhere.
- Education or training.
- Electrolysis.
- Experimental procedures such as radial keratotomy.
- Eyeglasses and contact lenses except under very limited circumstances, such as corneal lens removal.
- Food, food substitutes or supplements, or vitamins outside of a hospital except for home parenteral nutrition therapy such as prescribed for cancer patients.
- Foot care except when there's a medical problem or injury.
- Genetic tests not ordered by a doctor and under certain other conditions.
- Hearing aids except under the Program for the Handicapped.
- Hearing examinations unless in connection with surgery or some medical problem, or under the Program for the Handicapped.
- Megavitamins and orthomolecular psychiatric therapy.
- Mind expansion or elective psychotherapy (for example: Erhard Seminar Training (EST); transcendental meditation; and Z-therapy).
- Orthodontia except in limited cases, such as when related to the surgical correction of a cleft palate.
- Orthopedic shoes and arch supports, except when part of a brace.
- Preventive care such as school or annual physical, except for well-baby care.
- Private hospital rooms unless the doctor orders it for medical reasons, or a semiprivate room is not available. Hospitals that are subject to

CHAMPUS' new diagnosis-related groups (DRG) payment system may provide the patient with a private room but will still only receive the standard DRG amount. If a patient asks for a private room the hospital can bill the patient for the extra charges.
- Rest cure.
- Retirement homes.
- Runaway child treatment except under special circumstances.
- Sex changes.
- Speech therapy except when related to a specific illness or injury.
- Supplemental diagnostic services, such as laboratory tests, x-rays exams, pathological exams and machine tests that produce hard-copy results, that are requested by the attending military hospital physician, and are performed by a civilian provider of these services. The military hospital pays for such services.
- Sexual inadequacy treatment.
- Surgical sterilization reversals.
- Telephone services or advice including remote monitoring and consultation, except for transtelephonic monitoring of pacemakers.
- Weight control or weight reduction services and supplies are not covered, except for certain surgical procedures when specific conditions have been met.

Rules for the Provision of Health Benefits

1. *Physician* means a professionally qualified doctor of medicine or doctor of osteopathy who is licensed to provide the medical care for which payment is requested at the time and place the care is provided.

2. *Hospital Accommodations* — Hospitalization normally will be provided in semiprivate accommodations. A private room is an allowable benefit only when medically indicated or when it is the only type of room available.

3. *Outpatient Care Incident to Maternity Cases* — All care received during and for a pregnancy that results in hospitalization shall be treated for payment purposes as part of that hospitalization.

4. *Long-Term Care* — Such care is subjected to peer review every 30 days, to determine whether it should be continued. Requests for inpatient mental health care beyond 30 or 45 days in a year, should be sent to: Health Management Strategies International, Inc., CHAMPUS/CHAMPVA Division, 1725 Duke St., Suite 300C, Alexandria, VA 22314 (1-800-242-6764).

5. *Professional Services* — Payment of the Government's portion of charges for professional services is authorized as follows:

   a. Payment of physicians, including necessary consultants, doctors of optometry, and qualified clinical psychologists will be made on the basis of the reasonable charge for service provided.

   b. Payment of private duty nurses will be made on the basis of the reasonable charge for the service provided when the attending physician certifies that such services were required for the proper care and treatment of the patient but only if the hospital has no intensive care unit.

   c. Payment of other professional persons will be made on the basis of reasonable charge for the service provided when the services were ordered by the attending physician.

6. *Drugs* — In the United States and Puerto Rico, payment for drugs is based on the acquisition cost of the drug plus an established professional fee schedule. In other areas, the standard charge in the locality concerned will be used as a guide in determining the amount payable.

7. *Patients Who Lose Entitlements to Health Benefits* — In the case of a dependent or retired member who is receiving health benefits under CHAMPUS at the time entitlement to receive such benefits ceases, the Government's responsibility for payment ceases as of midnight of the date entitlement ceases.

Participation in CHAMPUS

Participation in CHAMPUS is voluntary for the physician or any other source of medical care, except that all hospitals participating in MEDICARE and hospital-based professionals which are employed by or contracted to such hospitals, must also participate in CHAMPUS for inpatient hospital services, pursuant to admissions to hospitals occurring on or after January 1, 1987 (PL 99-514, Section 1895 B(6). A physician or other source of care participates in CHAMPUS when he or she provides authorized services, signs, and submits a CHAMPUS claim.

The claim form the physician or other source of care signs contains a certification that, except for the percentage payable by the patient under CHAMPUS, the amount paid by the Government will be accepted as payment in full for the service and/or supplies listed on the form. Also, the beneficiary/sponsor is still responsible for charges which are above the allowed amount of any non-covered services.

Once a physician or other source accepts a patient as a beneficiary of CHAMPUS, and agrees to submit a claim directly by signing the claim form, the patient does not have to pay more than his or her share of costs as described in the section below under *DRG Hospital Payment Rules*.

For these reasons, except in true emergency cases, a beneficiary should confirm in advance of receiving care that the physician or other source of care will participate in CHAMPUS. Health Benefits Advisors sometimes maintain lists of local providers who have agreed to participate, but these providers may decide to participate or not to participate on a case-by-case basis.

Patients should not pay for authorized benefits received from participating providers of care except that portion of the charges which is their responsibility. However, when patients do pay more than their share of the charges or when they obtain services from a nonparticipating source of care, they may submit a claim for reimbursement of the applicable percentage of the reasonable charges that would have been paid to the provider of care had the provider of care submitted a claim. CHAMPUS will share costs based on the reasonable charges for the local areas in which the services were provided. These charges may be less than the provider's actual charges.

Providers of care who don't participate in CHAMPUS (also called "accepting CHAMPUS assignment") are limited in how much they can bill CHAMPUS patients.

For services provided on or after Nov. 1, 1993, the law says that providers who don't participate may bill CHAMPUS patients no more than 115 percent of the CHAMPUS allowable charge for a particular service. The 115 percent limit is the same as that used by Medicare.

Providers who don't comply with the limit on charges could lose their status as authorized providers of care under CHAMPUS. CHAMPUS-eligible persons who seek care from non-participating providers, and who believe that such a provider has over charged for care, may contact the appropriate CHAMPUS claims processing contractor, or may write to: OCHAMPUS, Office of Program Integrity, Aurora, CO 80045-6900.

Some people mistakenly believe that the government is supposed to pay all of the medical bills of the families of military members. This idea just won't go away, despite the fact that only active-duty service members are guaranteed free medical care. There's nothing anywhere in the law making CHAMPUS or any other government agency responsible for dependents' medical bills.

Legal responsibility for such charges rests solely with the patient (or the patient's parents or legal guardian).

CHAMPUS is a cost-sharing program whose job is to process claims as quickly and accurately as possible. But if a CHAMPUS claim is not filed, or if it is lost, mishandled or denied, the patient is still responsible for the bill. If a bill is not paid, it's the patient — not CHAMPUS — who could be sued.

The Defense Department has reduced some CHAMPUS maximum allowable payments to physicians and other individual professional providers (including clinical laboratories), to more closely match Medicare fees.

For services rendered on or after Nov. 1, 1993, medical procedures for which the prior year's national CHAMPUS Maximum Allowable Charge (CMAC) exceed the Medicare fee will be reduced by the lesser of: (1) the amount by which it exceeds the Medicare fee; or (2) fifteen percent.

If CHAMPUS payment is delayed for any reason, it might be advisable to go ahead and pay bills, especially small ones, even if you can only make partial monthly payments. Most creditors will accept these arrangements, and the laws in some states protect people from collections and harassment in such cases.

DRG Hospital Payment Rules

Under CHAMPUS' Diagnosis-Related Groups (DRG) Payment system, most hospitals in 49 states, the District of Columbia, and Puerto Rico, will be paid a fixed rate for inpatient services, regardless of how much the care actually costs. Maryland is currently exempt from the DRG payment system.

The DRG amounts paid for inpatient services are based generally on national averages of costs for specific services. The fixed amount that CHAMPUS pays to a hospital under the DRG system may be either more or less than a specific hospital charges for a given service.

(NOTE: Individual doctors' fees for services they provide aren't paid by DRG amounts. And, some hospitals even within the so-called "DRG states" are also exempt from DRG payment limits. These hospitals are: psychiatric, cancer, long-term care, and sole community hospitals exempt from Medicare. The new payment system also doesn't affect certain services, such as kidney-acquisition costs, heart and liver transplants, cystic fibrosis treatment for patients under 18, and children who test positive for the HIV (AIDS) virus. Additionally, Christian Science sanatoria and distinct parts of a hospital providing psychiatric and rehabilitation services, would not be affected. In non-DRG hospitals, CHAMPUS will pay as before.

Families of active-duty members pay at least $25 for each admission, or a small daily fee for each day in a civilian hospital — whichever total is *greater*. The daily fee, which is the same charged for inpatient care at military hospitals changes over time. (For 1996 the daily fee is $9.70.) But no matter how short your hospital stay, *you must pay at least $25*. CHAMPUS pays the rest of your covered inpatient bills, if all providers participate in CHAMPUS.

UNIFORMED SERVICES ALMANAC

Retirees, their families, the families of service members who have died, and some former spouses of service members, will pay the *lesser* of 25 percent of the billed charges or a fixed daily amount ($330 in Fiscal Year 1996). CHAMPUS will pay the rest of your covered hospital bills.

All families also pay in full for any care that is not covered by CHAMPUS.

Annual Deductible. For outpatient care, there is an annual deductible of $150 per fiscal year, if benefits are claimed for one eligible beneficiary or $300 if benefits are claimed for two or more eligible family members. These deductibles apply to Grades E-5 and above. The deductible for family members of active duty E-4s and below is $50 for an individual and $100 for the entire family. After the deductible has been met, dependents of active duty members are required to pay 20% of the allowable charges for authorized outpatient services and retired members and their dependents and the dependents of deceased members are required to pay 25% of the allowable charges.

CHAMPUS claims forms should be sent to the CHAMPUS claims processor as soon as possible after care is received. The claims forms must be received **within one year of the date the health care or services were received** or, in the case of inpatient care, the claim must be filed within one year of the date the patient is discharged from the inpatient facility.

The old rules still apply to services provided before the end of 1993. Claims for these services must be in the hands of the proper CHAMPUS contractor by Dec. 31 of the year after the year in which the services were provided. In other words, for treatment or services provided any time during 1993, you must get the claim to the CHAMPUS contractor by the end of 1994.

If you or a family member received care in more than one state and are sending claims to more than one CHAMPUS processor, you should include the EOB form sent by one claims processor to any other processor receiving a claim.

Losing CHAMPUS Eligibility

Military members and retirees are pretty well informed about their CHAMPUS eligibility but may not be aware of the ways they can lose it. Here's how it can happen:

• When you turn 65. That's when most people lose CHAMPUS and gain Medicare eligibility. As a general rule, you don't have a choice; it will happen. You usually can't have both CHAMPUS and Medicare at the same time, and you can't reject one in favor of the other.

The only time a retiree doesn't lose CHAMPUS eligibility at age 65 is if he's not eligible for Medicare, Part A (hospital services) in which case you must file a Social Security Administration Notice of Disallowance certifying your lack of Medicare eligibility with the uniformed service that issues your ID card, so they can issue you an ID card that shows CHAMPUS eligibility. You should also be sure you're entered in the DEERS files as CHAMPUS-eligible.

• If you're eligible for Medicare because of disability, CHAMPUS-eligible persons retain eligibility for CHAMPUS. CHAMPUS becomes second payor to Medicare.

• If a retiree's status changes. If a retiree ceases to be eligible for retired pay, that person and his dependents lose their CHAMPUS eligibility as of the end of the day on which the eligibility for retired pay stops.

• By divorce or annulment. When a marriage ends by divorce or annulment, the spouse's eligibility ends at the end of the day on which the divorce or annulment becomes final — unless the former spouse meets

several requirements which allow him or her to keep CHAMPUS eligibility, either indefinitely or for a specified period.
- Contact your health benefits advisor for details on how former military spouses may remain eligible for CHAMPUS benefits. The eligibility of any children of the military couple is not affected by a divorce or annulment.
- If you're a widow or widower who remarries. As the widow or widower, if you marry a person whose dependents are not eligible for CHAMPUS, your eligibility ends the day after you remarry. However, your child who was the stepchild of the deceased member at the time of death still has the same CHAMPUS eligibility as other CHAMPUS-eligible children. If your new marriage ends for any reason, you can't get your CHAMPUS eligibility back.
- The child of a military couple has several ways you can lose CHAMPUS eligibility: by getting married; by turning 21; by being an unadopted stepchild when a divorce occurs. If you're the stepchild of a military sponsor, and the sponsor's marriage ends in divorce before you are legally adopted by the sponsor, your CHAMPUS eligibility ends when the marriage ends.

By being adopted by someone other than your military sponsor if the sponsor is still living. If you're the child of a living sponsor, and you're legally adopted by another person whose dependents are not eligible for CHAMPUS, you lose your eligibility at the beginning of the day after the day on which the adoption becomes final. But, you don't lose eligibility if you're adopted by someone else after your military sponsor has died.

Some family members of abusive military sponsors may be able to keep limited CHAMPUS eligibility under certain conditions.

If the sponsor is court-martialed and separated from active service for an offense involving physical or emotional abuse, the abused spouse or child is entitled to CHAMPUS benefits for care related to the abuse, for up to one year after the sponsor's separation from the service.

Effective for care received on or after Oct. 23, 1992, CHAMPUS benefits may be retained by the spouse (or former spouse) or child or a retirement-eligible active-duty member, or a retired service member whose eligibility for retired pay has been ended because of misconduct toward a spouse or dependent child while the sponsor was on active duty.

In order to be CHAMPUS-eligible, the spouse (or former spouse) must be receiving part of the abusive sponsor's retirement annuity under a court order, and must have been a victim of the abuse and been married to the sponsor at the time of the abuse; or must be the parent of an abused dependent child of the abusive member or former member. For a child to be eligible, he or she must have been a member of the sponsor's household at the time of the abuse.

CHAMPUS eligibility may be reinstated if Medicare hospital (Part A) coverage stops for persons with kidney disease or disabilities.

Other Health Insurance Coverage

1. The law requires that all CHAMPUS-eligible persons enrolled in any other primary insurance or health plan must use the other insurance benefits before CHAMPUS can make any payment. CHAMPUS will then pay the remaining allowable charges, if such charges do not exceed the amount that would have been paid had there been no other insurance.

2. Some insurance plans exclude payments covering benefits for which the individual may be eligible under any Federal program. In such cases, if the other plan's exclusionary clause was in effect prior to October 1, 1966 and if the patient was insured under the other plan prior to that date and has

continued to be insured by the plan without interruption, CHAMPUS would then acknowledge that the other plan was "last pay." Under these circumstances, CHAMPUS would pay its full share of the allowable costs without regard to the other plan. This exception is not applicable to coverage under the Federal Employees Health Benefits Program; plans under the FEHBP are always "first pay."

3. The only exceptions for all CHAMPUS families to CHAMPUS' second pay are Medicaid and CHAMPUS supplemental plans. CHAMPUS supplemental plans cover the beneficiaries' cost share under CHAMPUS — such plans are offered through military, retiree associations and others. If CHAMPUS beneficiaries have either of these types of coverage, they should file with CHAMPUS as soon after getting care as possible. The beneficiary should write "Medicaid" or "CHAMPUS Supplemental" on the CHAMPUS claim form. In these cases, CHAMPUS pays first.

CHAMPUS Supplements

CHAMPUS supplemental insurance policies are offered by many military associations and other private firms and pay all or part of the civilian health care cost sharing. Such policies can provide a large measure of assistance if a sizeable balance is due after CHAMPUS pays its share of hospital charges for a serious illness or injury.

However, under the DRG payment system now in place in most areas, CHAMPUS pays only its share of the "allowable" amount specified by the DRG guidelines for the type of care received. Some of the CHAMPUS supplement policies only provide for payment of the "allowable" charges which may not cover the "billed" amount. Therefore, although having a CHAMPUS supplement policy is generally a good idea, members should examine the various plans carefully to select a plan that will cover all or most of the costs after CHAMPUS has paid its share of civilian health care. Members need only one such policy. It has been found that many members carry two or more of such policies, which is a waste of money. A number of the military and veterans organizations listed in Part IV offer CHAMPUS Supplement Plans.

Nondiscrimination Policy

Except under unusual circumstances, payment cannot be made by CHAMPUS for inpatient or outpatient care provided in and billed by civilian facilities found by the Department of Defense to practice discrimination in the admission and/or treatment of patients on the basis of race, color, or national origin.

Additionally, reimbursement cannot be made to an eligible patient who pays for care in such a facility and submits a claim for reimbursement.

This policy applies in the 50 States, District of Columbia, Puerto Rico, Virgin Islands, American Samoa, Wake Island, Canal Zone, and the territories and possessions of the U.S. This restriction on payment applies to bills submitted by ineligible facilities for all care authorized under CHAMPUS including benefits authorized under the Program for the Handicapped.

However, payment of attending physician and other professionals or paramedical personnel who bill independently of the facility will not be refused solely because their services were provided in an ineligible facility. Advise your physician of this policy before he or she plans your inpatient or outpatient hospital care.

UNIFORMED SERVICES ALMANAC
PROGRAM FOR PERSONS WITH DISABILITIES (PFPWD)

Eligibility

The Programs for Persons with Disabilities (PFPWD) is only for seriously disabled persons who are **dependents of active-duty members.** You must apply and get approval from your CHAMPUS claims processor before CHAMPUS can help pay the costs of care. Each case under the program is treated on a case-by-case basis. Because of this, the requirement to apply and/or stay in the program is very important to work closely with your HBA when applying and later on as well.

Sometimes, *not* using PFPWD benefits for diagnostic and treatment services can save you money. The PFPWD benefit is generally limited to $1,000 per month. You may be able to get these services under the basic CHAMPUS program, where your maximum costs in a fiscal year may be limited by the $1,000 "catastrophic cap" for active duty families. Because of this it is very important to work closely with your HBA when considering these benefits.

The PFPWD serves two kinds of serious disabilities: persons who are moderately or severely mentally retarded; persons who have a major physical disability; or a combination of both. Remember, though, they must be dependents of active-duty members.

- **Mentally retarded.** A person must be moderately or severely retarded to qualify for the PFPWD.
- **Physically handicapped.** Under PFPWD, a seriously physically handicapped person is one who: is expected to have the handicap at least a year or is expected to die from the handicap; and needs help just to do the basics of living — eating, getting dressed, going to the bathroom, etc.

Application

The active-duty member must apply for PFPWD care for a family member, and must have the care approved in advance. He or she must submit claims on the DD Form 2642 claim form. Individual providers of care must use the HCFA 1500. Institutions must use the UB-92. Your HBA or CHAMPUS claims processor should have DD 2642 forms. Send the form to your CHAMPUS claims processor.

In many communities, public funds or special programs are available for disabled residents. (Your HBA may be able to help you find out about help available in your community.) If so, you must get assistance this way first.

If public help is not available or isn't enough, CHAMPUS helps pay for allowable services from private, not-for-profit organizations. You must include with your request for PFPWD benefits a letter from the proper public official saying why public help is unavailable or insufficient. If you don't know who the right public official is, contact the HBA. The letter from the public official must be on the public agency's stationery, or on CHAMPUS Form 769.

Note: CHAMPUS cannot help pay for care at a private, for-profit facility. And as with the rest of the CHAMPUS program, all providers of services or supplies/equipment must be authorized.

CHAMPUS will tell you whether it approves or denies your application.

But CHAMPUS may approve only certain parts of the care. For example, CHAMPUS may change the date on which benefits start, or tell you that it can only share the bills for a specific time period.

If your application is approved. CHAMPUS will tell you how often a progress report is needed from the disabled person's doctor. The doctor must also send a new management plan with each progress report. Remind the doctor to send the progress report and the new management plan. Every year (or when you move from one CHAMPUS claims processing region to another) you need to send the claims processor a new letter from the appropriate public official that says that public assistance is still unavailable or insufficient.

Claims for pre-authorized benefits. All benefits under the PFPWD must be authorized in writing by CHAMPUS before any services or supplies/ equipment are received. A copy of the authorization must be attached to the claim form.

For all services and supplies under the Program for Persons with Disabilities, send the DD Form 2642 claim form to the claims processor for the state where the care was received, unless you live in any area where the TRICARE Managed Care Support Program is in operation. In such a case, check with your nearest HBA or TRICARE Service Center.

For general medical care for the disabled person, use the DD Form 2642, or other appropriate form. Anyone under the PFPWD - no matter what age - is covered for general medical care as described elsewhere in this section.

If the active-duty member is transferred. If the new duty station doesn't offer public help for the disabled or if it isn't enough, a letter from the proper local official must be sent to the CHAMPUS claims processor for the area within 60 days of the move. If this letter isn't received, the disabled person will not be covered any longer.

Changing health care centers. If you need to move the disabled person from one health care center to another, you must ask the claims processor for a new benefit authorization. Along with the new application, you must send a copy of the disabled person's medical records from the present facility and another letter from the right public official saying public assistance remains unavailable or insufficient.

How Much Will It Cost?

You must pay part of the monthly expenses for care of the disabled person before CHAMPUS can help. How much you must pay depends on the sponsor's pay grade. (NOTE: You must report any change in pay grade to the claims processor. An amended authorization will be issued for any increase or decrease in your cost-share resulting from the pay grade change.)

After you have paid your share, CHAMPUS will pay as much as $1,000 a month more for the care of a disabled person. If the costs are more than that, you must pay the extra.

In determining the CHAMPUS payment, CHAMPUS figures an allowable charge for the care the disabled person is receiving. CHAMPUS cannot pay more than the allowable charge for any care.

CHAMPUS sends you an Explanation of Benefits that spells out how much CHAMPUS will pay. The CHAMPUS cost-share is figured on a monthly basis.

Two or more disabled persons. If there are two or more persons in the family who qualify for the PFPWD, CHAMPUS will make sure you won't have to pay any more than you pay for one. CHAMPUS covers all allowable

UNIFORMED SERVICES ALMANAC

costs for the second disabled person, as long as you pay your full monthly share for the other disabled person. Check with your HBA for more information.

SCALE OF MONTHLY PAYMENTS FOR BENEFITS

Enlisted Personnel		Warrant Officers		Commissioned Officers	
Pay Grade	Amount $	Pay Grade	Amount $	Pay Grade	Amount $
E-1	25	E-6	30	W-1	45	O-1	35	O-6	75
E-2	25	E-7	35	W-2	45	O-2	40	O-7	100
E-3	25	E-8	40	W-3	50	O-3	45	O-8	150
E-4	25	E-9	45	W-4	50	O-4	50	O-9	200
E-5	25					O-5	65	O-10	250

ADMINISTRATION OF CIVILIAN HEALTH BENEFITS

Office of Secretary of Defense

The Assistant Secretary of Defense (Health Affairs) is responsible for overall policy direction and administration of CHAMPUS worldwide. The Director, Office of the Civilian Health and Medical Program of the Uniformed Services (OCHAMPUS), is responsible for day to day program operation.

DEERS

The Defense Enrollment Eligibility Reporting System (DEERS) was established in 1979 to provide a means for minimizing fraudulent use of military health benefits by unauthorized persons, improving the control and distribution of available military health care services, and projecting and allocating costs for existing and future health care programs. Under DEERS, an individual's eligibility can be quickly verified at a health care facility, making it less likely that an ineligible person would receive care — either by mistake or fraud. DEERS enrollment is mandatory for non-emergency medical care.

CHAMPUS claims are checked against DEERS for all uniformed services benefits. CHAMPUS claims will not be paid if the patient is not on the DEERS data base or if DEERS shows the patient to be ineligible. If a legitimate CHAMPUS claim is denied, however, the sponsor or family member should contact the CHAMPUS claims processor and resubmit the CHAMPUS claim with proof of eligibility.

Active duty service members and retirees who draw retired pay are automatically enrolled in DEERS. Family members are not automatically enrolled in DEERS. Newborns must be enrolled in DEERS within four days of birth at a USMTF or within fourteen days if born in a civilian hospital. All others enroll at the nearest personnel office of any of the uniformed services. Questions regarding DEERS enrollment may also be directed to the DEERS Beneficiary Center by calling (800) 538-9552 (except in California, Alaska, and Hawaii). In California the number is (800) 334-4162. From Hawaii or Alaska, call (800) 527-5602. DEERS also now applies to military families covered by CHAMPVA, administered by the Veterans Administration. CHAMPVA claims are now checked against DEERS. To resolve CHAMPVA eligibility problems, contact the CHAMPVA Center, 300 Jackson St., Denver, CO 80206-5023 or call 1-800-733-8387.

UNIFORMED SERVICES ALMANAC

HEALTH BENEFITS FOR RETIRED MEMBERS IN FEDERAL MEDICAL FACILITIES

Health Benefits in Uniformed Services Facilities

Retired members shall, upon request, be provided any type of health care in uniformed services facilities that is provided active duty members, *subject to the availability of space and facilities and the capabilities of the medical and dental staff,* and subject to the provisions of Executive Order 10122, April 14, 1950, as amended by Executive Order 10400, September 19, 1952, and Executive Order 11733, July 30, 1973.

Non-emergency care shall not be provided this group at times and places where it would interfere with providing care to spouses and children of members who are serving on active duty or who died while serving on such duty or where it would interfere with the performance of the primary mission of the facility.

There shall be no charge for outpatient care provided or for inpatient care provided to retired enlisted members. Retired officers shall pay the current subsistence charge for inpatient care.

Military Retiree Health Care

Former active duty members of the U.S. Armed Forces, regardless of rank, who are in receipt of retired or retainer pay potentially have dual eligibility for Department of Veterans Affairs (VA) medical benefits, as VA beneficiaries and as beneficiaries of the Department of Defense (DoD).

Applicants (including military retirees) who fall into the discretionary eligibility category are eligible for VA medical care as VA beneficiaries only after they agree to pay a modest co-payment for the medical benefit for which they apply. Should the military retiree not agree to make this co-payment, he or she would not be eligible as a veteran. The retiree may, however, be offered VA medical care as a beneficiary of the DoD and at DoD expense, but only on a space and resource available basis as determined by the facility director. Discretionary eligibility is defined in the VA section of this Almanac.

Note: Beneficiaries of the DoD, with the exception of those in need of emergency medical services, will be required to obtain DoD authorization prior to receiving VA medical care.

SATELLITE PRIMARY HEALTH CARE

The DoD Authorization Act of 1984 directed the Department of Defense to conduct studies and demonstration projects designed to improve access, quality, efficiency, and cost effectiveness of health services. A concept called Primary Care for the Uniformed Services (PRIMUS) was implemented first by the Army and soon followed by the Navy and Air Force.

The Army approved the establishment of the first contractor owned and operated PRIMUS center in October 1985 in Northern Virginia. Two more PRIMUS clinics were subsequently opened in Northern Virginia. In 1994 these were converted to PRIMUS PLUS and are now also staffed with military providers and operate on an appointment basis under the DeWitt Army Community Hospital at Fort Belvoir. Other PRIMUS Centers are in Savannah, GA, near Fort Stewart; two at Fort Hood, TX; and one each at Fort Benning, GA; and Fort Bragg, NC.

UNIFORMED SERVICES ALMANAC

The Navy has established several appointment based NAVCARE clinics to provide primary medical care for active duty military, retirees, and their dependents. The NAVCARE Clinics are located at Long Beach, CA; two at San Diego, CA; Oakland, CA; Camp Pendleton, CA; Camp Lejuene, NC; Charleston, SC and two at Norfolk, VA. Treatment at NAVCARE clinics is available on an appointment basis. The clinics are staffed by civilian physicians, nurses, and physician assistants who perform basic medical care and refer patients to specialists at Navy Hospitals when necessary within the Medical Treatment Facility capabilities. Patients are treated for ailments they might ordinarily go to a general or family practitioner's office for, such as colds, flus, earaches, minor gynecological problems, minor injuries, stable chronic care, routine physicals, or immunizations. Lab tests, x-rays, mammograms, and prescription medicines are all available free of charge. NAVCARE physicians are all board certified in internal medicine, family practice, gynecology or pediatrics.

The Air Force has PRIMUS Centers at or near; Davis-Monthan AFB, AZ; Offutt AFB, NE. The PRIMUS Centers at March AFB, CA; Mather AFB, CA and MacDill AFB, FL are either closed or closing soon.

PRIMUS and NAVCARE clinics are not emergency rooms, nor do they provide eye care, dental treatment, mental health care, obstetrical services or surgery.

The PRIMUS and NAVCARE Centers improve access by being located off the military base and near the user population. They facilitate the return to the direct care system of beneficiaries who would otherwise only use CHAMPUS. These Centers reduce long backlogs trying to access the outpatient clinics on military installations.

Clinic users must present a valid ID Card and be enrolled in the DEERS program. For information, contact the health benefits advisor at the nearest military treatment facility.

The user beneficiary does not share costs at the PRIMUS-NAVCARE Centers as they are part of the direct medical care system. Current budget reduction efforts and pending legislation may change the no-cost feature by collecting 3rd party insurance payments, as appropriate.

Note: At the time of TRICARE implementation, PRIMUS and NAVCARE Centers will become TRICARE outpatient clinics.

The USTF hospitals and clinics where the managed-care options are available are:

BALTIMORE, MD
Homewood Hospital Center
3100 Wyman Park Dr,
Baltimore, MD 21211, (301) 338-3000
In and Outpatient: All

BOSTON, MA
Brighton Marine Public Health Center
77 Warren St, Boston, MA 02135
(617) 782-3400
Inpatient: Active Duty Only
Outpatient: All

NASSAU BAY, TX
Hospital of St. John
2050 Space Park Dr, Nassau Bay, TX 77058, (713) 333-5503
In and Outpatient: All

SEATTLE, WA
Pacific Medical Center
1200 12th St S., Seattle, WA 98144
(206) 326-4000
In and Outpatient: All

STATEN ISLAND, NY
Bayley-Seton Hospital
Bay St & Vanderbilt Ave, Staten Island, NY 10304, (718) 390-6111
Inpatient: Active Duty Only
Outpatient: All

PORTLAND, ME
Martin's Point Health Care Center
331 Veranda St, Portland, ME 04103
(207) 774-5801
Outpatient Only: All

CLEVELAND, OH
Lutheran Medical Center
2609 Franklin Blvd., Cleveland, OH 44113, (216) 363-2153
Outpatient Only: All

GALVESTON, TX
St. Mary's Hospital
404 St. Mary's Blvd., Galveston, TX 77550, (409) 766-4302
Outpatient Only: All

HOUSTON, TX
St. Joseph Hospital
1919 La Branch St., Houston, TX 77002, (713) 757-7455
Outpatient Only: All

PORT ARTHUR, TX
St. Mary's Hospital
3600 Gates Blvd., Port Arthur, TX 77642, (409) 983-1621
Outpatient Only: All

UNIFORMED SERVICES ALMANAC
CHAMPUS CLAIMS PROCESSORS

January 1, 1996
CHAMPUS CLAIMS
PROCESSORS
(Toll-Free or Commercial Numbers)

Northern Region*
(Connecticut, Illinois, Indiana, Maine, Massachusetts, Michigan, New Hampshire, New Jersey, New York,, Rhode Island, Vermont, and Christian Science claims)
Claims processor: AdminaStar
Toll-free telephone: **1-800-842-4333**

Western Region
(Alaska, Arizona, Colorado, Idaho, Montana, Utah, Nebraska, Nevada, New Mexico, North/ South Dakota, Oregon, Washington, Wyoming)
Claims processor: Palmetto GBA
Toll-free telephone: **1-800-225-4816**

Mid-Atlantic Region
(Delaware, District of Columbia, Maryland, North and South Carolina, Pennsylvania, Virginia)
Claims processor: AdminaStar
Toll-free telephone: **1-800-842-4333**

Southeast Region
(Alabama, Florida, Georgia, Mississippi, Tennessee, Puerto Rico, Canada, Mexico, Central and South America, Bermuda, West Indies, China, Thailand, Korea, Australia, Japan and other Pacific-area countries)
Claims processor: Wisconsin Physicians Service
Toll-free telephone (stateside only): **1-800-866-6337**
Puerto Rico and areas outside U.S.: **1-608-259-4847**

South Central Region
(Arkansas, Kansas, Louisiana, Missouri, Oklahoma, Texas)
Claims processor: Wisconsin Physicians Service
Toll-free telephone: **1-800-388-6767**

Six State Region
(Minnesota, Wisconsin, Iowa, West Virginia, Kentucky, and Ohio)
Claims Processor: Palmetto GBA
Toll-free telephone: **1-800-471-0704**

Where to Send the Claim

Claims go to the CHAMPUS claims processor for the state or country where you received the care, no matter where you live. Remember this when you're traveling. (If you live in any area where CHAMPUS test programs or managed-care programs are in operation, such as California and Hawaii, claims submission requirements may be different; check on this with your nearest HBA).

Here are up-to-date standard CHAMPUS claims filing addresses for each state and for overseas areas. These addresses may change from time to time, so double check them before sending in claims:

Alabama
Wisconsin Physicians Service
P.O. Box 7889
Madison, WI 53707-7889

Alaska
Palmetto GBA
P.O. Box 100502
Florence, SC 29501-0502

Arizona
Palmetto GBA
P.O. Box 100502
Florence, SC 29501-0502

Arkansas
Wisconsin Physicians Service
P.O. Box 8932
Madison, Wisconsin 53708-8932

UNIFORMED SERVICES ALMANAC

California (including California residents who are traveling outside the state and nonresidents who receive care in California)--Palmetto GBA, CHAMPUS Claims, P.O. Box 870001, Surfside Beach, SC 29587-8701. Toll-free phone: 1-800-741-5048. This also includes claims for care received from non-network providers of care (standard CHAMPUS), regardless of the date the services were received. And, it includes claims for care received by residents and nonresidents on and after Feb. 1, 1994, from TRICARE network and non-network providers.

Claims for all California care received from CHAMPUS Reform Initiative network providers before Feb. 1, 1994, should be sent to: FHFS CHAMPUS Claims Department, P.O. Box 1600, Rancho Cordova, CA 95471-1600. Toll-free phone: 1-800-634-7148 (Northern California); or 1-800-451-8552 (Southern California).

Colorado
Palmetto GBA CHAMPUS Claims
P.O. Box 100502
Florence, SC 29501-0502

Connecticut
AdminaStar
P.O. Box 3066
Columbus, IN 47202-3066

Delaware
AdminaStar
P.O. Box 3076
Columbus, IN 47202-3076

District of Columbia
Palmetto GBA CHAMPUS Claims
P.O. Box 100502
Florence, SC 29501-0502

Florida
Wisconsin Physicians Service
P.O. Box 7889
Madison, WI 53707-7889

Georgia
Wisconsin Physicians Service
P.O. Box 7889
Madison, WI 53707-7889

Hawaii (including Hawaii residents who are traveling outside the state and nonresidents who receive care in Hawaii)--Palmetto GBA, CHAMPUS Claims, P.O. Box 870001, Surfside Beach, SC 29587-8701. Toll-free phone: 1-800-741-5048. This also includes claims for care received from non-network providers of care (standard CHAMPUS), regardless of the date the services were received. And, it includes claims for care received by residents and nonresidents on and after Feb. 1, 1994, from TRICARE network and non-network providers.

Claims for all Hawaii care received from CHAMPUS Reform Initiative network providers before Feb. 1, 1994, should be sent to: FHFS CHAMPUS Claims Department, P.O. Box 1600, Rancho Cordova, CA 95471-1600. Toll-free phone: 1-800-321-5469.

Idaho
(except zip codes 83854 & 83876)
Palmetto GBA CHAMPUS Claims
P.O. Box 100502
Florence, SC 29501-0502
(zip codes 83854 & 83876)
FHFS
P.O. Box 17600
Tucson, AZ 85731-7600

Illinois
AdminaStar
P.O. Box 3054
Columbus, IN 47202-3054

Indiana
AdminaStar
P.O. Box 3056
Columbus, IN 47202-3056

Iowa
Palmetto GBA CHAMPUS Claims
P.O. Box 100598
Florence, SC 29501-0598

Kansas
Wisconsin Physicians Service
P.O. Box 8932
Madison, WI 53708-8932

Kentucky
(except Fort Campbell area)
Palmetto GBA CHAMPUS Claims
P.O. Box 100598
Florence, SC 29501-0598
(Fort Campbell area only)
Wisconsin Physicians Service
P.O. Box 7889
Madison, WI 53707-7889

Louisiana
(except CHAMPUS reform areas)
Wisconsin Physicians Service
P.O. Box 8932
Madison, Wisconsin 53708-8932

UNIFORMED SERVICES ALMANAC

(New Orleans area)
FHFS Claims Dept.
P.O. Box 1718
Rancho Cordova, CA 95670-1718
(Alexandria/Fort Polk areas)
FHFS/Louisiana Claims
P.O. Box 2030
Rancho Cordova, CA 95670-2030

Maine
AdminaStar
P.O. Box 3064
Columbus, IN 47202-3064

Maryland
Palmetto GBA CHAMPUS Claims
P.O. Box 100502
Florence, SC 29501-0502

Massachusetts
AdminaStar
P.O. Box 3063
Columbus, IN 47202-3063

Michigan
AdminaStar
P.O. Box 3053
Columbus, IN 47202-3053

Minnesota
Palmetto GBA CHAMPUS Claims
P.O. Box 100598
Florence, SC 29501-0598

Mississippi
Wisconsin Physicians Service
P.O. Box 7889
Madison, WI 53707-7889

Missouri
Wisconsin Physicians Service
P.O. Box 8932
Madison, Wisconsin 53708-8932

Montana
Palmetto GBA CHAMPUS Claims
P.O. Box 100502
Florence, SC 29501-0502

Nebraska
Palmetto GBA CHAMPUS Claims
P.O. Box 100502
Florence, SC 29501-0502

Nevada
Palmetto GBA CHAMPUS Claims
P.O. Box 100502
Florence, SC 29501-0502

New Hampshire
AdminaStar
P.O. Box 3067
Columbus, IN 47202-3067

New Jersey
AdminaStar
P.O. Box 3052
Columbus, IN 47202-3052

New Mexico
Palmetto GBA CHAMPUS Claims
P.O. Box 100502
Florence, SC 29501-0502

New York
AdminaStar
For Zip Codes 10000-12999
P.O. Box 3051
For Zip Codes 13000-14999
P.O. Box 3050
Columbus, IN 47202

North Carolina
Palmetto GBA CHAMPUS Claims
P.O. Box 100502
Florence, SC 29501-0502

North Dakota
Palmetto GBA CHAMPUS Claims
P.O. Box 100502
Florence, SC 29501-0502

Ohio
Palmetto GBA CHAMPUS Claims
CHAMPUS claims
P.O. Box 100598
Florence, SC 29501-0598

Oklahoma
Wisconsin Physicians Service
P.O. Box 8932
Madison, WI 53708-8932

Oregon
FHFS CHAMPUS Claims Processing
P.O. Box 17600
Tucson, AZ 85731-7600

Pennsylvania
AdminaStar
P.O. Box 3074 for Zip Codes 15001-15299 & 19001-19199
Columbus, IN 47202-3074
P.O. Box 3075 for all other cities
Columbus, IN 47202-3075

Rhode Island
AdminaStar
P.O. Box 3065
Columbus, IN 47202-3065

South Carolina
Palmetto GBA CHAMPUS Claims
PO Box 100502
Florence, SC 29501-0502

UNIFORMED SERVICES ALMANAC

South Dakota
Palmetto GBA CHAMPUS Claims
P.O. Box 100502
Florence, SC 29501-0502
Tennessee
Wisconsin Physicians Service
P.O. Box 7889
Madison, WI 53707-7889
Texas (except Bergstrom/Carswell areas)
Wisconsin Physicians Service
PO Box 8932
Madison, WI 53708-8932
(Bergstrom/Carswell area only)
FHFS/Texas Claims
P.O. Box 1170
Rancho Cordova, CA 95670-1170
Utah
Palmetto GBA CHAMPUS Claims
P.O. Box 100502
Florence, SC 29501-0502
Vermont
AdminaStar
P.O. Box 3068
Columbus, IN 47202-3068
Virginia
Palmetto GBA CHAMPUS Claims
PO Box 100502
Florence, SC 29501-0502
Washington
FHFS CHAMPUS Claims Processing
P.O. Box 17600
Tucson, AZ 85731-7600
West Virginia
Palmetto GBA CHAMPUS Claims
P.O. Box 100598
Florence, SC 29501-0598
Wisconsin
Palmetto GBA CHAMPUS Claims
P.O. Box 100598
Florence, SC 29501-0598

Wyoming
Palmetto GBA CHAMPUS Claims
P.O. Box 100502
Florence, SC 29501-0502
Canada, Mexico, Central and South America, Bermuda, West Indies, Pacific area (China, Thailand, Korea, Australia, Japan, etc.)
Wisconsin Physicians Service
P.O. Box 7985
Madison, WI 53707-7985
Africa, Europe, Middle East (plus adjunctive dental claims for those areas)
OCHAMPUSEUR
144 KarlsruheStrasse
6900 Heidelberg, FRG or
OCHAMPUSEUR
Unit 29220
APO AE 09102
Telephone: DSN 371-2219/2575; Fax: 06221-342367
Puerto Rico
Wisconsin Physicians Service
P.O. Box 7985
Madison, WI 53707-7985
Christian Science Claims (except for California and Hawaii, New Orleans, and base closure sites in Texas and Louisiana)
AdminaStar
ATTN: Christian Science
P.O. Box 3063
Columbus, IN 47202-3063
Christian Science claims for services in regions where managed-care programs are in operation should be sent to the contractor for a particular region.
Adjunctive Dental Claims (worldwide except for Europe, Africa and Middle East, California and Hawaii, and base closure sites in Texas and Louisiana)
Palmetto GBA CHAMPUS Claims
P.O. Box 100599
Florence, SC 29501-0599
Telephone: (803) 665-2320

Have this information handy when checking on a claim — If you need to check on the status of a CHAMPUS claim with your state's claims processor listed above, the process will be speeded up considerably if you have the following information at hand when you call: patient's full name; sponsor's full name, rank, branch of service and status (active or retired); sponsor's Social Security number; sponsor's and patient's addresses and telephone numbers; name and address of provider of the care; and dates of the care.

UNIFORMED SERVICES ALMANAC

SURVIVOR BENEFIT PLAN

Enacted by Public Law 92-425 on September 21, 1972, the Survivor Benefit Plan (SBP) is a voluntary program in which a military retiree may elect to receive a reduced amount of retired (or retainer) pay to provide an annuity to eligible survivor(s). (This reduction is referred to as a "premium.") SBP is available to retired members of the Armed Forces, including the U.S. Coast Guard (USCG), Public Health Service (PHS), and the National Oceanic and Atmospheric Administration (NOAA). Service members retiring under the 15-year early retirement program are eligible to enroll in the SBP program. The same rules, regulations and laws apply to the 15-year as does the 20-plus year retirement. Survivors of SBP participants receive annuities of up to 55% of the participant's retired pay.

Retirement-eligible members of the above services who are serving on active duty are covered by SBP at the maximum level as long as they remain on active duty. Upon retirement, enrollment in SBP with the maximum level of coverage is automatic for all members unless a member elects to decline participation or to participate with a reduced "base amount" prior to the date on which the member becomes entitled to retired pay. Written concurrence of the member's spouse is required to decline participation or to elect a reduced level of coverage for spouse only, spouse and child(ren) or child(ren) only options.

A member's "base amount" is a dollar amount selected by a member at the time of enrollment on which the member's monthly premium and the survivor's monthly annuity will be computed. A base amount may be any amount between a $300.00 minimum and the member's full gross retired pay.

Members of the Reserve Forces, including the Army and Air National Guard, are eligible to participate in the Reserve Component Survivor Benefit Plan (RCSBP) upon completion of 20 years of qualifying service or upon early retirement (15-20 years). Under the provisions of P.L. 95-397, enacted September 30, 1978, Reservists can: (A) decline to make an election until attaining age 60 when they become eligible to receive retired pay and participate in SBP; (B) elect coverage for annuities to begin upon Reservist's death or upon date Reservist would become age 60, whichever is later; or (C) elect coverage for annuities to begin upon Reservist's death, regardless of Reservist's age when death occurs. Reservists who elect either options B or C at less than the maximum level of spouse coverage or for children only must provide the written concurrence of their spouses.

COVERAGES AVAILABLE

There are six categories of beneficiaries that may be elected to receive survivor protection under SBP. The category elected determines the amounts of a member's premium and the survivor's annuity. The categories are:

Spouse Only. Eligibility for this coverage requires that a surviving spouse be a widow or widower who was married to a retiree at the time of his or her retirement; or, if not married at the time of retirement, was married to the deceased retiree for at least one year prior to his or her death; or, if not married at time of retirement and was not married to the deceased retiree for at least one year prior to his or her death, was the parent of issue by that marriage.

SBP spouse coverage applies not only to the spouse a member has at time of enrollment, but also automatically to any future spouse the member might acquire, unless the member elects to decline coverage for a subsequent spouse within one year of the date of marriage. (Concurrence of the subsequent spouse is not required, but he or she will be notified of the member's declination.)

A surviving spouse's annuity is calculated at 55% of the participant's "base amount" until age 62, when it is reduced to 35% of the base amount. This reduction is due to the surviving spouse's entitlement to Social Security survivor benefits attributable to the member's income while serving on active duty. Survivors of members who retired, or were eligible for retirement, prior to October 1, 1985 may have their annuities reduced by the actual amount of the Social Security survivor benefits attributable to income earned on active duty after December 31, 1956 rather than to 35% of the member's base amount if it is to the annuitant's advantage.

An SBP annuitant may continue receiving an annuity until death or until remarriage under age 55; however, if that remarriage later ends by death, divorce, or annulment, entitlement to the annuity may be restored. Remarriage after age 55 does not terminate entitlement to an SBP annuity.

If a surviving spouse is also entitled to receive Dependency and Indemnity Compensation (DIC) from the Department of Veterans' Affairs (VA), the SBP annuity will be reduced dollar-for-dollar by the amount of DIC received. If a DIC recipient later loses his or her entitlement to DIC due to remarriage, full SBP entitlement may be restored if the surviving spouse is over age 55 at the time of remarriage.

A surviving spouse of two deceased retirees, both of whom were SBP participants, can choose between the two entitlements, selecting the more advantageous of the two.

Spouse and Child(ren). With this option, SBP protection is expanded to cover an eligible child or children if there is no surviving spouse, or if a surviving spouse subsequently dies or becomes ineligible to receive benefits due to remarriage before the age of 55. Thus, if there is a divorce or if the spouse predeceases the retiree, the full SBP annuity will be paid to the eligible surviving child or children in the same manner as if the member had elected "Child(ren) Only" coverage as discussed below.

Child(ren) Only. This option provides an annuity only for dependent children regardless of whether a member is married or not at time of enrollment (although a married member's spouse must concur with a child(ren) only election). Children remain beneficiaries until age 18 or age 22 if a full-time, unmarried student. Children mentally or physically incapable of self-support remain eligible for as long as the incapacitation exists or until marriage.

Children's annuities are calculated at 55% of the member's base amount for as long as the child(ren) remain eligible and are not reduced due to entitlement to any other Government benefits. The 55% annuity is divided equally among all eligible children. Annuities are paid to a child's parent or guardian until the child's 18th birthday, at which time the annuity is paid directly to the child or until age 22 if the child is an unmarried full-time student.

A retiree with no dependent children at time of retirement may elect coverage for a child subsequently acquired, but the child must be added within one year of being acquired (born, adopted, etc.). If a member has children upon retirement but does not elect coverage for them, the member may not later elect coverage for children acquired after retirement.

Former Spouse. The Uniformed Services Former Spouses' Protection Act of 1982, enacted September 8, 1982 (P.L. 97-252), amended the SBP program to permit retiring service members to voluntarily elect SBP coverage for former spouses (under the Insurable Interest option discussed later).

P.L. 98-94, enacted September 24, 1983, permitted already-retired members to change their spouse elections to cover their former spouses during an open season between September 24, 1983 and September 23, 1984.

P.L. 98-525, enacted October 19, 1984, permitted the enforcement of court orders in which members agree to voluntarily provide continued SBP coverage to former spouses. In order for such a court order to be enforced, the former spouse must request the election be deemed on the member's behalf within one year of the date of the court order.

P.L. 99-661, enacted November 14, 1986, permitted state courts to order members to elect former spouse coverage (applies only to court orders issued on or after November 14, 1986).

Former spouses become ineligible to receive SBP annuities if they remarry before age 55, and their annuities are subject to the same reduction at age 62 as spouse annuities.

A former spouse who was not a member's former spouse on the date a member became eligible to participate in SBP must have been married to the member for at least one year in order to be named as an SBP former spouse beneficiary. (In other words, a former spouse acquired after retirement must have been an eligible spouse beneficiary.)

Former spouse elections are permanent and irrevocable, except as follows: members who voluntarily elect coverage on behalf of a former spouse may only change their elections to spouse coverage within one year of remarrying; members who elect former spouse coverage in compliance with a written agreement, which has not been incorporated into a court order, may change their elections to spouse coverage within one year of remarrying only with the written concurrence of the former spouse; members who elect former spouse coverage in compliance with a court order which orders them to provide such coverage, or which incorporates an agreement to voluntarily provide such coverage, may change their elections to spouse coverage within one year of remarrying only if they obtain a court order which relieves them of the requirement imposed by the prior court order.

Former Spouse and Child(ren). P.L. 99-145, enacted November 8, 1985, with an effective date of March 1, 1986, provided for the cost and annuity amounts to be computed at the same rate as coverage for spouses and permitted children (from the marriage to the former spouse) to be included with the election.

Persons with Insurable Interest. Retiring members who have neither a spouse nor a dependent child at time of retirement may enroll in SBP to provide coverage for a person who has a bona fide financial interest in the continued life of the SBP participant. This person may be any close relative, such as a parent, brother or sister, a child not dependent on the retiree for support, or a close business associate. In addition, an unmarried member may elect coverage for a sole dependent child at the time of retirement.

The annuity an insurable interest beneficiary would receive is always 55 % of the participant's full retired pay after the premium amount is deducted. As with children's coverage, there is no offset for other Government benefits to which the named insured may also be entitled.

P.L. 103-337, The FY 95 Defense Authorization Act, permits a participant to discontinue insurable interest coverage.

A member with an insurable interest election may change that election to cover a subsequently acquired spouse and/or child(ren); Such a change must be made within one year of acquiring the spouse or child.

UNIFORMED SERVICES ALMANAC

REMARRIAGE — ITS EFFECT ON THE SURVIVOR BENEFIT PLAN (SBP)

A retiree initially participating in SBP with either spouse or spouse and child(ren) coverage has several options when that marriage ends in death, divorce, or annulment, and the retiree remarries.

Upon notification to the Finance Center of your change in marital status, your SBP participation and costs will be suspended, not terminated. Under the law, upon remarriage, your new spouse is automatically covered under SBP 1 year after your remarriage with the same level of coverage as your prior spouse. (An earlier date applies if a child is born of that marriage, or if you remarry your former spouse.)

Your options upon remarriage are: (1) resume spouse coverage at the same level and cost as you had for your first spouse (under the "automatic" provisions of the law); (2) elect not to resume spouse coverage, provided your election to do so is received by the Finance Center within 1 year after your remarriage; (3) increase your SBP coverage, if you previously were under reduced coverage (You must pay any difference prior to the first year anniversary of the remarriage.) ; and (4) add supplemental SBP coverage for your new spouse.

The important thing to remember is that you must notify the Finance Center when you remarry. If you do not notify them, your new spouse will be automatically covered under SBP, and you will be responsible for SBP costs retroactive to one year after your remarriage.

COST (Premiums)

Spouse/Former Spouse Coverage. Coverage for spouses and former spouses are the same. P.L. 101-189, enacted November 29, 1989, and effective March 1, 1990, reduced the cost of SBP coverage for the majority of participants. Premiums for members who ENTERED SERVICE ON OR AFTER March 1, 1990, are computed at 6.5% of the member's base amount. Premiums for members who ENTERED SERVICE BEFORE March 1, 1990 are computed at either 6.5% of the member's base amount or 2.5% of the first $421* of the base amount, plus 10% of the remaining base amount, whichever method results in a lower premium. For members retiring in 1995 who entered service before March 1, 1990, the 6.5% calculation method results in a lower premium for base amounts of $903 or greater. Members who retired before March 1, 1990 had their premiums recalculated as of that date and reduced to 6.5% of their base amounts if they had been paying more than that amount under the old formula. Participants' retired pay is reduced by the amount of SBP premium only during periods in which the participant has an eligible beneficiary.

*This amount increases at the same time and by the same rate as cost-of-living adjustments to active duty military pay. $421 is the rate effective as of January 1, 1996.

If a member elects to provide coverage on behalf of a former spouse, regardless of whether the election is voluntary or court-ordered, SBP premium reductions in retired pay begin the first day of the month following the month in which the member requests the election change. If a former spouse requests an election change be deemed on a member's behalf on the first of the month following the date of a court order which requires that a member elect former spouse coverage, and the member

fails to voluntarily change his or her election during the one-year period, SBP premium reductions in retired pay are applied retroactively to the date of the court order.

SURVIVOR BENEFIT PLAN SPOUSE ONLY MONTHLY AMOUNTS

Base Amount of Retired Pay $	Monthly Payment for Surviving Spouse* $ 55%	35%	SBP Premium** $ 2.5%+	6.5%
300.00	165.00	105.00	7.50	19.50
421.00	231.55	147.35	10.53	27.37
500.00	275.00	175.00	18.43	32.50
600.00	330.00	210.00	28.43	39.00
700.00	385.00	245.00	38.43	45.50
800.00	440.00	280.00	48.43	52.00
900.00	495.00	315.00	58.43	58.50
902.00	496.10	315.70	58.63	58.63
***903.00	496.65	316.05		58.70
1,000.00	550.00	350.00		65.00
1,200.00	660.00	420.00		78.00
1,400.00	770.00	490.00		91.00
1,500.00	825.00	525.00		97.50
1,800.00	990.00	630.00		117.00
2,000.00	1,100.00	700.00		130.00
2,500.00	1,375.00	875.00		162.50
3,000.00	1,650.00	1,050.00		195.00
3,500.00	1,925.00	1,225.00		227.50
4,000.00	2,200.00	1,400.00		260.00
4,500.00	2,475.00	1,575.00		292.50
5,000.00	2,750.00	1,750.00		325.00
5,500.00	3,025.00	1,925.00		357.50
6,000.00	3,300.00	2,100.00		390.00
6,500.00	3,575.00	2,275.00		422.50
7,000.00	3,850.00	2,450.00		455.00

*Amount in left column is amount of annuity for beneficiaries under age 62; amount on right is amount for beneficiaries over age 62. Amount in right column applies to survivors of members who retired after October 1, 1985. Survivors of members who retired before October 1, 1985 will also usually receive this amount, but a small number of survivors may receive slightly greater amounts under the old Social Security offset method. Service finance centers will compute the annuity both ways and pay the larger amount.
**Amount in left column applies to members who entered service before March 1, 1990; amount in right column applies to members who entered service on or after March 1, 1990.
***Premiums for members with base amounts of $903 or greater retiring in 1996 are the same regardless of when they entered service.

Child(ren) Only Coverage. A member's premium for Child(ren) Only coverage is calculated using an actuarial factor determined by a combination of the ages of the member and the member's youngest child at time of enrollment. Generally, premiums are about 2.5% of the annuity of the average, but could be higher or lower depending on the difference in the age span between the member and the youngest child. As with spouse/former spouse coverage, premium reductions in retired pay terminate upon the date the youngest child beneficiary loses eligibility to receive the annuity.

Spouse/Former Spouse and Child(ren) Coverage. A member's premium for spouse and child(ren) coverage or former spouse and child(ren) coverage is calculated at the same rate as spouse or former spouse coverage, plus a small additional charge for the child(ren) portion of the coverage. The amount of this additional charge is calculated using an actuarial factor determined by the combination of the ages of the member, the member's spouse, and the member's youngest child at time of enrollment. Generally, premiums are about one-half of 1% of the annuity amount on average, but could be higher or lower

UNIFORMED SERVICES ALMANAC

depending on the difference in the age span between the parents and the youngest child.

If a participant with this election loses a spouse or former spouse beneficiary, the participant's premium will be recalculated using the actuarial factor which applies to the ages of the member and the youngest child at the time.

ESTIMATED SBP COSTS TO RETIREES AND BENEFIT PAYMENTS TO DECEASED RETIREE FAMILIES FOR FISCAL YEARS 1973-1995
(EXCLUDES RSFPP) ($ in thousands)

FY*	Average Number of Retirees	Fiscal Year Cost to Retirees	Cumulative Cost to Retirees	Average Number of Deceased Retiree Families Collecting	Fiscal Year Payments to Families	Cumulative Payments to Families
73	129,963	36,145	36,145	1,950#	5,700#	5,700#
74	367,134	111,974	148,119	6,725#	19,661	25,361
75	496,368	177,593	325,712	14,281	41,751	67,112
76	533,507	226,726	552,438	20,852	66,899	134,011
77	588,052	338,736	891,174	29,907	99,676	233,687
78	576,464	311,088	1,202,262	35,017	128,863	362,550
79	601,544	362,604	1,564,866	41,581	167,469	530,019
80	624,463	429,662	1,994,528	48,797	223,165	753,184
81	638,168	500,754	2,495,282	56,765	292,913	1,046,097
82	668,872	570,505	3,065,787	62,947	350,311	1,396,408
83	755,159	652,536	3,718,323	68,930	406,887	1,803,295
84	761,427	664,993	4,383,316	77,284	460,955	2,264,250
85	767,623	686,997	5,070,313	87,329	515,788	2,780,038
86	772,355	686,555	5,756,868	97,525	573,940	3,353,978
87	775,581	691,442	6,448,310	108,395	627,986	3,981,964
88	781,323	717,655	7,165,965	119,885	704,853	4,686,817
89	792,765	746,627	7,912,592	130,455	791,170	5,477,987
90	801,809	708,000	8,620,592	141,119	883,457	6,361,444
91	809,955	691,816	9,312,408	151,583	989,282	7,350,726
92	824,037	722,157	10,034,565	162,139	1,083,409	8,434,135
93	863,204	822,955	10,857,520	172,425	1,177,185	9,611,320
94	886,662	878,449	11,736,019	182,484	1,235,924	10,847,244
95	899,868	897,274	12,633,293	192,480	1,365,805	12,249,297

*Fiscal years 73-76 are July to June. Fiscal year 77 is July to September (15 months). Fiscal years 78-94 are October to September.

Notes:
1. For FY80-89 and 91-95 costs are estimated by multiplying the midpoint, March, by 12. Prior to FY80 only the end month of the fiscal year costs are available. Mid-fiscal year costs are estimated by averaging the previous end-month fiscal year figures with current end-month fiscal year figures to obtain a midpoint and multiplying by 12 to obtain the annual. Legislation significantly reducing SBP costs to retirees became effective March 1, 1990. Cost-to-Retirees figures for FY90 were estimated by multiplying the December costs by 5 and the June cost by 7 and adding. Cost-to-Retiree figures may be slightly overstated since no attempt was made to factor out the cost of the CPI increases which occurred at various times over the fiscal year.
2. Retiree numbers are determined from the March file (FY80-95) or by averaging end fiscal year figures (FY73-79). Retirees counted include only those electing and making payments for survivor benefits.
3. "Payment to families" prior to FY79 were obtained form historical reports maintained by the office of the DoD actuary.

Insurable Interest Coverage. Premiums for insurable interest coverage are 10% of the member's gross retired pay, plus an additional 5% for each full five years the beneficiary is younger than the member. The premium may not exceed 40% of the member's retired pay. Premium reductions in retired pay continue as long as the beneficiary remains alive or until the member changes the election to cover a spouse and/or child(ren) acquired later or requests termination of the insurable interest coverage.

SOCIAL SECURITY OFFSET

SBP guarantees that surviving spouses of SBP participants will receive an income from the Federal Government equal to at least 55% of a participant's base amount. Under age 62, this benefit is provided solely by SBP; after age 62 it is a combination of SBP and the Social Security survivor's benefit.

Because the Federal Government pays part of the cost for both SBP and Social Security, SBP payments to a surviving spouse will be offset by the amount of the Social Security survivor's benefit which is attributable to the member's military service. The Social Security offset to SBP is based only on Social Security credit earned by the participant while on active duty after December 31, 1956. There is no offset to annuities paid to survivors of members who retired prior to January 1, 1957. Additionally, there is no offset if the annuitant is still employed and has earnings too high for Social Security benefits to be paid only until age 70. To gain exemption from the SBP offset, a working widow(er) must obtain a statement from the Social Security Administration stating that she (or he) is not eligible for benefits because of excess earnings. This statement must then be sent to the Defense Finance center which pays the SBP annuity. Once a working widow(er) stops working and begins receiving Social Security benefits, the offset is applied or is automatically applied at age 70.

Increases in Social Security benefits during the 1970's resulted in much larger offsets to SBP annuities than originally intended (sometimes eliminating them entirely). As a result, Congress enacted P.L. 96-401 on October 9, 1980, which placed a limit on the Social Security offset to 40% of the SBP annuity. In order to increase benefits and reduce the administrative burden involved with computing the offsets, Congress eliminated the Social Security offset in November 1985 (P.L. 99-145) and replaced it with a new "two-tier" method of calculating annuities after age 62. Under this new method, annuities are reduced at age 62 from 55% of the member's base amount to 35% of the member's base amount. As such, the offset is applied whether an annuitant's social security benefit is based completely or partially on her/his own social security wage record, or on the social security wage record of his/her military spouse. The two-tier method is used automatically for survivors of members who become eligible for retirement on or after October 1, 1985. Survivors of members who retired or were eligible for retirement before October 1, 1985 are grandfathered under the original Social Security offset method. Defense Finance centers calculate annuities using both methods when an annuitant attains age 62 and pay the higher amount. In most cases, survivors receive higher annuities under the new two-tier method than under the original method. Social Security offsets to SBP can never be more than the actual amount of the Social Security benefit received.

Government Pension Offset

Social Security spouse's benefits provide income to wives and husbands who have little or no Social Security benefits of their own. Since the beginning of the Social Security program, spouse's benefits were intended for women and men who were financially dependent on their husbands or wives who worked at jobs covered by Social Security.

Spouse's benefits are normally offset by the amount of any benefits that a spouse may receive based on his or her own earnings **covered** by Social Security. Under the government pension offset, the spouse's benefit is offset by a government pension based on earnings **not covered** by Social Security. The intent of the offset is to provide similar treatment with respect to the payment of Social Security spouse's or surviving spouse's benefits for a person who worked in covered employment and for one who worked in a noncovered governmental job.

Understanding how the SBP program is funded may help in understanding why the reduction in SBP annuities at age 62 must occur, even though a surviving spouse may receive Social Security benefits based upon his or her own earnings record rather than the member's. SBP was designed to operate with a 40% subsidy from the Federal Government, with participants paying the remaining 60% through monthly reductions in their retired pay. The rate of members' premiums was determined by calculating the amount of benefits surviving spouses are expected to receive during their lifetimes, which naturally includes benefits received both before and after age 62. In other words, the reduced benefit level after age 62, as well as the full 55% benefit level before age 62, were both factored into the formula which was used to determine the rate of participants' premiums. If the reduction in annuities at 62 did not occur, members' premiums would be significantly higher than 6.5%.

DIC OFFSET

When a member of the Uniformed Services dies of a service-connected cause, either while on active duty or in retirement, certain members of his or her family may be eligible for monthly DIC payments. (See the Section on Dependency and Indemnity Compensation for details.) Whenever a surviving spouse of an SBP participant is also entitled to DIC, the spouse's monthly SBP annuity will be reduced by the amount of the DIC payment. The portion representing the DIC payment is not taxable by the Federal Government. The total of the two payments, DIC and SBP, will be equal to the full amount of the SBP annuity. If the surviving spouse remarries and becomes ineligible for DIC, the full amount of SBP may be paid if the spouse is over age 55 when the remarriage occurs. When DIC is paid to the surviving spouse of an SBP participant, the percentage of the participant's SBP premiums which corresponds to the portion of the SBP annuity not payable will be refunded to the beneficiary. This refund must be repaid for SBP eligibility to be restored.

COLA ADJUSTMENTS

SBP premiums and survivor annuities are adjusted at the same time and by the same percentage as military retired pay. Military retired pay is usually adjusted annually at the same rate as the annual increase in the Consumer Price Index (CPI). This is a significant advantage of SBP which is generally not offered by alternative programs.

UNIFORMED SERVICES ALMANAC
TAX TREATMENT

Since SBP premiums are paid in the form of reductions in participants' retired pay, they are not counted as taxable income. This tax break is especially important when comparing SBP to life insurance alternatives. For example, if a member's SBP premium is $100 a month and the member is in the 28% tax bracket, the member's actual out-of-pocket cost for SBP coverage is only $72, i.e., if the member elected to decline SBP participation and receive the $100 instead, the member would only get to keep $72 after paying taxes on the $100. $72, therefore, is the amount which one should use in comparing the cost of SBP to the cost of a comparable amount of life insurance. Studies show that, except in unusually rare circumstances, no life insurance policy can guarantee equal or greater protection for equal or less cost than SBP.

SBP annuities are considered taxable income for Federal income tax purposes. Many states exempt SBP annuities in whole or in part from taxable income for state income tax purposes. (Refer to "State Income Tax Provisions for Military Personnel" table.) The "present value" of the SBP annuity is generally not includible in the gross estate of the deceased retiree. In addition, there are no Federal gift taxes imposed on SBP annuities. (Note: *Where SBP includes DIC, the DIC portion of the total is not considered taxable income.*)

MILITARY SURVIVORS' BENEFITS

Benefit	From Military Service Active	From Military Service Retired	From Veterans Administration Service Connected	From Veterans Administration Non-Service Connected	From Social Security Wife	From Social Security Children
Death Gratuity	Yes	No(1)	No	No	No	No
Burial Allowance	Yes	No(2)	Yes*	Yes*	Yes*	Yes*
Travel Allowance	Yes	No(3)	No	No	No	No
Shipment of HHG	Yes	No(3)	No	No	No	No
DIC	No	No	Yes	No	No	No
SBP	Yes(4)	Yes(5)	No	No	No	No
RSFPP	No	Yes(5)	No	No	No	No
ID Privileges (BX, Theater, Commis.)	Yes	Yes	No	No	No	No
National Cemetery	Yes	No	Yes	Yes	No	No
Government Headstone	Yes	No	Yes*	Yes*	No	No
Burial Flag	Yes	No	Yes*	Yes*	No	No
Pension	No	No	No	Yes(6)	No	No
Monthly Survivor Payments	No	No	No	No	Yes(7)	Yes(7)
Insurance	Yes(8)	No	Yes(8)	Yes(8)	No	No
Legal Assistance	Yes	Yes	No	No	No	No
Home Loan Guaranty	No	No	No	No	No	No
CHAMPUS	Yes	Yes	No	No	No	No

*If not covered by other source.
(1)Unless death occurs within 120 days of retirement and is determined by the VA to be Service-connected.
(2)Unless retired and retained in military hospital until death occurs.
(3)Unless death occurs within one year of retirement and move has not been made.
(4)Only if member has 20 or more years of service.
(5)If SBP was elected by member.
(6)Only is survivor's income is below VA income limitations.
(7)Dependent on age and income of survivors.
(8)If member participated in SGLI, VGLI, NSLI or earlier forms of insurance.

UNIFORMED SERVICES ALMANAC

SOCIAL SECURITY

There are more than 1,300 Social Security offices located throughout the 50 States, and in Puerto Rico and the District of Columbia. Any one of these offices will give you accurate information on Social Security matters any time you go in or call by telephone. You can get the street address and telephone number of your nearest Social Security office from a telephone directory (may be listed under U.S. Gov't., Department of Health and Human Services) or from the postmaster of any U.S. post office. Your military personnel branch can also help you in getting this information. Much time can be saved by calling the Social Security office before visiting. You may be able to transact your business completely by phone. In addition, Social Security has a nationwide toll-free number (1-800-772-1213) to call. Social Security representatives answer the number from 7:00 am-7:00 pm on workdays. The best times to call are between 7:00 am-9:00 am and between 5:00 pm and 7:00 pm. After 7:00 pm automated answering equipment provides information that the offices are closed and provides the best times to call back.

Before you or your family can get any Social Security benefits, you must apply for them. *Do not delay in filing a claim if you are retiring or you are a spouse or surviving spouse. Benefits cannot be paid retroactively in most cases,* and, if so, for not more than 12 months. Get in touch with any Social Security office if:

(1) You're unable to work because of an illness or injury that has lasted or is expected to last a year or longer, or to result in death.

(2) You're 62 or older and plan to retire.

(3) You're within 3 months of 65 even if you don't plan to retire. A delay in applying for monthly benefits can cause loss of some benefits.

(4) The worker in your family dies.

(5) If you or a dependent needs dialysis treatments or a kidney transplant because of a permanent kidney failure.

Make sure that your spouse or another member of your family is aware of these important incidents to contact the Social Security office.

IMPORTANT: Retirement, spouse, and surviving spouse benefits that are reduced for age may not, with certain exceptions, be paid for any period prior to the month a claim is filed. To avoid possible loss of benefits, do not delay filing a claim, or, telephoning your Social Security Office if you cannot visit in person.

PAYMENTS INTO SOCIAL SECURITY TRUST FUNDS

The Servicemen's and Veterans' Survivor Benefits Act of 1956 (P.L. 84-881) amended the Social Security Act to extend Social Security benefits to members of the Uniformed Services. Effective January 1, 1957, service performed by such members while on *active duty* or *active duty* for training constitutes covered employment for Social Security purposes. The service member's share of Social Security and Medicare taxes, referred to as FICA (Federal Insurance Contribution Act) taxes, are withheld from base pay. *Retirement pay, however, is not subject to these taxes.*

FICA taxes are applicable to all persons appointed, enlisted, or inducted into the Regular Services or their Reserve Components who are performing active duty or active duty for training; to cadets at the military academies; and to members of the Army, Naval, and Air Force Reserve Officers' Training Corps when ordered to ROTC training for periods of 14 days or more.

UNIFORMED SERVICES ALMANAC

The maximum wage base on which Social Security taxes are withheld is $62,700 for 1996. There is no wage base limitation for Medicare tax; all covered wages are subject to Medicare tax. The Social Security tax is 6.2 percent. The Medicare tax is 1.45 percent. Form W-2 (Withholding Tax Statement), prepared for each service member at the end of each calendar year, shows the amount of FICA tax withheld during the year. Where a nonpay status extends to any full calendar month, no FICA tax is deducted for that month.

Since military Chaplains are considered employees of the Federal Government and not self-employed ministers, FICA tax is withheld from their base pay in the same manner as from base pay of other service members.

The drill pay a service member earns while on inactive duty training as a reservist is subject to FICA taxes. Reserve and Guard drill pay is subject to the same 7.65 percent withholding as for active duty members.

After-hours compensation received for services performed in nonappropriated fund activities is also subject to FICA taxes. Social Security and Medicare taxes cannot be withheld from military allowances such as those for subsistence, uniforms, and housing, and neither can these allowances be counted as earnings for Social Security purposes. Hazardous duty and other special pay does not count for FICA tax or earnings purposes. However, from January 1957 through December 1977, an additional $300 of "deemed" wages for each quarter in which you received military pay is creditable. Since 1978, wages have been reported annually. A $100 credit will be added for each full $300 in reported military wages up to $3,600. Thus, the "deemed" credit for the year cannot exceed $1,200. This amount will be taken into consideration when benefits are applied for; however, it will not be subject to Social Security taxes. DoD reimburses the Social Security trust funds with tax equivalent funds. Section 977 of the DoD Authorization Act of 1981 provides for the denial of the "deemed" credit for a person who fails to complete two years (24 months) of an original enlistment if the original enlistment was after September 7, 1980. Subsequently, the DoD Act was changed again to provide a denial of "deemed" credit for veterans who failed to complete an enlistment after October 13, 1982. The total of wages and credits cannot exceed the Social Security maximum for a given year.

Military earnings and taxes were reported quarterly by the Services through 1977 but are now reported annually. Periodically, funds to cover Social Security and Medicare taxes on the base pay of all military personnel are transferred, through DoD funds, to three trust funds set up for financing the retirement, survivors, disability and health insurance programs. One fund is used to finance the retirement and survivors insurance programs; a second is used to finance the disability insurance program. A third, the Hospital Insurance Trust Fund, began in 1966. The Federal old-age, survivors, and disability insurance programs are administered by the Social Security Administration and the health insurance program is administered by the Health Care Financing Administration, under the Department of Health and Human Services.

Table 1 shows the FICA tax rates in effect for 1976 to present. Like civilian employers, the DoD as the servicemember's employer, matches the taxes contributed by its employees.

UNIFORMED SERVICES ALMANAC

TABLE 1. FICA TAX CONTRIBUTION RATE SCHEDULE

Years	Percent of Covered Earnings		
	Retirement, Survivors, and Disability Insurance Benefits	For Hospital Insurance	Total %
1976-77	4.95	0.90	5.85
1978	5.05	1.00	6.05
1979-80	5.08	1.05	6.13
1981	5.35	1.30	6.65
1982-83	5.40	1.30	6.70
1984	5.70	1.30	7.00
1985	5.70	1.35	7.05
1986-87	5.70	1.45	7.15
1988-89	6.06	1.45	7.51
1990 & After	6.20	1.45	7.65

SOCIAL SECURITY BENEFITS AVAILABLE TO YOU

Old-age, survivors, and disability insurance (OASDI) benefits are paid to: (1) a retired insured worker age 62 or over; (2) eligible survivors and dependents of retired or disabled workers; (3) a disabled insured worker under age 65; and (4) a lump sum death payment may be payable upon the death of the insured worker.

The purpose of the Social Security benefits is to provide a partial replacement of earnings for the Service member, or civilian worker, and his or her family when family income is reduced or stops because of the serviceman's or worker's retirement, disability, or death. The amount of monthly benefits is related to earnings covered under Social Security of the insured person and provides significant replacement for family income lost when one of these events happens.

The provisions of the Social Security law are of vital interest to Service personnel and veterans. This is true both for the Service members and veterans who have Social Security insurance protection through taxes withheld from military pay after 1956 and for the veteran who gained Social Security "wage credits" during active duty in the U.S. Armed Forces before and after World War II.

MEDICARE

Medicare is the federal health insurance program for Social Security recipients. There are two parts of the program that pay for different services: Part A (Hospital Insurance) helps pay for inpatient care in a hospital or skilled-nursing home and for home health and hospice care. Protection is also available for people who have chronic renal (kidney related) disease and to those receiving or are entitled to receive cash benefits for 24 consecutive months under the Social Security program because they are disabled. If you are working, Part A can supplement your employer's health plan. Part B (Medical Insurance) helps pay for doctor's services, outpatient hospital care, and a number of other medical services and supplies.

Although most people do not pay a monthly premium for Part A coverage, enrollees do pay deductible and coinsurance amounts. Part B enrollees pay a monthly premium **plus** the deductible and coinsurance amounts. The premium amounts are set each year by law. The government meets more than two-thirds of the cost of the program. This makes this plan an exceptionally "good buy" for most older members. The premium increases if enrollment is delayed beyond age 65. Contact your local Social Security office or call the toll free number 1-800-772-1213 for more details.

UNIFORMED SERVICES ALMANAC
SOCIAL SECURITY COVERAGE

To be eligible for OASDHI (old-age, survivors, disability and health insurance) benefits, a person must have "insured status." "Insured" means that the person involved must have worked and earned Social Security credits from military service or in civilian wage-employment, or self-employment, covered by the Social Security Act for a specified amount of time, depending on the individual's age. The Social Security Administration (SSA) determines if you are fully insured, currently insured or insured for disability.

CREDITS NECESSARY FOR RETIREMENT AND SURVIVOR BENEFITS

To be fully insured, the service person must have at least one quarter of coverage for each calendar year after 1950, or after the year he or she attains age 21 if later, and prior to attainment of age 62, death or disability.

Table 2 shows the number of credits, called quarters of coverage, necessary for fully insured status. A quarter of coverage, corresponds with a calendar quarter of military service or civilian work under the law. A calendar quarter is a 3-month period beginning either January 1, April 1, July 1, or October 1 each year. *Quarters earned through military service wage credits of $160 per month after September 15, 1940 and before 1951 can be counted toward the total needed if the same period is not used for military retirement if the discharge was not under dishonorable conditions.* Wage credits for service after 1950 and before 1957 will also be granted even though this period is also used for military retirement if the person has covered military service after 1956. Civilian employment covered by the law can be counted from January 1, 1937, and self-employment covered by the law can be counted from January 1, 1951.

Certain benefits can be paid when the serviceman or woman is "currently insured," but not fully insured. You will be currently insured if you have at least 6 quarters of coverage — through either military service or civilian work — during the 13 quarters (3 1/4 years) period ending with the quarter of death. If you have earned the necessary Social Security credits, your spouse and dependent children are eligible to get monthly benefits following your death regardless of your age at death.

If you have credit for as many as 20 quarters within the 10 years ending with the quarter of disability and are fully insured, you are insured for Social Security disability benefits if you should become disabled at any time before you reach age 64 1/2. Workers disabled before age 31 need less credit and workers disabled by blindness need only to be fully insured.

Once a person has credit for 40 quarters under Social Security — from military service, covered civilian work, or a combination of both — he or she is "permanently insured" for retirement and survivors insurance, but for disability the current coverage as described above is also needed. Ten years of active military service after 1956 gives these 40 quarters of Social Security credit. Benefits, including retirement benefits, in some amount will always be payable on his or her Social Security account.

UNIFORMED SERVICES ALMANAC

TABLE 2. CREDITS (QUARTERS OF COVERAGE) NEEDED TO BE FULLY INSURED

Year in which a worker reaches age 62 or dies	Will need credit for work during this number of calendar quarters	Which is equivalent to this period of work under social security	Year in which a worker reaches age 62 or dies	Will need credit for work during this number of calendar quarters	Which is equivalent to this period of work under social security
1975	24	6 years	1984	33	8¼ years
1976	25	6¼ years	1985	34	8½ years
1977	26	6½ years	1986	35	8¾ years
1978	27	6¾ years	1987	36	9 years
1979	28	7 years	1988	37	9¼ years
1980	29	7¼ years	1989	38	9½ years
1981	30	7½ years	1990	39	9¾ years
1982	31	7¾ years	1991 & later	40	10 years
1983	32	8 years			

DISABILITY BENEFITS

Extent of Disability and Amount of Work Needed

If you become so severely disabled that you are retired from the service and are not able to do other substantial work, you and your dependents may receive disability Social Security benefits if you qualify.

To be eligible for disability benefits, a person must have a disability that is so severe it, in the words of the law, makes him or her unable to "engage in any substantial gainful activity." It must be a physical or mental impairment that will show up in medical tests and examinations and one that is expected to continue for at least 12 consecutive months or to result in death. A waiting period of 5 months after the disability began is required before benefits begin. However, a disability claim may be filed as soon as the disability occurs.

Service men and women should bear in mind that disability has a specific meaning under the Social Security law. Thus, the fact that a serviceman or woman is entitled to payments for "total disability" from another Government agency does not mean that, in every case, the person will be found eligible for disability benefits under Social Security. These benefits, however, may be received by eligible persons in addition to military disability payments based on service since 1956.

Disabled Child

When a former service member receives retirement or disability insurance benefits or when he or she dies, Social Security benefits may also be paid to a child age 18 or over and continue to any age if the child was disabled before he or she reached age 22. See Table 3 for the amount of work needed and dependents who can receive disability benefits.

Disabled Widow or Widower

A disabled widow or widower of an eligible serviceman or woman may begin to receive benefits as early as age 50.

UNIFORMED SERVICES ALMANAC

TABLE 3. SOCIAL SECURITY BENEFITS AND "INSURED STATUS" NEEDED

RETIREMENT PAYMENTS

Monthly payments to—	If you are—
You as a retired worker	Fully insured.
And monthly payments to your—	
Spouse (or divorced spouse, if married for at least 10 years) 62 or over	
Dependent child (under 18 or any age if disabled before age 22)	
Student child 18 - 19 if full time student at a secondary school	
Spouse (regardless of age) if caring for entitled child under age 16 or disabled.	

SURVIVOR PAYMENTS

Monthly payments to your—	If at death you were—
Widow or widower 60 or over	Fully insured.
Widow or widower or divorced spouse (regardless of age) if caring for child	Either fully or currently insured.
Disabled widow or widower 50-59	Fully insured.
Dependent child (under 18 or any age if disabled before age 22)	Either fully or currently insured.
Dependent parent (mother or father 62)	Fully insured.
Divorced spouse 60 or older, or spouse 50-59 and disabled (if married for at least 10 years)	Fully insured.
Lump-sum payment to your	
Widow or widower, if living with you in the same household; otherwise can go to a spouse or child who was eligible for monthly benefits for the month of death .	Either fully or currently insured.

DISABILITY PAYMENTS

Monthly payments to—	If you are—
You and your dependents* if you are totally disabled for work	Fully insured and have 20 credits out of the 40 calendar quarters ending with the one in which you became disabled.**

Children under 18, children over 18 up to 19 if a full time student at a secondary school or in some cases under 22, disabled child 18 or older (who became disabled before 22nd birthday), spouse at any age if caring for child or children under 16 or disabled and entitled to benefits, husband or wife at age 62 whether or not a child entitled to benefits is in care.** If you are less than 31, you need fewer than 20 quarters of credit, depending on when your disability began.

HOW MEMBERS EARN SOCIAL SECURITY CREDIT

Before 1978 for most employed people—and for members of the Uniformed Services — credit for one quarter of coverage was given for each calendar quarter in which the person received $50 or more in covered earnings or base pay. *Military personnel will have a quarter of coverage with any amount of pay due to the addition of the $300 deemed wages after 1956 and through 1977, or may have quarters of coverage for service between September 16, 1940 and December 31, 1956,* as explained later in this section. For every calendar quarter in which military wages are received while on active duty or active duty for training, you get credit for 1 quarter under Social Security. Each calendar year of military service gives you credit for 4 quarters of coverage under Social Security.

Starting in 1978, wages have been reported on an annual basis and $100 in deemed wages is added for each full $300 in military wages up to $3,600. Thus, the deemed wages credit for the year cannot exceed $1,200. Also, starting in 1978, one quarter of coverage was earned for each $250 of the annual wages, including the deemed wages, no matter when during the year the wages were paid. In 1979, 1980, 1981, 1982, 1983, 1984, 1985, 1986, 1987, 1988, 1989, 1990, 1991, 1992, 1993, 1994 and 1995, $260, $290, $310, $340, $370, $390, $410, $440, $460, $470, $500, $520, $540, $570, $590, $620 and $630 was required respectively for a quarter of coverage. In 1996, $640 will be required for a quarter of coverage.

Since January 1, 1957, Social Security tax has been withheld from base pay due each member of the Uniformed Services on active duty. These withholdings give you the full protection of Social Security's retirement, survivors, and disability insurance. If you are entitled to Social Security benefits on the basis of active duty after 1956, or on the basis of active duty after 1956 plus civilian work after 1936 under Social Security, these benefits can be paid regardless of any other Government or private-plan benefits you or your survivors can receive. The career service member can count all active duty after 1956 toward Social Security benefits in addition to military retirement or disability payments and any civil service payments he or she may be entitled to. If you have not been in the Uniformed Services long enough to qualify for Social Security benefits through service since December 31, 1956, any Social Security credits you received in civilian work will also count toward giving you full protection.

If you have active service after 1956, you can also count for Social Security credit and military retirement purposes any active duty during 1951-56. This service is credited in the form of military wage credits. *This 1951-56 period credit, however, cannot be used for both Social Security and civil service purposes.* (See NOTE in section on Employment of Retired Military personnel.)

If you were on active duty in the military or naval forces of the United States (including the Army, Navy, Air Force, Marine Corps, and Coast Guard) or you were a commissioned officer in the Public Health Service or the Coast and Geodetic Survey (now NOAA) *between September 15, 1940, and January 1, 1957,* you have gratuitous Social Security "wage credits" of $160 for each month of active duty as long as your release or retirement was under other than dishonorable conditions. In addition, your period of service must have been for at least 90 days or, if less, you must have been retired or discharged from service because of disability or injury incurred or aggravated in the line of duty (with certain exceptions as noted in previous section). If your service is confined to this period — September 16, 1940 and December 31, 1956 — you cannot count the wage credits for Social Security credit if you receive military retirement pay (See 1951 — 1956 exception above, if you had active service after 1956) or if monthly benefits are payable by another Federal agency (except the Veterans Administration) based on the same military service. Payments from the Veterans Administration do not prevent the use of deemed military wages for service after 1956 toward Social Security benefits. Beginning January 1957 and through December 1977 you may count up to $300 in additional Social Security credit, called deemed military wages, for each quarter in which you received *any military pay* for active duty (see below), but not to exceed maximum annual taxable earnings subject to Social Security tax. Starting in 1978, deemed wages have been granted in $100 increments, as explained above.

A person who died while in service during this period also has Social Security credit in the form of wage credits for his or her period of service. Any Social Security credit gained by a veteran who left military service under other than dishonorable conditions following a military tour during World War II or the Korean Conflict is added to Social Security credits gained in Social Security-covered civilian work and count toward insured status.

United States citizens meeting certain dates of entry, U.S. citizenship and residence, length of service, and discharge conditions who had World War II military service with a foreign country that was at war on September 16, 1940, with a country with which the United States was at war during World War II, also may be given gratuitous wage credits.

A former member of the Woman's Army Auxiliary Corps may get military wage credits for service in this auxiliary if she had service after May 13, 1942, and before September 30, 1943, and had active service in the Uniformed Services after September 29, 1943. Wage credits were not granted for service with certain auxiliary organizations, including the Coast Guard Auxiliary, the temporary Coast Guard Reserve (unless service was full-time duty with military pay and allowances), the Civilian Auxiliary to the Military Police, and the Civil Air Patrol.

Service by midshipmen at the U.S. Naval Academy or cadets at the U.S. Military, Air Force, or Coast Guard Academy is termed military service under the Social Security law, giving them full credit under Social Security for periods of attendance.

Since January 1, 1957, *active duty for training* is also creditable for Social Security purposes. Active duty for training includes the full-time training duty performed by members of the Army, Navy, or Air Force ROTC. Authorized travel to and from this full-time duty, or to and from the ROTC training, is included in the period of active duty for training. If a 14 day or longer tour falls in two calendar quarters, or after 1977, in two calendar years, Social Security credit will be given for the period in which earnings are reported. *Evening and weekend drills attended by Reserve personnel with paid-duty slots are inactive duty for training.* Social Security tax is withheld from pay received for attendance at these drills since 1988.

Social Security credits received by members of the Uniformed Services while on active duty and active duty for training are combined where necessary with credits received through covered civilian work — wage-employment or self-employment — before or after military service to increase Social Security credits and the amounts of benefits due them and dependents or due survivors. Today, nine out of ten persons working in the United States are earning Social Security credits.

AMOUNTS OF SOCIAL SECURITY BENEFITS

Amounts of benefits payable on your Social Security record are determined from your average yearly taxable earnings over a certain period of time. Social Security benefits are computed by two methods of averaging earnings depending on when you are first eligible or the date you die. Usually, the basic amount payable is determined on the basis of the earnings adjusted to reflect earlier earnings in terms of the current dollar value. Social Security Administration will explain how the earnings are indexed; the averaging period and how benefits are computed. On the Social Security records of most people, this period is from January 1, 1951, (or January 1 of the year of the *22nd birthday* for those who have reached 21 since 1950) through the year *before* the person reaches 62 (with some adjustment for men reaching 62 before 1975), becomes disabled, or dies. Amounts of benefits payable on your record will depend on your average earnings over a certain number of these years. The lowest 5 years of earnings in the number of years to be used are excluded in figuring the average.

TABLE 4. PERCENTAGES FOR DEPENDENT AND SURVIVOR PAYMENTS

When you retire, become disabled, or die, monthly benefits can be paid to your—	This % times your monthly amount (before any reduction for age)*
Spouse or divorced spouse 62 or older, or spouse at any age with your entitled child (under 18 or disabled) in care[1][2]	50%
Child under 18 or 18-19 who qualifies as a student, or who is over 18 and is disabled before age 22	50% (if you are alive) 75% (if you are deceased)
Widow(er) or surviving divorced spouse who is at least age 60, or disabled and age 50-59	100%[1][2]
Child(ren)'s mother or father or surviving divorced mother or father	75%
First dependent parent	82½%
Second dependent parent (if two parents are entitled at the same time, each would receive 75%)	75%

[1] A divorced spouse must be 62 even with a child in care

[2] A divorced spouse must have been married to the worker for at least 10 years

[1] Reduced for months of entitlement before age 65
[2] not reduced below 75% If the widow(er) or surviving divorced spouse has your entitled child in care.
*Limited by a maximum amount payable to the family.

In every case, the benefit amount due the insured person is figured when he or she applies for Social Security retirement or disability benefits, or when his or her family members file claims for survivor benefits. All payments to dependents or survivors are based on this amount. Table 4 shows the percentages used in figuring various dependent and survivor payments.

Since military personnel usually complete active service prior to age 62, it will probably be several years before you file for Social Security retirement benefits. Shortly before you reach retirement age, when you file your Social Security claim, the exact amount of your benefit, based on all applicable earnings and the then-current benefit schedule, will be figured by trained personnel working for the Social Security Administration. You can estimate the amounts of disability and survivor benefits that could be paid to you based on your Social Security record.

If you want to know the approximate amounts of benefits on your record, refer to the material on the following page in the section headed "ESTIMATING RETIREMENT BENEFITS."

UNIFORMED SERVICES ALMANAC

REDUCED BENEFITS AS EARLY AS AGE 62

The Social Security law allows both men and women to apply for Social Security retirement and spouse benefits as early as age 62, (60 for widows, surviving divorced spouses, and widowers or 50 for surviving spouses and surviving divorced spouses if disabled).

When retirement benefits based on his or her Social Security record are paid to a former service member before age 65, the amount of the benefit is permanently reduced. Benefits paid to a spouse of a former service member before he or she reaches 65 are also reduced, unless that spouse has care of the service member's entitled child under age 16, or a child disabled before age 22.

The reduction at age 62 is 20 percent, 13 1/3 percent at age 63, and 6 2/3 percent at age 64. (A retiree entitled to $8,500 a year at age 65 will receive $6,800 a year at age 62).

To reach an informed decision on when to retire, an individual should determine:

  a. Whether you are fully insured.
  b. How much earnings have been credited to your Social Security record.
  c. What the Social Security Administration projects your estimated Primary Insurance Amount (PIA) will be at age 65. Your PIA is the monthly Social Security Payment that you would be entitled to at age 65 based on your total earnings history.

To obtain a benefit estimate, you can call toll-free (1-800-772-1213) and request SSA Form 7004. After you complete the SSA Form 7004, and return it to Social Security, you should receive a detailed Personal Earnings and Benefits Estimate Statement within six weeks.

BIGGER BENEFITS BY ADDITIONAL WORK

When an insured person works after he or she is eligible for retirement benefits, the amount he or she can receive in benefits will depend upon how much he or she earns in employment or self-employment. Beginning with the month he or she reaches 70, however, a person can receive all benefits due him or her regardless of how much he or she earns or works each year.

If you return to work after you start receiving retirement benefits, your added earnings may result in higher benefits. Social Security will automatically refigure your benefit after the additional earnings are credited to your record. Only earned income is subject to Social Security payment. Retired pay is not earned income.

In addition, a special credit can mean a larger benefit. For each month past 65 that you delay receiving retirement benefits, a credit increases the amount of your benefit. These increases, known as delayed retirement credits, apply up to the month you are 70.

The rate of delayed retirement credits depends on a person's year of birth, as shown in the following table.

Survivor benefits are payable to dependent parents at age 62, surviving spouses and surviving divorced spouses at age 60, and disabled surviving spouses and surviving divorced spouses as early as age 50. Benefits to them, however, are reduced because of age under 65. Parents' benefits are not reduced for age.

UNIFORMED SERVICES ALMANAC

CHART OF DELAYED RETIREMENT CREDIT RATES

Attain Age 65	Monthly Percentage	Yearly Percentage
Prior to 1982	1/12 of 1%	1%
1982-1989	1/4 of 1%	3%
1990-1991	7/24 of 1%	3.5%
1992-1993	1/3 of 1%	4%
1994-1995	3/8 of 1%	4.5%
1996-1997	5/12 of 1%	5%
1998-1999	11/24 of 1%	5.5%
2000-2001	1/2 of 1%	6%
2002-2003	13/24 of 1%	6.5%
2004-2005	7/12 of 1%	7%
2006-2007	5/8 of 1%	7.5%
2008 or later	2/3 of 1%	8%

BENEFITS MAY BE TAXABLE

The Omnibus Budget Reconciliation Act of 1993 (P.L. 103-66) increases the percentage of Social Security and Railroad Retirement Tier I benefits that may be subject to income taxes from 50 percent to 85 percent for single taxpayers with incomes over $34,000 and for married taxpayers filing jointly with incomes over $44,000. The law retains the present law, under which no more than 50 percent of benefits may be subject to income taxes, for single taxpayers with incomes from $25,000 to $34,000 and for married taxpayers filing jointly with incomes from $32,000 to $44,000. Income for benefit taxation purposes would continue to be the sum of the taxpayer's adjusted gross income, any tax-exempt income, and 50 percent of the taxpayer's Social Security or Tier I benefits.

After the end of each year, you will receive a *Social Security Benefit Statement* (Form SSA-1099) in the mail showing the amount of benefits you received. The statement is to be used only for completing your Federal income tax return if any of your benefits are subject to tax.

Most people who are neither residents nor citizens of the United States will be taxed by having up to 15 percent of their benefits withheld. If you are subject to this tax and you become a U.S. resident or citizen, you should notify any Social Security office.

If you have taxable income, some Internal Revenue Service publications may be of help, especially Publication 554, *Tax Benefits for Older Americans*, and Publication 915, *Tax Information on Social Security (and Tier 1 Railroad Retirement) Benefits*. These and other publications are available at local Internal Revenue Service offices.

THE LUMP-SUM PAYMENT

Upon the death of an insured person, a lump-sum payment may be made. It is paid in addition to any monthly benefits due survivors. The lump-sum payment is made to the widow or widower if she or he was living in the same household as the insured person at the time of his or her death, or is entitled to or eligible for widow(er)'s benefits for the month of death. Otherwise, the lump sum is paid to a child who was entitled to or eligible for monthly benefits for the month of death. The lump-sum payment is $255.

UNIFORMED SERVICES ALMANAC

NOTE: It would be advisable to request a Social Security earnings statement every 3 years, which is the limit within which corrections to your record can be made by Social Security Administration if there are any errors. There are certain exemptions to permit earnings records corrections after 3 years.

ESTIMATING RETIREMENT BENEFITS

The following table, although it does not reflect the specific amounts you will receive, gives you some ideas of amounts of maximum and average payments as of January 1, 1996.

EXAMPLES OF MONTHLY PAYMENTS

Benefit Category	January 1996 Payments
I. Maximum Social Security benefit	
Maximum benefit, worker retiring at age 65	$1,248
II. Average Social Security benefit	
All retired workers	$720
Aged couple, both receiving benefits	$1,215
Widowed mother and two children	$1,407
Aged widow alone	$680
Disabled worker, spouse, and children	$1,148
All disabled workers	$682
III. Maximum Federal SSI payments*	
Individual	$470
Couple	$705

EARNED INCOME AFTER SOCIAL SECURITY STARTS

If you go back to work and are under age 70, your earnings may affect your Social Security benefits. You don't have to stop working completely, though, to get Social Security benefits. You can receive all benefits if your earnings do not exceed the annual exempt amount. Retirement pay is not earned income.

In 1996 for those between 65-69, the withholding is $1 of benefits for every $3 of earnings above the limit. It remains $1 for every $2 for people under 65. Since January 1978, a person may use the monthly test *only in the first year* he or she has a month in which earnings do not exceed 1/12 of the annual exempt amount and does not perform substantial services in self-employment. For 1996, if such a month occurs, a benefit can be paid for any month in which you earn $960 or less (if age 65-69) or $690 (if under 65) and you don't perform substantial services in self-employment even though your total yearly earnings exceeds the annual amount. For people 65 and over, the calendar year exempt amount was $9,720 in 1991; $10,200 in 1992; $10,560 in 1993; $11,160 in 1994; $11,280 in 1995; and $11,520 in 1996. After that, the limit will increase automatically as the level of average wages rises. The limit for people under 65 ($8,280 in 1996) will also continue to increase.

(Note: Different rules apply to work performed by people getting benefits because they are disabled. For more information, ask for a copy of the leaflet, "If You Become Disabled," at any Social Security office.)

If you are getting retirement checks, your earnings may affect your dependent's checks as well as your own. If you get checks as a dependent or survivor, your earnings can affect only your own check.

UNIFORMED SERVICES ALMANAC

SOCIAL SECURITY FINANCING SCHEDULE
CALENDAR YEARS 1937-1996[1]

Calendar Year	Maximum annual taxable earning $	Tax Rate: Employer and Employee, Each			Maximum Employee Tax $
		OASDI* %	HI** %	Total %	
1937-49	3,000	1.0	—	1.0	30
1950	3,000	1.5	—	1.5	45
1951-53	3,600	1.5	—	1.5	54
1954	3,600	2.0	—	2.0	72
1955-56	4,200	2.0	—	2.0	84
1957-58	4,200	2.25	—	2.25	94.50
1959	4,800	2.5	—	2.5	120
1960-61	4,800	3.0	—	3.0	144
1962	4,800	3.125	—	3.125	150
1963-64	4,800	3.625	—	3.625	174
1966	6,600	3.85	—	4.2	277.20
1967	6,600	3.9	.35	4.4	290.40
1968	7,800	3.8	.5	4.4	343.40
1969-70	7,800	4.2	.6	4.8	374.40
1971	7,800	4.6	.6	5.2	405.60
1972	9,000	4.6	.6	5.2	468
1973	10,800	4.85	.6	5.85	631.80
1974	13,200	4.95	1.0	5.85	772.20
1975	14,100	4.95	.9	5.85	824.85
1976	15,300	4.95	.9	5.95	895.05
1977	16,500	4.95	.9	5.85	965.25
1978	17,700	5.05	.9	6.05	1,070.85
1979	22,900	5.08	1.0	6.13	1,403.77
1980	25,900	5.08	1.05	6.13	1,587.67
1981	29,700	5.35	1.05	6.65	1,975.05
1982	32,400	5.40	1.30	6.70	2,170.80
1983	35,700	5.40	1.30	6.70	2,391.90
1984	37,800	5.70	1.30	7.0	2,646.00#
1985	39,600	5.70	1.30	7.05	2,791.80
1986	42,000	5.70	1.35	7.15	3,003.00
1987	43,800	5.70	1.45	7.15	3,131.70
1988	45,000	6.06	1.45	7.51	3,379.50
1989	48,000	6.06	1.45	7.51	3,604.80
1990	51,300	6.20	1.45	7.65	3,924.45
1991	53,400	6.20	1.45	7.65	4,085.10
1992	55,500	6.20	1.45	7.65	4,245.75
1993	57,600	6.20	1.45	7.65	4,406.40
1994	60,600	6.20	1.45	7.65	4,635.90
1995	61,200	6.20	1.45	7.65	4,681.80
1996	62,700†	6.20	1.45	7.65	4,796.55

[1]After 1983 the base will increase per average wage levels.
*Old Age, Survivors and Disability Insurance.
**Hospital Insurance.
#The maximum tax actually paid by employees was $2,532.60. Amendments of 1983 raised the tax rate in 1984 from 6.7 percent to 7.0. A one-time credit of 0.3 percent of covered wages was allowed against 1984 employees taxes. Thus the effective tax rate for employees was 6.7 percent in 1984.
†Earnings above this amount will continue to be taxed for Hospital Insurance (Medicare) purposes.

UNIFORMED SERVICES ALMANAC

PART III

VETERANS BENEFITS

(**NOTE**: The FY 96 Appropriations Act for the Department of Veterans Affairs (VA) was not enacted at the time this edition went to press. A 2.6 percent increase for disabled veterans receiving disability compensation was approved as was an increase in DIC payments to eligible surviving spouses and children. These new figures are reflected in this section. Due to the ongoing impasse between the Congress and the Administration, we have no way of knowing when, or if, a budget bill for the VA will be approved for FY 96. The information on pensions, educational assistance and home loan amounts are accurate as of press time.)

This section is designed to provide general information concerning the most important Federal benefits that the Congress has provided specifically for all veterans, their dependents and beneficiaries. More detailed information concerning any benefit may be obtained from the Federal agency administering it. Applications for VA benefits may be filed at, or further information may be obtained from, your nearest VA office. Dial 1-800-827-1000, a toll-free number, to reach a regional representative. VA has a number of other nationwide toll-free telephone services, including: Life Insurance, 1-800-669-8477; Debt Management Center, 1-800-827-0648; Telecommunication Device for the Deaf (TDD), 1-800-829-4833; CHAMPVA, 1-800-733-8387. Please do not write the VA Central Office in Washington, D.C.

COMPENSATION FOR SERVICE CONNECTED DISABILITY

Nature of Benefit — Disability compensation means a monthly payment by the VA to a veteran for a service connected disability. The payments are made for disabilities of 10% up to 100%. Certain serious disabilities are given special monthly rates. When the extent of disability falls between two such groups, an intermediate rate may be awarded. The current nontaxable minimum compensation is $91 per month and the maximum is currently $1,870 per month. VA compensation is not counted as taxable income by the Federal government. Social Security payments do not affect VA compensation.

Basis of Eligibility — Disability must result from disease or injury incurred in or aggravated during active duty or active duty for training. Benefits also may be paid for injury sustained during inactive duty for training. In all cases the disability must have occurred in line of duty, and discharge or release from duty must have been under other than dishonorable conditions.

UNIFORMED SERVICES ALMANAC

Monthly Rates of Compensation.

Service-Connected Disability   **Effective Dec 1, 95**

1. 10 percent .... $ 91
2. 20 percent 174
3. 30 percent 266
4. 40 percent 380
5. 50 percent 542
6. 60 percent 683
7. 70 percent 862
8. 80 percent 999
9. 90 percent 1,124
10. 100 percent 1,870

Additional Amounts Payable for:

a. Total disability, plus additional service-connected disabilities independently rated at 60% or veteran is permanently house-bound by reason of service-connected disability 2,093

b. Loss, or loss of use, of a creative organ, or 1 foot, or 1 hand, or both buttocks, or blindness of 1 eye, or has suffered a complete loss of speech or bilateral deafness (but in no event to exceed $2,779 exclusive of additional compensation for dependents 80

c. Loss, or loss of use, of both feet, or 1 hand and 1 foot, or blindness of both eyes, or is permanently bedridden or so helpless as to be in need of regular aid and attendance 2,326

d. Loss, or loss of use, of both hands, or both legs at a level, or with complications, preventing natural knee action with prostheses in place, or of one arm and one leg at levels, or with complications, preventing natural elbow and knee action with prostheses or suffered blindness in both eyes, rendering him or her so helpless as to be in need of regular aid and attendance 2,565

e. Loss, or loss of use, of both arms at levels, or with complications, preventing natural elbow action with prostheses in place, has suffered the anatomical loss of both legs so near the hip as to prevent the use of prosthetic appliances, or has suffered the anatomical loss of one arm and one leg so near the shoulder and hip as to prevent the use of prosthetic appliances, or suffered total blindness or anatomical loss of both eyes 2,918

f. Suffered disability under conditions which would entitle him to 2 or more rates in a. to d. above, no condition being considered twice, or suffered bilateral deafness (and hearing impairment in either or both ears is service-connected) rated at 60% or more, plus disabling and service-connected total blindness, or if the veteran has suffered the anatomic loss of both arms so near the shoulder as to prevent the use of prosthetic appliances 3,261

Allowances for Dependents. Veterans whose service-connected disabilities are rated at 30 percent or more are entitled to additional compensation for dependents. The additional amount is determined by the number of dependents and the degree of disability.

The current rates are listed below and are based upon 100 percent disability. The rates for 30 percent or more are payable at the same ratio that the degree of disability bears to 100 percent.

UNIFORMED SERVICES ALMANAC

Dependency	Rate
Spouse and —	
No children	$109
1 child	186
2 children	243
3 children	300
Additional children (each)	57
No spouse and	
1 child	75
2 children	132
3 children	189
Additional children (each)	57
Dependent parents	
1 parent	88
2 parents	176
Child over age 18 attending school (in lieu of benefits shown above)	172
Spouse requiring aid and attendance (in lieu of above) depending upon rate of disability of veteran	29 to 96

COMPENSATION FOR PERSIAN GULF VETERANS

Legislation signed into law November 2, 1994 allows compensation payments to Persian Gulf veterans suffering from mystery illnesses. The new law gives the Department of Veterans Affairs the authority to compensate any Persian Gulf veteran suffering from a chronic disability that became evident during or after service in the region. The VA is directed to develop and implement a uniform case assessment protocol and case definitions or diagnoses of Persian Gulf veterans. Also authorized is a survey of Persian Gulf War veterans and their families and an epidemiological study of ailments associated with Persian Gulf War veterans.

PENSION

Veterans may be eligible for support if they have limited income when they have 90 days or more of active military service, at least one day of which was during a period of war. Their discharge from active duty must have been under conditions other than dishonorable. They must be permanently and totally disabled for reasons neither traceable to military nor to willful misconduct. Payments are made to qualified veterans to bring their total income, including other retirement or Social Security income, to an established support level. Countable income may be reduced by unreimbursed medical expenses. Pension is not payable to those who have assets that can be used to provide adequate maintenance.

Nature of Benefit — Effective December 1, 1995 the improved pension program provides for the following annual rates, generally payable monthly, reduced by the amount of the annual countable income of the veteran, spouse and dependent children if any.

UNIFORMED SERVICES ALMANAC

Pension Rates for Veterans:
Veteran without dependent spouse or child $8,246
Veteran with one dependent (spouse or child) $10,801
Veteran in need of regular aid and attendance w/o dependents ... $13,190
Veteran in need of regular aid and attendance with 1 dependent . $15,744
Veteran permanently housebound without dependent $10,080
Veteran permanently housebound with one dependent................ $12,634
Two veterans married to one another $10,801
World War I veteran add.. $1,867
                                                    to the applicable annual rate
Increase for each additional dependent child $1,404

EDUCATIONAL ASSISTANCE — SONS AND DAUGHTERS, OR SPOUSES OF CERTAIN TOTALLY DISABLED AND DECEASED VETERANS

Nature of Benefit — Educational or special restorative training for a maximum of 45 months. Period of eligibility for children generally is from the 18th birthday, or graduation from high school, if earlier, to 26th birthday, but there are exceptions to both age limits. A spouse or surviving spouse must complete training within 10 years from the date he or she first becomes eligible. Survivors become eligible up to one year from the veteran's discharge from active duty. An assistance allowance is paid to the spouse or surviving spouse, or parent or guardian of an eligible child pursuing a program of education at the following rates: $404 for full-time training; $304 for 3/4-time training; and $202 for 1/2-time training. Payment of a special training allowance for the pursuit of special restorative training at the basic rate of $404 which amount may be increased under certain conditions is available for eligible sons and daughters. Assistance allowance may be paid to an eligible dependent pursuing education on a less than 1/2-time basis; payments are computed at the rates of the school's established charges for tuition and fees, or $404 per month for a full-time course, whichever is the lesser.

Basis of Eligibility — Death or a permanent and total disability of the veteran resulting from a service-connected disability arising out of active service in the Armed Forces, or who died from any cause while a disability (so evaluated) was in existence, but only if the veteran's service did not terminate under dishonorable conditions. Spouses and children of current prisoners of war, of members listed as missing in action or interned in line of duty by a foreign power for more than 90 days may also qualify for these benefits.

Counseling — The eligible child may receive VA educational or vocational counseling to assist in selection of a goal and the development of a program of education. Counseling is available to spouses and survivors on request.

MONTGOMERY GI BILL

The Montgomery GI Bill establishes a program of education benefits for individuals entering military service after June 30, 1985. Servicemembers entering active duty after that date will have their basic pay reduced by $100 a month for the first 12 months of active duty, unless they specifically elect not to participate in the program. **The reduction is non-refundable.** An exception is made under specific conditions for servicemembers who are involuntarily separated from active duty with an honorable discharge after

UNIFORMED SERVICES ALMANAC

February 2, 1991. Those who previously decided not to participate in this program and who voluntarily separate from active duty after December 4, 1991, under the Special Separation Benefit or the Voluntary Separation Incentive Programs also may elect to participate. If the servicemember decides to participate before separation, military pay will be reduced before separation, and education or training may take place following separation. A death benefit may be payable to a designated survivor if the servicemember's death is in service and is service-connected. The servicemember must have been eligible at the time of death or would have been eligible but for the high school diploma and/or length of service requirements. VA will pay an amount equal to the participant's actual military pay reduction less any education benefits previously paid or any accrued benefits paid.

Servicemembers eligible for post-Korean Conflict GI Bill benefits as of December 31, 1989, who served 3 years of continuous active duty after June 30, 1985, as well as those who served 2 years on active duty followed by 4 years satisfactory participation in the Selected Reserve after June 30, 1985, are eligible, but will not have their basic pay reduced. These members must have been on active duty on October 19, 1984, and continued without a break in service through the individual's qualifying period. Married servicemembers both of whom are veterans may claim each other as a dependent for education benefits, provided a certified copy of the marriage certificate appears in both VA files. Servicemembers who, after December 31, 1976, received commissions as officers from service academies or Senior ROTC scholarship programs are not eligible for this program.

Active duty for 3 years, or 2 years active duty plus 4 years in the Reserve or National Guard, will entitle an individual to $416.62 a month in basic benefits for 36 months. Individuals who serve at least 2 years of continuous active duty, if the initial period of service is less than 3 years, will receive $338.51 a month. Future rate increases will be tied to the Consumer Price Index. There is also a discretionary kicker of up to an additional $700 available if directed by DoD. Also, servicemembers who serve an additional 5 years may receive a supplemental benefit of up to $300 with a discretionary kicker of up to $300 more for 36 months if directed by DoD. Rate increases are tied to the Consumer Price Index. By law, there was no rate change for the 1994 Federal fiscal year; the 1995 and the 1996 fiscal year increases were reduced by one-half.

If an individual is released for the convenience of the government the servicemember must have served at least 20 months of an obligation of less than 3 years, or 30 months of an obligation of 3 years or longer. Participants who do not complete the required obligated service must have been discharged for a service-connected disability for hardship, for a pre-existing medical condition or involuntarily separated due to reduction in force.

The veteran who completes his or her obligated period of service must be discharged with an honorable discharge. Before completing the initial obligated tour of service, the participant must have met the requirements of a secondary school diploma or the equivalent. Individuals with entitlement under the noncontributory GI Bill, who convert to the new program, may satisfy the high school requirement if they successfully complete the equivalent of 12 semester hours in a program leading to a standard college degree.

UNIFORMED SERVICES ALMANAC

Eligibility will end 10 years from the date of the veteran's last discharge or release from active duty. Participants in a program requiring 2 years active duty followed by 4 years in the Selected Reserve will have 10 years in which to train after completing the 4-year reserve requirement. Individuals with entitlement under the noncontributory GI Bill, who convert to the new program, will have until January 1, 2000, to use their entitlement, but must have been discharged before December 31, 1989.

Those who are involuntarily separated from active duty with an honorable discharge and who were on active duty on September 30, 1990, and discharged after February 2, 1991, or who were on active duty on or after November 30, 1993, may elect to receive benefits under the MGIB.

Benefits are payable for attendance at institutions of higher learning, noncollege degree programs, apprenticeship/on-the-job training, pursuit of correspondence training, flight training to include solo flying hours for the remainder of the current program for which enrolled, and cooperative courses. Veterans may pursue refresher, remedial and deficiency courses, qualify for tutorial assistance, or receive work-study benefits. Questions regarding the Montgomery G.I. Bill should be directed to any VA regional office.

An educational entitlement program to include tutorial assistance, referred to as the Montgomery GI Bill-Selected Reserve, is available for members of the Selected Reserve, and National Guard. Those eligible after June 30, 1985, are members who enlist, reenlist, or extend an enlistment in the Selected Reserve for a period of 6 years or more; and those who are appointed or are serving as a reserve officer and agree to serve in the Selected Reserve for not less than 6 years in addition to any other period of obligated Selected Reserve service after June 30, 1985.

To receive benefits, an individual must complete his or her initial period of active duty training. In addition, a reservist must have completed the requirements for a secondary school diploma or the equivalent before completing initial active duty, or before completing a reenlistment or extending an enlistment. The reserve member must continue to satisfactorily participate in the Selected Reserve.

An eligible reservist is entitled to $197.90 a month. Future rate increases will generally be tied to the Consumer Price Index. Eligibility will end the date of separation from the Selected Reserve or 10 years from the date eligibility began whichever occurs first.

Educational assistance is payable for courses leading to a certificate or diploma from business, technical, or vocational schools, cooperative training, apprenticeship/on-the-job training, correspondence training, independent study programs and flight training. Reservists may also receive work-study benefits.

A reservist who fails to participate satisfactorily in the Selected Reserve is no longer eligible for educational assistance and may be required to repay a portion of the educational benefits received.

VOCATIONAL REHABILITATION PROGRAM

Nature of Benefit — The vocational rehabilitation program provides all services and assistance necessary to enable service-disabled veterans to achieve maximum independence in daily living and, to the maximum extent feasible, to become employable and to obtain and maintain suitable employment.

The services and assistance which may be provided under title 38 U.S.C., chapter 31 include the following:
Evaluation to determine potential for rehabilitation;
Subsistence allowance;
Clothing allowance for special cases;
Payment of tuition, books, fees, tools, equipment and supplies;
Work-study allowance;
Counseling and Placement Services;
Personal adjustment and work adjustment training;
Vocational and other training services;
No-interest loans;
Treatment, care, and services;
Prosthetic appliances, eyeglasses;
Lipreading training and signing for the deaf;
Assistance to a veteran's family;
Transportation expenses;
Special services related to blindness and deafness;
Services necessary to enable a veteran to achieve maximum independence for daily living; and
Other incidental goods and services determined by the VA to be necessary to accomplish rehabilitation.

Eligibility and Entitlement

A veteran is eligible for vocational rehabilitation if he or she has a service-connected disability incurred or disabilities which VA has rated at least 20 percent disabling and which the veteran on or after September 16, 1940; has an other than dishonorable discharge, and is determined to be in need of rehabilitation services because of an employment handicap. **Note:** If a veteran first filed an application for vocational rehabilitation before November 1, 1990, he or she may be eligible with a less than 20 percent compensable disability rating. Effective October 1, 1993, veterans with a 10 percent disability, with a serious employment handicap, may also be eligible. A veteran must complete a rehabilitation program within the 12-year period from the date of notification of entitlement to VA compensation. This period may be adjusted if the veteran was unable to train for a period because of medical conditions, including the disabling effects of chronic alcoholism. The 12-year period may be extended to complete the training program if the veteran is determined to have a serious employment handicap.

Up to 48 months and more of training, education and other supportive rehabilitation services may be authorized in colleges and universities, apprentice, on-the-job and on-the-farm training sites, as well as in special rehabilitation facilities or in the veteran's home if necessary. A veteran with a serious disability may receive services under an extended evaluation program to improve his or her training potential. Eligible veterans may receive job counseling, placement and adjustment services for a maximum period of 18 months. For those veterans for whom a vocational goal is not currently feasible, the veteran may be furnished services needed to improve his or her capacity for independent living in the community.

UNIFORMED SERVICES ALMANAC

LOANS GUARANTEED, INSURED, OR MADE BY DEPARTMENT OF VETERANS AFFAIRS —HOME LOANS AND OTHER

Nature of Benefits — Since President Franklin D. Roosevelt signed the VA home loan program into law in June 1944, VA has guaranteed the repayment of loans made by private lenders to eligible veterans. Loans may be to build or purchase a conventionally constructed home or manufactured homes; to make alterations, repairs or improvements in homes already owned and occupied by the veteran; to purchase a farm home; to purchase a residential condominium; to refinance an existing home loan or an existing VA loan to reduce the interest rate; or to improve a home through the installation of a solar heating and/or cooling system or for other weatherization improvements. This benefit is for eligible veterans (eligibility requirements for different periods of service vary. Consult with the local VA office for details); for the spouses of personnel officially listed as MIA, or captured, for more than 90 days; unremarried surviving spouses of veterans who died on active duty or as a result of a service-connected disability; and for active duty servicemembers who have served at least 90 days. Home loans may be made for terms up to 30 years and 32 days.

The Veteran's Entitlement. The word "entitlement" means the guaranty benefits available to an eligible veteran. The basic entitlement available to an eligible veteran is $36,000. However, as much as $50,750 of entitlement may be available to veterans purchasing or constructing homes to be financed with a loan of more than $144,000 or who refinance an existing VA loan for interest rate reduction and more than $36,000 entitlement was originally used.

The VA does not establish maximum loan amounts. However, no loan for the acquisition of a home may exceed the reasonable value of the property. A loan for the purpose of refinancing existing mortgage loans or other liens secured on record of a dwelling owned and occupied by the veteran as the veteran's home is generally limited to 90 percent of the appraised value of the dwelling as determined by VA. A loan for the purchase of a manufactured home and/or lot is limited to 95 percent of the amount that would be subject to finance charges. In addition to these limits, the VA funding fee and up to $6,000 in energy efficient improvements may be included.

The maximum amount of entitlement which may be used depends on the loan purpose and loan amount and will be the lesser of the percentage or dollar limits in the following table.

Loan Amount	Guaranty Percent	Dollar Amount
Up to $45,000	50%	$22,500
$45,001 to $56,250	40%-50%	$22,500
$56,251 to $144,000	40%	$36,000
Over $144,000 (Purchase or construction loan only)	25%	$50,750
Manufactured home and/or Lot loan	40%	$20,000

VA does not require a down payment if the lender agrees. VA does require a down payment for manufactured homes and if the purchase price exceeds the reasonable value of the property or the loan has a graduated payment feature. The maximum loan amount is limited to the lesser of the sales price or the reasonable value of the property, as determined by the VA plus the funding fee, if required. Certain refinancing loans may not exceed 90 percent of the reasonable value of the home plus the funding fee, if required.

VA also guarantees loans for the purchase of a lot in combination with a loan for a manufactured home or, if the veteran already owns a manufactured home, for a lot upon which to place the unit. Manufactured home loans may include an appropriate amount for necessary site preparation of a lot being purchased or already owned by the veteran. The guaranty on manufactured home loans is 40 percent up to $20,000. For loans closed after January 31, 1988, no loan may exceed 95 percent of the purchase price of the manufactured home, based on P.L. 100-198. The maximum maturity for manufactured home loans is 20 years and 32 days for a single-wide unit either with or without a lot, 23 years and 32 days for a double-wide unit without a lot, and 25 years and 32 days for a double-wide unit and lot. A loan for the purchase only of a manufactured home lot has a maximum maturity of 15 years and 32 days.

VA is also authorized to guarantee loans involving manufactured homes that are on a permanent foundation. If consistent with State law, these loans are subject to the longer term, lower interest rate, and increased guaranty available on loans involving conventionally constructed homes.

Current VA mortgage holders who desire to refinance their loans to decrease the interest rate will only be charged a 0.5% funding fee. Those who obtain home improvement loans will pay a 1.25 % funding fee. Loans for manufactured homes either for the home only, lot only, or home and lot will pay a 1% VA funding fee. The authority for the negotiated rate expired December 31, 1995, however, these authorities should be reinstated after the 1996 budget is passed.

P.L. 102-547, the Veterans' Home Loan Revitalization Program Act of 1992, significantly changed the VA home loan program. As of October 28, 1992, no interest rate will be set for VA loans, but members may negotiate the rate as well as points with the lender. VA points will no longer have to be paid by the seller but can be paid by the buyer or seller or split between the two.

The program operates by substituting the guaranty of the Federal Government for the investment protection afforded, under conventional mortgage terms, by substantial down payment requirements and relatively shorter terms of loan. Thus eligible veterans are enabled to finance home purchases even though they may not have the resources to qualify for conventional loans.

When a veteran gets a GI loan, he or she may be obligated to repay the Government any amount VA is required to pay to the holder of the loan because of a default on the loan. Veterans who used their entitlement before October 1, 1980, may have additional entitlement available for GI home loan purposes.

Veterans may have previously used entitlement "restored" to purchase another home if the property has been disposed of and the loan has been paid in full, or VA has been relieved of the obligation under the guaranty. In certain other cases involving assumption, a veteran may qualify for restoration if the buyer is a veteran and is approved by VA to substitute his or her entitlement for that used by the original veteran borrower.

Basis of Eligibility — GI loan benefits remain available until used, and are not subject to an expiration date.

All veterans, whether or not eligible for guaranteed VA loans, may be eligible under the Housing Act of 1965 to obtain a home loan through the Federal Housing Administration if they meet minimum active duty requirements. This includes National Guard and Reserve members, who have served at least six years.

Equal opportunity in housing under VA and FHA must be observed by all involved in supplying housing and all phases of it. (See Section on Home Buying for the Servicemember.)

Safeguards. VA protects veteran borrowers in the following ways:

a. Homes completed less than a year before acquisition with GI financing must meet or exceed VA minimum property requirements for planning, construction and general acceptability.

b. VA may suspend from participation in the loan program those who take unfair advantage of veteran borrowers or decline to sell a new home to, or make a loan to, a creditworthy, eligible veteran because of race, color, religion, sex, disability, financial status or national origin. Also, all credit transactions involving VA financing must meet the requirements of the Equal Credit Opportunity Act and the Federal Reserve Board.

c. On a new home completed under VA or FHA's inspection, the builder is required to give the veteran purchaser a 1-year warranty that the home has been constructed in substantial conformity with VA approved plans and specifications. A similar warranty is required to be given to the veteran in respect to new manufactured homes.

d. In the cases of new construction completed under VA or FHA inspection, VA may pay or otherwise compensate the veteran borrower for correction of structural defects seriously affecting livability which develop within 4 years of the time a home loan is guaranteed or made.

e. The borrower obtaining a GI loan may only be charged the fees and charges prescribed by VA as allowable.

f. The borrower has the right to prepay at any time, without premium or penalty, the entire loan or any part not less than the amount of one installment or $100.

SPECIALLY ADAPTED HOUSING FOR DISABLED VETERANS

Disabled veterans may be entitled to a grant from VA for a home specially adapted to their needs or for adaptations.

For $38,000 Grant. VA may approve a grant of not more than 50 percent of the cost of building, buying or remodeling adapted homes or paying indebtedness on those homes already acquired, up to a maximum of $38,000. Veterans must be entitled to compensation for permanent and total service-connected disability due to:

(a) loss, or loss of use of both lower extremities, such as to preclude locomotion without the aid of braces, crutches, canes, or wheelchair; or

(b) disability which includes (1) blindness in both eyes, having only light perception, , plus (2) loss, or loss of use, of one lower extremity; or

(c) loss, or loss of use of one lower extremity together with (1) residuals of organic disease or injury, or (2) the loss or loss of use of one upper extremity, which also affects the functions of balance or propulsion as to preclude locomotion without the aid of braces, crutches, canes or a wheelchair.

For $6,500 Grant. VA may approve a grant for the actual cost, up to a maximum of $6,500, for adaptations to a veteran's residence which are determined by VA to be reasonably necessary. The grant also may be used to assist eligible veterans in acquiring a residence which has already been adapted with special features for the veteran's disability. In the latter situation, the amount of the grant is based on the fair market value of the existing special features, and not their cost. Veterans must be entitled to compensation for total service-connected disability due to:

(a) Blindness in both eyes with 5/200 visual acuity or less, or

(b) Anatomical loss, or loss of use, of both hands.

Supplemental Financing. Veterans with available loan guaranty entitlement may also obtain a guaranteed loan or a direct loan from VA to supplement the grant to acquire a specially adapted home.

Housing Insurance. Veterans with a specially adapted housing grant may be eligible for Veterans Mortgage Life Insurance.

These special areas of assistance are in addition to GI loan benefits to which the veteran may be entitled. Consult the VA office for more detailed information.

AUTOMOBILES OR OTHER CONVEYANCES

Veterans and current service personnel qualify for this benefit if they have service-connected loss of one or both hands or feet, or permanent loss of use, or permanent impairment of vision of both eyes. There is a onetime payment by VA of not more than $5,500 toward the purchase of an automobile or other conveyance. To apply, contact a VA regional office or the prosthetic service at a VA medical center.

CLOTHING ALLOWANCE

Any veteran who is entitled to receive compensation for a service-connected disability for which he or she uses prosthetic or orthopedic appliances, including a wheelchair that tends to wear out or tear clothing, may receive an annual clothing allowance of $491.

HOSPITALIZATION

Eligibility for VA hospitalization and nursing home care is divided into two categories "Mandatory" and "Discretionary." (Eligibility for outpatient medical care is explained elsewhere). Within these two categories, eligibility assessment procedures, based on income levels, are used for determining whether nonservice-connected veterans are eligible for cost-free VA medical care. These income levels are adjusted on January 1 of each year by the percentage that the improved pension benefits are increased. VA *shall* provide hospital care and may provide nursing home care to veterans in the "Mandatory" category, and *may* provide hospital and nursing home care to veterans in the "Discretionary" category if space and resources are available.

VA is required by law to provide hospital care to veterans in the "Mandatory" category at the nearest VA facility capable of furnishing the care in a timely fashion. If no VA facility is available, care shall be furnished in a DoD facility or other facility with which VA has a sharing or contractual relationship. If space and resources are available after caring for "Mandatory" category veterans, VA may furnish care to those in the "Discretionary" category. Veterans in the "Discretionary" category must agree to pay VA a co-payment for their care before they will be considered eligible.

Veterans in the "Mandatory" category not subject to the eligibility assessment are service-connected veterans; former prisoners of war; veterans who were exposed to herbicides while serving in Vietnam or to ionizing radiation during atmospheric testing and in the occupation of Hiroshima and Nagasaki, and need treatment for a condition that might be related to the exposure; veterans receiving VA pension; veterans of the Mexican Border period or World War I; veterans eligible for Medicaid. Veterans who lose their pension are eligible for mandatory care.

The eligibility assessment, which follows, applies to all other nonservice-connected veterans, *regardless of age:*

"Mandatory" Veterans: Your hospital care is considered "Mandatory" if you are not subject to the eligibility assessment (as listed above) or if you are a nonservice-connected veteran and your income is $21,001 or less if single, or $25,204 or less if married, plus $1,404 for each additional dependent. Hospital care in VA facilities *shall* be provided to veterans in the "Mandatory" category. Nursing home care *may* be provided in VA facilities, *if space and resources are available.*

"Discretionary" Veterans: Your hospital care is considered "discretionary" if you are a nonservice-connected veteran and your income is above $21,001 if single, or $25,204 if married, plus $1,404 for each additional dependent. You must agree to pay a deductible amount for your care equal to what you would have to pay under Medicare. The Medicare deductible currently is $736 and is adjusted annually. VA may provide hospital, outpatient, and nursing home care in VA facilities to veterans in the "discretionary" category, *if space and resources are available.*

If your medical care is considered "discretionary", you will be charged, and are personally responsible for the cost of care that you receive or $736, whichever is less, for the first 90 days of care during any 365-day period. For each additional 90 days of hospital care, you will pay half the Medicare deductible. For each 90 days of nursing home care, you will pay the Medicare deductible.

In addition to the above co-payment, you will be charged a co-payment of $10 per day for inpatient hospital care and a co-payment of $5 per day for nursing home care.

How Income Is Assessed. Your total income and net worth under the eligibility assessment, include Social Security; U.S. Civil Service retirement; U.S. Railroad retirement; military retirement; unemployment insurance; any other retirement income; total wages from all employers; interest and dividends; workers' compensation; black lung benefits; and any other gross income for the calendar year prior to your application for care. The income of your spouse and dependents as well as the market value of your stocks, bonds, notes, individual retirement accounts, bank deposits, savings accounts, cash, etc. are also used. Your debts are subtracted from your assets to determine your net worth. Your primary residence and personal property, however, are excluded. You will not be required to provide proof of income or net worth beyond filling out VA Form-10-10f, Financial Worksheet, at the time you apply for care; however, VA has the authority to compare information you provide with information obtained from the Department of Health and Human Services and the Internal Revenue Service.

Note: The Department of Veterans Affairs is authorized to bill insurance carriers for the cost of medical care furnished to all veterans for nonservice-connected conditions covered by health insurance policies. Veterans are not responsible and will not be charged for any co-payment or coinsurance required by their health insurance policies.

PERSIAN GULF, AGENT ORANGE AND IONIZING RADIATION

Public Law 97-72 authorizes the Department of Veterans Affairs (VA) to "provide certain health care services to any veteran of the Vietnam Era (August 5, 1964 through May 7, 1975) who, while serving in Vietnam, may have been exposed to dioxin or to a toxic substance in a herbicide or defoliant used for military purposes. Health care services may not be provided, under this law, for the care of conditions which are found to have resulted from a cause other than exposure to these substances."

VA has a continuing program for examining veterans who are concerned about the possible health effects of Agent Orange or nuclear radiation exposure. The findings of these examinations are entered into a registry. Vietnam veterans and those veterans concerned about radiation exposure are encouraged to request an examination at the nearest VA health-care facility. A veteran who participates will receive a comprehensive physical examination and be asked to complete a questionnaire about service experience. Following the examination, the veteran will be advised of the results. The examination could help to detect any illness or injury the veteran may have, regardless of origin, and may provide a basis for follow-up. VA recently announced as service connected, soft tissue sarcomas based on exposure to dioxin-containing herbicides.

The Department of Veterans Affairs (VA) has published an amendment to regulations adding rectal cancer and lymphomas other than Hodgkins' disease to the list of diseases that may be considered for disability compensation due to ionizing radiation exposure.

Under the regulation, which is used to determine if the disease resulted from in-service radiation exposure, VA must consider the condition the veteran claims, the radiation dose a veteran received, and the time elapsed between exposure and the onset of the disease. Veterans do not have to prove that ionizing radiation may have caused any of the listed diseases.

Diseases already recognized as radiogenic under the regulation include all forms of leukemia, except chronic lymphatic (lymphocytic) leukemia; multiple myeloma; posterior subcapsular cataracts; nonmalignant thyroid nodular disease; parathyroid adenoma; tumors of the brain and central nervous system; and cancer of the thyroid, breast, lung, bone, liver, skin, esophagus, stomach, colon, pancreas, kidney, urinary bladder, salivary gland, and ovaries.

The list is not exclusive. In February 1995, VA revised the regulation so that is will consider veterans' claims based on diseases other than those listed in the regulation, provided the claimant presents scientific or medical evidence showing the claimed condition may be caused by radiation.

UNIFORMED SERVICES ALMANAC

The same process applies to any veteran found to have been exposed to ionizing radiation from the detonation of a nuclear device in connection with the veteran's participation in the test of a nuclear device or with the American occupation of Hiroshima and Nagasaki, Japan during the period beginning on September 11, 1945, and ending on July 1, 1946. VA also provides priority treatment to any Persian Gulf veteran who requires treatment for a condition medically determined to be related to service in the Persian Gulf area.

The veteran should contact the nearest VA medical center or call toll free 1-800-827-1000 for an examination. An appointment can be arranged, generally within two to three weeks.

DOMICILIARY CARE
For Veterans Who Have a Permanent Disability

Benefit. To provide care on an ambulatory self-care basis for veterans disabled by age or disease who are not in need of acute hospitalization and who do not need the skilled nursing services provided in nursing homes, but who are unable to care for themselves adequately in the community.

Eligibility. VA provides domiciliary care to veterans whose annual income does not exceed the maximum annual rate of VA pension, and to veterans the Secretary of VA determines have no adequate means of support.

Where to Apply. At any VA office. Prior approval needed for admission.

NURSING HOME CARE
All Veterans

Benefit. To provide skilled nursing care and related medical care in VA or private nursing homes for convalescents or persons who are not acutely ill and not in need of hospital care.

Eligibility. *Admission or transfer to VA Nursing Home Care Units, is essentially the same as for hospitalization.* Direct admission to private nursing homes at VA expense is limited to (1) veterans who require nursing care for a service-connected disability after medical determination by the VA, and (2) any person in an Armed Forces hospital who requires a protracted period of nursing care and who will become a veteran upon discharge from the Armed Forces. VA may transfer hospitalized veterans who need a protracted period of nursing care to a private nursing home at VA expense. Normally VA authorized care may not be provided in excess of six months except for veterans whose hospitalization was primarily for a service-connected disability. Nonservice-connected veterans who exceed certain income threshold amounts must agree to pay the VA copayments for nursing home care.

ALCOHOL AND DRUG DEPENDENCE
All Veterans

Eligibility — General. Discharge or release from active military service under conditions other than dishonorable. Nonservice connected veterans whose incomes exceed the threshold amount may be authorized for treatment only if the veteran agrees to pay the applicable copayment.

UNIFORMED SERVICES ALMANAC

Nature of Benefit. After hospitalization for alcohol or drug treatment, veterans may be eligible for outpatient care, or may be authorized to continue treatment or rehabilitation in facilities such as halfway houses, therapeutic communities, or mental health centers at VA expense.

READJUSTMENT COUNSELING
Vet Centers

Veterans who served on active duty during the Vietnam era, or served in the war or conflict zones of Lebanon, Grenada, Panama, Somalia or Persian Gulf areas during hostilities may be provided counseling to assist the veteran in readjusting to civilian life. Application may be made any time.

The intent of the readjustment counseling program is to provide outreach, counseling, and referral services to those Vietnam era veterans, or those who served in the war or conflict zones of Lebanon, Grenada, Panama and Persian Gulf areas who have encountered readjustment difficulties at any time following their service in the military during the above conflicts.

Readjustment counseling includes an assessment to determine whether the veteran has psychological, social, or employment problems stemming from military service or the transition therefrom. Services include individual, group, and family counseling. A wide range of difficulties can be addressed, including post traumatic stress disorder, difficulties in progressing with educational career or employment, family conflicts, and difficulties in accessing care from other VA sources or in the community generally. In addition to outreach, Vet Centers also actively assist veterans in obtaining services elsewhere and provide counseling to veterans who have difficulties due to sexual assault or harassment while on active duty.

Readjustment counseling is usually provided in community-based centers, the location of which can be found in the phone book under "Vet Center" or Vietnam Veteran Center" in both the white and blue pages. In addition, the nearest VA medical facility can provide information on the location of the nearest vet center. In areas distant from a vet center, the VA may provide readjustment counseling services to veterans through a contract/fee arrangement with professionals in the community.

OUTPATIENT MEDICAL TREATMENT CENTER

Outpatient medical treatment includes medical examinations and related medical services, drugs and medicines, rehabilitation services, and mental health services. As part of outpatient medical treatment, veterans may be eligible for home health services for the treatment of disabilities. The following are the different categories of outpatient eligibility:

1. VA must furnish outpatient care without limitation to veterans for service-connected disabilities and to veterans who have suffered an injury as a result of VA hospitalization, for that condition only, to veteran's with a 50 percent or more service-connected disability for any ailment, and to veterans who served in the Persian Gulf War and whose condition the Secretary finds may be the result of exposure to a toxic substance or environmental hazard.

2. VA must furnish outpatient care for any condition to prevent the need for hospitalization; to prepare for hospitalization, or to complete treatment after hospital care, nursing-home care or domiciliary care to 30-40 percent

UNIFORMED SERVICES ALMANAC

service-connected disabled veterans; and to veterans whose annual income is not greater than the maximum annual pension rate of a veteran in need of regular aid and attendance.

3. VA may furnish outpatient care without limitation to veterans in a VA-approved vocational rehabilitation program; former prisoners of war; WWI or Mexican Border Period veterans; and to veterans who receive increased pension or compensation based on the need for regular aid and attendance of another person, or who are permanently housebound.

4. VA may furnish outpatient care to prevent the need for hospitalization; to prepare for hospitalization, or for a condition for which the veteran was hospitalized, to veterans who are 0-20 percent service-connected disabled; to veterans exposed to a toxic substance during service in Vietnam or to ionizing radiation following the detonation of a nuclear device; to mandatory category veterans whose income is more than the pension rate of a veteran in need of regular aid and attendance; to discretionary category veterans, subject to a copayment of $39 per outpatient visit; and to allied beneficiaries and to employees of other federal agencies for which charges shall be made as required by law.

5. VA provides counseling to women veterans to overcome psychological trauma resulting from physical assault, battery of a sexual nature or sexual harassment during active duty. The counseling is provided at VA medical centers and Vet Centers. Treatment is authorized for physical conditions resulting from sexual trauma.

OUTPATIENT PHARMACY SERVICES CENTER

Pharmacy services are provided without charge to (1) veterans receiving medication for treatment of service-connected conditions; (2) veterans rated with 50 percent or more service-connected disability; and (3) veterans whose annual income does not exceed the maximum VA pension. Veterans who have a service-connected condition rated less than 50 percent and are receiving medication on an outpatient basis from VA facilities for the treatment of nonservice-connected disabilities or ailments are charged a set amount for each 30-day supply or less.

OUTPATIENT DENTAL TREATMENT

Outpatient dental treatment provided by VA includes examinations and the full spectrum of diagnostic, surgical, restorative and preventive techniques. Nonservice-connected veterans who are authorized outpatient dental care may be billed the applicable copayment if their income exceeds the maximum threshold. The following may be eligible for free dental care:

(1) Dental conditions or disabilities that are service-connected and compensable in degree will be treated.

(2) Service-connected dental conditions or disabilities that are not compensable in degree may receive onetime treatment if the conditions can be shown to have existed at discharge or within 180 days of release from active service. Veterans who served on active duty for 90 days or more during the Persian Gulf War are included in this category. Veterans must apply to VA for care for the service-connected dental condition within 90 days following separation. Veterans will not be considered eligible if their separation document indicates that necessary treatment was completed by military dentists during the 90 days prior to separation.

(3) Service-connected, noncompensable, dental conditions resulting from combat wounds or service injuries, and service-connected, noncompensable, dental conditions of former prisoners of war who were incarcerated less than 90 days may be treated.

(4) Veterans who were prisoners of war for more than 90 days may receive complete dental care.

(5) Veterans may receive complete dental care if they are receiving disability compensation at the 100 percent rate for service-connected conditions or are eligible to receive it by reason of unemployability.

(6) Nonservice-connected dental conditions that are determined by VA to be associated with an aggravated, service-connected medical problem may be treated.

(7) Disabled veterans participating in a vocational rehabilitation program may be treated.

(8) Veterans may be treated for nonservice-connected dental conditions or disabilities when treatment was begun while in a VA medical center, when it is professionally determined to be reasonably necessary to complete such dental treatment on an outpatient basis.

(9) Veterans scheduled for admission in inpatient services or who are receiving medical services may be provided outpatient dental care if the dental condition is professionally determined to be complicating a medical condition currently under treatment by VA.

BENEFICIARY TRAVEL
Eligibility/Benefit

Beneficiary travel payment or reimbursement may be made to the following veterans in connection with receiving VA medical care. In addition, eligible veterans may be authorized beneficiary travel payments in a medical emergency when, in sound medical judgment, delay in immediate transportation would have been hazardous to the patient's health and life; or when specialized modes of transportation such as ambulance or wheelchair van are medically indicated:

(a) A veteran rated at 30% or more service-connected.

(b) A rated veteran traveling in connection with treatment of a service-connected condition.

(c) A veteran who is in receipt of a VA pension.

(d) A veteran traveling in connection with a compensation and pension examination.

(e) A veteran whose income is less than or equal to the maximum base VA pension rate with aid and attendance.

(f) A veteran whose medical condition requires use of a special mode of transportation, if travel is pre-authorized.

Travel related to medical emergencies, compensation and pension examinations, interfacility transfers, and cases requiring special modes of transportation will be paid in full. All other travel is subject to a deductible of $3 for each one-way trip with a monthly cap of $18.

UNIFORMED SERVICES ALMANAC
MEDICAL CARE FOR DEPENDENTS AND SURVIVORS (CHAMPVA)

The Civilian Health and Medical Program of the Department of Veterans Affairs (CHAMPVA) is a medical benefits program through which the VA helps pay for medical services and supplies obtained from civilian sources by eligible dependents and survivors of certain veterans. The following persons are eligible for CHAMPVA provided they are not eligible for medical care under CHAMPUS or Medicare:

- The spouse or child of a veteran who has a total disability, permanent in nature, resulting from a service-connected disability;
- The surviving spouse or child of a veteran who died as a result of a service-connected disability, or who at the time of death had a total disability, permanent in nature, resulting from a service-connected disability;
- The surviving spouse or child of a person who died while in the active military, naval or air service in the line of duty.

Normally, care under the CHAMPVA program is not usually provided in VA facilities. VA facilities may be utilized for treatment when: (1) they are equipped to provide the care and (2) use of these facilities does not interfere with care and treatment of veterans.

Where to Apply. CHAMPVA Registration Center, P.O. Box 65023, Denver, CO 80206 or call 1-800-733-8387.

CIVIL SERVICE PREFERENCE
(Office of Personnel Management)

See Section titled VETERAN PREFERENCE IN GOVERNMENT which also includes REEMPLOYMENT AFTER MILITARY DUTY.

IMPROVED PENSION FOR NONSERVICE-CONNECTED DEATH

Benefit — The Improved Pension program provides a monthly payment to bring an eligible persons's income to a support level established by law. The payment is reduced by the annual income from other sources such as Social Security that may be payable to either the surviving spouse or dependent children. Countable income may be reduced by medical expenses. Pension is not payable to those who have assets that can be used to provide adequate maintenance.

Pension Rates for Surviving Spouse:

Surviving spouse without dependent children	$5,527
Surviving spouse with one dependent child	$7,240
Surviving spouse in need of regular aid and attendance without dependent children	$8,839
Surviving spouse in need of regular aid and attendance with one dependent child	$10,548
Surviving spouse permanently housebound without dependent children	$6,758
Surviving spouse permanently housebound with one dependent child	$8,466
Increase for each additional dependent child	$1,404

UNIFORMED SERVICES ALMANAC
APPEALS

Eligibility/Benefit—VA claimants have the right to appeal determinations made by a VA regional office or medical center which they believe are unfavorable to them. Compensation or pension benefits, education benefits, waiver of recovery of overpayments, and reimbursement of unauthorized medical services are issues which may be appealed to the Board of Veterans Appeals.

Time Limits: When to File — A claimant has one year from the date of the mailing of the notification of the determination within which to file an appeal. An appeal is initiated by filing a "Notice of Disagreement" in which the claimant expresses his or her dissatisfaction and requests appellate review. This Notice of Disagreement should be filed with the VA facility responsible for making the determination.

Following receipt of a Notice of Disagreement, the DVA office will furnish the claimant a "Statement of the Case" setting forth the issue, facts, applicable law and regulations, and the reasons for the determination.

In order to complete the request for appeal, the claimant must file a "Substantive Appeal" within 60 days after the date of the Statement of the Case, or within one year from the notification of the original determination, whichever is later.

Board of Veterans' Appeals — The Board of Veterans' Appeals conducts the appellate program for the Secretary of Veterans Affairs and makes final VA decisions on appeals involving all benefits administered by VA. A claimant may be represented by a veterans service organization, an agent or an attorney. Attorneys and recognized agents may charge a fee for representing a claimant or appellant before VA, including the Board of Veterans' Appeals, under certain circumstances. The Board reviews the reasonableness of fee agreements of attorneys and agents recognized by VA. The Board also makes decisions concerning the eligibility of attorneys for payment of fees from the claimant's past-due benefits.

Hearings on appeal before a member of the Board of Veterans' Appeals may be arranged following the filing of a Notice of Disagreement. At the election of the appellant, the hearing may be held in Washington, D.C., or at a VA regional office. The appellate decisions of the Board of Veterans' Appeals have been indexed to facilitate access to the contents of decisions. The board produces a CD-ROM with the text of its decisions, available at most VA Regional Offices. Cases which pertain to the same issues are grouped together in the index under alphabetically arranged subject terms. The index is available at VA regional offices and at the Board of Veterans' Appeals in Washington, D.C. Microfiche copies can be purchased from Promisel and Korn, Inc., 7201 Wisconsin Avenue, Suite 480, Bethesda, MD 20814.

United States Court of Veterans' Appeals. The Court of Veterans' Appeals has exclusive jurisdiction to review decisions of the Board of Veterans' Appeals. The Court is located at 625 Indiana Avenue, NW, Suite 900, Washington DC 20004 or call 1-800-869-8654.

Access to the Court is limited to claimants who have submitted their claim for review by the Board of Veterans' Appeals and have received an adverse decision from the Board concerning the claim. The notice of appeal must be filed with the Court of Veterans' Appeals within 120 days after the date on which notice of the decision is mailed by the Board of Veterans' Appeals.

DEPENDENCY AND INDEMNITY COMPENSATION

General

Dependency and Indemnity Compensation (DIC) may be authorized to the survivors of military personnel who die in line of duty while on active duty or active duty for training. If death occurs during inactive duty for training, benefits are payable in some cases.

This compensation may be authorized when death occurs *following* service mentioned above if death is due to a service-connected disability. DIC payments are authorized for surviving spouses, unmarried children under 18 (as well as certain helpless children and those between 18 and 23 if attending a VA-approved school), and parents of deceased veterans. DIC may also be paid in certain cases involving death unrelated to military service. This is possible only if the veteran was totally disabled immediately prior to death as a result of disability related to military service, and was recognized by the VA as having such disability. More information about this special provision is available from your nearest VA regional office.

Rates of Dependency and Indemnity Compensation

Spouses' Payments — The rate which a surviving spouse will receive formerly depended on the veteran's highest military rank while on active duty. The following table shows the rates based on "pay grades" which correspond to military ranks. Payments are not affected by income which the spouse may receive from earnings or other sources. If the spouse receives SBP benefits under the "Survivor Benefits Plan" administered by the Department of Defense, the law requires offset of SBP payments against DIC payments. (See the Section on Survivor Benefit Plan.)

If the surviving spouse remarries, DIC is normally terminated. However, Public Law 102-86, 1991, restores DIC payments to certain remarried spouses and dependent children who were eligible for such benefits on October 31, 1990, (whose marital or dependent status has remained unchanged.)

The Veterans' Benefits Act of 1992, P.L. 102-568 standardized and equalized the DIC payment to surviving spouses of veterans whose service-connected deaths occur on or after January 1, 1993, by eliminating the schedule of benefits which had been based on the military rank of the deceased veteran. Effective January 1, 1996, a monthly base rate of $810 will be payable to the surviving spouses of all such veterans. That rate would be increased by $177 per month if the veteran was totally disabled due to service-connected disabilities, continuously for at least 8 years prior to death. Surviving spouses of veterans who died before January 1, 1993, will receive the higher of either the new rate or the benefit under the old schedule.

Spouses will receive additional DIC for any children under 18 who are in the spouse's custody. A spouse may qualify for special additional payments based on disability status. If the spouse is a patient in a nursing home or if the VA determines that the spouse needs regular health care and assistance from another person, the "aid and attendance allowance" will be paid. For less severe disability, if the spouse is substantially confined to the residence, VA will pay the "housebound allowance."

UNIFORMED SERVICES ALMANAC

MONTHLY DIC PAYMENTS TO SURVIVING SPOUSES OF VETERANS WHO DIED BEFORE JANUARY 1, 1993

COMMISSIONED OFFICERS		WARRANT OFFICERS		ENLISTED PERSONS	
Pay Grade	Monthly Rate	Pay Grade	Monthly Rate	Pay Grade	Monthly Rate
O-1	$855	W-1	$855	E-1	$810
O-2	883	W-2	889	E-2	810
O-3	945	W-3	916	E-3	810
O-4	999	W-4	969	E-4	810
O-5	1,100			E-5	810
O-6	1,240			E-6	810
O-7	1,339			E-7	837
O-8	1,467			E-8	883
O-9	1,572			*E-9	922
O-10*	1,724				

*Special rates may apply for certain individuals in these grades.

Children's Payments. Normally, payments for minor children (under age 18) will be included with a surviving spouse's payment. In 1995, the rate of payment for each minor child was $200.00 per month, for 1996 $205.00 per month. Payments are made for older children under certain circumstances. Children between the ages of 18 and 23 are eligible for payments if they remain unmarried and are attending an educational program approved by VA. Such programs can include secondary school, college level programs and trade, technical or business training programs. Payments also may be made for unmarried children over age 18 who became helpless, as determined by VA, prior to age 18 as a result of physical or mental disability. Payment for a school child over 18 is $174 per month and $344 for a helpless child.

When no spouse is entitled to receive payments, children will still be paid provided they remain unmarried and meet general requirements for age, school attendance, or helplessness according to the following rates:

NO SURVIVING SPOUSE		
No. of Children	Each Child	Total
1	344.00	344.00
2	248.00	496.00
3	214.33	643.00
4	192.25	769.00
5	179.00	895.00
6	170.16	1021.00
7	168.95	1147.00
8	159.12	1273.00
9	155.44	1399.00

For each additional child add $126.00.
For each helpless child over age 18 add $205.00.

Social Security Eligibility — Eligibility for DIC does not affect eligibility for Social Security, and eligibility for Social Security does not affect eligibility for DIC, for either surviving spouses or children.

Dependents are eligible for REPS (Reinstated Entitlement Program) payments if they are eligible for DIC and the veteran's death occurred in service prior to August 13, 1981, or resulted from disability related to military service and acquired before August 13, 1981. Eligible spouses may be paid REPS benefits only when Social Security eligibility ceases because the youngest child has reached age 16, and the spouse has a child between the ages of 16 and 18. Children over 18 may receive REPS payments to age 22 if they are unmarried and attending a post-secondary educational program which meets certain requirements, including full-time attendance.

Parents' Payments — Parents of deceased veterans may be paid DIC provided they meet certain income tests. The rate of payment will depend on whether both parents survive and whether a surviving parent is currently married. The income limit for two parents together is $12,611; the limit for one parent or two parents not together is $9,381.

BURIAL

FOR MEMBERS OF THE ARMED FORCES

When a member dies while on active duty, (including members who are retired and retained in a military hospital and who continue hospitalized as patients therein to date of death or on active duty for training), the military will provide for care and disposition of remains. When military authorities arrange for disposition of remains, services of preparation at the place of death-removal, embalming preparation and preservation, casket, and transportation to a common carrier are normally obtained under contract; however, when no contract is available, military authorities negotiate with local funeral directors to obtain these services. The military authorities also will provide the following as required.

1. Cremation (if cremation is requested in writing by the Person Authorized to Direct Disposition (PADD) of the remains).
2. A suitable urn for the cremated remains.
3. A U.S. flag to drape the casket.
4. Transportation of remains, accompanied by an escort, from the place of death to the place designated by the PADD. This transportation may be by hearse or commercial air cargo, whichever the Transportation Officer determines the most expeditious.
5. Military honors, if available, will be provided at the place of interment if requested by the next of kin of the deceased. Honors must be arranged for by the family or their representative.

If the PADD should desire, it is her (his) prerogative to make private arrangements for care and disposition of remains and to subsequently request reimbursement in the amount allowable. The standard of services provided under military contract is high, and it is generally advantageous to leave arrangements for preparation of remains at the place of death to military authorities. When the PADD makes private arrangements for the care and disposition of remains, reimbursement will be limited to those items normally obtained by the military under contract (removal, embalming and other preservation, casket and outside case, and hearse services to a local cemetery or common-carrier terminal) and in the amount for which the Government could have obtained the services from the contractor. If there is no Government contractor in the vicinity where death occurs, reimbursement is limited to a maximum of $1,750.00.

UNIFORMED SERVICES ALMANAC

Armed Forces members of the United States or a former member who was discharged under conditions other than dishonorable and the surviving spouse, minor children, and, in certain instances, unmarried adult children are eligible for burial in any national cemetery, under the jurisdiction of the Veterans Administration, having grave space available. No grave sites are reserved in national cemeteries. One gravesite is normally authorized for eligible members of a family unit. The remains of additional eligible family members are interred in the same gravesite as previously deceased member of the family. If the spouse or eligible child of a member dies first, the member must sign an agreement indicating that the member will eventually be buried in the same grave.

At the time of death of the member or eligible dependent, the next-of-kin or representative making the funeral arrangements should contact the superintendent of the national cemetery in which interment is desired.

Interment in the Arlington National Cemetery, which is under the jurisdiction of the U.S. Army, is limited to the following individuals:

1. Persons dying on active duty in the Armed Forces.
2. Retired military personnel, defined as retired members of the Army, Navy, Air Force, Marine Corps, or Coast Guard who are carried on an official service retired list and who are eligible to receive compensation stemming from service in that Armed Force.
3. Medal of Honor, Distinguished Service Cross, Air Force Cross or Navy Cross; Distinguished Service Medal; Silver Star; and Purple Heart recipients.
4. Persons otherwise eligible by reason of honorable military service who have also held elective office in the U.S. Government or served on the Supreme Court or in the Cabinet or in an office compensated at Level II under the Executive Salary Act.
5. Members of the Armed Forces separated for physical disability of 30% or greater prior to Oct. 1, 1949, who served on active duty (other than for training) and would have been eligible for retirement under the provisions of 10 USC 1201 if statute was in effect on the date of separation.
6. The spouses, minor children, and dependent adult children of the persons listed in 1 through 4 above and of persons already buried in Arlington.
7. A veteran of any of the United States Armed Forces honorably discharged who selects cremation, may have his or her cremated remains interred in the Columbarium at the Arlington National Cemetery.

The next-of-kin or representative making the funeral arrangements should contact the Office of the Arlington National Cemetery Superintendent.

In addition there is an allowance to assist in defraying costs incident to burial of the remains in the maximum amount of $3,100 when burial is in a civilian cemetery; $2,000 when remains are consigned to a funeral director designated by the next of kin and subsequently interred in a national or post cemetery; and $110 when shipped directly for burial to a national or post cemetery. Note: Interment allowance for a State Veterans' Cemetery is the same as for a Government cemetery. This allowance is to cover such items as (1) hearse hire to the home, funeral home, church, or cemetery, (2) flowers, (3) vault, (4) church service or minister's fee, (5) obituary notices, (6) a passenger car for the immediate family to and from the cemetery, (7) services of the funeral director, including the use of funeral home facilities, (8) grave site, (9) opening and closing of the grave, and (10) use of cemetery equipment when interment is in a private cemetery. When burial is in a national or post cemetery, reimbursement will be made only for actual expenses of items listed above that were not furnished by the government.

The Government will mark all graves in national and post cemeteries with regulation headstones and markers of the types authorized.

When interment is made in a private or civilian cemetery, the PADD may obtain a regulation Government headstone or marker, without expense, to mark the grave of a deceased member of the Armed Forces or a former member of the Armed Forces who was discharged under conditions other than dishonorable. Applicants may select either an upright headstone of marble or a flat marker of marble, granite, bronze, dependent upon the type permissible in the cemetery.

RETIRED CASUALTY ASSISTANCE SERVICES

When a retiree dies, the next of kin should immediately call the Defense Finance and Accounting Service (DFAS) — Cleveland Center. The Retired Casualty Section at DFAS can be reached can be reached toll-free, at 1-800-269-5170, from anywhere in the United States. DFAS will conduct a thorough review of and close the retiree's pay account. They will also mail a survivor benefits packet to the decedent's next-of-kin. The packet typically consists of a condolence letter and, if appropriate, forms for applying for the retiree's unpaid pay and the Survivor Benefit Plan annuity. These forms must be completed as soon as possible and returned to DFAS with a photocopy of the death certificate.

Local Retired Activities Offices (RAOs) are available to render additional assistance. This includes providing information, counseling on eligibility for various survivor benefits, referral services and any other questions you may have.

Another equally important issue that must be considered, is a retiree's entitlement to military funeral honors. Observing a full military honor funeral in the movies, on television, or in person, may cause an incorrect assumption that a comparable detail is available for the funerals of all deceased military veterans and retirees.

In fact, as resources allow, a retiree is eligible for the same honors detail as an active duty member. This detail consists of pallbearers, a firing party, a bugler, a military chaplain and an officer-in-charge or noncommissioned officer-in-charge, depending on the grade of the deceased.

Department of Defense policy, outlined in DoD Directive 1300.15, establishes that retirees are entitled to a full-honors detail, *if the necessary support is available at a local command.* If not, the Service must provide a minimum of one uniformed representative to attend the funeral. This representative, if desired by the next of kin, will present the U.S. flag to a designated person, on behalf of the Commander-in-Chief of the United States Armed Forces and a grateful Nation.

If the local commander must deny a request for full military honors, he or she can - and should - offer assistance in obtaining the requested support from another activity of the same military service, the National Guard or Reserves, an ROTC Unit, a veteran's organization, or another military service.

UNIFORMED SERVICES ALMANAC
REMAINS OF RETIREES AND DEPENDENTS

Remains of retirees and authorized dependents of military personnel serving on active duty, (other than for training) may be transported from place of death to place of interment. Transportation only at Government expense is authorized.

When death of a dependent occurs in an overseas command in which an Armed Forces mortuary is operated, remains of such dependents may be prepared (embalmed and certain supplies furnished) at such mortuaries, on a reimbursable basis, as a convenience to the sponsor. The sponsor, however, must bear the costs of preparation, casket, and interment.

Reimbursement for the cost of transporting the remains of a retiree or their dependent who dies while properly admitted as an inpatient in a government medical treatment facility is authorized. Reimbursement is limited to the cost of transporting the remains from a government medical treatment facility to a place no further than the decendent's last permanent residence.

The remains of retirees or their dependents who die while OCONUS may be transported to CONUS aboard military aircraft at no cost, space-available basis. Additionally, mortuary services for the remains may be obtained from a military OCONUS mortuary on a reimbursable space-available basis. The person making arrangements for the remains should contact the Department of State's Citizen's Emergency Assistance Office (202) 647-5226 for information and assistance in obtaining mortuary services and transportation.

MEMORIAL SERVICES — REMAINS NOT RECOVERED

When a member of the Armed Forces dies while on active duty (whose death occurs after January 1, 1961) and whose remains are non-recoverable, reimbursement for memorial service expenses incurred by next of kin is authorized up to $2,000. Upon request, a flag of the United States will be furnished to the primary next of kin and to parents, if other than primary next of kin. In addition, a memorial marker may be provided for erection by next of kin in a civilian cemetery or placement in a national cemetery.

REIMBURSEMENT OF BURIAL EXPENSE
(Department of Veterans Affairs)

VA will pay a burial allowance up to $1500 if the veteran's death is service-connected. VA also will pay the cost of transporting the remains of a service-disabled veteran to the national cemetery nearest the home of the deceased that has available gravesites. In such cases, the person who bore the veteran's burial expenses may claim reimbursement from VA.

VA will pay a $300 burial and funeral expense allowance for veterans who, at time of death, were entitled to receive pension or compensation or would have been entitled to compensation but for receipt of military retirement pay. Eligibility also is established when death occurs in a VA facility or a nursing home with which VA contracted. Additional costs of transportation of the remains may be reimbursed in those cases. Concerning service-connected deaths, there is no time for filing reimbursement claims. In other deaths, claims must be filed within two years after permanent burial or cremation.

UNIFORMED SERVICES ALMANAC

VA will pay a $150 burial allowance when the veteran is not buried in a cemetery that is under U.S. government jurisdiction if the veteran is discharged from active duty because of disability incurred or aggravated in line of duty or if the veteran was in receipt of compensation or would have been in receipt of compensation but for receipt of military retired pay, or if the veteran died while hospitalized by VA. As of November 1, 1990, the plot allowance is no longer payable based solely on wartime service. If the veteran is buried without charge for the cost of a plot or interment in a state-owned cemetery reserved solely for veteran burials, the $150 plot allowance may be paid to the state. If burial expenses were paid by the deceased's employer or state agency, the burial allowance will not be reimbursed to those making interment arrangements.

BURIAL FLAGS (DVA)

VA provides an American flag to drape the casket of a veteran who was discharged under conditions other than dishonorable and to a person entitled to retired military pay, including reservists. After the funeral service, the flag may be given to the next of kin or a close associate of the deceased. VA also will issue a flag on behalf of a servicemember who was missing in action and later presumed dead. Flags are issued at VA regional offices, VA national cemeteries and most local post offices.

BURIAL IN NATIONAL CEMETERIES
(Director of National Cemetery where burial is desired)

Nature of Benefit — Burial in a National Cemetery. A gravesite, opening and closing of the grave, perpetual care, and a government headstone or marker is provided at no cost to the next-of-kin. Services provided by funeral directors and other related costs are a private expense incurred by the next-of-kin.

Committal services are commonly held in shelters located away from the gravesite. Viewing facilities are not available. Interment takes place following committal services. Contact Director of National Cemetery where burial is desired. Gravesites cannot be reserved. The only casketed burials that can be accommodated at some national cemeteries are those of the spouses or dependent children of those already buried in the cemetery. Most cemeteries can accommodate burials or inurnments of cremated remains.

Basis for Eligibility — Members of the Armed Forces who die on active duty, including members of the reserve components, Army National Guard and Air National Guard, and all veterans (including retirees) discharged under conditions other than dishonorable; additionally, spouse, minor child and, if authorized by VA's Director of the National Cemetery System (NCS), dependent adult children of those eligible because of military service.

The number, 1-800-697-6947, connects callers to VA's National Cemetery System's Office of Memorial Programs in Washington, D.C., Mon. through Fri., 8:00 a.m. - 4:30 p.m. (ET).

NCS operates 114 cemeteries throughout the United States and Puerto Rico. All veterans with discharges other than dishonorable, their spouses and dependent children are eligible for burial in a VA national cemetery. They also are eligible for a government-provided headstone or marker and a Presidential Memorial Certificate.

UNIFORMED SERVICES ALMANAC

HEADSTONE OR GRAVE MARKER
(National Cemetery System, DVA)

Nature of Benefit — Permanent Monument. Upright, marble headstone; flat bronze, granite or marble marker; bronze niche marker. These monuments are furnished without application if burial occurs in a national cemetery or a state veterans cemetery. VA provides standard inscriptions including name, branch of service, year of birth and death. Optional inscriptions at VA expense are rank, war service, dates of birth and death, valor awards and Purple Heart, if applicable. For personalized inscriptions, contact National Cemetery System, Office of Memorial Programs.

Basis of Eligibility — Members of the Armed Forces who die on active duty, including reserve components, Army National Guard and Air National Guard, and all veterans discharged under conditions other than dishonorable.

The Department of Veterans Affairs (VA) has established a single, nationwide, toll-free telephone number to make it easier for veterans and their dependents to inquire about the veterans headstone and gravemarker program, (800) 697-6947.

VA customer service representatives can provide immediate information about the status of applications, headstone or marker delivery and general information about memorial programs.

DEATH GRATUITY

The law fixes $800 as the minimum lump-sum payment in the event of death while a member of the Armed Forces is on active duty for training, or inactive duty training. The gratuity is also payable if a member or former member dies of a service-connected cause within 120 days after his or her discharge or release from active duty for training. In the case of inactive duty training, the gratuity is payable if death occurs within 120 days and is the result of injury received during that training.

The six-month death gratuity is paid by the service concerned as soon as possible after the servicemember's death. This goes to the spouse, or children or, if no spouse or children, to parents, brothers, or sisters as designated. The amount is computed as follows:

Total monthly pay (including special incentive, hazard, and basic pay, but not allowances)   X 6 =   death* gratuity
*not to exceed $6,000

In addition, the families of a member who dies on active duty, will be allowed 90 days Basic Allowance for Quarters (BAQ): 90 day rent free occupancy of government quarters, or 90 day BAQ/VHA for area of residence.

PRESIDENTIAL MEMORIAL CERTIFICATES
(Department of Veterans Affairs)

Benefit — The Presidential Memorial Certificate is a parchment certificate with a calligraphic inscription expressing the nation's grateful recognition of the veteran's service. The veteran's name is inscribed and the certificate bears the signature of the President.

Certificates are issued in the name of honorably discharged, deceased veterans. Eligible recipients include next of kin, other relatives and friends. The award of a certificate to one eligible recipient does not preclude certificates to other eligible recipients. The veteran may have died at any time in the past. The local VA regional office generally originates the application for a Presidential Memorial Certificate if a veteran's death is brought to official attention. The next of kin may request a certificate when a servicemember dies on active duty, or if the veteran was not receiving a VA benefit. Requests should be accompanied by a copy of a document such as a discharge to establish honorable service. VA regional offices can assist in applying for certificates.

MEMORIAL MARKERS
National Cemetery System
(Department of Veterans Affairs)

Nature of Benefit — Permanent Monument. Upon application by next of kin, or descendant accepted as next of kin, a memorial headstone or marker for active duty servicemember or veteran whose remains were: not recovered; not identified; buried at sea; donated to science; scattered as "ashes" following cremation. National cemeteries provide plots for placement. Eligibility is the same as for burial in a national cemetery.

VA AND MILITARY INSURANCE PROGRAMS

GENERAL

Department of Veterans Affairs has established a national hotline for veterans seeking information about their government insurance. By calling 1-800-669-8477, insurance holders and beneficiaries can obtain immediate service on address or policy changes, dividend information and general insurance information. In addition specialists are available between 8:00 a.m. and 6:30 p.m. to report death of an individual policyholder. After hours a caller may leave a recorded message, which will be answered on the next workday.

If the policy number is unknown, send the veteran's VA file number, Social Security number, military serial number or military service branch and dates of service with date of birth to one of two VA insurance centers. For states east of the Mississippi River, or for any policy which is being paid by a deduction from VA benefits, military retired pay or a checking account, send to: Department of Veterans Affairs, Regional Office and Insurance Center, P.O. Box 8079, Philadelphia, PA 19101. For states west of the Mississippi River, and the states of Minnesota, Wisconsin, Illinois, Indiana and Mississippi, send to: Department of Veterans Affairs, Regional Office and Insurance Center, Bishop Henry Whipple Bldg., Fort Snelling, St. Paul, MN 55111.

Dividends Can Increase Total Insurance

Since July 1, 1972, the maximum amount of government life insurance, exclusive of SGLI, VGLI, and VMLI, can be increased from a ceiling of $10,000. Policyholders with WWII National Service Life Insurance (V) can use their dividends to purchase additional paid-up coverage, permitting insureds to have more than $10,000 coverage. Policyholders with Veterans Special Life Insurance (RS, W) and Veterans Reopened Insurance (J, JR, JS) also can purchase additions to coverage.

UNIFORMED SERVICES ALMANAC

Status of Life Insurance Programs

Program	Beginning Date	Ending Date for New Issues	Policy Letter Prefix
U.S. Government (USGLI)	May 1919	April 24, 1951	K
National Service (NSLI)	Oct. 8, 1940	April 24, 1951	V, H
Veterans Special (VSLI)	April 25, 1951	Dec. 31, 1956	RS, W
Service Disabled (SDVI)	April 25, 1951	Still Open	RH
Veterans Reopened (VRI)	May 1, 1965	May 2, 1966	J, JR, JS
Servicemen's Group (SGLI)	Sept. 29, 1965	Still Open	
Veterans Mortgage (VMLI)	Aug. 11, 1971	Still Open	
Veterans Group (VGLI)	Aug. 1, 1974	Still Open	

Service-Disabled Veterans Insurance

Veterans who are granted a service-connected disability but are otherwise in good health may apply to VA for up to $10,000 life insurance coverage at standard insurance rates within two years from the date VA notifies the veteran that the disability has been rated as service-connected. This insurance is limited to veterans who left service after April 24, 1951. Veterans who are totally disabled may apply for a waiver of premiums. For those veterans who are eligible for this waiver, an additional policy of up to $20,000 is available. Premiums, however, cannot be waived on the additional insurance.

Reinstatement of Lapsed Insurance

Lapsed term policies may be reinstated within five years from the date of lapse. However, NSLI on the Limited Convertible Term Plan (Policy prefix W) may not be reinstated if the term insurance expired after the policyholder's 50th birthday. Lapsed permanent plan policies may be reinstated at any time except that J and JR policies must be reinstated within five years from date of lapse, and an endowment plan must be reinstated within the endowment period.

Automatic Renewal

A five-year term policy which is not lapsed at the end of the term period is automatically renewed for an additional five-year period. The exception is the NSLI Limited Convertible Term Plan (policy prefix W) which may be converted to a permanent plan, but cannot be renewed after the insured's 50th birthday. The premium rate for each renewal is based on the attained age of the insured, except "V" and "RS" prefixed policies renewed beyond age 70. The rate on these policies is based on the age 70 renewal rate, with no further increases occurring over the remaining life of the contract.

Convertibility

Any term policy which is in force may be converted to a permanent plan if requirements are met. NSLI policyholders, however, are not eligible to convert to an endowment plan while totally disabled. Upon reaching renewal at age 70 or older, NSLI "V" and "RS" term policies on total disability premium waiver are automatically converted to a permanent plan of insurance which provides cash and loan value as well as higher annual dividends.

Modified Life

A "modified life at age 65" plan of insurance is available to NSLI policyholders. The comparatively low premium rates for this plan remain the same throughout the premium-paying period, while the face value reduces by

50 percent at age 65. The reduced amount may be replaced with a "special ordinary life" plan, for an additional premium. In 1972, a "modified life at age 70" plan became available, which is like the modified life at age 65 plan except that face value reduction does not occur until age 70. The premium rate is only slightly higher than for the modified life at age 65 plan.

Dividends

Dividends are paid to holders of "K," "V," "RS," "W," "J," "JR," and "JS" insurance on the policy anniversary date. Dividends are not paid to holders of "H" or "RH" policies, or to holders of the current policies, SGLI, VMLI and VGLI. The Internal Revenue Service has announced that interest on insurance dividends left on deposit with the VA is not taxable. For details on this ruling contact the IRS.

Guaranteed Permanent Plan Policy Values

When a permanent plan policy has had premiums paid or waived for at least one year, and it is not lapsed, the guaranteed values include cash surrender, loan and reduced paid-up provisions. If a permanent plan policy lapses after being in force for at least three months, it will automatically be extended as term insurance. The period of this protection is determined by the net cash value of the policy. The amount of extended coverage is the face value less any indebtedness.

Total Disability Income Provision (TDIP)

Full information about adding the TDIP rider to a policy is available from the VA Regional Office and Insurance Center which maintains the veteran's insurance records, or the nearest VA office. The provision currently provides that an NSLI policyholder will be paid $10 per month, per $1,000 insurance, after being totally disabled for six consecutive months. A few older riders pay $5 per month. In either instance, disability must have commenced before the insured reached the 60th or 65th birthday, depending upon the insurance. USGLI policies also carry a TDIP provision. The amount of the monthly payment, however, differs from that paid to NSLI policyholders. TDIP payments do not reduce the face value of the policy. TDIP is not available for policies with the prefix "RH," "JR," or "JS."

Waiver of Premiums

All NSLI policies contain a provision for waiver of payment of premiums if the insured becomes totally disabled for at least 6 consecutive months. Before January 1, 1965 a waiver of premiums was granted as the result of a total disability that commenced before the insured's 60th birthday. On or after January 1, 1965, premiums may be waived as the result of total disability occurring up to the insured's 65th birthday. Total disability is defined as any impairment of mind or body which continuously renders it impossible for the insured to follow any substantially gainful occupation.

Policy Loan

Government Life Insurance policyholders with permanent plans of insurance can take out a loan against the cash surrender value of their policy. The policy cannot be lapsed, and premiums must be paid or waived at least one year before a policy has loan value. Policy loans may be granted up to 94% of the cash surrender value less any indebtedness.

Since November 2, 1987, all policy loans have a variable interest rate with a minimum rate of 5% and a maximum rate of 12%. The current interest rate for these adjustable rate loans is 8%. Each October 1, the interest rate may be

UNIFORMED SERVICES ALMANAC

increased or decreased depending on the ten year constant maturities, US Treasury Securities index. Policyholders with outstanding loans at the 11% rate have the opportunity to take advantage of the variable rate. The current interest rate is available at any VA office or may be obtained by calling the toll-free number 1-800-669-8477.

USGLI ("K" prefix) policy loans are not eligible for variable interest rates. Interest on USGLI loans was fixed, by law, at 5%.

Veterans Mortgage Life Insurance (VMLI)

P.L. 92-95, effective August 11, 1971, authorized Mortgage Protection Life Insurance for veterans who have received a grant from the VA for specially adapted housing and was limited to a maximum of $40,000 on the original or successor home. On October 1, 1992, the amount was increased to $90,000 by P.L. 102-568. Coverage continues on a decreasing basis until the mortgage is paid off, or the home is sold, or the insured veteran reaches age 70 or dies, which ever occurs first. If a mortgage is terminated through sale or liquidation, VMLI may be obtained on a mortgage of a second or subsequent home. If an eligible veterans elects not to be insured, he or she may be insured later upon application and proof of good health.

Servicemen's Group Life Insurance (SGLI)

All members of the Uniformed Services, including commissioned officers of the Public Health Service and the National Oceanic and Atmospheric Administration, and cadets and midshipmen of the service academies, are automatically insured under Servicemen's Group Life Insurance (SGLI) for the maximum amount of $100,000 unless an election is filed reducing the insurance by $10,000 increments or cancelling it entirely. Members may also purchase an additional $100,000 for a total of $200,000 outlined in P.L. 102-568. SGLI has no loan, cash, paid-up or extended values.

The current cost for this coverage is $.90 per $10,000 or $18.00 per month for the maximum of $200,000.

Public Law 93-289 on May 24, 1974, also extended full- and part-time coverage in the maximum amount to those persons who volunteer for assignment to the Ready Reserve of a Uniformed Service (including members of the Army and Air National Guard) and are assigned to a unit or position in which they may be required to perform at least 12 periods of inactive duty training that is creditable for retirement purposes under Chapter 67 of title 10. The current cost for this coverage is $18.00 per month up to the maximum $200,000. Effective October 5, 1994, those retired under the temporary special retirement authority with 15 or more but less than 20 years of service are eligible for SGLI coverage as retired reservists and must apply to OSGLI for coverage.

In addition to extending full time coverage to the Ready Reservists as stated above, those persons assigned to or who, upon application, would be eligible for assignment to the Retired Reserve of a Uniformed Service who have not received the first increment of retired pay and have not reached their 61st birthday but have completed at least 20 years of satisfactory service creditable for retirement purposes under Chapter 67 of title 10 are also eligible for full time coverage in the maximum amount. This coverage ends upon reaching their 61st birthday or receiving their first retirement check, whichever comes first. The coverage for these individuals commences upon approval of the acceptable application and receipt of the required initial premium. The premium for Retired Reservists is as follows: $.34 per $1,000 per month up to age 44, $.42 per $1,000 per month for those age 45 through 49, and $.56 per

$1,000 per month for those age 50 to 54 and $.72 for those over 55. The insurance may only be purchased in multiples of $10,000 up to a maximum of $200,000. Applications and premiums must be sent directly to OSGLI (Office of Servicemen's Group Life Insurance), 213 Washington Street, Newark, New Jersey 07102.

Public Law 93-289 increased the 90 day disability extension of coverage to 120 days for reservists performing active duty or inactive duty training who do not qualify for full time coverage. Public Law 102-568 increased the maximum coverage from $100,000 up to $200,000.

Veterans Group Life Insurance (VGLI)

The VGLI program was established August 1, 1974, by Public Law 93-289. This is a 5-year term insurance available upon application to all members being separated or released from active duty under call or order to duty that does not specify a period of less than 31 days. Also eligible are Reservists who, while performing active duty or inactive duty for training under a call or order specifying a period of less than 31 days, suffer an injury or disability which renders them uninsurable at standard premium rates. VGLI may be issued in multiples of $10,000. P.L. 102-568 increased **maximum renewable coverage up to $200,000** effective December 1, 1992. Also, VGLI is renewable for life in five-year term periods and can be converted to commercial insurance at the end of any five-year term period. However, no person may be issued VGLI in an amount greater than the amount of SGLI carried at the time of separation from service.

Members wishing to continue group coverage under the VGLI program must submit application and payment of first premium within 120 days of separation. If application (unless totally disabled) is not made within the 120 day period, application may be made within 1 year after SGLI coverage terminates provided evidence of good health is provided. If the member is totally disabled on the date of separation, application for VGLI may be made anytime during the 1 year extended SGLI coverage period. The effective date of VGLI will be the day following the end of the 1-year period or the day following the date disability ends, which ever is earlier. A medical examination and evidence of continuing disability may be required in such cases.

P.L. 99-166 also extended full-time VGLI coverage to members of the Individual Ready Reserve (IRR) and the Inactive National Guard (ING) who then had coverage only for the annual training and travel to and from drills. Those individuals who remain in the IRR/ING throughout their 5-year term period may renew their VGLI contract for a subsequent 5 year period.

Insurance applications and premiums are sent directly to OSGLI, 213 Washington Street, Newark, New Jersey 07102, Tel. 1-800-419-1473. VGLI premiums are based on the amount of insurance issued and age at the time insurance is granted.

The VGLI premium rate structure was changed from six age categories to eleven categories effective September 1, 1993. The monthly premium rates per $1,000 of coverage for those individuals who became eligible for VGLI on and after September 1, 1993 are as follows:

AGE 29 and Under	30-34	35-39	40-44	45-49	50-54	55-59	60-64	65-69	70-74	75 and Over
$.12	$.20	$.26	$.34	$.44	$.65	$.88	$1.12½	$1.50	$2.25	$4.50

SGLI can no longer be converted to an individual policy upon separation or release from active duty. VGLI can be renewed at the end of the 5 year term expiration, but once converted to a commercial policy it cannot be renewed. The exception to this is that a member of the Ready Reserves who upon completion of 20 years of duty for retirement purposes may at that time convert to an individual policy in lieu of continuing SGLI as a Retired Reservist.

VETERANS PREFERENCE IN GOVERNMENT EMPLOYMENT

The principle of veterans preference was written into law in 1865, when Congress gave preference to veterans with service-incurred disabilities. Since then the national policy has been broadened and strengthened by law, executive order and regulation. In 1944, the various statutes, White House directives and Civil Service Commission regulations were unified into a single law, known as the Veterans Preference Act, covering the rights of veterans (including certain spouses, widows or widowers, and mothers of veterans).

Under the Veterans Education and Employment Assistance Act of 1976 (P.L. 94-502), individuals entering the military services after October 14, 1976 do not receive veterans preference unless they serve in a campaign for which a service medal is awarded or become disabled during or as a result of military service. In addition, a 2 year minimum active duty service condition for those who enlisted after September 7, 1980 or entered on active duty other than enlistment on or after October 14, 1982 must be met. **The minimum active duty service condition does not apply for disabled veterans.**

The Civil Service Reform Act of 1978 (P.L. 95-454) contains additional provisions regarding Veterans Preference in Government employment. As of January 1979, a disabled veteran with a compensable service-connected disability of 30 percent or more, who meets the appropriate qualifications standard, may be given a noncompetitive appointment which may lead to conversion to career or career-conditional employment. Veterans with disability ratings of 30 percent or higher, whose performances have been rated acceptable are entitled to preference in retention over other competing veterans and non-veterans.

Veterans with disabilities of 30% or more also have the right to be notified in advance and respond to any decision in which: they are considered ineligible for a position due to physical requirements of the position; they would be passed over by an agency in the course of filling a position from civil service certificates; or they are deemed ineligible for retention in a position during a reduction-in-force due to the physical requirements of the position.

Effective October 1, 1980, veterans preference was eliminated, except in certain adverse action appeals, for non-disabled military retirees who retire from the service at or above the rank of Major or Lieutenant Commander.

PREFERENCE IN EMPLOYMENT AND RETENTION

Preference in Retention During Layoffs. In Government reduction in force programs brought about by the economy or other factors, Congress has given employees with veterans preference (except for certain retired military personnel — see "Employment of Retired Military Personnel" following) in the Federal service job priority rights over certain non-veterans.

Career civil service veterans have job retention rights over all other Federal workers in the same occupational series and grade at their place of employment.

Veterans with career-conditional or indefinite status do not have job retention rights over non-veterans who have career civil service status. However, they do have retention rights over non-veteran workers with the same status. Veterans with Temporary Appointment Pending Establishment of a Register (TAPER) appointments have retention rights over non-veteran TAPERS.

Thus, between two persons who are doing similar work in identical positions and serving under the same tenure, the veteran is retained over the non-veteran if one must go. Veterans who are reached for a RIF action also have a wider range of bumping rights than non-veterans.

Appeal Rights in Adverse Actions. Veterans have appeal rights on adverse agency actions. A veteran in the competitive service who has completed a probationary period, and a veteran in the excepted service who has completed one year of continuous service, are entitled to appeal to the Merit Systems Protection Board the following actions taken by his or her Agency: removal, suspension for more than 30 days, furlough without pay or demotion. If the Board rules in favor of the veteran, its decision is binding on the agency.

Veterans Preference in Hiring. In civil-service examinations, 5 points are added to the earned rating of an applicant who makes a passing grade and who was honorably separated from the Armed Forces of the United States: (a) any time between December 7, 1941, and July 1, 1955; (b) after more than 180 consecutive days of active duty any part of which occurred between January 31, 1955, and October 14, 1976 (service during an initial period of active duty for training under the "six-month" Reserve or National Guard programs does not qualify); or (c) after active duty in any campaign or expedition for which a campaign badge has been authorized. However, a 2 year minimum active duty service condition for those entering military service after September 7, 1980, or entered on active duty other than by enlistment on or after October 14, 1982 must be met. The minimum active duty service condition does not apply to disabled veterans. Reserve and Guard members who received campaign badges or services medals need not have served two years provided they served the full period called or ordered to active duty.

Ten points are added to the earned rating of a disabled veteran applicant who makes a passing grade and who was honorably separated (regardless of the time active duty was performed). Ten points are also added in some cases to the passing grade of an unmarried widow or widower of a veteran, the spouse of a disabled veteran, or the mother of a deceased or disabled veteran.

Under certain conditions, an applicant granted 10 point preference may file an application at any time to reopen closed competitive examinations.

In jobs where experience is necessary, the veteran gets full credit for his or her military service. It is counted either as additional experience in his or her pre-service job or as experience gained in the service depending upon which is more beneficial to the veteran.

Candidates for jobs are listed on civil-service registers in order of the examination ratings they have earned plus their preference points; except that those disabled veterans who have compensable service-connected disabilities of 10% or more rise to the top of the register. However, this last does not apply in professional and scientific jobs in grade GS-9 or higher. Among themselves, the veterans disabled to a compensable degree who have gone to the top of the register are listed in order of their earned examination ratings plus 10 points.

UNIFORMED SERVICES ALMANAC

Under the rule of three, an agency is permitted to hire any one of the top three persons on a register; except that it may not pass over a preference eligible to select a non-preferenced eligible unless the preference eligible is not qualified for the position. OPM retains final approval authority on objections and passovers of compensable preference eligibles with a disability of 30 percent or more.

Some Government examinations are reserved for veterans as long as they are available. These are guards, elevator operators, messengers, custodians, and related occupations.

Veterans Readjustment Appointment (VRA). Veterans' Readjustment Appointments (VRA) allows veterans who served after August 4, 1964 to be appointed to any job for which they qualify up to grade GS-11 or equivalent without competition. A VRA appointment is not a right and is made at the agency discretion..

A Vietnam-era veteran must have served for a period of more than 180 days active duty and have other than a dishonorable discharge. VRA eligibility extends for a period of 10 years following the veteran's last discharge or December 31, 1995, whichever is later. Non Vietnam War veterans who entered active service after May 7, 1975, you have 10 years from the date of last separation, or until December 31, 1999, whichever is later. If you have a service-connected disability of 30 percent or more there is no time limit.

Veterans seeking a VRA should apply directly to the agency where they wish to work. Agencies can recruit candidates and make VRAs directly without using OPM lists.

VRA eligibles are not guaranteed appointment. Agencies can choose candidates from civil service examination lists, agency employees, or current or former federal employees with civil service status.

Disabled veterans and others with veterans preference must be given preference consideration over veterans who are not eligible for preference.

If you have less than 15 years of formal education, agencies are required to provide a training program for you. If you have 15 years or more, you may get training on the same basis as other employees including on-the-job training or classroom training.

The requirement for more than 180 days of active service does not apply to veterans separated because of a service- connected disability, or to Reserve and Guard members who served on active duty during a period of war, such as the Persian Gulf war, or in a military operation for which a campaign or expeditionary medal is authorized.

UNIFORMED SERVICES EMPLOYMENT AND REEMPLOYMENT RIGHTS

Employment and restoration rights have been provided for federal employees who leave their jobs to serve on active duty or on active duty for training in the Armed Forces.

Public Law 103-353, the Uniformed Services Employment and Reemployment Rights Act of 1994, clarifies and strengthens the prohibitions against discrimination or acts of reprisal against an employee or applicant for employment because of a past, current or future military obligation.

This Act reaffirms that the timing, frequency, duration and nature of an individual's military training or service shall not be a basis for denying employment or reemployment protection.

It also reaffirms that a protected individual is generally entitled to reemployment with the seniority, promotions and pay raises the person would have attained if he or she had been continuously employed.

The law provides that a protected person would, upon request, continue to be covered by employer-provided insurance for up to 31 days at the employer's expense and up to 18 months at the employees expense.

EMPLOYMENT OF RETIRED MILITARY PERSONNEL

The Dual Compensation Act (P.L. 88-448) overhauled antiquated dual-pay, dual-employment laws governing the employment of retired military personnel in Federal civilian jobs and the employment of Government workers in more than one Federal job.

Specifically, the law contains these major provisions:

1. All retired military officers are allowed to take Federal civilian jobs.

2. All retired military personnel who take Government civilian jobs receive the full pay of the position.

3. Retired regular officers and warrant officers receive only a portion of their military retired pay plus 50 percent of any remainder. As of December 1, 1995, the exempt amount on retired pay is $9,819.69 for retired officers who entered the Uniformed Services prior to August 1, 1986 and $8,999.27 for those who entered the uniformed services on or after August 1, 1986.

4. Retired reserve officers, all retired enlisted personnel (reserve and regular), and regular officers retired for combat disability keep all their retired pay when they work in Federal civilian jobs, unless they retired after January 11, 1979 and their combined retired pay and civil service salary exceed the cap based on the salary rate for Level V of the Executive Schedule.

5. With certain exceptions, military retirees are not entitled to placement in the veterans preference subgroup of their tenure group for reduction-in-force purposes, and they get credit only for length of military service performed during a war or in any campaign or expedition for which a campaign badge has been issued. Excepted from this provision are military personnel whose retirement is based on a disability incurred in the line of duty as a result of armed conflict or saused by an instrumentality of war. Those whose retirement is based on less than 20 years of active service, and those employed on November 30, 1964, in positions in the Federal civilian service to which the laws on veterans preference apply and who have not had a break in service of more than 30 days since then. Military retirees below the rank of major (0-4) get veterans preference in examinations and appointments even though they do not get a preference in RIFs.

6. Credit for military service of military retirees for annual leave purposes is limited to service during a war, or in a campaign or expedition for which a campaign badge has been issued, unless the member was retired for combat disability or was employed on November 30, 1964, in a Federal civilian position to which the annual and sick leave laws apply, and has not had a break in service for more than 30 days since that date.

7. Military retirees must wait at least 180 days after retirement before taking a civilian position in the DoD unless prior approval is obtained from the Service

UNIFORMED SERVICES ALMANAC

Secretary. This restriction can be waived for shortage category jobs or in a national emergency.

When the combined pay (military retired pay and federal wages) exceed the Executive Level V limit, the retired or retainer pay will be reduced accordingly.

P.L. 98-270, the Omnibus Budget Reconciliation Act of 1983, provided that future COLAs will be effective December 1 of each year and payable in the January check; the COLA is based on the change in the CPI between the third quarter average of the calendar year it is to take effect and the third quarter average of the preceding calendar year. The COLAs which were to be effective in May of 1984 and June of 1985 were eliminated.

The Deficit Reduction Act of 1984, P.L. 98-369, repealed the provision which reduced the civil service pay of military retirees by the amount of any COLA increase and the Second Supplemental Appropriations Act of 1984, P.L. 98-396, did away with the "half COLA" provisions which limited cost of living increases for retirees under age 62. P.L. 99-509, the Omnibus Budget Reconciliation Act of 1986, insured a COLA for retirees for FY 1987, 1988, and 1989 by exempting such increases from mandatory budget cuts resulting from the Gramm-Rudman-Hollings deficit reduction amendment. A 3.7 percent COLA for both CSRS and FERS retirees was authorized for FY 1992, effective December 1, 1991. A 3.0 percent COLA for both CSRS and FERS retirees was authorized for FY 1993, effective December 1, 1992 and a 2.6 percent increase effective December 1, 1993. Federal civilian retirees will receive a COLA increase of 2.0 percent for 1996, however, payments will be delayed until April 1, 1996.

1996 PAY SCHEDULE FOR GENERAL SCHEDULE EMPLOYEES*

Longevity Steps / Grade GS	1	2	3	4	5	6	7	8	9	10
1	12,384	12,797	13,208	13,619	14,032	14,274	14,679	15,089	15,107	15,489
2	13,923	14,255	14,717	15,107	15,274	15,723	16,172	16,621	17,070	17,519
3	15,193	15,699	16,205	16,711	17,217	17,723	18,229	18,735	19,241	19,747
4	17,055	17,624	18,193	18,762	19,331	19,900	20,469	21,038	21,607	22,176
5	19,081	19,717	20,353	20,989	21,625	22,261	22,897	23,533	24,169	24,805
6	21,269	21,978	22,687	23,396	24,105	24,814	25,523	26,232	26,941	27,650
7	23,634	24,422	25,210	25,998	26,786	27,574	28,362	29,150	29,938	30,726
8	26,175	27,048	27,921	28,794	29,667	30,540	31,413	32,286	33,159	34,032
9	28,912	29,876	30,840	31,804	32,768	33,732	34,696	35,650	36,624	37,588
10	31,839	32,900	33,961	35,022	36,083	37,144	38,205	39,266	40,327	41,388
11	34,981	36,147	37,313	38,479	39,645	40,811	41,977	43,143	44,309	45,475
12	41,926	43,324	44,722	46,120	47,518	48,916	50,314	51,712	53,110	54,508
13	49,856	51,518	53,180	54,842	56,504	58,166	59,828	61,490	63,152	64,814
14	58,915	60,879	62,843	64,807	66,771	68,735	70,699	72,663	74,627	76,591
15	69,300	71,610	73,920	76,230	78,540	80,850	83,160	85,470	87,780	90,090

*Rates shown do not include locality payments payable in the 48 conitguous states and the District of Columbia. There are 27 separate locality pay areas with locality payments ranging from 4.13 percent to 9.40 percent in 1996.

Note: For more detailed Federal pay tables and other vital information on civil service employment, order the **FEDERAL PERSONNEL GUIDE**. Call (703) 532-1631 to place credit card orders or for more information.

Q. *What limitations are placed on dual compensation under the law?*

A. There are two limitations. The first limitation applies to all regular officers. That limitation provides that a retired officer of the Uniformed Services who holds a federal government civilian position will receive the full salary of the civilian position. During periods when the limitation applies, the officer receives the first $9,819.69 (effective December 1, 1995) of his or her retired pay plus one-half of any remainder of that pay. Officers who entered the uniformed services on or after August 1, 1986, receive the first $8,999.27 plus one-half of any remainder.

The second limitation applies to all retired military personnel (regular or reserve, officer or enlisted) who first receive retired or retainer pay after January 11, 1979. This additional limitation provides that, when an individual's combined federal civilian salary and military retired or retainer pay, after reduction in the case of a retired regular officer, exceeds the base salary rate for Level V of the Executive Schedule, the retired or retainer pay will be reduced by the amount needed to bring the total down to the Level V ceiling.

Q. *Will the retired pay of Reserve officers and enlisted personnel be reduced under the law?*

A. Only if they first receive retired or retainer pay after January 11, 1979 and their combined retired or retainer pay and federal civilian salary exceed the statutory Level V ceiling described above. Retired Reserve officers and all enlisted personnel continue to be exempt from the reduction in retired pay applied to retired regular officers.

Q. *Are any retired regular officers exempt from the reduction in military retirement pay provision?*

A. Yes. Any regular officer is exempt whose retirement was based on disability resulting from injury or disease received in line of duty as a direct result of armed conflict or disability caused by an instrumentality of war and incurred in the line of duty during a period of war.

Q. *Are there any other exceptions to the reduction in retirement pay provisions?*

A. Yes. The Federal Employees Pay Comparability Act of 1990, P.L. 101-509, permits exceptions to the reduction in retired pay provisions when necessary to respond to an emergency posing direct threat to life or property or to exceptional difficulty in filling a particular job. Exceptions must be requested by the agency head, or a designee at the agency headquarters level, and must be approved by OPM.

Q. *Did the Dual Compensation Act change the reduction-in-force rights of retired military personnel?*

A. Yes. Now a retired member of any of the uniformed services who is entitled to veterans preference under section 2108 of Title 5, US Code will be placed in veterans subgroup of his or her tenure group on reduction-in force only if:

1. His or her retirement was based on disability resulting from injury or disease received in line of duty as a direct result of armed conflict or disability caused by an instrumentality of war and incurred in the line of duty during a period of war; or

2. His or her retirement is based upon less than 20 years of active military service; or

3. He or she was employed in a civilian position to which the laws on veterans preference apply on November 30, 1964 and has not had a break in service of more than 30 days since that date.

CREDITING OF MILITARY SERVICE ("Catch 62")

Generally, military service is creditable for Civil Service retirement, however, since it is also creditable for Social Security benefits (after 31 December 1956), the law requires that those retirees who combine military service with civil service for a single annuity, have their civil service retirement annuity recomputed at age 62 when they become eligible for Social Security. This has often resulted in a significant reduction of retirement benefits.

The Budget Reconciliation Act of 1982 (P.L. 97-253, September 8, 1982), provided some relief for the majority of those subject to the "Catch 62" provisions.

CREDIT DEPOSITS FOR POST-1956 MILITARY SERVICE

The Omnibus Budget Reconciliation Act of 1982 (Public Law 97-253 September 8, 1982) established new requirements for credit for Post-1956 military service for Civil Service Retirement (CSR) purposes. The law distinguishes between employees employed before and after October 1, 1982.

Employed Before October 1, 1982. Individuals who first became employed in a position under CSRS before October 1, 1982, have the option of either (1) making the deposit for post-1956 military service or (2) receiving credit as in the past (without making the deposit) and having their annuity recomputed at age 62 to eliminate post-1956 military service if they are eligible for Social Security old-age or survivor benefits. Included are individuals who were, previous to October 1, 1982 covered under the CSRS and again employed under CSRS on or after October 1, 1982.

Employed on or After October 1, 1982. Individuals who first became employed under the CSRS on or after October 1, 1982, or after January 1, 1984, who are subject to the Federal Employee Retirement System (FERS), will receive credit for their post-1956 military service only if a deposit for the military service is made.

Amount of Deposit. The deposit under CSRS will be 7 percent of basic military pay received, plus interest. For individuals mandatorily subject to the new Federal Employees Retirement System (FERS) the deposit will be 3 % of basic military pay. The interest-free grace period will extend until 2 years after the initial appointment.

Payment Procedures. Employees making service credit deposits for their post-1956 service may elect, at their option to make such deposits in either a lump-sum payment, installment payments, or through payroll deductions.

Employees making a service credit deposit should evaluate their own situation to determine whether such deposits would prove advantageous.

Employees interested in making such a deposit should contact their personnel office for additional instructions.

Individuals who are mandatorily covered by FERS making the post-1986 military deposit should contact their personnel office for instructions.

Q. *Is military service creditable under the CSRS or FERS?*

A. As a general rule, military service is creditable provided it was active service, was terminated under honorable conditions, and was performed before separation from a civilian position under the Retirement System. For exceptions to this general rule, see the questions immediately following.

Q. *Does the receipt of pension or compensation under laws administered by the Veterans' Administration bar the crediting of military service?*

A. If an individual is receiving military retired or retainer pay, no retirement credit can be given for the military service (including pre-1957 military service) unless the retired pay is waived or was (1) awarded because of a service-connected disability incurred either in combat with an enemy of the United States or caused by an instrumentality of war and incurred in the line of duty during a period of war, or (2) awarded under the reserve retiree provisions (chapter 67, title 10, U.S. Code).

An applicant for disability retirement who is receiving military retired or retainer pay (or Veterans' Administration pension or compensation in lieu of such military retired or retainer pay) under conditions requiring that it be waived in order to make the military service available for civil service retirement credit is not eligible for computation under the guaranteed minimum provisions of the law unless he or she waives the military retired or retainer pay (and renounces the Veterans' Administration pension or compensation, if any).

Q. *May military retired pay be waived so that the military service will be credited under the CSRS or FERS?*

A. Yes.

LEAVE CREDIT AND REDUCTION-IN-FORCE CREDIT

With certain exceptions, military retirees are not entitled to placement in the veterans preference subgroup of their tenure group for reduction-in-force purposes, and they get credit only for length of military service performed during a war or in any campaign or expedition for which a campaign badge has been issued. Excepted from this provision are military personnel whose armed forces retirement is based upon a disability that is the direct result of an act of war, those whose retirement is based on less than 20 years of active service, and those employed on November 30, 1964, in positions in the federal civilian service to which the laws on veterans preference apply and who have not had a break in service of more than 30 days since then. Generally, military retirees get veterans preference in examinations and appointments even though they do not get preference in reductions in force.

Credit for military service of military retirees for annual leave purposes is limited to service during a war, or in a campaign or expedition for which a campaign badge has been issued, unless the member was retired for combat disability or was employed on November 30, 1964, in a federal civilian position to which the annual and sick leave laws apply, and has not had a break in service of more than 30 days since that date.

SURVIVOR OPTIONS

Q. *May the survivor of a deceased federal employee waive the military retired pay the employee was receiving at time of death?*

A. No.

Q. *What choice does an employee's survivor (widow, widower or dependent child) have between crediting military service toward retirement or towards social security?*

A. With regard to military service before January 1, 1957, there is a choice: the survivor can choose to have military service used under the CSRS or FERS or credited toward the Social Security benefit. When a surviving spouse appears eligible for a survivor annuity, and the deceased employee had post-1956 military service for which deposit was not made or completed, the surviving spouse may elect to make or complete the deposit in order to have the military service credited under the CSRS or FERS. The employing agency is responsible for advising the survivor of his or her right to make the deposit and for counseling the survivor about the effect of the decision to make or not make the deposit. If the survivor decides to make (or complete) the deposit, the agency must collect the amount due in one lump sum.

Q. *What is the effect of an election by a survivor to credit military service performed before January 1, 1957 toward social security rather than using it for retirement, and vice versa?*

A. The survivor cannot receive any annuity under the retirement system, if he or she elects to credit such military service toward social security. The survivor may still be eligible to receive social security even though the election was made to use the military service for retirement if there is sufficient other covered employment, but no credit for the military service will be allowed in computing the social security benefit.

UNEMPLOYMENT COMPENSATION FOR THOSE LEAVING ACTIVE DUTY

Military personnel about to complete an active duty tour or career should be aware of the availability of a compensation program for ex-servicemembers (UCX) which can provide a weekly income for a limited period of time for qualified personnel to help them meet basic needs while searching for new jobs.

Benefits are paid by the States from funds provided by DoD. Therefore, both Federal and State laws are applicable in determining qualifications for such benefits.

In order to receive UCX benefits, the individual must have performed active federal military service which is defined by PL 102-164, dated Nov. 15, 1991, as follows:

"Federal service" means active service (not including active duty in a reserve status unless for a continuous period of 90 days or more) in the armed forces or the commissioned corps of the National Oceanic and Atmospheric Administration (NOAA); if with respect to such service —

(A) the individual was discharged or released under honorable conditions (and, if an officer, did not resign for the good of the service); and

(B) the individual was discharged or released after completing his or her first full term of active service which the individual agreed to serve, or the individual was discharged before completing such term: (a) for the convenience of the Government under an early release program, (b) because of medical disqualification, pregnancy, parenthood, or service-incurred injury or disability, (c) because of hardship, or (d) because of personality disorder or inaptitude, but only if the service was continuous for 365 days or more.

All State laws require that you have qualifying earnings during a past period specified by the law; register for work, file a claim, report regularly as directed; and are able and available for work.

The amount of the weekly benefit and the number of weeks benefits may be paid are determined by State law based on pay grade and allowances at the time of separation from the service. Some States increase the weekly amount by allowances for dependents. The maximum amount of benefits payable based on military service is the same as the maximum amount payable under State law. Most States pay a maximum of 26 weeks. When unemployment is high and an individual has received all of the regular benefits to which he/she was entitled, he/she may become eligible for additional weeks of benefits.

Income while unemployed may affect eligibility for unemployment insurance. For example, military retirement payments are deducted from UCX benefits. Some States reduce or deny benefits if pay for unused leave, or severance pay is received. The following table lists those States which prorate or deny

UNIFORMED SERVICES ALMANAC

SIGNIFICANT STATE UNEMPLOYMENT INSURANCE PROVISIONS(1)
(As of July 1995)

State	Initial Waiting Period	Weekly benefit amount for total unemployment Minimum	Weekly benefit amount for total unemployment Maximum	Benefit weeks of total unemployment Minimum(2)	Benefit weeks of total unemployment Maximum(3)
Alabama	0	$22	$180	15+	26
Alaska	1	44-68	212-284	*16	*26
Arizona	1	40	185	12+	26
Arkansas	1	47	264	9	26
California	*1	40	230	*14+	*26
Colorado	1	25	272	13+	26
Connecticut	0	15-25	335-385	*26	*26
Delaware	0	20	300	24	26
District of Columbia	1	50	*347	26	26
Florida	1	10	250	10	26
Georgia	*0	37	205	9+	26
Hawaii	1	5	344	*26	*26
Idaho	1	44	248	10	26
Illinois	1	51	242-321	26	26
Indiana	1	50	217	14	26
Iowa	0	33-40	224-274	11+	26
Kansas	1	65	260	10	26
Kentucky	0	22	238	15	26
Louisiana	1	10	181	8	26
Maine	1	35-52	192-288	21+ -22	26
Maryland	0	25-33	*250	26	26
Massachusetts	1	14-21	336-504	10+30	30
Michigan	0	42	*293	15	26
Minnesota	*1	38	304	10+	26
Mississippi	1	30	180	13+	26
Missouri	1	45	175	11+	26
Montana	1	57	228	8	26
Nebraska	1	20	184	20	26
Nevada	0	16	237	12+	26
New Hampshire	0	32	204	26	26
New Jersey	*1	75	*354	15	26
New Mexico	1	41	205	19	26
New York	*1	40	300	26	26
North Carolina	1	25	289	13-26	26
North Dakota	1	43	243	12	26
Ohio	1	66	245-328	20	26
Oklahoma	1	16	247	*20+	*26
Oregon	1	70	301	4+	*26
Pennsylvania	1	35-40	*340-348	16	26
Puerto Rico	1	7	133	*26	*26
Rhode Island	1	41-51	324-404	15+	26
South Carolina	1	20	213	15	26
South Dakota	1	28	180	15+	26
Tennessee	1	30	200	12+	26
Texas	*1	42	252	9+	26
Utah	1	17	253	10	26
Vermont	1	25	212	26	26
Virgin Islands	1	32	223	12+	26
Virginia	1	65	208	12	26
Washington	1	75	350	16+ -30	30
West Virginia	1	24	290	26	26
Wisconsin	0	50	266	12+	26
Wyoming	1	16	233	12-26	26

(1) State laws may require that regular, as well as disability retirement payments to military personnel based on military service performed be deducted from unemployment compensation claims paid.
(2) When 2 amounts are shown, it reflects a range based on claimants qualifications.
(3) Maximum based on military service is as shown above in state of residence.
NOTE: Some states may prorate or deny unemployment compensation for ex-service personnel if receiving terminal or accrued leave pay or severance pay.
*Indicates additional qualifications. Consult State employment service office or unemployment insurance claims office.

payment for unemployment insurance because of unused leave or severance payments.

To file a UCX claim, go to the nearest State employment service office or unemployment insurance claims office. Register for work, and if a suitable job is not available, apply for unemployment insurance benefits. You will need Copy Number 4 of DD Form 214 and your social security card. However, if copy Number 4 was not made available to you upon separation, or was lost, you may utilize: a certified copy Number 2, 3, 6, 7, or 8 as an official copy to file a claim for UCX benefits. Benefit rights are determined by the state laws where you first file your claim after separation.

Benefits may be denied if, after military service, you quit a job without good cause, are fired for misconduct connected with your work or refuse a suitable job without good cause. Fines and/or imprisonment may result if intentional misinformation or falsification of facts are provided to State authorities for the purposes of obtaining benefits. If you discover any errors made when applying for benefits, notify the appropriate office immediately.

This section is necessarily general in presenting information concerning unemployment insurance benefits. The text is based on the best available information at time of publication but is subject to change at any time.

VETERANS EMPLOYMENT AND TRAINING PROGRAMS

The Department of Labor (DOL) is involved in a variety of measures to make certain no veteran who wants to work goes without a job or the training and assistance needed to get that job. There is special emphasis on assisting disabled veterans and veterans of the Vietnam era.

The Uniformed Services Employment and Reemployment Rights Act of 1994 (USERRA) clarifies and strengthens the veterans' reemployment rights (VRR) law.

USERRA continues the protection of civilian job rights and benefits for veterans and members of Reserve components. However, USERRA makes major improvements in the protection of rights and benefits by clarifying the law, improving enforcement mechanisms, and providing Federal Government employees Department of Labor assistance with processing claims.

The new law also expands to 5 years the cumulative length of time that an individual may be absent for military duty and retain reemployment rights (the old law provided 4 years of active duty, plus an additional year if the additional time was for the convenience of the Government). Similar to the old law, there are important exceptions to the 5 year limit. These include initial enlistments lasting more than 5 years, periodic training duty, and involuntary active duty extensions and recalls, especially because of a war or national emergency. USERRA clearly establishes that reemployment protection does not depend on the timing, frequency, duration, or nature of an individual's service.

USERRA also provides for enhanced protection for disabled veterans, such as the requirement that employers make reasonable efforts to accommodate the disability. Servicemembers convalescing from injuries received during service or training may have up to two years to return to their jobs (as opposed to the one year provided by the old law).

As under the old law, USERRA provides that returning servicemembers be reemployed in the job that they would have attained had they not been absent for military service (the long-standing 'escalator' principle), with the same seniority, status and pay, as well as other rights and benefits determined by seniority.

However, USERRA also requires that reasonable efforts be made (such as training or retraining) that would enable returning servicemembers to refresh or upgrade their skills so that they might qualify for reemployment. It clearly provides alternative reemployment positions if the servicemember cannot qualify for the 'escalator' position.

USERRA also reaffirms and clarifies that while an individual is performing military service, he or she is deemed to be on a furlough or leave of absence and is entitled to the non-seniority rights accorded other individuals on nonmilitary leaves of absence.

Health and pension plan coverage for servicemembers is clarified under USERRA. Individuals performing military duty of more than 30 days may elect to continue employer-sponsored health care for up to 18 months; however, they may be required to pay up to 102 percent of the full premium. For military service of less than 31 days, health care coverage is provided as if the servicemembers had never left. USERRA does provide grace periods for plans that are in compliance with USERRA provisions.

The application period after military service is now based on time spent on military duty not on the category of service performed. For service of less than 31 days, the servicemember must report at the beginning of the scheduled, first calendar work day after release from service, taking into account safe travel home plus an 8 hour rest period. For service of more than 30 days but less than 181 days, the servicemember must submit an application for reemployment within 14 days of release from service. For service of more than 180 days, an application for reemployment must be submitted within 90 days of release from service.

USERRA also requires that servicemembers provide advance written or verbal notice to their employers for all military duty. Under the old law, notice was only required for training duty. Additionally, for the first time, servicemembers will be able (but can be required) to use accrued vacation or annual leave while performing military duty.

Under the USERRA, the Department of Labor, through the Veterans' Employment and Training Service (VETS) must provide assistance to all persons having claims under USERRA, including Federal and Postal Service employees. If resolution is unsuccessful following an investigation, the servicemember with a claim against a State government or against a private sector employer may have their claim referred to the Department of Justice for consideration of representation in the appropriate District Court, at no cost to the claimant. For the first time, if violations under USERRA are shown to be willful, the court may award liquidated damages. Federal and Postal Service employees may have their claims referred to the Office of Special Counsel for representation consideration before the Merit Systems Protection Board (MSPB). Individuals who pursue their own claims in court or before the MSPB may be awarded reasonable attorney and expert witness fees if they prevail.

Veterans' Employment and Training Service (VETS)

The VETS is a nationwide network of Federal employees, whose responsibility is to ensure the Veterans programs described herein, are carried out according to current laws and regulations. There is one VETS Director stationed in every state, capital city, Puerto Rico, and District of Columbia.

UNIFORMED SERVICES ALMANAC

- **Job Service** — The public Job Service offices across the country are administered by each State government to provide veterans with priority in counseling, aptitude testing, job development, referral, placement in job openings and training opportunities.
- **Disabled Veterans Outreach Program (DVOP)** — Located in most Job Service offices, it's responsibility is to provide special assistance to other veterans and help them obtain employment and training services.
- **Servicemembers Occupational Conversion and Training Act (SMOCTA)** — SMOCTA established a job training program to help eligible veterans obtain stable, long-term employment. SMOCTA encourages employers to hire recently separated veterans by paying them directly for part of the costs associated with training employees who are hired under the program.

You may be eligible to participate in SMOCTA if you were discharged under other than dishonorable conditions after August 1, 1990, and served on active duty for more than 90 days or were released earlier because of a service-connected disability. You must meet one of the following criteria to be eligible for SMOCTA: (a) Have a primary or secondary military occupational speciality which is not readily transferable to the civilian work force. (b) Be unemployed at the time you apply for the program and for at least 8 of the 15 weeks immediately preceding application. (c) Be entitled to compensation from VA for a service-connected disability(ies) rated 30 percent or more, or would be if not for the receipt of military retired pay.

You must obtain a Certificate of Eligibility for SMOCTA to present to employers as verification of eligibility to participate in the program. The certificate expires 180 days after issuance but may be renewed upon request if you are still eligible. Initial application for a certificate must be made prior to September 30, 1995. You must begin in an approved training program before March 31, 1996, in order for your employer to be eligible for reimbursement.

You **may not** receive VA education benefits at the same time that your employer receives payment for your training under this program. Certain programs of job training are precluded from SMOCTA.

You may apply for participation in the program by completing VA Form 22-8932, Application for a Certificate of Eligibility. An application can be obtained at the nearest state employment or job service office, or your local VA regional office. Contact your local employment or job service office for help in identifying a suitable job training program. VA will provide vocational and educational counseling at no cost to you if you want help in making a career choice.

- **Training Programs** — Job Training Partnership Act funded programs at the state and local level also provide opportunities for eligible veterans. Veterans should contact a Job Service office listed under State government or a VETS Office listed under the U.S. Department of Labor for specific information.
- **Transition Assistance Program (TAP)** — The Department of Labor, in conjunction with the DoD and DVA, supports the TAP and the Disabled Transition Assistance Program (DTAP). These programs are geared toward military personnel, and their spouses, who are within 180 days of separation. TAP and DTAP are three to four day workshops that provide service personnel with benefits counseling, employment and training assistance, and information on the civilian labor market.

UNIFORMED SERVICES ALMANAC

- **Targeted Jobs Tax Credit (TJTC)** — This tax credit program is designed to hire certain target groups of workers including low-income Vietnam-era veterans and certain disabled veterans. The credit employers can receive is equal to forty percent of first year wages up to $6,000 for each eligible employee. Information regarding TJTC may be obtained from any Job Service office.
- **Veterans Affirmative Action** — Employers with Federal contracts of at least $10,000 are required by law to take affirmative action on behalf of special disabled and Vietnam-era veterans and to list job openings with the Job Service. The Job Service gives these groups of veterans priority when referring applicants to Federal contractor job openings. Job Service staff also assist employers in meeting their program obligations.
- **Information Sources** — Veterans needing assistance should contact their Local Veterans Employment Representative or Disabled Veterans' Outreach Program Specialist at a local Job Service office. General questions may be directed to the Office of the Assistant Secretary for Veterans' Employment and Training, (202) 219-9110, or by looking for the instate location listing in the blue pages of major city areas telephone directories.

SOLDIERS' AND SAILORS' CIVIL RELIEF ACT

Authority: 50 U.S.C. App. Sec. 501-648; 560-591; AFP 100-3, Chapter 18;

Scope of Protection: The Soldiers' and Sailors' Civil Relief Act of 1940 (SSCRA), as amended, was passed by Congress to provide protection for individuals entering or called to active duty in the military service. It is intended to postpone or suspend certain *civil* obligations to enable service members to devote full attention to duty. The Act applies to the United States, the States, the District of Columbia, all U.S. territories and in all courts therein. Reservists and the members of the National Guard are protected under the SSCRA while on active duty. The protection begins on the date of entering active duty and generally terminates within 30 to 90 days after the date of discharge from active duty.

Key Concept — For certain important provisions of the SSCRA to be of benefit, the ability of the servicemember to either defend or pursue an action must be *materially affected* by his or her military service. This can be due to geographic prejudice, i.e., the military member's duty location prevents personal attendance at the judicial proceeding to protect his or her rights. It can also be due to economic prejudice, i.e., the military member cannot meet financial obligations due to military service (reduction in income as a result of entering military service results in inability to meet obligations).

The court compares the servicemember's financial condition prior to entry on active duty with the financial condition while on active duty.

Basic Relief:

Termination of Leases — A lease for property occupied for dwelling, professional, business, agricultural or similar purposes may be terminated by a servicemember if the following two conditions are met:

—The lease was entered into by the member before he or she started active duty; and

UNIFORMED SERVICES ALMANAC

—The leased premises have been occupied for the above purposes by the member or his/her dependents.

—To terminate the lease, the member must deliver written notice to the landlord at any time after call to active duty or receipt of orders for active duty. Oral notice is not sufficient. The effective date of termination is determined as follows:

—For month to month rentals, the termination becomes effective 30 days after the first date on which the next rental payment is due subsequent to the date when the notice of termination is delivered. For example, if the rent is due on the first day of each month, and notice is mailed on August 1, then the next rental payment is due and payable on September 1. Thirty days after that date would be October 1, the effective date of termination.

—For all other leases, termination becomes effective on the last day of the month following the month in which proper notice is delivered. For example, if the lease requires a yearly rental and proper notice of termination is given on July 20, the effective date of termination would be August 31.

—The servicemember is required to pay rent for only those months before the lease is terminated. If rent has been paid in advance, the landlord must prorate and refund the unearned portion. If a security deposit was required, it must be returned to the servicemember upon termination of the lease.

Rent — Effective July 31, 1990, landlords cannot, unless they obtain permission from a court, evict dependents from rented housing where the rent does not exceed $1,200.00 per month. The Court may stay such proceedings for up to three months. Protection will likely be afforded in cases where the rental amount exceeds $1,200.00 when the agreed rent is modest and, taking inflation into account, is equal to or less than $1,200.00 limit. (Sec. 530).

Installment Contracts and Mortgage Foreclosures — A servicemember who, prior to entry into active duty, entered an installment contract for the purchase of real or personal property, will be protected under the SSCRA if the servicemember's ability to make the payments is "materially affected" by the military service.

—The servicemember must have paid, prior to entry onto active duty, a deposit or installment under the contract.

—The seller is then prohibited from exercising any right or option under the contract to rescind or terminate the contract, to resume possession of the property for nonpayment of any installment due, or to breach the terms of the contract, unless authorized by the court.

—The SSCRA protects servicemembers against foreclosures of mortgages, as long as the following facts are established:

—The relief is sought on an obligation secured by a mortgage, trust deed; or other security in the nature of a mortgage on either real or personal property;

—The obligation originated prior to entry on active duty;

—The property was owned by the servicemember or family member prior to entry on active duty;

—The property is still owned by the servicemember or family member at the time relief is sought.

—The ability to meet the financial obligation is materially affected by the servicemember's active duty obligation.

Default judgments — Before a court can enter a default judgment (for failure to respond to a lawsuit or failure to appear at trial) against a military member, the person who is suing the servicemember must provide the court with an affidavit stating the defendant is not in military service. If the plaintiff files no

UNIFORMED SERVICES ALMANAC

affidavit and defendant is in military, court will appoint an attorney to represent the defendant's interests (usually by seeking a delay in the proceedings). The Court may also require plaintiff to secure bond to protect defendant against harm. If a default judgment is entered against a military member, the judgment may be reopened if the member makes an application within 90 days after leaving active duty, shows he or she was prejudiced, and shows he or she had legal defense. (Sec. 520).

Stay of proceedings — Court has direction to delay a civil court proceeding when the requirements of military service prevent the member from either asserting or protecting a legal right. The stay provisions are applicable during the period of service plus 60 days thereafter. Normally granted unless court finds ability to defend or pursue action not materially affected by military service. Stay can last for the maximum of period of military service plus 3 months. (Sec. 521).

Health Insurance. For persons called to active duty on or after August 1, 1990, reinstatement of health insurance is automatic.

Taxation — The member's state of legal domicile may tax military income and personal property. Legal domicile is not changed solely by virtue of military service. Collection of income tax may be deferred for period of service plus 6 months if the ability to pay is impaired by military service. Property cannot be sold to satisfy a tax obligation or assessment except upon application to court. Court then determines if stay is appropriate. (Sec. 560, 503, 574).

Maximum rate of interest — If, prior to entering service, a member incurs a loan or obligation with an interest rate in excess of 6%, the member will, upon application to the lender, not be obligated to pay interest in excess of 6% per annum during any part of the period of military service unless the court finds the member's ability to pay has not been materially affected. (Sec. 526).

Miscellaneous Relief:

Stay of Execution of Judgments/Attachments — If the person against whom action brought is, or within the last 60 days was, in military service the court may stay the execution of judgments, court actions, attachments and garnishments. If the member requests a stay, it must be granted unless the court finds the member's ability to comply with the order or judgment is not materially affected by military status. (Sec. 521)

Statute of Limitations — Member's time in service cannot be used to compute the time limits for bringing any action or proceeding by or against a member, whether in court or elsewhere. However, this does not apply to time limitations established under federal tax laws. (Sec. 524).

Insurance — Member's private life insurance policy is protected against lapse, termination, and forfeiture for nonpayment of premiums or if any indebtedness for period of military service plus two years. Professional liability insurance of persons called to active duty will be suspended upon written request to the insurance carrier for the period of the individual's active duty. Insured or beneficiary must make application to the Veterans' Administration for protection (Sec. 540-548).

UNIFORMED SERVICES ALMANAC
SELECTIVE SERVICE SYSTEM (STATUS AS OF DECEMBER 31, 1995)

The Selective Service System is an independent agency of the Executive Branch of the federal government, operating under the authority of the Military Selective Service Act (50 USC App. 451 et. seq.). Although the authority for men to be inducted into the armed forces expired in July 1973, the Act requires that the Selective Service System be maintained as an effective standby organization capable of immediate operation in an emergency. The System has a two-part mission: to provide personnel for military service to the Department of Defense in the numbers and timeframes necessary in a crisis; and, to provide a program of alternative service for draftees who are classified as conscientious objectors.

Prior to the establishment of the all-volunteer force, the last man to be involuntarily inducted through the Selective service entered the Army on June 30, 1973. Although the draft ended and registration was suspended shortly thereafter, the requirement for men to register with Selective Service was resumed by presidential executive order in July 1980. Under the current program, men born after December 31, 1959 are required to register within 30 days of their 18th birthday. Late registrations are accepted, but once a man reaches age 26, he is too old to register. To register, a man completes a simple form, providing his name, address, date of birth, social security account number, and telephone number.

A man on full-time active duty in the armed forces is exempt from registering, provided he began his active duty before turning 18 and finishing after turning 26. Cadets and midshipmen at the U.S. military academies are also exempt. If a serviceman leaves active duty prior to reaching age 26, he must register within 30 days if he had not registered before entering the service. In most cases, Selective Service registration is one of the outprocessing steps a man undergoes during from the service.

National Guardsmen and Reservists must register if they are not on full-time active duty. Women are not required to register and would not be drafted under current law. In 1981, the Supreme Court upheld the decision of Congress that requires only men to register and be subject to a draft in a crisis.

Registration forms are available at U.S. post offices and at American embassies and consulates overseas. These days, most men are given the opportunity to register by mail. A registration reminder card from Selective Service is mailed to their homes shortly before they reach age 18. After a person registers, his only obligation is to keep the Selective Service System notified of his current address, until he turns 26.

It was never intended that the all-volunteer force would stand alone in time of emergency. In the event of a conflict, the Reserves and National Guard would be activated, and Selective Service could be brought out of standby to provide the next level of augmentation with draftees. Selective Service planning focuses on emergency conditions which may exist six months after a mobilization. A peacetime draft is not contemplated.

UNIFORMED SERVICES ALMANAC

PART IV

FEDERAL INCOME TAX INFORMATION FOR MILITARY PERSONNEL

INTRODUCTION

This section covers the special tax situations of active members of the U.S. Armed Forces. It does not cover military retirees or veterans' benefits or give the basic tax rules that apply to **all** taxpayers. If you need the basic tax rules or information on a subject not covered here, you can order IRS publications and forms by calling toll-free 1-800-829-3676 or write to the IRS Forms Distribution Center for your area.

For federal tax purposes, the U.S. Armed Forces includes commissioned officers, warrant officers and enlisted personnel in all regular and reserve units under the control of the Secretaries of the Defense, Army, Navy, and Air Force. The Armed Forces also includes the Coast Guard.

MONTHLY TAX WITHHOLDING COMPUTATION
(For 1996 taxable income)

The military services use the percentage method for computing monthly taxes. In some cases there may be a slight variation from the computerized figures that are shown in the detailed pay tables in Section I of this Almanac. However, any differences will equalize when filing your return after the close of the taxable year.

COMPUTATION

The amount of wages referred to below represents monthly gross taxable wages less $212.50 per exemption for 1996. To make the computation to determine your monthly income tax withholding, multiply the number of exemptions claimed by $212.50. Subtract this amount from your monthly gross wages (basic pay). Then use the result to calculate your taxes from the tax tables.

Monthly Payroll Period Table

SINGLE PERSON:

If the monthly wage is:	The amount of income tax to be withheld shall be:
Not over $219	0
Over $219 but not over $2,121	15% of excess over $219
Over $2,121 but not over $4,477	$285.30 plus 28% of excess over $2,121
Over $4,477 but not over $10,229	$944.98 plus 31% of excess over $4,477
Over $10,229 but not over $22,100	$2,728.10 plus $36% of excess over $10,229
Over $22,100	$7,001.66 plus 39.6% of excess over $22,100

UNIFORMED SERVICES ALMANAC

MARRIED PERSON:

If the monthly wage is: / The amount of income tax to be withheld shall be:
Not over $535 0
Over $535 but not over $3,688 .... 15% of excess over $535
Over $3,688 but not over $7,473 .... $472.95 plus 28% of excess over $3,688
Over $7,473 but not over $12,654 .... $1,532.75 plus 31% of excess over $7,473
Over $12,654 but not over $22,325 .... $3,138.86 plus 36% of excess over $12,654
Over $22,325 .... $6,620.42 plus 39.6% of excess over $22,325

Example: Married officer O-4 with over 14 years of service claiming 3 exemptions, with a taxable pay of $3,881.10 per month.
 a. $3,881.10 less $637.50 (3 x $212.50) $3,243.60
 b. Tax = 15% of $2,708 ($3,243.60-$535)
 c. Total tax to be withheld monthly $406.29

DEPENDENCY EXEMPTIONS

Exemptions reduce your income subject to tax. In 1995 each exemption reduced income by $2,500. For 1996, each exemption will reduce your income by $2,550. You generally can claim an exemption for yourself, your spouse, and each person who qualifies as your **dependent**. If another taxpayer can claim an exemption for you or your spouse, you cannot also claim the exemption on your tax return. If you can claim an exemption for a dependent, that dependent cannot claim a personal exemption on his or her own tax return.

If you claim a dependent on your tax return, you must list the dependent's social security number if he or she is at least 1 year old by the end of your tax year.

DEPENDENTS

A person is your **dependent** for tax purposes, if all 5 of the following tests are met:
- Member of household or Relationship test
- Citizenship test
- Joint return test
- Gross income test, and
- Support test

For specific information on these tests, get Publication 501, Exemptions, Standard Deduction, and Filing Information.

ALIEN STATUS

For tax purposes, an alien is an individual who is not a U.S. citizen. An alien is in one of three categories: resident, non-resident, or dual-status. Determining the correct status is crucial in determining what income to report and what forms to file. For details about alien status, get Publication 519, U.S. Tax Guide for Aliens.

UNIFORMED SERVICES ALMANAC

GROSS INCOME

Members of the Armed Forces receive many different types of pay and allowances. Some are includible in gross income while others are excludable from gross income. Includible items are subject to tax and must be reported on your tax return. Excludable items are not subject to tax, but may have to be shown on your tax return.

INCLUDIBLE ITEMS

These items are includible in gross income, **unless** the pay is for service in a combat zone declared by an Executive Order of the President.

Basic pay for such items as: Active duty; Attendance at a designated service school; Back wages; Drills; Reserve training, and Training duty.

Special pay for such items as: Aviation career incentives; Diving duty; Foreign duty; Hazardous duty; Imminent danger; Medical and dental officers; Nuclear-qualified officers, and Special duty assignment pay.

Bonuses for such items as: Enlistment and Reenlistment.

Payments for such items as: Accrued leave; non-disability or separation pay; Personal money allowances paid to high-ranking officers; Scholarships such as the Armed Forces Health Professions Scholarship Program (AFHPSP) and similar programs, granted after August 16, 1986, and Student loan repayment from programs such as the General Educational Loan Repayment Program.

EXCLUDABLE ITEMS

The items in the following list are excludable from gross income. The exclusion applies whether the item is furnished in-kind or is a reimbursement or allowance. There is no exclusion for your personal use of a government-provided vehicle.

• Living allowances for: BAQ (Basic Allowance for Quarters) You can deduct mortgage interest and real estate taxes on your home even if you pay these expenses with money from your BAQ; BAS (Basic Allowance for Subsistence); Housing and cost-of-living allowances abroad whether paid by the U.S. Government or by a foreign government, and VHA (Variable Housing Allowance).

• Family allowances for: Certain educational expenses for dependents; Emergencies; Evacuation to a place of safety, and Separation.

• Death allowances for: Burial services; Death gratuity payments to eligible survivors (not more than $5,000), and Travel of dependents to burial sites.

• Moving allowances for: Dislocation; Moving household and personal items; Moving trailers or mobile homes, Storage, and Temporary lodging.

• Travel allowances for: Annual round trip for dependent students; Leave between consecutive overseas tours; Reassignment in a dependent-restricted status and; Transportation for you or your dependents during ship overhaul or inactivation.

• Qualified Military Benefits: Disability; ROTC educational and subsistence allowances; Uniform allowances paid to officers, and Uniforms furnished to enlisted personnel; Legal assistance; Space-available travel on government aircraft; and Medical/dental care.

UNIFORMED SERVICES ALMANAC
COMBAT ZONE EXCLUSION

If you are a member of the U.S. Armed Forces who serves in a combat zone, you may exclude certain pay from your income. You do not have to receive the pay while in a combat zone, but it must be paid for service there, or for a period during which you were hospitalized as a result of your service there. The following military pay can be excluded from your income.

1) Active duty pay earned in any month you served in a combat zone.

2) A reenlistment bonus if the voluntary extension or reenlistment occurs in a month you served in a combat zone.

3) Pay for accrued leave earned in any month you served in a combat zone. The Department of Defense must determine that the unused leave was earned during that period.

4) Pay received for duties as a member of the Armed Forces in clubs, messes, post and station theaters, and other nonappropriated fund activities. The pay must be earned in a month you served in a combat zone.

5) Awards for suggestions, inventions, or scientific achievements you are entitled to because of a submission you made in a month you served in a combat zone.

Retirement pay does not qualify for the combat zone exclusion.

SERVING IN A COMBAT ZONE

Service performed in the Persian Gulf area combat zone only if it is performed on or after January 17, 1991. Service in the combat zone includes any periods you are absent from duty because of sickness, wounds, or leave. If as a result of serving in a combat zone, a person becomes a prisoner of war or is missing in action, that person is considered to be serving in the combat zone as long as he or she keeps that status for military pay purposes.

Qualifying service outside combat zone. Military service outside of a combat zone is considered to be performed in a combat zone if:

1) The service is in direct support of military operations in the combat zone, as determined by the Secretary of Defense, and

2) The service qualifies you for special military pay for duty subject to hostile fire or imminent danger.

Military pay received for this service will qualify for the combat zone exclusion if the other requirements are met.

Nonqualifying service in combat zone. The following military service does not qualify as service in a combat zone.

1) Presence in a combat zone while on leave from a duty station located outside the combat zone.

2) Passage over or through a combat zone in a non-duty status during a trip between 2 points that are outside a combat zone.

3) Presence in a combat zone solely for your personal convenience.

This service will not, therefore, qualify you for the combat zone exclusion.

AMOUNT OF EXCLUSION

If your grade is below commissioned officer and you serve in a combat zone during any part of the month, all of your military pay for that month is excluded from gross income subject to tax. You can also exclude military pay earned while you are hospitalized as a result of wounds, disease, or injury incurred in the combat zone. The exclusion of your military pay while you are hospitalized does not apply to any month that begins more than 2 years after the end of combat activities in that combat zone. Your hospitalization does not have to be in the combat zone.

UNIFORMED SERVICES ALMANAC

Hospitalized while serving in the combat zone. If you are hospitalized while serving in the combat zone, the wound, disease, or injury causing the hospitalization will be presumed to have been incurred while serving in the combat zone unless there is clear evidence to the contrary.

Hospitalized after leaving the combat zone. In some cases the wound, disease or injury may have been incurred while you were serving in the combat zone even though you were not hospitalized until after you left.

If you are a commissioned officer, you may exclude your pay as above. However, the exclusion is limited to $500 of your military pay each month during any part of which you served in a combat zone.

COMBAT ZONE/MILITARY ACTION FORGIVENESS

If a member of the U.S. Armed Forces dies while on active service in a combat zone or from wounds, disease, or other injury received in a combat zone, or as a result of military action, the decedent's entire income tax liability is forgiven for the year death occurred, and for any earlier tax year beginning with the year before the year in which the wounds, disease, or other injury occurred. That tax liability is forgiven for any earlier tax year in which the member served at least one day in a combat zone or the year proceeding the year of death due to military action. Any forgiven tax liability that has been paid will be refunded, and any unpaid tax liability at the date of death will be forgiven.

In addition, any unpaid taxes for prior years will be forgiven and any prior year taxes that are paid after date of death will be refunded.

This forgiveness provision also applies to a member of the Armed Forces serving outside the combat zone if the service:

1) Was in direct support of military operations in the zone, and
2) Qualified the member for special military pay for duty subject to hostile fire or imminent danger.

COMMUNITY PROPERTY

The pay you earn as a member of the Armed Forces may be subject to community property laws depending on your **marital status**, your **domicile**, and the **nature of the payment**. The community property states are Arizona, California, Idaho, Louisiana, Nevada, New Mexico, Texas, Washington, and Wisconsin.

Marital status. Community property rules apply to married persons whose domicile during the tax year was in a community property state. The rules may affect your tax liability if you file separate returns or are divorced during the year.

Domicile. Domicile describes your legal, permanent home. It is not always where you presently live.

Nature of the payment. Active duty military pay may be subject to community property laws. Armed Forces retired or retainer pay may be subject to community property laws.

For more information on community property laws, get Publication 555, Federal Tax Information on Community Property.

UNIFORMED SERVICES ALMANAC
ADJUSTMENTS TO INCOME

There are certain adjustments to income you can claim. The one that may affect you the most is a deduction for contributions to an Individual Retirement Arrangement (IRA). For information on IRA's get Publication 590, Individual Retirement Arrangements (IRAs).

Armed Forces members (including reservists on active duty for more than 90 days) are considered active participants in an employer-maintained retirement plan.

EARNED INCOME CREDIT

The Budget Reconciliation Act of 1993 changed the earned income credit rules. The basic credit is based on how many children you have and the amount of income you earn. A provision of the GATT accords extends the credit to military members residing overseas for tax year 1995 and after.

The basic credit is based on how many qualifying children you have and other factors. For a detailed discussion of the new rules and an explanation of the new Schedule EIC (Form 1040 A or 1040), see Publication 596, Earned Income Credit. The credit is $2,094 for families with one child and $3,110 for families with more than one child.

ELIGIBILITY

In order to take any of these credits, you must meet **all 9** of the following rules:

1) You must have a qualifying child who lived with you for more than 6 months (12 months for a foster child). See Birth or death of a child, later, for more information.

2) You must have earned income during the year.

3) Your 1995 earned income and adjusted gross income must each be less than $24,396. For 1996, this figure increases to $25,078.

4) Your return must cover a 12-month period. This does not apply if a short period return is filed because of an individual's death.

5) Your filing status cannot be married filing separate. See Married taxpayers, later, for an exception to the joint return rule.

6) You cannot be a qualifying child of another person.

7) Your qualifying child cannot be the qualifying child of another person whose adjusted gross income is more than yours.

8) You usually must claim a qualifying child who is married as a dependent.

9) You did not exclude from your gross income any income earned in foreign countries, or deduct or exclude a foreign housing amount. See Publication 54, Tax Guide for U.S. Citizens and Resident Aliens, for more information.

Important Note. If either your 1995 earned income or adjusted gross income is $24,396 or more, you do not qualify for the earned income credit.

Earned Income

For purposes of the earned income credit, earned income includes:
- Wages, salaries, tips,
- Long term-disability benefits you received prior to minimum retirement age,
- Voluntary salary deferrals,
- Quarters allowances and subsistence allowances and in-kind quarters and subsistence received by military members,

UNIFORMED SERVICES ALMANAC

- Pay for service in a combat zone,
- Net earnings from self-employment,
- Anything else of value, even if not taxable, that you received for providing services.

For purposes of the earned income credit, the terms "quarters allowances and subsistence allowances" mean the Basic Allowance for Quarters and the Basic Allowance for Subsistence received by military personnel (with respect to grade and status) and the value of meals and lodging furnished in-kind to military personnel residing on military bases. To calculate the value of meals and lodging furnished in-kind, you may assume that the value is equal to the combined Basic Allowance for Quarters (BAQ) and the Basic Allowance for Subsistence (BAS) the military member would have received had he or she been entitled to the allowance.

Earned income does not include interest, dividends, Social Security payments, welfare benefits, pensions, annuities, veterans' benefits, variable housing allowances, workers' compensation, or unemployment compensation.

Married taxpayers. If you are married, you and your spouse usually must file a joint return to claim the earned income credit. Even though you are married, you may file as head of household and claim the credit on your return if:

1) Your spouse did not live in your home at any time during the last 6 months of the year,

2) You paid more than half the cost to keep your home for the entire year, and

3) Your home was, for more than 6 months, the main home of your child for whom you will be entitled to claim an exemption.

You will meet (3), even if you cannot claim your child as an exemption because you released your claim in writing to the other parent or there is a pre-1985 agreement (decree of divorce or separate maintenance or written agreement) granting the exemption to your child's other parent.

QUALIFYING CHILD

You have a qualifying child if your child meets three tests:
1) Relationship,
2) Residency, and
3) Age.

Each test has separate rules. See Publication 596, Earned Income Credit for details.

Note: To be eligible for the EIC, you must have a qualifying child. If your child does not meet all 3 tests, then you cannot claim the credit.

Advanced Earned Income Credit

If you expect to qualify for the earned income credit (EIC) for 1996, you can choose to get part of the credit in advance by giving a completed Form W-5, *Earned Income Credit Advance Payment Certificate*, to your appropriate finance office. The credit will be included regularly in your pay. These advance payments could be as much as 60% of the EIC for one qualifying child.

How to claim credit. To receive your credit, you must file a tax return. You can use either Form 1040 or Form 1040A and attach Schedule EIC. You cannot use Form 1040EZ.

UNIFORMED SERVICES ALMANAC
ITEMIZED DEDUCTIONS

To figure your taxable income, you subtract either the standard deduction or itemized deductions. The standard deduction for 1995 was $3,900 for single returns and $6,550 for joint returns. For 1996 the standard deduction is $4,000 for single returns and $6700 for joint returns. For head of household the standard deduction increases from $5,750 in 1995 to $5,900 in 1996. For information on the standard deduction, get Publication 501, Exemptions, Standard Deduction, and Filing Information.

Itemized deductions are taken on Schedule A (Form 1040). This section discusses itemized deductions of particular interest to members of the Armed Forces. For information on other itemized deductions, get the publications listed below:

Publication 502, Medical and Dental Expenses
Publication 526, Charitable Contributions
Publication 545, Interest Expense
Publication 547, Nonbusiness Disasters, Casualties, and Thefts
Publication 550, Investment Income and Expenses

MISCELLANEOUS ITEMIZED DEDUCTIONS

Most miscellaneous itemized deductions are subject to a limit. You must subtract 2% of your adjusted gross income (AGI) from the total to figure the amount you can deduct. Some miscellaneous deductions are not subject to this 2% limit. For information on deductions not discussed here, get Publication 529, Miscellaneous Deductions.

Employee Business Expenses. Deductible employee business expenses are miscellaneous itemized deductions subject to the 2% limit.

For information on employee business expenses, get Publication 463, Travel, Entertainment, and Gift and Publication 917, Business Use of a Car.

Generally, you must file Form 2106, Employee Business Expenses, to claim these expenses. You do not have to file a Form 2106 if you are claiming only expenses for uniforms, professional society dues, and work-related educational expenses. You can deduct these expenses directly on Schedule A (Form 1040).

Reimbursement. Generally, for you to receive reimbursement, per diem, or another allowance from the government, you must adequately account for your expenses and return any excess reimbursement. Therefore, the amount you receive is not included on your Form W-2 and the expenses for which you receive this reimbursement are not deductible.

If your expenses exceed your reimbursement, or you do not receive any reimbursement, the excess expenses are deductible (subject to the 2 % limit) if you can substantiate them. If this is your situation, you must file Form 2106.

Travel expenses. You can deduct unreimbursed travel expenses only if incurred while traveling **away from home.** To be deductible, your travel expenses must be work-related. You cannot deduct any expenses for personal travel such as visits to family while on furlough, leave, or liberty.

Away from home. Home is your permanent duty station (which can be your ship or base), regardless of where you or your family live. You are away from home if your are away from your permanent duty station long enough to need significant rest or sleep to be able to complete your duties.

Common travel expenses include:
1) Expenses for meals (subject to the 50% limit), lodging, taxicabs, business telephone calls, tips, laundry, and cleaning while you are away from home on temporary duty or temporary additional duty,
2) Expenses of carrying out official business while on "No Cost" orders.

Note: Away from home assignments that last more than one year are not considered temporary in nature. Therefore members can no longer deduct travel expenses paid while on any assignment of more than one year. See Publication 463.

Reservists. You can deduct travel expenses if you are under competent orders, with or without compensation, and are away from your main place of business overnight to perform drills and training duty.

If you are called to active duty, you can deduct travel expenses if you keep your regular job while on active duty, return to your job after release, and are stationed away from the general area of your regular job or business. However, you can only deduct these expenses if you pay for them at your official military post and only to the extent the expenses exceed BAQ and BAS. (Additional details can be found in the RESERVE FORCES ALMANAC and the NATIONAL GUARD ALMANAC.)

Transportation expenses. Transportation expenses are the expenses of getting from one place to another while not traveling away from home. These expenses include the costs of operating and maintaining a car, but not meals and lodging. If you are required while on duty to go from one place to another (for example, as a courier or messenger, or to attend meetings or briefings) without being away from home (as explained earlier), your unreimbursed transportation expenses are deductible. If you must use your own vehicle, you can deduct the expenses of using it. However, commuting expenses (expenses to your regular place of work from home and returning home are not deductible.)

Temporary work location. If you have a regular place of business and commute to a temporary work location, you can deduct the expenses of the daily roundtrip transportation between your residence and the temporary location. A temporary location is one where you work on an irregular or short-term (generally a matter of days or weeks) basis.

Uniforms. You usually **cannot** deduct the expenses for uniform cost and upkeep. Generally, you **must** wear uniforms when on duty and you **can** wear them off duty. If military regulations prohibit you from wearing certain uniforms off duty, you can deduct their cost and upkeep, but you must reduce the cost by any allowances or reimbursements you receive.

Expenses for the cost and upkeep of the following articles are deductible. In all cases, you must reduce your expenses by any allowances or reimbursements you receive to pay for them.
1) Military fatigue uniforms if you cannot wear them off duty.
2) Articles not replacing regular clothing, including insignia of rank, corps devices, epaulets, aiguillettes, and swords, and;
3) Reservists' uniforms if you can wear the uniform only while performing duties as a reservist.

Professional dues. You can deduct dues paid to professional societies directly related to your military position.

However, you **cannot** deduct amounts paid to an officer's club or a noncommissioned officers' club.

Educational expenses. You can claim certain educational expenses. However, you must meet certain rules for the expenses to qualify as deductions.

UNIFORMED SERVICES ALMANAC

Also, you must reduce deductible educational expenses by any allowances and reimbursements you receive to pay for them.

You cannot deduct the cost of travel that is itself a form of education. However, if your educational expenses qualify for a deduction, then travel for that education, including transportation, meals (subject to the 50% limit), and lodging can be deducted. Educational services provided in-kind such as base-provided transportation to or from class are not deductible.

Qualifications. You **can** deduct educational expenses if the education:
 1) Is required by your employer or by law or regulations for you to keep your salary, status, or job, or
 2) Maintains or improves the skills required in your present work.

Even if the above requirements are met, you **cannot** deduct educational expenses if the education is necessary to meet the minimum educational requirements needed to qualify you in your trade or business, or is part of a course of study that will qualify you for a new trade or business, even if you have no plans to enter that trade or business.

MOVING EXPENSES

To deduct moving expenses, you must generally meet certain time and distance tests. However, members of the Armed Forces who move because of a permanent change of station do not have to meet these tests. In addition, members of the Armed Forces are not required to report the value of moving reimbursements. Moving expenses are shown on Form 3903, Moving Expenses, or Form 3903F, Foreign Moving Expenses, as well as on Schedule A (Form 1040) See Reporting Moving Expenses, later.

For more information, get Publication 521, Moving Expenses.

PERMANENT CHANGE OF STATION

A permanent change of station includes:
 1) A move from home to the first port of active duty,
 2) A move from one permanent post of duty to another,
 3) A move from the last post of duty to your home or to a nearer point in the United States, if you move within one year of ending active duty or according to the Joint Travel Regulations.

Desertion, imprisonment, or death. If a member of the Armed Forces deserts, is imprisoned, or dies, a permanent change of station for the spouse or dependent includes a move to the place of enlistment or to the member's, spouse's, or dependent's home of record or nearer point in the United States.

Separate moves. If the government moves you and your spouse or dependents to or from separate locations, the moves are considered a single move to your post of duty. All expenses are combined.

REIMBURSEMENT

Do not include in income the value of moving and storage services provided by the government in connection with a permanent change of station. Although the 1993 Budget Reconciliation Act redefined 'moving expenses' and made moving expenses an adjustment not requiring itemization of deductions, the law did not change or affect the following allowances: dislocation allowance; temporary lodging; temporary lodging expenses; or MIHA. These allowances are excludable from gross income. If your reimbursements or allowances are less than your actual moving expenses, do not include the reimbursements or allowances in income. You can deduct the expenses, subject to the dollar limits discussed later, that exceed your reimbursements.

If you are required to relocate and your spouse and dependents move to or from a different location, do not include in income reimbursements, allowances, or the value of moving and storage services provided by the government to move you and your spouse and dependents to and from the separate locations.

DEDUCTIBLE MOVING EXPENSES

You can deduct only reasonable unreimbursed moving expenses that are incurred by you and members of your household. A member of your household is anyone who has both your former and your new home as his or her home. It does not include a tenant or employee, unless you can claim that person as a dependent. You cannot deduct costs for unnecessary side trips or lavish and extravagant meals and lodging.

Some moving expenses have no limits and are fully deductible. Still others have specific dollar limits.

No dollar limits. You can fully deduct expenses for:

Moving household goods and personal effects, including expenses for hauling a trailer, packing, crating, in-transit storage, and insurance. You **cannot** deduct expenses for moving furniture or other goods you bought on the way from the old home to the new home.

Reasonable travel and lodging expenses from the old home to the new home, including automobile expenses, air fare, but not meals (subject to the 50% limit).

Specific dollar limits. You cannot deduct more than $3,000 for all other moving expenses combined. See Publication 521, Moving Expenses. Other expenses include those for:

Selling the old home, including state transfer taxes, title fees, real estate commission, attorneys' fees, and points (loan placement charges) you must pay. You **cannot** deduct expenses for a loss on the sale of a main home or home improvements made to help sell the home.

Buying a new home, including attorneys' fees, escrow fees, appraisal fees, title fees, and points (load placement charges **not** representing interest). You cannot deduct the purchase price or the cost of home improvements.

Settling an unexpired lease or acquiring a new lease, including attorneys' fees and commissions. You can also deduct the loss of a security deposit if the lease was broken because of the move. You cannot deduct payments or prepayments of rents, a security deposit to obtain a new lease, or a security deposit that was lost because the vacated space needed cleaning or redecorating when the lease was ended.

Foreign moves. A foreign move is one from the United States or its possessions to a foreign country, or from one foreign country to another foreign country. It is not a move from a foreign country to the United States or its possessions.

The limit for moving expenses other than the costs of moving household goods and traveling to the new residence is $6,000 for foreign moves. Of this total, no more than $4,500 can be for pre-move housekeeping trips and temporary living quarters combined. Figure your temporary living quarters expenses for any 90 consecutive days before you move into permanent quarters.

Note: Do not include any services provided in-kind by the government in figuring the dollar limits.

UNIFORMED SERVICES ALMANAC

REPORTING MOVING EXPENSES

Figure moving expenses deductions on Form 3903 for moves to a home in the United States or its possessions, even if you are moving from a location overseas. Use Form 3903F if the home to which you are moving is outside the United States or its possessions. Carry the deduction from Form 3903 or Form 3903F to Schedule A (Form 1040). For more information, get Publication 521.

No double deduction. You can claim the expenses of buying or selling a home as a moving expense, or in determining gain on the sale of your home, but not both. However, any amount not deducted as a moving expense because of the dollar limits can be used on Form 2119. See Publication 523, Tax Information on Selling your Home.

SALE OF HOME

If you sell your home, get Publication 523, Tax Information on Selling Your Home. The rules discussed in that publication apply to all taxpayers.

You may postpone paying tax on some or all of the gain on the sale of your home if you meet certain requirements. One requirement is that you buy and live in a new home within the replacement period. As a member of the Armed Forces, your replacement period after the sale of your old home is suspended for a limited time if you are on extended active duty. A longer suspension period may apply if you are on an overseas assignment. These replacement periods are discussed next.

The other requirement depends on the cost (including construction cost) of the new home and sales price of the old home. This is discussed in detail in Publication 523.

If you sell your home, you must file Form 2119, Sale of Your Home, even if you are postponing the payment of tax on the gain. Individuals age 55 or older may make a one time exclusion of capital gains up to $125,000 on sale of a residence.

REPLACEMENT PERIOD

When you sell your home and replace it with another, you must buy (or build) and live in the new home within a specified period of time (replacement period) to be able to postpone tax on any gain from the sale of the old home.

The normal replacement period is 2 years before or 2 years after the sale of the old home. This replacement period is suspended for members of the Armed Forces, as described under Extended active duty, Overseas assignment, or Operation Desert Shield/Desert Storm, later.

If you have a gain on the sale of your old home and do not replace it within the replacement period, you have no more time to do so. This is true even if the delay is from conditions beyond your control, such as a military requirement to live in government quarters for a period that is longer than the suspended replacement period.

You must physically live in the new home as your main home within the required period. If you move furniture or other personal belongings into the new home but do not actually live in it, you do not meet this requirement.

Extended active duty. This means you are called or ordered to active duty for an indefinite period or for a period of more than 90 days. If you are on extended active duty, your replacement period after the sale of your old home

UNIFORMED SERVICES ALMANAC

is suspended. The suspension applies only if your extended active duty begins before the 2-year period after the sale ends. Your replacement period plus any period of suspension is limited to 4 years from the sale of your old home. If your duty is outside the United States, see Overseas assignment, or Operation Desert Shield/Storm, next.

Overseas assignment. If you are on extended active duty outside the United States, your replacement period is suspended while you are overseas and up to 1 year after the last day you are stationed overseas. However, your total replacement period cannot be more than 8 years after you sell your old home.

Remote site. If you return from an overseas assignment and must live in on-base quarters because adequate off-base housing is unavailable at the remote site, your replacement period is suspended while you must live in these quarters and up to 1 year after the last day you were required to live in these quarters. To qualify for this provision, the Secretary of Defense must determine that adequate off-base housing is unavailable at the remote site. As of November, 1992, only Adak, Alaska has been designated as a remote base site for these purposes. However, the total replacement period, including the time you are overseas and at the remote site, cannot be more than 8 years after you sell your old home.

Operation Desert Shield/Desert Storm. The running of the replacement period for extended active duty in the U.S., or the replacement period for extended active duty overseas, is suspended for any period you served in the Persian Gulf Area combat zone. For this suspension, the designation of the area as a combat zone is effective August 2, 1990.

If you performed military service in an area outside the combat zone but in direct support of military operations in the combat zone, and you received special pay for duty subject to hostile fire or imminent danger, you are treated as if you served in the combat zone.

The suspension ends 180 days after the later of:

1) The last day you were in the combat zone (or if earlier, the last day the area qualified as a combat zone), or

2) The last day of any continuous hospitalization (limited to 5 years if hospitalized in the U.S.) for an injury sustained while serving in the combat zone.

Spouse. This suspension generally applies to your spouse (even if you file separate returns). However, any suspension for hospitalization within the U.S. does not apply to your spouse. Also, the suspension for your spouse does not apply for any tax year beginning more than 2 years after the last day the area qualifies as a combat zone.

For more information on extension of the replacement period and information on other tax benefits available to those who served in a combat zone, get Publication 945, Tax Information for Those Affected by Operation Desert Storm.

Married taxpayers. As long as one spouse is a member of the Armed Forces, the suspension of the replacement period applies whether the old home is owned by one of the spouses or by both spouses. However, both the old home and the new home must be used by both spouses as the main home.

If you are divorced or separated during the suspension period, the suspension period ends for the nonmilitary member spouse on the day of the divorce or separation.

Note: If you report and pay tax on the gain from the sale of your old home and later replace your home within an extended replacement period and meet

UNIFORMED SERVICES ALMANAC

the requirements to postpone gain, you should file an amended return (Form 1040X) for the year of sale to claim a refund. However, due to the extended replacement period, your claim for refund may be barred by the statute of limitation for filing a claim for refund. To avoid difficulties, you should file a protective claim for refund when you file your return and pay the tax. For more information, get Publication 523.

SPECIAL SITUATIONS

Some special situations about home ownership can affect military personnel.

Rental. If you **temporarily** rent out either your old home before selling it or your new home before moving into it (for convenience or for some other **nonbusiness** purpose), you can still postpone paying tax on the gain under the rules just discussed. If you own rental property, even if it once was your main home, get Publication 527, Residential Rental Property.

Property used for business. Some taxpayers use part of their home for business. For example, a military members's spouse uses a room of their house for a pet-grooming business. If the house is sold, the rules for postponing the tax apply only to the part used as a home. Rules for the sale of business property apply to the part used for business. To determine what part of the gain to treat each way, see Property used partly as your home and partly for business in Publication 523.

More than one main home. If you buy more than one principal residence during the normal replacement period, only the last home bought can qualify as your new home for the purpose of postponing the tax. All other homes bought and sold during the replacement period are subject to the regular capital gain and loss rules. However, see Exception for work-related move, next.

Exception for work-related move. If you sell your principal residence because of a work-related move for which moving expenses are deductible (see Deductible Moving Expenses), you can postpone paying tax on the gain on the sale of more than one home during the replacement period.

WHERE TO FILE

Send your federal return to the Internal Revenue Service Center for the place where you reside. The instructions for Forms 1040, 1040A, and 1040EZ give the addresses for the service centers. If you are overseas and have an APO or FPO address, file your return with the Philadelphia Service Center.

WHEN TO FILE

Most individual tax returns cover a calendar year, January through December. The normal due date for these tax returns is April 15 of the following year. If April 15 falls on a Saturday, Sunday, or legal holiday, the due date is the next business day. For 1995 tax returns, the due date is April 15, 1996.

EXTENSIONS

You can receive an extension of time to file your return. Different rules apply if you live within the United States or outside the United States.

UNIFORMED SERVICES ALMANAC

Within the United States. You can receive an automatic 4-month extension to file Form 1040, Form 1040A or Form 1040EZ by filing Form 4868, Application for Automatic Extension of Time To File U.S. Individual Income Tax Return. File the application by the normal due date for the return with the service center where you will file your return.

If you use the automatic extension, you cannot choose to have the IRS figure your tax.

The extension of time to file is automatic and you will not receive any notice of approval. However, if you file Form 4868 late or if you do not pay the balance due in full, your request for extension will be denied. The IRS will inform you of the denial.

Having an extension to file does not mean you have an extension to pay any tax due. On Form 4868, you must estimate your tax, taking into account any withholding or estimated tax payments. **You must send in any tax due when you file Form 4868.** Enter any amount you send on Form 1040, Form 1040A, or Form 1040EZ. You will have to pay interest on any tax due when you file your return. You may also have to pay penalties if you underestimate your tax due. For more details, see the instructions on Form 4868.

Outside the United States and Puerto Rico. A U.S. citizen or resident can qualify for an automatic extension of time until June 15, if either of the following are met:

1) Both your tax home and abode are outside the United States and Puerto Rico.

2) You are in military or naval service on an assigned tour of duty outside of the United States and Puerto Rico for a period that includes the entire due date of the return.

Interest will be charged on any amount not paid by the normal due date, until the date the tax is paid.

If you use this automatic extension, you must attach a statement to the return showing that you met the requirement.

In this case, your extension is only until June 15, but you can request an additional 2-month extension to file on or before August 15 by filing Form 4868 on or before June 15. To obtain the additional extension, you must pay, with Form 4868, any tax due and must write in the top margin of the Form 4868 "Taxpayer Abroad."

Joint returns. For married persons filing a joint return, only one spouse needs to meet the requirements to take advantage of the automatic extension to June 15.

Separate returns. For married persons filing separate returns, only the spouse who met the requirements qualifies for the automatic extension.

Additional extension beyond August 15. You can request an extension beyond the 4-month period by filing Form 2688, Application for Additional Extension of Time To File U.S. Individual Income Tax Return, or by letter. Except in undue hardship cases, this additional extension will be granted only if Form 4868 has already been filed. Form 2688 or your letter will not be considered if filed after the extended due date. If you file Form 2688 and an extension is granted, and later it is discovered that the information you gave was false or misleading, the extension is void. You may then be subject to a penalty for filing late.

UNIFORMED SERVICES ALMANAC
STATE INCOME TAXES

Members of the Armed Forces of the United States are not excused or exempt from state or local income taxes except to the extent that either the Soldier's and Sailor's Civil Relief Act (SSCRA) or the law of the particular state or locality so provides. The Act provides that a member of the Armed Forces who is a legal resident of one state but who is living in another solely by reason of military orders, is not liable to the second state for income taxes on his on his/her service pay.

NOTE, however, the SSCRA does not exempt military retired pay, separate income of a spouse or other members of the service member's family, nor the income of service personnel derived from off-duty employment, investments, business, rents, bank deposits or other sources.

The Tax Reform Act of 1976 (P.L. 94-555), authorizes the Federal Government to withhold State taxes from active duty personnel whose "home" state requests such withholding. Military retired or retainer pay is not subject to mandatory withholding; however, if desired, State taxes can be withheld on a voluntary basis for all states with state income taxes.

Most states which tax military income have executed mandatory withholding agreements with the U.S. Treasury.

Military personnel are required to obtain necessary forms, file returns and pay State taxes directly to the State tax authority. The Soldiers' and Sailors' Civil Relief Act reserves the right to tax a service member's income to the State or legal residence or domicile, sometimes referred to as the "home" State. The Act protects the member from taxation by a State where residing by virtue of military orders, but of which such member is not a legal resident, except on business income or civilian employment within such State, including off-duty employment at non-appropriated fund activities such as clubs. Taxes on such off-duty income may be withheld and remitted to the host State. Each member is required to file a return to his or her State of domicile and to the State where residing when such off-duty income is earned.

Spouses and dependents of service members are not covered by the act and may occasionally be subject to income tax by two or more States. Information and advice concerning the application of the Act in individual cases should be obtained from the Legal Assistance Office.

The income-taxing States are making a concerted effort to locate delinquent taxpayers and are imposing penalties on late returns. Computerization of Federal and State taxes has revealed many of these delinquent taxpayers. Additionally, most states have entered into agreements with the IRS for the exchange of tax data.

It should be noted that a legal "domicile" and the "home-of-record" as used within the Armed Forces are not always identical. The "home-of-record" is normally used to designate the place to which the member may be entitled to mileage reimbursement upon separation, and is not always the legal domicile. In determining its right to tax an individual, a State frequently looks to see whether the individual has claimed benefits based on domicile or has exercised his or her right to vote — a strong indication of domicile. Many States are now challenging any change of domicile and requiring proof of such changed domicile. The burden of proof is upon the member.

The following compilation of State tax information represents the best information available at time of publication. Some states were considering new tax legislation, so care should be exercised and questions should be resolved

UNIFORMED SERVICES ALMANAC

by checking with the state tax authority. *This data should be considered as a general guide to State income tax requirements.* The possible requirement for filing a declaration of estimated taxes has not been included. For specific information regarding your State, contact the Legal Assistance office or the State tax office for your State. For your convenience, a listing of the State tax authorities for the States having some form of income tax may be found following the State Tax Tables.

States with no personal income taxes:

Alaska	New Hampshire*	Texas
Florida**	South Dakota	Washington
Nevada	Tennessee***	Wyoming

*Imposes tax on capital gains, interest or dividend income.
**Imposes an intangible personal property tax.
***Imposes tax on certain dividend and interest income.

States which exempt all military disability retired pay.

Arizona	Maine	Ohio
Arkansas	Maryland	Oklahoma
California	Massachusetts	Oregon
Colorado	Minnesota	Puerto Rico
Connecticut	Missouri	Rhode Island
Delaware	Montana	South Carolina
District of Columbia	Nebraska	Vermont
Georgia	New Jersey	Virginia
Idaho	New Mexico	West Virginia
Indiana	North Carolina	
Iowa	North Dakota	

States which exempt all military retired pay.

Alabama	Kentucky	New York
Hawaii	Louisiana	Pennsylvania
Illinois	Michigan*	Wisconsin
Kansas	Mississippi	

*Does not exempt USPHS or NOAA Retired Pay.

States which exempt all active-duty military pay.

Illinois	New Hampshire	Tennessee
Michigan	Pennsylvania*	Vermont*
Montana		

*Exempts all military pay earned outside the state.

NOTE: The material contained in these tax tables represents the best information available at time of publication. This is a general guide to State income tax requirements. For specific information regarding your State, contact the Legal Assistance Office or your State Tax Office. (See the listing of State Tax Authorities following these tables.)

UNIFORMED SERVICES ALMANAC

SPECIAL STATE INCOME TAX PROVISIONS FOR SERVICE PERSONNEL AND RESUME OF STATE INCOME TAX FILING REQUIREMENTS

Income upon which Filing is Required by Residents	Personal Exemptions and Credits*	Due Date for Filing and Making Payments on the Return	Special Provisions Applicable to Armed Services Personnel
ALABAMA Net income of: $1,500 or more if single; $3,000 if married or head of family	$1,500 is single; $3,000 if married or head of family; $300 for each dependent	Return and payment due April 15th.	Military retired pay and military survivors benefit are exempt. Active Duty Pay is taxable for service inside or outside state. Combat zone pay is exempt.
ALASKA -- No State Income Tax			
ARIZONA AZ Adj Gross income of: $5,500 if single or married filing separately; $11,000 if married filing jointly; gross income of $15,000.	$2,100 if single; $4,200 if married or head of household; $2,300 for each dependent.	Return and payment due April 15th	Exclusion authorized for RSFPP and/or SBP contributions. See State instructions. Combat pay is exempt for AZ taxation.
ARKANSAS Gross income of $5,500 if single; $11,000 if married filing joint or gross income of $15,000 or more regardless of the amount of taxable income.	Credit from tax: $20, if single; $40 if married or head of household; $20 for each dependent; over 65 or blind, $20.	Return and payment due May 15th.	First $6,000 service pay excluded. $6,000 of retired pay or survivor benefit is exempt. Disability income is fully exempt. Military members from Texarkana are exempt for State Taxes. (Must file return)
CALIFORNIA Adj Gross income of $8,000 or more if single; $16,000 if married.	$66 is single, married filing separate or head of household; If married filing joint or widow (er)$132.	Return and payment due April 15th.	Same as Federal with some exceptions. See below for source tax provisions.
If domiciled in state, but on permanent duty outside of state, considered as a non-resident for tax purposes only. Therefore, does not have to file on income derived outside state. In addition, if a taxpayer has California source income, the taxpayer must file Form 540NR, California Non resident or Part-Year Resident Income Tax Return, and pay taxes on the California source income.			
COLORADO Must file if filing federal.	Same as federal. Some credits possible. See State instructions.	Return and payment due April 15th	Same as Federal. $20,000 military pension exclusion applies only to persons aged 55 or older as of close of tax year, and to secondary beneficiaries regardless of age.
CONNECTICUT Tax on adjusted gross income in excess of $12,000 (Single filer), $24,000 (Married Filing jointly); and $19,000 (Head of Household).	As much as $12,000 (Singlel); $24,000 (Married filing jointly) and $19,000 (Head of Household). (Exemptions are phased out as income increases.) Tax credits as much as 75% of tax due are available depending upon inc.	Return and payment due April 15th. Estimated taxes due April 15, June 15, Sept. 15, and Jan. 15.	Same as Federal. See State instructions for definition of residency and estimated tax requirements. Publication for military personnel, IP92(2.1) may be requested. Taxes may be waived if death occurs in combat zone.
DELAWARE Adjusted gross income after modifications (Line 30) of at least $4,550 if filing single, or $6,100 if married filing joint return.	$1,250 each for taxpayer, spouse, and each dep. An additional standard deduction is allowed in the amount of $1,000 for persons 65 years of age or over or blind or $2,000 for persons 65 years of age or over and blind.	Return and payment due April 30th.	Same as Federal, Exclusion of pensions for taxpayers under 60 years of age is $2,000; over 60 years of age is $3,000. All disability retirement pay is exempt if excludable on Fed tax return.

217

UNIFORMED SERVICES ALMANAC

SPECIAL STATE INCOME TAX PROVISIONS FOR SERVICE PERSONNEL AND RESUME OF STATE INCOME TAX FILING REQUIREMENTS

Income upon which Filing is Required by Residents	Personal Exemptions and Credits*	Due Date for Filing and Making Payments on the Return	Special Provisions Applicable to Armed Services Personnel
DISTRICT OF COLUMBIA Same as Federal	$1,370 if single; $2,740 if married or head of family, $1,370 for each dependent. Limited prop. tax credit available for homeowners or renters with household income of $20,000 or less.	Return and payment due April 15th.	Same as Federal ret pensions, annuities for injuries incurred in military. Can defer filing 6 mos. or up to 1 yr if outside the U.S. Disability retired pay is exempt. RSFPP/SBP benefits not taxable.
FLORIDA--No State Personal Income Tax. Has intangible personal property tax.			
GEORGIA Same as Federal with some adjustments.	$1,500 if single or head of household; $3,000 if married; $2,500 for each dependent.	Return and payment due April 15th.	First $12,000 of retirement income is exempt if over 62 or disabled. VA disability pay is exempt.
GUAM--No State Income Tax.			
HAWAII Gross Income equal or greater than sum of personal exemption plus applicable standard deduction amount.	$1,040 personal exemption. Also, food/excise tax credit, and other credits possible. See State instructions.	Return and payment due April 20th.	Same as Federal. 1st $1,750 for reserves excluded. Retired pay is exempt.
IDAHO Single or head of household $3,300; married joint return $5,400; married filing separately $1,000.	$15 grocery credit per filer. Same as Federal.	Same as Federal.	All active svc pay is excl for 120 days or more contin duty out of Idaho. Variable exemptions at age 65 (62 if disabled) for mil retirees. The max ret bene which may be deduc are: (a) Age 65 fil jointly w/spouse, or age 62, disab and file jointly w/spouse, $21,576; (b) Age 65 and not married, or age 62, disab and not married, $14,388; (c) Unremarried widow of a ret U.S. servicemember age 65 or age 62 and disab $14,388.
ILLINOIS If required to file Fed rtn or if income was more than $1,000 times number of exemptions allowed for Federal tax purposes.	$1,000 for each exemption allowable under Federal law. Part year residents prorate.	Same as Federal.	All active service pay is exempt, but must file return. Postponements for filing. See State definition of resident. Retired Pay is exempt.
INDIANA Gross income in excess of exemptions.	$1,000 for each exemption allowable under Federal law. $1,000 for blind; $1,000 for over 65.	Return and payment due same as Federal.	First $2,000 taxable active and reserve pay exempt. $2,000 retired pay exempt if over age 60, and does not claim for the elderly. Disability retired pay and RSFPP/SBP premiums excludable.
IOWA Net income of more than $9,000 (single) or $13,500 (filing status other than single). Subject to either IA lump-sum tax or IA minimum tax.	Credit from tax; $20 if single; $40 if married or head of household; $40 for each dependent. See State instruction for standard deduction.	Return and payment due April 30th.	Same as for Federal.

UNIFORMED SERVICES ALMANAC

SPECIAL STATE INCOME TAX PROVISIONS FOR SERVICE PERSONNEL AND RESUME OF STATE INCOME TAX FILING REQUIREMENTS

Income upon which Filing is Required by Residents	Personal Exemptions and Credits*	Due Date for Filing and Making Payments on the Return	Special Provisions Applicable to Armed Services Personnel
KANSAS Gross income of $5,000 if single; $9,000 if married, filing joint or if required to file Federal return.	$2,000 per Fed exemption. Addl. $2,000 allowable if filing as head of household. Some credits for child care & handicapped.	Return and payment due April 15th.	Same as Federal including combat zone exclusion. Military retired pay is exempt from tax for all taxable years commencing after 12-31-91.
KENTUCKY Adjusted gross income exceeding $5,000.	Credit from tax: $20 each for taxpayer, spouse, and each dep, if legally blind, 2 addl, credits; active NG member, one addl. credit.	Return and payment due April 15th.	Same as Federal. Military retired pay is exempt from tax. Service connected disability pension payments also exempt.
LOUISIANA Gross income of $12,000 or if tax table income is $4,500 is single or $9,000 if married filing jointly.	$4,500 single or separate return; $9,000 joint return surviving spouse, head of household. $1,000 for each dependent.	Return and payment due May 15th.	Same as Federal. Benefits received from a retirement system for retirees of the U.S. government are exempt.
MAINE Same as Federal; or Maine adj gross income which results in a state income tax liability.	$2,100 for each exemption allowable on Federal return.	April 15th.	Same as Federal. Check state definition of resident.
MARYLAND Same as Federal.	$1,200 for each personal exemption allowed on federal return. Additional $1,000 over 65 and/or another $1,000 if blind. Exemption value for dependent children and other dependents is $1,200.	Return and payment due April 15th.	Same as Federal. If outside U.S. may defer filing, and exclude up to $15,000 of mil income; however, this amount is reduced dollar for dollar for income in excess of $15,000; thus at income $30,000, exclusion is reduced to zero. Disability retired pay is exempt to same extent as Federal. Up to $2,500 mil ret inc exempt if age 65 and enlisted at retirement unless AGI exceeds $22,500.
MASSACHUSETTS Gross income above $2,000.	$2,200 if single or if married filing separate; $4,400 if married filing jointly; $2,200 exemption for each spouse who is blind; $1,000 for ea dep; addl $750 if 65 or older.	Return and payment due April 15th.	Same as Federal. May defer filing due to cause. Tax benefits to POW/MIA's and mil and spt pers who served in Operation Desert Shield/Storm. Cbt pay while serving in combat zone is exluded from fed gross inc.
MICHIGAN When Fed adj gross inc exceeds personal exemptions, or income subject to MI tax exceeds your MI exemption allowance.	$2,400 for each exeption on Federal return. Some credits.	Return and payment due April 15th.	All active-duty military and retired pay is exempt.
MINNESOTA Same as Federal.	Same as Federal.	Return & payment due April 15th.	Same as Federal. Taxes waived if member dies while on AD.
MISSISSIPPI Gross income is excess of personal exemptions plus standard deduction.	$6,000 if single; $9,500 joint return or head of family; $4,750 married/sep returns; $1,500 for deps, blind, and over 65.	Return and payment due April 15th.	Same as Federal.. Retired pay is exempt.

UNIFORMED SERVICES ALMANAC

SPECIAL STATE INCOME TAX PROVISIONS FOR SERVICE PERSONNEL AND RESUME OF STATE INCOME TAX FILING REQUIREMENTS

Income upon which Filing is Required by Residents	Personal Exemptions and Credits*	Due Date for Filing and Making Payments on the Return	Special Provisions Applicable to Armed Services Personnel
MISSOURI Same as federal. Non-residents with income of $600 from MO sources.	$1,200 if single; $2,400 if married, $2,000 head of household; $400 for each dependent.	Return and payment due April 15th.	Same as Federal. Check Stae def. of resident. Some mil. pay may be exempt.
MONTANA Gross income of $1,845 or more if single; $3,690 or more if married.	$1,480 if single, $2,800 if married. $1,400 for each dependent.	Return and payment due April 15th.	Compensation for active duty service is exempt; however, active duty personnel must file if gross income test is met.
NEBRASKA Same as Federal.	$65 personal credit exemption for each Federal exemption. Percentages are scaled according to income and tax filing status.	Return and payment due April 15th.	Same as Federal. Operation Desert Shield/ Storm spec provisions exempt mil pay by enl pers while serving in the cbt zone. Off pay up to $500 a mo. can be excl from income. Eff 1/1/91.
NEVADA--No State Income Tax.			
NEW HAMPSHIRE Must file if interest and dividends income exceeds $1,200 form all sources ($2,400 joint filing).	$1,200 for each taxpayer. $2,400 for married couples.	Return and payment due April 15th.	Military pay is not taxed by NH. Interest and dividend income is reportable.
NEW JERSEY Gross income of $7,500 or more; ($3,750 if married filing separately).	$1,500 for any qual dep, $1,000 for all other exemp, i.e., blind, disabled, etc.	Return and payment due April 15th.	Check State definition of resident and ruling on occupying Gov't qtrs. Some mil. pay may be exempt.
NEW MEXICO Same as Federal.	Same as Federal.	Return and payment due April 15th.	Same as Federal.
NEW YORK If Fed rtn is required or if you had fed adj gross income (plus NY addl) of more than $4,000 or more than $2,800 if single and can be claimed as a depn on another taxpayer's federal return.	$1,000 for each dependent exemption claimed on federal return.	Return and payment due April 15th.	Same as Federal. Taxes abated if death from combat zone activity. Check state definition of resident, and ruling on living in Gov't qtrs. Military pensions exempt from NY State tax as of 1 January 1989.
NORTH CAROLINA Same as Federal exclusive of inflation adjustments for standard deductions and personal exemption. Also, certain transitional adjustments requried under NC law.	Same as Federal, exclusive of inflation adjustments for standard deductions and personal exemption.	Return and payment due April 15th.	Mil dis pay is not taxable. Max of $4,000 ret pay is exempt.. Automatic 6-month extension is provided if extension form and tax due is filed by 4/15.
NORTH DAKOTA Same as Federal.	Same as Federal.	Return and payment due April 15th.	Long form only. Up to $1,000 exclusion for active duty, reserve, and Nat'l Guard pay, plus $300 per month if stationed outside 50 states; Ltd to actual mil pay. Field grade and gen offs do not qualify for the add'l $300 exclusion.

UNIFORMED SERVICES ALMANAC

SPECIAL STATE INCOME TAX PROVISIONS FOR SERVICE PERSONNEL AND RESUME OF STATE INCOME TAX FILING REQUIREMENTS

Income upon which Filing is Required by Residents	Personal Exemptions and Credits*	Due Date for Filing and Making Payments on the Return	Special Provisions Applicable to Armed Services Personnel
OHIO Adj gross income unless exemptions and exclusions exceed tax liability.	$650 for self, spouse and each dependent. Plus $20 tax credit for each exemption.	Return and payment due April 15th.	Same as federal including disability retired military pay.
OKLAHOMA Same as Federal.	$1,000 for each exemption.	Return and payment due April 15th.	See state definition of "resident". First $1,500 of military pay may be deductible.
OREGON If Federal return is required or income exceeds $4,200 if single; $7,800 married filing jointly; $3,900 married filing separate; head of household, $5,040; $400 if self employed. Over 65: single, $5,400; married filing jointly, $9,800; married filing separately, $4,900; head of household, $6,124 and qual widow(er) under 65, $7,800.	Credit of $120 per each federal exemption, plus severely disabled taxpayer or spouse, plus disabled child age 17 and under. An additional standard deduction for nonitemizers who are 65 or older, or blind, as follows: If marr filing jointly, or marr filing separately, $1,000 if blind and $1,000 if age 65 or older--up to $2,000 per person; If single or head of household, $1,200, if blind $1,200 if age 65 or older --up to $2,400 per person.	Same as Federal.	First $3,000 active duty pay exempt. In tax year of intial draft or enlistment or tax year of discharge from or termination of full time active duty, compensation received for mil svcs performed outside of Oregon is subtracted from AGI. A possible 9% credit, if age 60 or older, of the lesser of retirement income or the product of a formula. Household income must be less than $45,000 if married filing joint return, or $22,500 for all other filing statuses. Check state defin of "household income" and instruc for calculation of credit.
PENNSYLVANIA $35 or more of state taxable income, or if claiming loss on any of the classes of taxable income. Check State requirements for taxes or losses on certain types of income.	None except certain credits, different than federal are available.	Same as Federal.	Residents: Military pay is fully taxable unless earned outside of PA while on Federal Active Duty outside PA or on Federal Active Duty for training outside PA. Mil pay earned within PA is taxable. Non-Residents: Only mil pay earned in PA is not taxable. Any other income earned is fully taxable. Mil ret pay and mil dis ret pay is exempt
RHODE ISLAND If required to file Fed rtn.	Same as Federal.	Same as Federal.	Same as Federal. Check definition of State resident.
SOUTH CAROLINA Same as Federal.	Same as Federal.	Return and payment due April 15th.	Res and NG pay and expenses related to Res pay is exempt. Up to $3,000 mil ret pay may be deducted.
SOUTH DAKOTA--No State Income Tax.			
TENNESSEE Income over $1,250 for individuals and $2,500 for married joint returns for certain types of dividends and interest.	First $1,250 of taxable income for individuals and $2,500 for joint returns.	Return and payment due April 15th.	All military compensation is exempt.
TEXAS--No State Income Tax.			

UNIFORMED SERVICES ALMANAC

SPECIAL STATE INCOME TAX PROVISIONS FOR SERVICE PERSONNEL AND RESUME OF STATE INCOME TAX FILING REQUIREMENTS

Income upon which Filing is Required by Residents	Personal Exemptions and Credits*	Due Date for Filing and Making Payments on the Return	Special Provisions Applicable to Armed Services Personnel
UTAH If required to file Fed rtn.	Same as Federal except 25% of pers exempt must be added back to income.	Return and payment due April 15.	Mil mbrs claiming UT as home state must file returns on all income. Credit allowed for non-mil income tax paid to another state.
VERMONT If required to file Fed income tax return, and more than $100 VT income or earned or received more than $1,000 in gross income from other sources.	Same as Federal.	Return and payment due April 15th.	All active duty military pay earned outside the state of Vermont is not considered Vermont income.
VIRGINIA $5,000 if single; $8,000 if married filing jointly; $4,000 if separate returns.	$800 for each exemption on Federal return.	Return and payment due May 1st. Fiscal year filers: 15th day of the 4th month after the close of your taxable year.	Same as Federal, to include Soldiers and Sailors Civil Relief Act Provision.
WASHINGTON--No State Income Tax.			
WEST VIRGINIA If legal residence was WV at time of entry in mil svc, then fed adj income is taxable. If mbr maintains a perm place of residence in WV or spends more than 30 days in WV, then Fed adj income is taxable. If mbr spends less than 30 days during a tax year and does not maintain a perm place of residence in WV, the mil income earned is exempt.	$2,000 for each exemption on Federal return.	Same as Federal.	First $2,000 of military retirement benefits and first $2,000 of mil retirement which has been converted to the Fed Civil Service Retirement Program.
WISCONSIN $5,200 is single & under 65; $5,710 if single & 65 or over; $8,900 if married filing jointly & both under 65; $9,410 if one spouse 65 or over; $9,920 if both 65 or over; $4,230 if married filing separately.	$50 for each dependent; $25 for each taxpayer 65 or over.	Return and payment due April 15th, or in installments if tax if over $200.	Same as Federal.
WYOMING--No State Income Tax.			
PUERTO RICO Gross income over $3,200 if single; or separated. $6,000 if married and living with spouse. $1,500 if married filing separately.	$1,300 if single or separated; $3,000 if married or head of family. $1,300 for each dependent ($1,600 if university student.)	Return due April 15th. Tax payable may be paid in 2 equal installments, one with return, one by Oct. 15th.	$500 deductions for all honorably discharged veterans. Disability compensation are exempt. Grants credit for taxes paid to U.S. or its possessions for services performed within CONUS.

222

UNIFORMED SERVICES ALMANAC
STATE TAX AUTHORITIES

Alabama
Alabama Department of Revenue, Income Tax Division, P.O. Box 327460, Montgomery, AL 36132-7460

Alaska
Department of Revenue, Juneau, Alaska 99811

Arizona
Department of Revenue, 1600 W. Monroe, Phoenix, Arizona 85007-2650

Arkansas
Department of Finance and Administration, P.O. Box 3628, Little Rock, Arkansas 72203-3628

California
California Franchise Tax Board, P.O. Box 942840, Sacramento, California 94240-0000

Colorado
Department of Revenue, 1375 Sherman St/State Capitol Annex, Denver, Colorado 80261

Connecticut
Department of Revenue Services, 92 Farmington Avenue, Hartford, Connecticut 06105

Delaware
Division of Revenue, Carvel State Office Bldg., 820 N. French Street, Wilmington, Delaware 19801-8911

District of Columbia
Department of Finance & Revenue, 441 4th Street, N.W., Washington, D.C. 20001

Florida
Department of Revenue, 5050 W. Tennessee Street, Tallahassee, FL 32399-0100

Georgia
Department of Revenue, Income Tax Division, Room 216-F, Trinity-Washington Bldg., 270 Washington St., S.W., Atlanta, Georgia 30334

Guam
Dept. of Revenue & Taxation, 378 Chalan San Antonio, Tamuning, Agana, Guam 96911

Hawaii
Department of Taxation, P.O. Box 259, 425 Queen St., Honolulu, Hawaii 96809

Idaho
Idaho State Tax Commission, 800 Park Plaza IV, P.O. Box 36, Boise, Idaho 83722

Illinois
Department of Revenue, 101 W. Jefferson St., P.O. Box 19001, Springfield, Illinois 62794-9001

Indiana
Department of Revenue, State Office Bldg., 100 N. Senate Ave., Indianapolis, Indiana 46204-2253

Iowa
Iowa Department of Revenue & Finance, Hoover State Office Bldg., Des Moines, Iowa 50319

Kansas
Director of Taxation, Kansas Dept. of Revenue, Docking State Office Building, 915 S.W. Harrison St., Topeka, Kansas 66612-1588

Kentucky
Revenue Cabinet, 200 Fair Oaks Lane, Frankfort, Kentucky 40620

Louisiana
Department of Revenue & Taxation, Income Tax Section, P.O. Box 201, Baton Rouge, Louisiana 70821-0201

Maine
Bureau of Taxation, State House Station 24, Augusta, Maine 04333

Maryland
Revenue Administration Division, Comptroller of the Treasury, Annapolis, Maryland 21411

Massachusetts
Department of Revenue, 100 Cambridge St., Boston, Massachusetts 02204

Michigan
Michigan Department of Treasury, Individual Taxes Division, Treasury Bldg., Lansing, MI 48922

Minnesota
Department of Revenue, Minnesota Income Tax Division, Mail Station 4453, St. Paul, Minnesota, 55146-4453

Mississippi
State Tax Commission, P.O. Box 960, Jackson, Mississippi 39205

Missouri
Department of Revenue, Tax Administration Bureau, P.O. Box 2200, Jefferson City, Missouri 65105-2200

Montana
Department of Revenue, Income & Miscellaneous Tax Division, P.O. Box 5805, Helena, Montana 59604-5805

Nebraska
Department of Revenue, PO Box 94818, Lincoln, Nebraska 68509-4818

New Hampshire
Dept. of Revenue Administration, P.O. Box 637, Concord, New Hampshire 03302-0637

New Jersey
Division of Taxation, 50 Barrack St. CN269, Trenton, New Jersey 08646-0269

New Mexico
Taxation & Revenue Department, PO Box 25122, Santa Fe, New Mexico 87504-5122

New York
Department of Taxation & Finance, W.A. Harriman Campus, Albany, New York 12227

North Carolina
Department of Revenue, P.O. Box 25000, Raleigh, North Carolina 27640-0001

North Dakota
Tax Commissioner, State Capitol, 600 E. Blvd. Ave., Bismarck, North Dakota 58505-0599

Ohio
Department of Taxation, P.O. Box 2476, Columbus, Ohio 43266-0076

Oklahoma
Oklahoma Tax Commission, 2501 Lincoln Boulevard, Oklahoma City, Okla. 73194

Oregon
Oregon Department of Revenue, Revenue Building, 955 Center St., N.E., Salem, Oregon 97310

Pennsylvania
Department of Revenue, Bureau of Individual Taxes, Harrisburg, Pennsylvania 17128-0600

Puerto Rico
Department of the Treasury, P.O. Box 4515, San Juan, PR 00905-4515

Rhode Island
Division of Taxation, One Capitol Hill, Providence, Rhode Island 02908-5800

South Carolina
Department of Revenue and Taxation, Box 125, Columbia, SC 29214

Tennessee
Department of Revenue, Andrew Jackson State Off. Bldg., 500 Deaderick Street, Nashville, Tennessee 37242-1099

Utah
State Tax Commission, 210 North 1950 West., Salt Lake City, Utah 84134

Vermont
Department of Taxes, Pavilion Off. Bldg., Montpelier, Vermont 05602

Virginia
Virginia Department of Taxation, P.O. Box 1880, Richmond, Virginia 23282-1880

West Virginia
Department of Tax and Revenue Division, P.O. Box 2389, Charleston, WV 25328-2389

Wisconsin
Department of Revenue, P.O. Box 8906, Madison, Wisconsin 53708-8906

UNIFORMED SERVICES ALMANAC

PART V

THE RESERVE FORCES

This section deals with the reserve forces of the United States, including the Army and Air National Guard. It provides a general overview of these forces. Space limitations preclude the development of detailed, comprehensive coverage of these vital elements of our national defense in this book. To meet the need for providing Reservists and Guardsmen with specific information regarding their benefits, entitlements, organization, history and other vital subjects of interest and concern, the **NATIONAL GUARD ALMANAC** and the **RESERVE FORCES ALMANAC** are available. These editions contain the most comprehensive compilation of data for members of these components. Information regarding ordering these publications can be found inside the front cover of this Almanac.

The United States has had reserve as well as active Armed Forces since the beginning of our history. The Militia, later known and organized into the National Guard, has been in existence as both a state and federal force since Colonial times. In the early part of the 20th century, various federal reserve components, with no state responsibilities, were also created by the Congress. The National Defense Act of 1916, establishing the Reserve Officer Training Corps (ROTC) was most important. The ROTC provides both regular and reserve officers and is one of the most valuable systems in our nation's history. The Navy Reserve Act of 1925 applied this source of officer procurement to the Navy and Marine Corps.

The 1952 Armed Forces Reserve Act as amended by the 1955 Reserve Forces Act placed on the statute books the first law in the history of this country that provides a source for enlisted reserves. The portion of this law pertaining to enlistment of personnel under 18 1/2 years of age with an initial ADT requirement expired on 31 July 1963. However, Public Law 88-110 enacted a similar program for personnel without prior military service between the ages of 17 and 26 enlisting in the reserve components.

Since January 1, 1968, Public Law 90-168, often referred to as the Reserve Forces Bill of Rights, has required annual strength authorizations for the Selected Reserve. This law requires that each of the Selected Reserve components shall consist in part of units organized and trained to serve as such, and prohibits any reorganization of the Selected Reserve which would result in any of its components being composed solely of individuals. The law also requires a Selected Reserve within the Army Reserve, Air Force Reserve, Army National Guard, Air National Guard, and Coast Guard Reserve. Finally, the Reserve Forces Bill of Rights provides that each unit or individual in the Selected Reserve may be required to perform at least 48 drills and serve not less than 14 days of active duty training annually.

Each year, an end strength ceiling must be authorized for each component of the Selected Reserve for the appropriation of reserve pay and allowances, according to 10 USC 138. This reserve strength is part of the annual DoD Authorization Act. Legislation containing these authorizations must be passed by both Houses of Congress and signed by the President *before* any money can actually be appropriated for these purposes. The authorizations set maximum strength levels for the Selected Reserves; however, the Congress may appropriate less money than needed to fund the full authorized strength.

UNIFORMED SERVICES ALMANAC

Funds are appropriated for the Armed Forces by the annual Department of Defense Appropriation Act. *No funds may be appropriated for any item requiring an authorization until the authorization has become law.*

The DoD Appropriations Act for FY 1996, established the following end strengths for the Selected Reserves: Army National Guard, 373,000; Army Reserve, 230,000; Naval Reserve, 98,608; Marine Corps Reserve, 42,000; Air National Guard, 109,458; Air Force Reserve, 73,969; Coast Guard Reserve, 8,000. The average strengths are to be proportionately adjusted in case of call-up or return to Reserve status of units ordered to active duty.

Within the end strengths above, the Reserve components are appropriated the following number of Reserves and Guard personnel to serve on full-time active duty for the purpose of organizing, administering, recruiting, and training the Reserve components: Army National Guard, 23,390; Army Reserve, 11,575; Naval Reserve, 17,490; Marine Corps Reserve, 2,285; Air National Guard, 9,817; Air Force Reserve, 628.

TOTAL FORCE POLICY

The Total Force Policy, which places increased reliance on the National Guard and other Reserves to meet national defense requirements, is not new. It was first announced by the Secretary of Defense in 1969. A strengthened policy coupled with drastic manpower and equipment reductions from the active forces, has gone far to integrate the active duty, National Guard, and Reserve organizations into a single military force. The DoD is providing greater support to the Guard and Reserve in terms of funding, equipment, and training assistance.

Reserve Administration

Our laws contain a number of statutory changes concerning the administration of the reserve components within DoD. Each of these changes is aimed at clarifying and strengthening the organization for the administration of the reserve components.

The FY 1984 DoD Authorization Act (P.L. 98-94) upgraded the office of the Deputy Assistant Secretary of Defense for Reserve Affairs to the Assistant Secretary of Defense level. The Congress stated in its vote that the National Guard and Reserve are integral parts of the Total Force, and these components deserve the same level of access and exchange with the Secretary of Defense as the other Assistant Secretaries. Prior to this, the office of the Assistant Secretary of Defense for Manpower, Reserve Affairs, and Installations was the chief spokesman for the seven reserve components, with an office of Deputy Assistant Secretary of Defense for Reserve Affairs under it.

The Assistant Secretary of Defense for Reserve Affairs is responsible for all matters relating to reserve affairs within the office of the Secretary of Defense. The Assistant Secretary of Defense for Reserve Affairs is appointed by the President with the advice and consent of the Senate.

An additional Assistant Secretary for Manpower and Reserve Affairs is also authorized in the Department of the Army, Navy, and Air Force each with a Deputy for Reserve Affairs.

The law provides for an Office of Army Reserve and an Office of Air Force Reserve each headed by a Chief who is the advisor to his or her respective Chief of Staff on reserve matters. The Chiefs of Reserves are appointed by the President with the advice and consent of the Senate and are appointed in the rank of major general.

UNIFORMED SERVICES ALMANAC

TOTAL RESERVE STRENGTH
As of September 30, 1995

TOTAL RESERVE MANPOWER

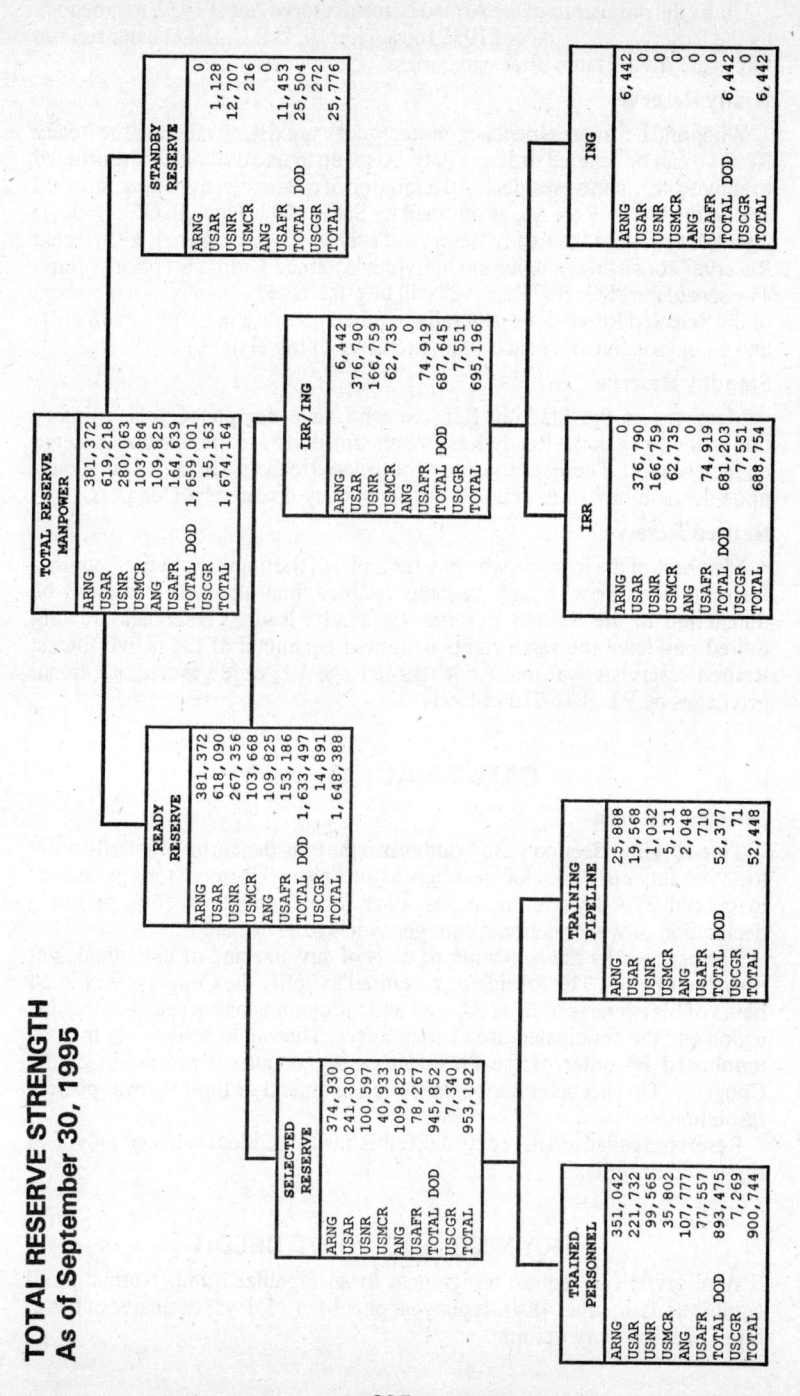

ARNG	381,372
USAR	619,218
USNR	280,063
USMCR	103,884
ANG	109,825
USAFR	164,639
TOTAL DOD	1,659,001
USCGR	15,163
TOTAL	1,674,164

STANDBY RESERVE

ARNG	0
USAR	1,128
USNR	12,707
USMCR	216
ANG	0
USAFR	11,453
TOTAL DOD	25,504
USCGR	272
TOTAL	25,776

READY RESERVE

ARNG	381,372
USAR	618,090
USNR	267,356
USMCR	103,668
ANG	109,825
USAFR	153,186
TOTAL DOD	1,633,497
USCGR	14,891
TOTAL	1,648,388

IRR/ING

ARNG	6,442
USAR	376,790
USNR	166,759
USMCR	62,735
ANG	0
USAFR	74,919
TOTAL DOD	687,645
USCGR	7,551
TOTAL	695,196

IRR

ARNG	0
USAR	376,790
USNR	166,759
USMCR	62,735
ANG	0
USAFR	74,919
TOTAL DOD	681,203
USCGR	7,551
TOTAL	688,754

ING

ARNG	6,442
USAR	0
USNR	0
USMCR	0
ANG	0
USAFR	0
TOTAL DOD	6,442
USCGR	0
TOTAL	6,442

SELECTED RESERVE

ARNG	374,930
USAR	241,300
USNR	100,597
USMCR	40,933
ANG	109,825
USAFR	78,267
TOTAL DOD	945,852
USCGR	7,340
TOTAL	953,192

TRAINING PIPELINE

ARNG	25,888
USAR	19,568
USNR	1,032
USMCR	5,131
ANG	2,048
USAFR	710
TOTAL DOD	52,377
USCGR	71
TOTAL	52,448

TRAINED PERSONNEL

ARNG	351,042
USAR	221,732
USNR	99,565
USMCR	35,802
ANG	107,777
USAFR	77,557
TOTAL DOD	893,475
USCGR	7,269
TOTAL	900,744

UNIFORMED SERVICES ALMANAC

CATEGORIES OF THE RESERVE FORCES

Under the provisions of the Armed Forces Reserve Act of 1952, as amended by the Reserve Forces Act of 1955 (now Title 10, U.S.C. 10141), our reserve forces are divided into three categories.

Ready Reserve

When and if Congress declares an emergency to exist, members of the Ready Reserve can be ordered to active duty. Also, up to one million can be ordered to active duty upon a presidential declaration of an emergency. The authorized size of the Ready Reserve, as outlined by Sec. 10142, Title 10, U.S. Code, is 2,900,000. Within the Ready Reserve of each component there is a "Selected Reserve" consisting of units and individuals trained for highest priority duty. The size of the "Selected Reserve" will be established annually. All members of the Selected Reserve are generally required to train a minimum of 48 drills and 14 days active duty each year (exclusive of travel time.)

Standby Reserve

Members of the Standby Reserve who have completed their military obligation to be in the Ready Reserve are transferred to the Standby Reserve on their request. These reservists can be ordered to extended active duty, only upon declaration of war or an all-out emergency declared by Congress.

Retired Reserve

Members of the Reserve who have completed the number of years required for retirement, or who have become disabled, may upon their request, be transferred to the Retired Reserve. Generally, Retired reservists drawing retired pay have the same rights as retired personnel of the active forces. Retired reservists who have not reached age 60, were granted additional privileges by P.L. 101-510 in 1991.

CALL TO ACTIVE DUTY

Selected Reserve

Title 10, USC, Section 12304, authorizes the President to involuntarily order to active duty up to 200,000 members of the Selected Reserve for a period not to exceed 270 days for purposes other than training, whether or not a declaration of war or national emergency has been declared.

The act permits the activation of units of any size and of individuals not assigned to units. The President is required to notify the Congress within 24 hours of his exercise of this authority and the circumstances necessitating his action and the anticipated use of such forces. The call to active duty may be terminated by order of the President or by concurrent resolution of the Congress. This act shall not be construed to amend or limit the war powers resolution.

Reservists called to active duty under this law are entitled to all reemployment rights and benefits.

TRAINING AND POINT CREDIT

A reservist can request assignment to an organized unit. Normally, all combat units conduct 48 drills per year plus 14 or 15 days (exclusive of travel time) of active duty training.

UNIFORMED SERVICES ALMANAC

A reservist could be assigned to train with a National Guard unit only with the consent of the National Guard authorities of the state concerned.

The reservist in drill pay status receives one day's pay for each drill period plus his/her pay for his/her active duty training.

The services conduct schools to which reservists can request to be assigned. By attending these schools, they add to their military proficiency and also receive one point retirement credit for each session they attend. Also, they may be ordered to 15 to 30 days' active duty training with pay.

Correspondence courses are available to members of the reserves. By completing these correspondence courses, the Ready Reservist can earn retirement points and also increase his/her military knowledge.

Membership Points

Under provision of Ch. 67, Title 20, U.S.C., each member of the active reserve is given 15 membership points. The Army and Navy require each reservist to earn an additional 12 points making a total of 27, in order to be retained in the active reserve. The Air Force requires the reservist to earn 15 points in order to be so retained.

Retirement Points

Under the provisions of Ch. 67, Title 20, U.S.C., a reservist must earn 50 points per year (including the 15 points gratuitously given) in order to earn a satisfactory year for retirement.

An individual in this category can be credited with only 60 points in any one year for inactive duty training including the 15 gratuitous points but, he or she is entitled to one point for each day of active duty for training.

LONGEVITY AND RETIREMENT CREDIT

Reserve officers receive credit for longevity for being in the reserves, and the daily pay and allowance for reservists is generally the same as pay and allowance for regular service.

Ch. 67, Title 10, U.S.C., provides that any reservist who accumulates 20 years of satisfactory service and meets certain other criteria will, when reaching age 60, receive a certain amount of retired pay.

Each year in the active reserves, whether on active or inactive duty prior to the first of July, 1949, counts as a year of satisfactory service. Starting with the first of July, 1949, each reservist in the service must earn 50 points a year to receive credit for a satisfactory year. Once a reservist has accumulated 20 satisfactory years, he or she can do one of three things as listed below:

1. Remain active in the reserves and accumulate additional point credit for retirement.

2. Request to be transferred to the retired reserve. When an individual transfers to the retired reserve, he or she cannot earn additional points for retirement purposes.

3. Request discharge from the reserves.

In either case, when he or she reaches age 60, based on the number of points he or she has earned, he or she is eligible to receive retired pay, but must make application therefor. No individual can receive more than 75% of his/her base and longevity pay.

All reservists and former reservists who have accumulated 20 years of qualifying service and who were members of a reserve component prior to August 16, 1945 must have served on active duty during World War I, World War II, Korea, the Berlin airlift or Cuban missile crisis, Vietnam era, or Desert

UNIFORMED SERVICES ALMANAC

Shield/Storm to be eligible to receive reserve retirement pay at age 60. It must be noted that while a member of the regular service can count time in the regular service for pay purposes, the last eight years of qualifying service must be in the reserve.

Any reservist who has completed his/her 20 years of satisfactory service should write to the retirement section of the service to which he or she belongs approximately six to nine months before he or she reaches age 60 and request that application forms be furnished him or her in order to apply for retirement.

All service, whether in the reserves or on active duty or inactive duty, is considered in computing the satisfactory service required under the provisions of Ch. 67, Title 10, U.S.C.

Reserve retirement legislation provides incentives for participation in the reserve components of the Armed Forces. The amount of participation by an individual determines how much the individual will receive on retirement.

Under a ruling by the Court of Claims and later decision of the Comptroller General, reserve officers who qualify for Reserve retirement do not come under the provisions of the Economy Act of 1933, and individuals in this category can draw retired pay and, at the same time, draw full pay as government employees and are not subject to dual compensation.

RESERVE OFFICERS ON EXTENDED ACTIVE DUTY

At the present time, more than 50% of the officers composing the active duty force are reserve officers serving on extended active duty. Extended Active Duty is defined as Active Duty performed by a member of the National Guard or a Reservist when strength accountability passes from the Reserve Component to the active military service.

Officers in this category are given the same protection on disability retirement, medical care, survivor benefits, and retirement under provisions of Title II, Public Law 810, as are members of the regular services.

Under the provisions of Ch. 67, Title 10, U.S.C., any commissioned officer who accumulates 20 years' federal active duty, 10 of which are as an officer, may request retirement.

The present policy of most of the services is to retire most reserve officers who qualify with 20 years' federal active duty.

Under the provisions of Sec. 687, Title 10, U.S. Code as amended, reserve officers on extended active duty who have completed their initial service obligation and a total of six years' continuous active duty service will, if involuntarily relieved from active duty under honorable conditions, have ten percent of the product of the member's years of active duty service and twelve times the monthly basic pay with no cap. In addition, P.L. 102-190, the DoD Authorization Act, December 1991, provided for voluntary separation incentives. *Members who qualify for and accept separation pay will be required to serve in the Ready Reserve for a period of not less than three years.*

Under the provisions of the Defense Officer Personnel Management Act— DOPMA, a reserve officer who, on or after September 15, 1981, is discharged or released from active duty and who has completed his or her initial service obligation and completed six or more, but less than 18 years of active service immediately before that discharge or release is entitled, unless the Secretary concerned determines that the conditions under which the officer is discharged or separated do not warrant it, to separation pay. Separation pay is calculated based upon ten percent of the product of the member's years of active duty service and twelve times the monthly basic pay *with no cap*. Members who qualify for and accept separation pay will be required to serve in the Ready Reserves for a period of not less than three years. An officer on active duty on or before September 14, 1981 is allowed to elect the severance or readjustment pay to which he or she would have been entitled before enactment or the separation pay provided to DOPMA, whichever is greater.

THE NATIONAL GUARD

Today's Guard members trace their heritage back to 1636, when three militia regiments were formed for the protection and "publick safety" of the settlements in the area of Boston, MA. Nearly 140 years later, militiamen from all 13 colonies formed the Continental Army to fight in the American Revolution, and these citizen-soldiers have since provided the margin for victory in all the wars fought by our nation. In the 19th Century, militia units across the nation referred to themselves as "National Guard" units, after a New York militia unit adopted the name in deference to France's "Garde Nationale."

More than 480,000 members of the Army and Air National Guard train an average of 39 days per year to provide significant, low-cost augmentation to America's active military forces, and to serve their states and local community when natural disasters and civil disorders occur. Under the Defense Department's "Total Force Policy," the Army National Guard (ARNG) comprises about 50% of the U.S. Army's combat forces. The Air National Guard (ANG) plays an equally significant role in support of the Air Force, providing about 33% of its total structure.

Operating at the highest level of combat readiness in its over 359-year history, the Guard contributes 23% of the nation's military forces for less than 5% of the national defense budget. The ARNG operates on about 10% of the total Army budget and the ANG on about 5% of the Air Force budget. The training is accomplished with an increasingly modern equipment inventory and facilities valued at more than $15 billion.

Under control of the governors during peacetime, Guard members and their equipment are located in more than 3,000 communities in the 50 states, Puerto Rico, the Virgin Islands, Guam, and the District of Columbia. This unique, wide dispersion enables many Americans to serve their country while pursuing civilian careers, and it also facilitates rapid response to emergencies occurring in any area of the nation.

In Operation Desert Shield/Storm Army and Air National Guard units demonstrated their capabilities and readiness, bringing further honors to the well-documented history of both.

ARMY NATIONAL GUARD

The 371,920 Army National Guard members comprise the largest reserve component and the oldest military force in the United States. These Guard members train at 3,132 armories and state or federal training facilities which are located in nearly 2500 communities.

Programmed major units of the Army National Guard in FY96 will include two armored divisions; three standard infantry divisions; one light infantry division; 14 separate armored, mechanized or infantry brigades; one armored cavalry regiment; one divisional brigade for strategic reserve; one infantry scout group; and two special forces groups. As part of the Total Force the Army National Guard comprises 54% of combat forces, 35% of combat support, and 35% of combat service support.

UNIFORMED SERVICES ALMANAC
AIR NATIONAL GUARD

The Air National Guard, with over 109,418 members, is composed of 89 flying units with about 1,200 aircraft, and 242 non-flying units that provide major mission support. Support organizations bring the total number of Air Guard units to more than 1,000.

The Air Guard possesses 33 percent of the Air Force's Tactical Fighter Assets, provides 100 percent of the United States' peacetime alert forces, has 23 percent of the tactical air support, and 45 percent of the tactical airlift.

In addition, it also provides almost one-third of the Air Force's tactical fighters, 43 percent of the K-135 aerial refueling tankers, and 28 percent of the rescue and recovery capability.

The flying units operate 13 different types of aircraft, representing about 33 percent of the total Air Force aircraft inventory.

ARMY RESERVE

As of September 30, 1995, the Total Army Ready Reserve consisted of 618,090 men and women, of which 241,300 were Selected Reservists organized into units; there were another 1,128 total Standby Reservists.

Major Army Reserve units commanded by general officers included 23 Army Reserve commands, nine training divisions, five exercise divisions, two separate infantry brigades, two engineer commands, two engineer brigades, two Theater Army area commands, two Theater Army area command augmentations, one corps support command, one corps support command augmentation, one military police command, three military police brigades, one transportation command, three transportation brigades, three civil affairs commands, one signal command, one signal brigade, two chemical brigades, three major hospitals, and seven medical brigades.

NAVAL RESERVE

As of September 30, 1995, there were 267,356 Naval Ready Reservists, of which 100,597 were paid-status Selected Reserve personnel. Another 12,707 Total Standby Reservists rounded out the Naval Reserve rolls.

The Naval Selected Reserve contains approximately 2,200 units of battalion/squadron size or smaller.

AIR FORCE RESERVE

As of September 30, 1995, there were 153,186 members of the Air Force Ready Reserve. A total of 78,267 of them were Selected Reserve members. There were also an additional 11,453 members of the Total Standby Reserve.

The Air Force Reserve's major units include seven unit-equipped and six associate airlift wings; five fighter wings; one air refueling wing; one air rescue wing; one special operations wing; one composite wing; and other smaller flying units, plus numerous ground units.

UNIFORMED SERVICES ALMANAC

MARINE CORPS RESERVE

On September 30, 1995, there were 103,668 Marine Corps Ready Reservists, which included 40,933 paid members of the Selected Marine Corps Reserve (SMCR) and 62,418 unpaid members of the Individual Ready Reserve (IRR). There were an additional 216 members in the Standby Reserve.

The SMCR is comprised of the warfighting units of Marine Forces (MARFORRES), headquartered in New Orleans, LA. Warfighting Major Subordinate Commands (MSC) of MARFORRES are the 4th Marine Division, 4th Marine Aircraft Wing, and 4th Force Service Support Group. The 4th MarDiv is comprised of a headquarters battalion, three infantry regiments, one artillery regiment, one reconnaissance battalion, two tank battalions, one light armored reconnaissance battalion, one assault amphibious battalion, and one engineer battalion. The 4th MAW is comprised of a headquarters squadron, three flying groups, one control group, and one support group. The 4th FSSG has 8 battalions which provide the traditional medical, dental, supply, engineer, motor transport, maintenance, and landing support. The MARFORRES MSC, the Marine Corps Reserve Support Command (MCRSC), is responsible for the administration and mobilization of the IRR.

COAST GUARD RESERVE

As of November 30, 1995, a total of 7,340 Coast Guard Selected Reservists were assigned within 8,000 Selected Reserve billets, Of these, there were 1,002 commissioned officers on board within 1,050 billets and 157 commissioned warrant officers within 160 billets. In addition, there were a total of 7,551 reservists assigned to the Individual Ready Reserve, bringing the total Coast Guard Ready Reserve strength to 14,891.

Under Team Coast Guard, the majority of Coast Guard reservists are now assigned directly to the active component unit where they train. In the field, respective active component commanders exercise operational control over assigned reservists. Reserve and active pay and personnel systems have been merged. As a result, most Reserve units are being disestablished in order to eliminate parallel and redundant command and administrative organizations. Likewise, reserve organizations at the district level have been disestablished with their various divisions integrated into other district office areas.

UNIFORMED SERVICES ALMANAC

SELECTED RESERVE STRENGTH (As of September 30, 1995)

	Army National Guard	Army Reserve	Naval Reserve	Marine Corps Reserve	Air National Guard	Air Force Reserve	Total DoD
Selected Reserve*							
Officer	43,371	49,742	20,770	4,641	13,520	16,123	148,167
Enlisted	331,559	191,558	79,827	36,292	96,305	62,144	797,685
Total	374,930	241,300	100,597	40,933	109,825	78,267	945,852
Individual Ready Reserve/ Inactive National Guard**							
Officer	535	64,713	21,180	4,073	0	14,389	104,890
Enlisted	5,907	312,077	145,579	58,662	0	60,530	582,755
Total	6,442	376,790	166,759	62,735	0	74,919	687,645
Total Ready Reserve							
Officer	43,906	114,455	41,950	8,714	13,520	30,512	253,057
Enlisted	337,466	503,635	225,406	94,954	96,305	122,674	1,380,440
Total	381,372	618,090	267,356	103,668	109,825	153,186	1,633,497

*Includes those in the training pipeline receiving pay.
**Includes those in the training pipeline not receiving pay.
Members of Selected Reserve units train throughout the year and participate annually in active duty training. Pretrained individual Reservists include Individual Mobilization Augmentees, members of the Inactive National Guard, and Individual Ready Reservists. The Individual Ready Reserve generally consists of people who have served recently in the active forces or Selected Reserve and have some period of obligated service remaining on their contract. The majority of the members in the Individual Ready Reserve do not participate in organized training.

STANDBY RESERVE (As of September 30, 1995)

	Army Reserve	Naval Reserve	Marine Corps Reserve	Air Force Reserve	Total DoD
Active Standby Reserve					
Officer	271	112	45	520	948
Enlisted	599	767	22	821	2,209
Total	870	879	67	1,341	3,157
Inactive Standby Reserve					
Officer	126	5,142	149	9,023	14,440
Enlisted	132	6,686	0	1,089	7,907
Total	258	11,828	149	10,112	22,347
Total Standby Reserve					
Officer	397	5,254	194	9,543	15,388
Enlisted	731	7,453	22	1,910	10,116
Total	1,128	12,707	216	11,453	25,504

The Standby Reserve generally consists of members who have completed their statutory six-year military obligation and have chosen to remain in the Standby Reserve. Members of the Standby Reserve do not generally participate in Reserve training or readiness programs. They may be mobilized by authority of Congress.

Detailed information regarding pay, benefits, organizations, etc., pertaining to the Reserve Forces and the National Guard can be found in the **RESERVE FORCES ALMANAC** and the **NATIONAL GUARD ALMANAC**. See inside front cover for prices and ordering information.

UNIFORMED SERVICES ALMANAC

PART VI

NATIONAL MILITARY AND VETERANS ORGANIZATIONS

NATIONAL MILITARY ORGANIZATIONS

ASSOCIATION OF THE U.S. ARMY, 2425 Wilson Blvd., Arlington, VA 22201. Jack N. Merritt, GEN USA (Ret), President; William F. Paul, Chief Executive Officer/Deputy Chairman, Council of Trustees (703) 841-4300.

AIR FORCE ASSOCIATION, 1501 Lee Highway, Arlington, VA 22209. R. E. G. Smith, President; Gen John A. Shaud, USAF (Ret.), Executive Director (703) 247-5800.

AIR FORCE SERGEANTS ASSOCIATION, P.O. Box 50, Temple Hills, MD 20757. CMSgt Claude Klobus (Ret), President; James D. Staton, CMSgt. (Ret), Executive Director (301) 899-3500.

COAST GUARD CHIEF PETTY OFFICERS ASSOCIATION, 5520G Hempstead Way, Springfield, VA 22151. T.R. Scaramastro, Chief Administrator (703) 941-0395.

COAST GUARD ENLISTED ASSOCIATION, 5520G Hempstead Way, Springfield, VA 22151. T.R. Scaramastro, Chief Administrator (703) 941-0395.

ENLISTED ASSOCIATION OF THE NATIONAL GUARD OF THE UNITED STATES, 1219 Prince St., Alexandria, VA 22314, MSGT Blaine Ross, President; MSG Michael P. Cline, USA (Ret), Executive Director 1-800-234-EANG.

FLEET RESERVE ASSOCIATION, 125 N. West Street, Alexandria, VA 22314-2754. James C. Eblen, President; Charles L. Calkins, National Executive Secretary; (703) 683-1400, (800) FRA-1924, FAX (703) 549-6610.

MARINE CORPS ASSOCIATION, P.O. Box 1775, MCCDC, Quantico, VA 22134. LtGen. A. Lukeman, USMC (Ret), Executive Director (703) 640-6161 and 1-800-336-0291.

MARINE CORPS MUSTANG ASSOCIATION, INC., Suite 23, Washington Bldg., 101 Route 130 South, Cinnaminson, NJ 08077. Capt. Bob Richter, USMC (Ret), President/Executive Director., Maj. Bill Max, USMC (Ret), Membership Secretary, (800) 321-USMC, FAX (609) 786-4155.

MARINE CORPS RESERVE OFFICERS ASSOCIATION, INC., 110 N. Royal St., Suite 406, Alexandria, VA 22314. Col. James T. Ragsdale, USMCR, National President; Col. Raymond A. Hord, USMC (Ret.), Executive Director (703) 548-7607.

NATIONAL ASSOCIATION FOR UNIFORMED SERVICES, 5535 Hempstead Way, Springfield, VA 22151. VADM Earl B. Fowler, USN (Ret) and CMSgt Norman Parnes, USAF (Ret), Co-Chairmen; MG James C. Pennington, USA (Ret.), President (703) 750-1342.

NATIONAL GUARD ASSOCIATION OF THE U.S., 1 Massachusetts Ave., N.W., Washington, D.C. 20001. Maj Gen John L. France, USAF (Ret.), President; Maj Gen Edward J. Philbin, ANGUS (Ret.), Executive Director (202) 789-0031, FAX (202) 682-9358.

NAVAL RESERVE ASSOCIATION, 1619 King St., Alexandria, VA 22314. RADM James J. Carey, USNR (Ret.), President; RADM James E. Forrest, SC, USN (Ret.), Executive Director (703) 548-5800.

UNIFORMED SERVICES ALMANAC

NAVAL ENLISTED RESERVE ASSOCIATION, 6703 Farragut Ave., Falls Church, VA 22042. MS1(SS) Eddie Oca, USNR, President (703) 534-1329 (24 hours), 800-776-9020 or FAX (703) 534-3617.

NAVY LEAGUE OF U.S., 2300 Wilson Blvd., Arlington, VA 22201. Hugh H. Mayberry, National President, RADM John R. Dalrymple, USN (Ret), Executive Director.

NON COMMISSIONED OFFICERS ASSOCIATION OF USA, P.O. Box 33610, San Antonio, TX 78265. Charles R. Jackson, President; Thomas F. Silk, Executive Vice President (210) 653-6161.

RESERVE OFFICERS ASSOCIATION, 1 Constitution Ave., N.E., Washington, D.C. 20002. Maj Gen James C. Wahleithner, USAF (Ret), President; MG Roger W. Sandler, AUS (Ret.), Executive Director (202) 479-2200.

THE SOCIETY OF AMERICAN MILITARY ENGINEERS, 607 Prince St., Alexandria, VA 22314. LTG Arthur E. Williams, USA, President; VADM A. Bruce Beran, USCG (Ret.), Executive Director, (800) 336-3097 or (703) 549-3800, FAX (703) 684-0231.

THE RETIRED ENLISTED ASSOCIATION NATIONAL HEADQUARTERS (TREA), 1111 S. Abilene Court, Aurora, CO 80012. Dorothy W. Holmes, National President; John E. Muench, National Executive Director, (800) 338-9337.

THE RETIRED OFFICERS ASSOCIATION, 201 N. Washington St., Alexandria, VA 22314. GEN Louis C. Wagner, Jr., USA (Ret), Chairman; LtGen Michael A. Nelson, USAF (Ret.), President (703) 549-2311.

U.S. ARMY WARRANT OFFICERS ASSOCIATION, 462 Herndon Pkwy., Suite 207, Herndon, VA 22070. CW5 Ray Bell, President; Don Hess, Executive Vice President. (703) 742-7727, FAX (703) 742-7728.

CHIEF WARRANT OFFICERS ASSOCIATION, USCG, c/o James Creek Marina, 200 V St. S.W., Washington, D.C. 20024. CWO Bob Lewis, USCG (Ret), Executive Director, (202) 554-7753.

VA RECOGNIZED NATIONAL SERVICE ORGANIZATIONS

THE AMERICAN LEGION, 1608 K Street, N.W., Washington, D.C. 20006. Daniel A. Ludwig, National Commander; Robert W. Spanogle, National Adjutant (202) 861-2700.

AMERICAN RED CROSS, Military/Social Services, National Hq., 17th and D Street, N.W., Washington, D.C. 20006. Sue A. Richter, Vice President, Military Social Services (202) 737-8300.

AMVETS (American Veterans of World War II-Korea-Vietnam), 4647 Forbes Blvd. Lanham, MD 20706-4380. Kenneth E. Wolford, National Commander; James J. Kenney, National Executive Director, (301) 459-9600.

CATHOLIC WAR VETERANS OF U.S., 441 North Lee St., Alexandria, VA 22314. John H. Walsh, National Commander; Linda M. Torreyson, Executive Assistant (703) 549-3622.

DISABLED AMERICAN VETERANS, 807 Maine Ave., S.W., Washington, D.C. 20024. Thomas A. McMasters, III, National Commander; Arthur H. Wilson, National Adjutant (202) 554-3501.

GOLD STAR WIVES OF AMERICA, INC., 1964 E. Oak Rd, Unit I-4, Vineland, NJ, 08360, JoAnne Danna, National President, (609) 696-4500. Rose Lee, Washington Representative, 540 N. Lombardy St., Arlington, VA 22203, (703) 527-7706.

UNIFORMED SERVICES ALMANAC

JEWISH WAR VETERANS OF THE UNITED STATES, 1811 R Street, N.W., Washington, D.C. 20009; Neil Goldman, National Commander, Col Herb Rosenbleeth, USA (Ret), National Executive Director, (202) 265-6280.

THE MARINE CORPS LEAGUE, 8626 Lee Highway, Suite 201, Fairfax, VA 22031. Paul J. Seton, National Commandant; William "Brooks" Corley, Jr., Executive Director (703) 207-9588.

MILITARY ORDER PURPLE HEART U.S.A. NATIONAL HEADQUARTERS, 5413-B Backlick Rd., Springfield, VA 22151-3960. Carroll M. Fyffe, National Commander; Michael B. Prothero, Adjutant General.

MILITARY ORDER OF THE WORLD WARS, 435 N. Lee Street, Alexandria, VA 22314. Col. B. Dean Smith, USAF (Ret) Commander-in-Chief; MG John S. Guthrie, Jr., AUS (Ret), Chief of Staff (703) 683-4911 FAX: (703) 683-4501.

PARALYZED VETERANS OF AMERICA, 801-18th St., N.W., Washington, D.C. 20006. Richard Grant, President; Gordon H. Mansfield, Executive Director (202) 872-1300.

VETERANS OF FOREIGN WARS, 200 Maryland Ave., N.E., Washington, D.C. 20002. Paul A. Spera, Commander-in-Chief; James R. Currieo, Executive Director (202) 543-2239.

WOMEN'S ARMY CORPS VETERANS ASSOCIATION, 2221 Atkinson, Detroit, MI 48206, Lurlene Dokes, National President.

OTHER NATIONAL SERVICE ORGANIZATIONS

AMERICAN EX-PRISONERS OF WAR, 3201 E. Pioneer Pkwy, Suite 40, Arlington, TX 76010-5396. Larry Moses, National Commander, Clydie J. Morgan, National Adjutant (817) 649-2979.

AMERICAN MILITARY RETIREES ASSOC., INC., Administrative Office, 68 Clinton St., Plattsburgh, NY 12901-2818. COL David G. Fitz-Enz, USA (Ret) President; Robert W. Roe, Executive Director (518) 563-9479, (800) 424-2969.

AMERICAN RETIREES ASSOCIATION HQS., 7564 Trade St., San Diego, CA 92121, (619) 239-9000. Washington, D.C. Office: 2009 N. 14th St., Suite 300, Arlington, VA 22201, Capt Frank W. Ault, USN (Ret), Executive Director, (703) 527-3065.

THE ARMY DISTAFF FOUNDATION, INC., 6200 Oregon Ave., N.W., Washington, D.C. 20015. MG Calvert P. Benedict, USA (Ret.), Executive Director (202) 541-0105.

ASSOCIATION OF PERSONNEL AFFAIRS, P.O. Box 3357, Austin, TX 78764. CDR Byron Varner, USN (Ret), Executive Director, 1-800-950-8297.

THE COMMISSIONED OFFICERS ASSOCIATION OF THE U.S. PUBLIC HEALTH SERVICE, 2111 Wilson Blvd., Suite 321, Arlington, VA 22201. Michael W. Lord, Executive Director (703) 243-1301.

NATIONAL MILITARY FAMILY ASSOCIATION, INC., 6000 Stevenson Ave., Suite 304, Alexandria, VA 22304-3526. Sylvia Kidd, President (703) 823-NMFA.

SOCIETY OF MILITARY WIDOWS, 5535 Hempstead Way, Springfield, VA 22151. Mrs. Kitty Goodman, President (813) 785-5532. Affiliated with the National Association for Uniformed Services.

EDITOR'S NOTE: The above list is not all-inclusive. If any national organization has been omitted or any change of officers or address has occurred, please get in touch with us by November 15 so that the necessary revisions can be made in time for next year's issue of the UNIFORMED SERVICES ALMANAC.

UNIFORMED SERVICES ALMANAC

U.S. SERVICE ACADEMIES

The U.S. Military Academy (1802), U.S. Naval Academy (1845), U.S. Coast Guard Academy (1876), and the U.S. Air Force Academy (1955), offer qualified young applicants, including members of the Armed Forces and their children, opportunities for obtaining a high-quality college education leading to rewarding careers in the service of our country. Applicants must meet not only demanding physical, mental, and academic standards, but must have the character and desire necessary to meet the challenge of a rigorous and demanding program.

Eligibility requirements for all the academies are essentially the same:

Age: Applicant must be at least 17 and not have passed his/her 22nd birthday by July 1 of the year to be admitted as a cadet or midshipman.

Citizenship: Applicant must be a citizen of the United States at the time of entry into the Academy.

Marital Status: Applicant must be unmarried and have no legal dependents and must not be pregnant.

In addition to the basic legal requirements, applicants must also meet certain medical, physical, and academic requirements. Generally, applicants are expected to have above-average high school, college, or preparatory school academic records, and score well on the Scholastic Assessment Test (SAT) or the American College Testing Program (ACT).

Applicants must also pass a very thorough Medical Examination and achieve an acceptable score on a strenuous Physical Aptitude Examination which measures strength, endurance, and agility. The Physical Aptitude Examination is conducted separately and is not a part of the Medical Examination. Candidates are strongly advised to ensure that they are physically fit prior to taking this examination.

Except for the Coast Guard Academy, which tenders appointments solely on the basis of an annual nationwide competition, an applicant must obtain a nomination to be considered for an appointment as a cadet or midshipman. Although there are several nominating categories, the primary source of nominations are from Senators who may nominate from their states at large, and from Representatives who nominate applicants from their districts. The Vice President, Congressional Delegates from the District of Columbia, Guam and the Virgin Islands, and the Governors of Puerto Rico, and American Samoa may also nominate applicants.

Each Senator and Representative is authorized to have at least five cadets or midshipmen at each of the academies at one time. For each vacancy that occurs, the Congressman may nominate a maximum of ten candidates to be considered for the appointment. If the Congressman does not have a vacancy available, he/she will not nominate candidates during that year. The other nominating authorities also have limitations on the number of cadets or midshipmen at the Academies at any one time.

Children of career military personnel — enlisted, warrant, and commissioned, may be appointed by the President of the United States. Up to 100 cadets or midshipmen may be appointed to each of the academies, except for the Coast Guard Academy, under this competitive category. Candidates from this category who have a parent on active duty for at least eight continuous years, retired with retirement pay or deceased, from any of the uniformed services are selected from the best qualified applicants. Children of deceased or 100% VA disabled veterans and children of a parent who is in a "missing status," may also be considered for a competitive appointment. Other competitive categories include enlisted members of the Regular or Reserve components, ROTC and Junior ROTC programs, honor graduates of military or naval schools, and children of Medal of Honor recipients.

At the end of four years, graduates are awarded bachelor of science degrees. Graduates of the four academies become second lieutenants or ensigns in their services and are obliged to serve a six-year tour of active duty. (five year active duty tour for Coast Guard Academy)

Detailed information regarding eligibility and nominating procedures can be obtained by writing to:

Director of Admissions
U.S. Military Academy
606 Thayer Rd.
West Point, NY 10996-1797

HQ USAFA/RRS
2304 Cadet Drive, Suite 200
U.S. Air Force Academy, CO
80840-5025

Director of Admissions
U.S. Naval Academy
117 Decatur Road
Annapolis, MD 21402-5018

Director of Admissions
U.S. Coast Guard Academy
15 Mohegan Ave.
New London, CT 06320-4195

ARMED FORCES RETIREMENT HOMES

UNITED STATES NAVAL HOME

The United States Naval Home (USNH) was relocated in Gulfport, Mississippi in 1976 from Philadelphia where it was first established in 1833. The USNH is a modern 11-story, carpeted and air-conditioned building with 550 rooms.

In 1990, Congressional action incorporated the U.S. Naval Home and the U.S. Soldiers' and Airmen's Home into an independent establishment in the Executive branch of the Federal Government known as the Armed Forces Retirement Home. Each facility of the Retirement Home, maintained as a separate establishment of the Retirement Home for administrative purposes, shall be operated by a Director under the overall supervision of the Armed Forces Retirement Home Board.

Persons eligible for residency are those who served as members of the Armed Forces, at least one-half of whose service was not active commissioned service (other than as a Warrant Officer or Limited-Duty Officer), and who meet the following additional criteria:

(1) Persons who—(a) are 60 years of age or over; and (b) were discharged or released from service in the Armed Forces under honorable conditions after 20 or more years of active service.

(2) Persons who are determined under rules prescribed by the Retirement Home Board to be incapable of earning a livelihood because of a service connected disability incurred in the line of duty in the Armed Forces.

(3) Persons who—(a) served in a war theater during a time of war declared by Congress or were eligible for hostile fire special pay under section 310 or title 37, United States Code; (b) were discharged or released from service in the Armed Forces under honorable conditions; and (c) are determined under rules prescribed by the Retirement Home Board to be incapable of earning a livelihood because of injuries, disease, or disability.

(4) Persons who — (a) served in a women's component of the Armed Forces before the enactment of the Women's Armed Services Integration Act of 1948; and (b) are determined under rules prescribed by the Retirement Home Board to be eligible for admission because of *compelling personal circumstances.*

Coast Guard veterans who had service during wartime while the Coast Guard was operated as part of the Navy are also eligible for admission.

The eligibility of Active-Status Reservists for residency at USNH will fall into category three. "Active Duty" is defined in part as full-time in the active military service of the United States. Such full time duty includes the annual active duty for training that military reservists must fulfill. It does not, however, include reserve inactive-duty training commonly known as reserve drills, nor does it include years spent as a drilling reservist; the key is active duty time only.

User Fees Paid By Residents. The U.S. Naval Home will collect from each resident a monthly user fee for residency. The fee will be a percentage of Federal payments made to a resident. A person who becomes a resident of the Naval Home will be required to pay a monthly fee that is equal to 25 % of Federal payments made to the resident.

Although residents must be self-sufficient, mentally and physically, at time of admission, they are provided for by the USNH thereafter either in the Home's limited medical care facility, or, at the nearby Keesler Air Force Base or the Veterans Administration Hospitals in Biloxi, Mississippi (if eligible and when available). *All USNH residents are solely responsible for the cost of any medical care required beyond the capabilities of the Home.*

Financial responsibility for medical care. There is no charge for medical care rendered by the USNH medical care facility. Residents are financially responsible for care received from other medical facilities or from visiting civilian medical practitioners. Residents maintain medical insurance including a supplemental policy to cover medical care in the event that military/veteran medical facilities are not available.

In addition to medical care, the USNH also provides residents with a private room, board, movie theater, exercise room, swimming pool, library, hobby shops, and other recreational facilities. Other services, such as barber and beauty shops, are also available.

The single rooms are furnished with a bed, desk, night stand, lamp and a chair. Each room has a half-bath with lavatory and toilet. Showers and baths are located on each floor.

Additional information and applications for admission may be obtained by writing to the Director, United States Naval Home, 1800 Beach Drive, Gulfport, Mississippi 39507-1597 (1-800-332-3527).

UNITED STATES SOLDIERS' AND AIRMEN'S HOME

Nestled in the heart of our Nation's Capital, is 300-acres of secure-park-like setting, in which nearly 2,000 servicemen and women have found a retirement home.

No longer called "The Old Soldiers' Home," USSAH has evolved from an "asylum for the old and disabled soldier," to a retirement community that offers a secure and comfortable life-style filled with activity. Although called the Soldiers' and Airmen's Home, the Home is now open to eligible veterans from all the services.

UNIFORMED SERVICES ALMANAC

Whereas "inmates" once lived in eight-man squad rooms, most of today's members have private rooms, and many have private baths and walk-in closets. Ongoing renovation will enable all members to have private baths and amenities such as cable TV, air-conditioning and elevators.

Three meals a day are served in a modern cafeteria that seats 1,400 people. The facility offers a wide variety of food, including short-order, special diet lines, and a salad bar.

Health care services range from community nursing and assisted living for those in the dormitories, to primary, intermediate, and skilled care at the King Health Center. This 385-bed, well-equipped, long-term care facility is dedicated exclusively to the members at no additional cost and is accredited by the Joint Commission on Accreditation of Healthcare Organizations.

A city within a city, USSAH has its own laundry, banking facilities, and post office, as well as three chapels, a large gymnasium and a six-lane bowling alley. Residents can get their shirts cleaned, their pants pressed and then hop the Home's private bus for a day at one of the Smithsonian museums, the Capitol, or any of the many local attractions in the area.

For those interested in hobbies, there are arts and crafts shops that cater to everyone's talents, such as: woodworking, ceramics, photography, oil painting, and picture framing. Near the well-groomed, nine-hole golf course and driving range, are garden plots and two tranquil lakes, which offer sportfishing for Crappie, Bass, Bream and Catfish.

Financed by enlisted servicemembers, and operated exclusively for their benefit, this unique institution is an independent federal agency in the nature of a congressional trust and has never been funded by taxpayers dollars. The trust is supported by active-duty, monthly payroll deductions of $1.00; fines and forfeitures imposed on wayward military members; interest from the trust fund; and a 25 percent user fee paid by the residents on all federal annuities.

Membership of USSAH is made up of veterans from the Armed Services whose active-duty service was at least 50 percent enlisted or warrant officer and who are:

- Retirees at least 60 years of age.
- Veterans unable to earn a livelihood due to service-connected disability.
- Veterans unable to earn a livelihood due to nonservice disability and who served in a war theater.

The Home is, after all, a special place for special people.

For additional information or an application packet call 1-800-422-9988, or write: Admissions Office, USSAH, Washington, D.C. 20317.

RETIREMENT RESIDENCES FOR MILITARY PERSONNEL AND WIDOWS

During the past several years, each service has established Foundations whose major purposes are to provide military widows, retirees, and others who qualify, with housing facilities and other accommodations designed primarily for the aged and those in need of comfort, security, and companionship. The foundations and the residences they maintain are privately endowed and are supported primarily by contributions from wives' clubs, military associations, corporate and foundation gifts, bequests, trusts, and fees. The Air Force Enlisted Men's Widows and Dependents Home Foundations, Inc., receives the main portion of its funding from the annual Air Force Assistance Fund Campaign.

UNIFORMED SERVICES ALMANAC

Knollwood, originally the Army Distaff Hall, was opened in 1962 in Washington, D.C. A continuing care retirement community for retired military officers and their close relatives, it is sponsored and operated by the Army Distaff Foundation. Eligibility for residence has been extended to retired officers (male or female) from any service branch, spouses (and other close relatives) of retired officers, reserve officers with 20 years of active military service, and reserve officers retired under Title III, Title 10, USC. The community includes 190 1- and 2-bedroom independent living apartments, 40 apartments in The Terrace, Knollwood's assisted living unit, and a 50 bed skilled nursing facility. Amenities include scenic grounds, scheduled transportation to Walter Reed Medical Center and nearby commissaries, pool, spa, Wellness Center and 3 dining rooms. For more information about Knollwood, please contact the Army Distaff Foundation at 1-800-541-4255 or 202-541-0149 or write 6200 Oregon Avenue, N.W., Washington, D.C. 20015.

Vinson Hall, located in McLean, Virginia, was established 26 years ago by the Navy Marine Coast Guard Residence Foundation. A Continuing Care Retirement Community, Vinson Hall serves Retired Officers and other affiliated members of the uniformed services. Residency is also open to their spouses, widowed spouses, parents and other individuals on a case by case basis. There are 179 apartments, an infirmary, dining room, chapel and many other amenities. Also located on the same grounds is the Arleigh Burke Pavilion which includes an assisted living center, intermediate and skilled nursing care. The newly opened memory-impaired unit offers guided independence. Financing options include a 90% refundable plan. For more information call (703) 536-4344 or 1-800-451-5121 or write to Vinson Hall Corp., 6251 Old Dominion Drive, McLean, VA 22101-4818.

Air Force Village, located in San Antonio, Texas has been open since 1970 to widows of Air Force officers, retired Air Force officers (single or with spouse) and young widows of Air Force officers with or without children during an adjustment period of up to one year. Air Force Village is owned and operated by the Air Force Village Foundation, Inc. There are 374 apartment living units and a health care facility including a licensed skilled care 112 bed nursing home. Air Force Village II, located just seven miles from Air Force Village, opened in February 1987, with similar amenities and services. Village II has 388 residential apartments and construction of a 20 unit garden home addition is planned. Retired officers of all Uniformed Services are eligible for residency at both villages. This policy may change in the future at the discretion of the Board of Trustees. Additional information regarding costs, applications procedures, and other details may be obtained by writing to the Air Force Village Foundation, Inc. 5100 John D. Ryan Blvd., San Antonio, TX 78245-3502 or calling 1-800-762-1122.

The Air Force Enlisted Men's Widows and Dependents Home Foundation, Inc., has as its primary objective, the providing of homes for the widows of Air Force enlisted persons. The foundation is the parent organization of **Teresa Village,** a 123-unit complex, and **Bob Hope Village,** which consists of 256 apartments. Any widow or widower, age 55 or older, whose spouse was a retired enlisted person from the Regular Air Force, Air National Guard, or Air Force Reserve, is eligible to reside in the facilities. Younger widows may be admitted under special circumstances, and a limited number of retired couples, age 62 or older, whose spouse is 55 years of age or older, may be admitted. Write to the Air Force Enlisted Men's Widows and Dependents Home Foundation, Inc., 92 Sunset Lane, Shalimar, FL 32579 for additional details regarding costs, application procedures, or other information, or you may call (904) 651-3766/1401/9858.

HOME-BUYING FOR THE SERVICE MEMBER

There are numerous ways whereby service personnel can make arrangements for purchasing and financing of a home, including regular FHA loans, VA loans, and financing. Neither HUD or VA lends money, builds houses, or furnishes house plans. One exception is that VA has a direct loan program for "specially adapted housing" for veterans with specific disabilities.

Active Duty VA Loan Benefits. In order to be entitled to VA loan benefits, persons who originally *enlist* in a regular component of the Armed Forces after September 7, 1980 or who *enter on active duty* (e.g., as commissioned officers) after October 16, 1981, must complete the lesser of: 24 continuous months of active duty; or, the full period for which the person was called or ordered to active duty. These minimum service requirements do not apply to those members on active duty who have completed 181 days of service, or those who are discharged or released from active duty for the convenience of the government or for disability incurred or aggravated in line of duty, or, those who have a compensable service-connected disability.

FHA In-Service Insured Loans. Section 222 provides mortgage insurance for loans financing the purchase of a single family dwelling or condominium unit by service members on active duty, in the Coast Guard or employees of the National Oceanic and Atmospheric Administration.

FHA Regular Insured Loans. Most FHA insured mortgages will be subject to an upfront mortgage insurance premium and an annual premium. The upfront premium may be added to the mortgage amount and financed. The annual premium will be calculated on the unpaid principal balance. The standard mortgage limit for a single family home under this program is $78,600. Certain areas are eligible for mortgage amounts ranging up to $155,250 because of the high cost of housing.

Special terms are available for qualified veterans purchasing single-family homes. The veteran must get a Certificate of Eligibility from the VA to obtain these special terms. Qualifications are less stringent than those for eligibility under the VA home loan programs, and there is no limit on the number of times an eligible veteran can use his/her eligibility in HUD programs.

FHA and VA Graduated Payment Mortgage. HUD insures and VA guarantees mortgages to facilitate early homeownership to households that expect their incomes to rise substantially. These "graduated payment" mortgages allow homeowners to make smaller monthly payments initially and to increase their size gradually over time.

VA Loans are guaranteed by the Government through the Department of Veterans Affairs in the maximum amount of $50,750, except that a smaller guaranty applies to mobile or manufactured home loans. Since this is a guaranteed loan, there is no monthly insurance premium paid by the borrower. However, a fee of up to 2.0% of the loan amount will be collected by the VA on all guaranteed loans except interest reduction refinances, vendee loans, direct loans, manufactured home loans and loan assumptions, with the exception of those to veterans receiving VA compensation for service-connected disabilities. As of October 28, 1992, adjustable rate mortgages may be included in the VA home loan program. No interest rate will be set for VA loans, but members may negotiate the rate as well as points with the lender. VA points will no longer have to be paid by the seller but can be paid by the buyer or seller or split between the two. There is no maximum total loan amount nor down payment set by Department of Veterans Affairs.

• **Conventional Financing.** Requires up to 30% down payment, but unlike FHA and VA financing the purchaser can use a second trust as an aid to making the purchase — especially to meet the downpayment. The conventional loan is neither insured nor guaranteed by the Government. It is a loan between the home buyer and the lender with the risk assumed entirely by such lender although such risk is minimized through the use of private Mortgage Insurance.

• There are also many homes for sale with assumable VA and FHA loans, where the financing is already set up and paid on for several years. One can assume the remaining loan, take over the payments, and either pay cash above the exiting first trust balance, or pay a lesser amount of cash and negotiate a second trust to make up the difference.

FHA AND VA ASSISTANCE

FHA and VA regulations require that housing provided with FHA or VA assistance be made available without discrimination because of race, color, creed, national origin, religion, sex, handicap, or familial status. Discrimination in the sale, rental, or financing of housing is illegal without regard to whether FHA or VA assistance is involved.

Requirements for Borrower and Property

Requirements for the borrower and for the property are the same for servicemen as they are for civilians who buy homes with mortgages insured under HUD programs. The serviceman or woman as borrower, or mortgagor, must have a good credit standing and be able to make the required down payment, and his or her monthly mortgage payments must bear a proper relation to his or her present and anticipated income and expenses.

Builder's Warranty

When HUD agrees to insure a loan to purchase a home before it is constructed, the builder is required to warrant that the house conforms with HUD or VA approved plans. This warranty is for one year following the date on which title is conveyed to the original buyer or the date on which the house was first occupied, whichever occurs first.

Use and Terms of the Mortgage

The serviceman or woman may use a mortgage insured by HUD or guaranteed by the VA to buy an existing home or build a new home, or buy a unit in a condominium or cooperative project. A veteran may refinance a home he or she already owns and should check with the lender for terms and conditions. The same applies to a veteran with a VA loan. The veteran must certify that he or she is the owner and an occupant of the dwelling.

The amount of a standard FHA mortgage can be up to 97.75% of the lesser of the appraised value or the sales price. If the property is valued at $50,000 or less, the mortgage can be 98.75% of the lesser of the appraised value or sales price. If the mortgage covers a dwelling appraised for mortgage insurance after building begins, and before the house is a year old, the mortgage limit is 90% of value unless the property is covered by an acceptable insurance backed protection plan.

Although the mortgage amount varies, no limit is placed upon the value of the house that can be purchased. The serviceman or woman must, however, make a large enough down payment to cover the difference between the maximum allowable mortgage and the cost of the house.

The longest repayment period the mortgage may have is 30 years (in a few special cases, 35 years). The serviceman or woman repays the mortgage to the lender in regular monthly installments. Each month the total amount he or she pays includes payment to principal, interest, hazard insurance, taxes and special assessments, and miscellaneous items, and a portion of the mortgage insurance premium.

There is no longer a set maximum interest rate on FHA insured home mortgages. Changes in the interest rates on FHA insured mortgages are keyed to the same market forces that determine conventional rates. The current maximum mortgage amount is $78,600 up to $155,250 in certain designated high-cost areas. Once a mortgage is insured, it continues to bear interest at the rate or rates set forth in the mortgage note unless it is insured under the Adjustable Rate Mortgage (ARM) program. An ARM is subject to an annual adjustment.

Mortgage Insurance Premium

On all mortgages that it insures, HUD now charges an upfront MIP and an annual premium. (Contact the local FHA office for further information.)

VA Funding Fee

Effective October 1, 1993, a fee of up to 2% of the loan amount was authorized to be collected by VA in connection with all guaranteed loans except interest rate reduction refinances, vendee loans, direct loans, manufactured home loans and loan assumptions, with the exception of those to veterans receiving VA compensation for service connected disabilities.

VA funding fees are 2% of the loan for those who make a down payment under 5% of the property's cost; 1.50% for a down payment of between 5% and 10%; and 1.25% for a down payment of 10% or more.

Multiple users (2nd time and subsequent users), VA funding fees are 3% of the loan for those who make a down payment under 5% of property cost; 1.5% when down payments are between 5% but less than 10% and 1.25 with a 10% or higher down payment.

Current VA mortgage holders who desire to refinance their loans to decrease the interest rate will only be charged a 0.5% funding fee. Those who obtain home improvement loans will pay a 1.25% funding fee. Loans for manufactured homes either for the home only, lot only, or home and lot will pay a 1% VA funding fee.

Selected Reservists with six years of service either on active duty, in the reserves, or a combination, will be eligible for VA home loans for the first time. Prior to the enactment of P.L. 102-547, reservists must have served a prescribed length of time on active duty to qualify. VA funding fees for Selected Reservists will be somewhat higher than for other VA loan recipients. A 2.75% funding fee will be required for loans when the down payment less than 5%; 2.25% when down payments are between 5% and 10%; and 2% with a 10% or higher down payment.

UNIFORMED SERVICES ALMANAC

SELECTED PERSONNEL STATISTICS

ACTIVE DUTY MILITARY PERSONNEL BY GRADE AND SERVICE

Grade	Army	Navy	Marine Corps	Air Force	Total DoD
Commissioned Officers					
O-10	11	11	3	10	35
O-9	39	21	9	34	103
O-8	97	74	22	90	283
O-7	151	106	34	140	431
O-6	3,751	3,314	626	4,158	11,849
O-5	9,421	7,084	1,637	10,659	28,801
O-4	14,127	11,189	3,161	15,516	43,993
O-3	25,088	21,056	5,457	32,817	84,418
O-2	8,362	7,162	2,859	7,551	25,934
O-1	9,610	6,383	2,044	7,469	25,506
Warrant Officers					
W-5	401	0	34		435
W-4	1,447	430	299		2176
W-3	2,982	922	574		4478
W-2	5,656	942	867		7465
W-1	1,886	5	156		2047
Total Officers	83,029	58,699	17,782	78,444	237,954
Enlisted					
E-9	3,258	3,282	1,394	3,175	11,109
E-8	10,966	8,181	3,354	6,307	28,808
E-7	39,822	27,677	8,779	32,997	109,275
E-6	59,120	66,349	13,770	40,994	180,233
E-5	80,276	82,500	21,378	77,002	261,156
E-4	127,554	73,991	30,883	84,223	316,651
E-3	50,617	56,486	45,667	43,461	196,231
E-2	29,881	32,139	19,748	18,603	100,371
E-1	19,921	20,292	11,806	11,176	63,195
Total Enl.	421,415	370,897	156,779	317,938	1,267,029
Grand Total	504,444	429,596	174,561	396,382	1,504,983

As of September 30, 1995

AVERAGE TIME IN SERVICE FOR PROMOTION BY SERVICE
[YEARS] (As of September 30, 1995)

GRADE	ARMY	NAVY	USAF	USMC
O-7	26.7	26.7	24.8	26.2
O-6	21.2	19.4	19.8	21.9
O-5	16.9	14.4	15.3	17.4
O-4	11.5	9.4	10.7	11.8
O-3	4.6	3.6	3.5	4.9
O-2	2.9	2.0	1.8	2.0
W-5	22.7	0.0		12.7
W-4	14.4	7.7		8.9
W-3	8.7	3.8		5.6
W-2	2.9	0.2		0.8
E-9	21.0	19.3	21.2	21.7
E-8	17.7	16.1	18.5	18.3
E-7	13.0	11.9	15.2	14.4
E-6	8.4	8.5	12.3	10.1
E-5	4.6	4.7	7.1	5.4
E-4	1.9	2.1	2.8	2.6

UNIFORMED SERVICES ALMANAC

ACTIVE DUTY FEMALE MILITARY PERSONNEL
BY GRADE AND SERVICE

Grade	Army	Navy	Marine Corps	Air Force	Total DoD
\multicolumn{6}{c}{Commissioned Officers}
O-8	0	0	1	1	2
O-7	3	4	0	5	12
O-6	210	214	11	204	639
O-5	947	888	50	1,062	2,947
O-4	1,982	1,541	102	2,333	5,958
O-3	3,814	2,964	153	5,414	12,345
O-2	1,513	1,155	104	1,516	4,288
O-1	1,728	1,006	145	1,533	4,412
\multicolumn{6}{c}{Warrant Officers}
W-5	1	0	1		2
W-4	25	5	14		44
W-3	114	37	34		185
W-2	276	81	62		419
W-1	208	1	13		222
Officer Total	10,821	7,896	690	12,068	31,475
\multicolumn{6}{c}{Enlisted}
E-9	113	86	20	192	411
E-8	793	410	121	582	1,906
E-7	4,224	1,931	437	3,510	10,102
E-6	6,539	5,314	719	4,890	17,462
E-5	9,986	8,125	1,209	10,087	29,407
E-4	19,338	8,744	1,422	15,993	45,497
E-3	7,774	10,226	1,906	9,628	29,534
E-2	4,961	5,877	1,074	4,090	16,002
E-1	2,937	3,661	494	2,506	9,598
Total Enl.	56,665	44,374	7,402	51,478	159,919
Grand Total	67,486	52,270	8,092	63,546	191,394

As of September 30, 1995

ACTIVE DUTY MILITARY PERSONNEL AND THEIR DEPENDENTS

	Military Personnel	Spouses	Children	Parents & All Others	Total Dependents
ARMY					
Officers	83,781	65,245	107,880	2,269	175,394
Enlisted	448,450	242,282	430,292	6,273	678,847
Total	532,231	307,527	538,172	8,542	854,241
NAVY					
Officers	59,309	45,306	62,710	273	108,289
Enlisted	391,269	229,817	328,356	3,296	561,469
Total	450,578	275,123	391,066	3,569	669,758
USMC					
Officers	17,907	12,837	20,073	40	32,950
Enlisted	154,822	65,660	89,728	380	155,768
Total	172,729	78,497	109,801	420	188,718
USAF					
Officers	79,013	60,815	86,398	671	147,884
Enlisted	332,966	218,794	278,410	2,270	499,474
Total	411,797	279,609	364,808	2,941	647,358
DoD					
Officers	240,010	184,203	277,061	3,253	464,517
Enlisted	1,327,507	756,553	1,126,786	12,219	1,895,558
Total	1,567,517	940,756	1,403,847	15,472	2,360,075

As of June 30, 1995

UNIFORMED SERVICES ALMANAC

RETIREES BY STATE (As of September 30, 1995)

State	Army	Navy	Marine Corps	Air Force	Total DoD
Alabama	22,911	6,445	1,507	15,090	45,953
Alaska	2,477	583	132	4,006	7,198
Arizona	13,022	7,253	2,717	22,117	45,109
Arkansas	7,796	4,660	976	10,517	23,949
California	37,158	85,618	18,473	65,393	206,642
Colorado	16,029	4,940	1,219	20,751	42,939
Connecticut	3,002	5,023	591	2,210	10,826
Delaware	1,455	857	185	3,734	6,231
District of Columbia	2,180	730	161	1,369	4,440
Florida	42,468	55,461	7,394	65,302	170,625
Georgia	36,522	10,153	3,125	19,543	69,343
Guam	567	789	70	491	1,917
Hawaii	5,568	3,851	918	3,441	13,778
Idaho	2,260	2,346	459	4,423	9,488
Illinois	10,306	7,607	1,764	11,566	31,243
Indiana	8,593	4,166	1,268	6,308	20,335
Iowa	3,506	2,428	551	2,864	9,349
Kansas	8,360	2,817	718	6,228	18,123
Kentucky	13,367	3,155	871	4,845	22,238
Louisiana	9,359	4,917	1,271	11,482	27,029
Maine	2,797	3,800	506	3,714	10,817
Maryland	15,970	11,926	1,875	11,772	41,543
Massachusetts	7,512	6,177	1,301	6,541	21,531
Michigan	8,922	5,596	1,459	8,054	24,031
Minnesota	5,119	3,740	829	4,595	14,283
Mississippi	6,643	5,328	899	10,118	22,988
Missouri	12,508	6,615	1,934	10,921	31,978
Montana	1,770	1,455	343	3,047	6,615
Nebraska	2,209	1,695	338	7,611	11,853
Nevada	4,259	4,958	1,307	11,832	22,356
New Hampshire	2,735	2,012	421	3,994	9,162
New Jersey	10,712	5,613	1,271	5,507	23,103
New Mexico	5,355	2,826	682	10,736	19,599
New York	14,203	8,364	2,313	10,943	35,823
North Carolina	27,928	10,534	9,042	16,582	64,086
North Dakota	841	423	67	2,032	3,363
Ohio	11,881	7,436	2,291	17,317	38,925
Oklahoma	13,157	4,321	1,125	13,441	32,044
Oregon	5,653	6,755	1,390	6,653	20,451
Pennsylvania	17,824	11,502	3,181	11,954	44,461
Puerto Rico	7,066	381	141	835	8,423
Rhode Island	1,361	3,377	262	930	5,930
South Carolina	16,449	11,979	2,647	15,645	46,720
South Dakota	1,350	708	126	2,804	4,988
Tennessee	16,879	9,436	2,189	11,732	40,236
Texas	62,155	22,098	5,771	77,294	167,318
Utah	3,042	1,717	410	5,365	10,534
Vermont	1,312	634	128	945	3,019
Virginia	36,282	43,733	6,862	23,550	110,427
Virgin Islands	164	56	6	47	273
Washington	22,104	20,510	2,149	20,137	64,900
West Virginia	3,776	2,193	670	2,867	9,506
Wisconsin	6,136	3,677	922	4,628	15,363
Wyoming	895	662	127	2,173	3,857
Other	10,485	7,152	813	8,807	27,257
Total	614,360	453,188	100,167	636,803	1,804,518

LOCATION OF MILITARY DEPENDENTS

Location	ARMY	NAVY	USMC	USAF	Total DoD
Continental US	724,763	619,298	168,217	545,939	2,058,217
Alaska	6,606	435	28	15,213	22,282
Hawaii	13,213	14,325	5,889	6,727	40,154
US Terr./Spec. Locations	736	7,958	148	2,687	11,529
Foreign Countries	108,923	27,742	14,436	76,792	227,893
Total	854,241	669,758	188,718	647,358	2,360,075

As of June 30, 1995

UNIFORMED SERVICES ALMANAC

WHERE THEY SERVE
(As of June 30, 1995)

	ARMY	NAVY	MARINE CORPS	AIR FORCE	TOTAL DoD
UNITED STATES, U.S. TERRITORIES, SPECIAL LOCATIONS					
Continental United States	388,550	224,263	136,262	323,482	1,072,557
Alaska	7,019	1,076	19	9,987	18,101
Hawaii	18,113	10,957	6,177	4,646	39,893
Guam	47	3,389	46	2,129	5,611
Johnston Atoll	269	2	0	13	284
Puerto Rico	287	2,292	103	36	2,718
Transients	9,840	12,988	6,488	6,354	35,670
Other	54	5	0	1	54
Afloat	0	146,162	0	0	146,162
TOTAL	424,173	401,134	149,095	346,661	1,321,063
EUROPE					
Belgium	1,055	103	30	503	1,691
Germany	62,606	282	137	16,238	79,263
Greece	21	257	59	173	510
Greenland	0	0	0	122	122
Iceland	3	1,306	75	906	2,290
Italy	2,747	4,613	542	3,980	11,882
Netherlands	442	15	15	294	766
Portugal	25	64	9	981	1,079
Spain	11	2,483	122	218	2,834
Turkey	296	27	18	2,846	3,187
United Kingdom	232	1,859	204	11,175	13,470
Other	89	46	192	86	388
Afloat	0	6,119	3,832	0	9,951
TOTAL	67,539	17,174	5,235	37,522	127,470
EAST ASIA and PACIFIC					
Australia	19	64	11	268	362
Japan	1,961	7,025	15,848	15,176	40,010
Republic of Korea	25,697	286	64	8,672	34,719
Singapore	5	107	8	44	164
Philippines	15	93	11	11	130
Thailand	50	9	21	27	107
Other	64	87	64	41	245
Afloat	0	14,240	0	0	14,240
TOTAL	27,811	21,911	16,027	24,228	89,977
NORTH AFRICA, NEAR EAST and SOUTH ASIA					
Bahrain	11	420	20	13	464
Diego Garcia	8	752	83	24	867
Egypt	1,001	34	31	61	1,127
Kuwait	518	17	8	7	550
Saudi Arabia	1,121	44	54	211	1,430
Other	78	22	120	59	257
Afloat	0	1,535	0	0	1,535
TOTAL	2,737	3,248	316	375	6,676
WESTERN HEMISPHERE					
Bermuda	1	359	0	0	360
Canada	18	97	11	96	222
Cuba (Guantanamo)	364	1,490	1,328	1	3,183
Haiti	1,670	0	11	0	1,681
Honduras	234	2	13	39	288
Panama	5,847	399	170	2,149	8,565
Suriname	145	0	6	0	151
Other	252	122	226	65	665
Afloat	0	1,697	0	0	1,697
TOTAL	8,531	4,166	1,765	2,350	16,812

UNIFORMED SERVICES ALMANAC

EDUCATIONAL LEVEL DISTRIBUTION BY SERVICE
(As of September 30, 1995)

	Non HS Grad	HS Grad	B.A. Degree	M.A. Degree	Ph D.
ARMY					
OFF	0	486	40,308	26,754	767
WO	0	6,316	2,944	412	3
EM	1,227	384,723	14,829	1,139	62
TOTAL	1,227	391,525	58,081	28,305	832
NAVY					
OFF	0	891	30,434	18,108	547
WO	0	2,436	159	62	21
EM	8,772	335,776	8,827	402	17
TOTAL	8,772	339,103	39,420	18,572	585
USMC					
OFF	35	618	12,276	2,695	63
WO	1	1,405	256	40	1
EM	176	146,748	1,760	179	5
TOTAL	212	148,771	14,292	2,914	69
USAF					
OFF	0	340	35,133	38,975	1,358
WO	0	0	0	0	0
EM	31	302,469	12,829	1,661	24
TOTAL	31	302,809	47,962	40,636	1,382
USCG					
OFF	10	803	4,039	737	76
WO	20	1,254	72	11	0
EM	448	25,883	636	29	4
TOTAL	478	27,940	4,747	777	80
TOTALS					
OFF	45	4,683	122,190	87,269	2,811
WO	21	9,866	3,431	525	25
EM	10,654	1,195,599	38,881	3,410	112
TOTAL	10,720	1,210,148	164,502	91,204	2,948

ACTIVE DUTY MILITARY PERSONNEL BY ETHNIC GROUP
(As of September 30, 1995)

	White No.	%	AI/AN No.	%	AA/PI No.	%	Black No.	%	Hisp No.	%	O/U No.	%
ARMY												
OFF	67068	80.6	409	0.5	2002	2.4	9522	11.4	2625	3.2	1560	1.9
ENL	244912	58.1	2552	0.6	9138	2.2	126838	30.1	23685	5.6	14399	3.4
TOT	311980	61.8	2961	0.6	11140	2.2	136360	27.0	26310	5.2	15959	3.2
NAVY												
OFF	50880	86.7	226	0.4	1721	2.9	3245	5.5	1905	3.2	730	1.2
ENL	250586	67.6	2061	0.6	19804	5.3	68968	18.6	28136	7.6	1368	0.4
TOT	301466	70.2	2287	0.5	21525	5.0	72213	16.8	30041	7.0	2098	0.5
USMC												
OFF	15676	88.2	110	0.6	250	1.4	1029	5.8	642	3.6	75	0.4
ENL	108400	69.1	1342	0.9	2775	1.8	26641	17.0	15853	10.1	1768	1.1
TOT	124076	71.2	1452	0.8	3025	1.7	27670	15.9	16495	9.4	1843	1.1
USAF												
OFF	69299	88.3	310	0.4	1364	1.7	4389	5.6	1549	2.0	1533	2.0
ENL	239958	75.5	1777	0.6	6452	2.0	53614	16.9	13258	4.2	2879	0.9
TOT	309257	78.0	2087	0.5	7816	2.0	58003	14.6	14807	3.7	4412	1.1
USCG												
OFF	6648	91.2	40	0.5	187	2.6	215	3.0	198	2.7	0.0	0.0
ENL	23005	81.3	769	2.7	579	2.0	2166	7.7	1775	6.3	0.0	0.0
TOT	29653	83.3	809	2.3	766	2.2	2381	6.7	1973	5.5	0.0	0.0

Legend: AI = American Indian   AN = Alaskan Native   AA = Asian
PI = Pacific Islander   HISP = Hispanic   O/U = Other/Unknown

UNIFORMED SERVICES ALMANAC

TOTAL RETIRED MILITARY LIFETIME RETIREMENT PAY
(LUMP-SUM EQUIVALENT) (As of January 1, 1996)

PAY GRADE	Over 15	Over 16	Over 17	Over 18	Over 19
COMMISSIONED OFFICERS					
O-10	862,809	983,130	1,040,716	1,096,745	1,151,669
O-9	754,622	869,340	920,108	969,889	1,018,567
O-8	724,437	802,423	849,197	934,095	980,780
O-7	628,802	735,505	778,576	877,110	920,997
O-6	455,164	560,399	593,159	657,188	690,043
O-5	437,232	499,672	528,932	589,608	618,980
O-4	413,025	458,401	485,338	525,464	551,865
O-3	383,139	407,402	431,283	454,448	477,418
O-2	284,216	302,161	319,974	337,328	354,186
O-1	224,145	238,486	252,260	266,025	279,457
COMMISSIONED OFFICERS WITH MORE THAN 4 YEARS ACTIVE SERVICE AS ENLISTED MEMBERS					
O-3E	388,817	413,593	437,676	461,320	484,468
O-2E	329,344	349,918	370,543	390,590	410,021
O-1E	278,538	296,266	313,290	330,455	346,854
WARRANT OFFICERS					
W-5	409,438	435,407	460,926	485,947	510,130
W-4	355,321	369,079	390,596	422,662	443,861
W-3	293,182	321,323	340,027	369,400	388,026
W-2	263,296	289,780	306,606	333,892	350,802
W-1	242,376	267,376	283,066	308,692	324,013
ENLISTED MEMBERS					
E-9	286,909	311,905	329,980	355,717	373,194
E-8	249,027	271,939	287,733	310,162	325,576
E-7	220,835	241,531	255,477	276,700	290,416
E-6	197,636	216,914	229,501	245,487	257,748
E-5	175,611	186,795	197,531	208,368	218,712
E-4	141,546	150,595	159,281	167,876	176,077
E-3	121,283	129,164	136,445	143,974	151,160
E-2	102,489	108,892	115,322	121,478	127,628
E-1	91,329	97,018	102,762	108,262	113,785

See footnotes on page 249.

SENIOR OFFICIALS
THE JOINT CHIEFS OF STAFF

Chairman—General John M. Shalikashvili, USA
Vice Chairman—Admiral William A. Owens, USN
Chief of Staff, US Army—General Dennis J. Reimer, USA
Chief of Naval Operations—Admiral Jeremy M. Boorda, USN
Chief of Staff, US Air Force—General Ronald R. Foglemam, USAF
Commandant of the Marine Corps—General Charles C. Kurlak, USMC
Commandant of the Coast Guard—Admiral Robert E. Kramek, USCG

As of January 1, 1996

KEY CONGRESSIONAL COMMITTEES

SENATE ARMED SERVICES COMMITTEE—Sen. Strom Thurmond, R-SC, Chairman; Sen. Sam Nunn, D-GA, Ranking Minority Member. (202) 224-3871
HOUSE COMMITTEE ON NATIONAL SECURITIES—Rep. Floyd D. Spence, R-SC, Chairman; Rep. Ronald V. Dellums, D-CA, Ranking Minority Member. (202) 225-4151.
SENATE VETERANS AFFAIRS COMMITTEE—Sen. Alan Simpson, R-WY, Chairman; Sen. John D. Rockefeller, D-WV, Ranking Minority Member. (202) 224-9126.
HOUSE VETERANS AFFAIRS COMMITTEE—Rep. Bob Stump, R-AZ, Chairman; Rep. G.V. (Sonny) Montgomery, D-MS, Ranking Minority Member. (202) 225-3527.

As of January 3, 1996

These committees may be addressed by writing to them at the Capitol, Washington D.C. The zip code is 20515 for House committees and 20510 for Senate committees.

UNIFORMED SERVICES ALMANAC

TOTAL MILITARY LIFETIME RETIREMENT PAY
(LUMP-SUM EQUIVALENT) (As of January 1, 1996)

GRADE	Over 20	Over 21	Over 22	Over 23	Over 24	Over 25	Over 26	Over 27	Over 28	Over 29	Over 30
COMMISSIONED OFFICERS
O-10	1,251,130	1,292,115	1,330,968	1,367,109	1,401,013	1,432,101	1,460,608	1,486,730	1,509,945	1,530,689	1,548,453
O-9	1,124,851	1,151,620	1,196,503	1,229,185	1,255,358	1,287,493	1,407,268	1,432,254	1,454,677	1,474,491	1,491,663
O-8	1,065,736	1,100,741	1,161,612	1,193,320	1,222,844	1,250,134	1,274,916	1,297,652	1,318,062	1,336,100	1,351,519
O-7	963,603	995,363	1,025,267	1,053,022	1,079,101	1,103,229	1,125,117	1,145,217	1,163,263	1,178,984	1,199,826
O-6	737,967	762,220	830,413	853,125	903,796	923,813	988,527	1,006,218	1,021,863	1,033,913	1,047,874
O-5	667,473	689,328	734,864	755,022	773,535	790,896	806,575	821,048	833,807	845,309	855,061
O-4	577,551	596,508	614,355	631,075	646,641	661,028	674,472	686,446	697,192	706,688	714,917
O-3	499,564	515,972	531,421	545,894	559,369	571,824	583,246	593,617	602,925	611,151	618,282
O-2	370,510	382,748	394,272	405,069	414,866	424,166	432,699	440,449	447,409	453,329	458,674
O-1	292,245	301,939	311,069	319,361	327,335	334,708	341,224	347,376	352,903	357,559	361,809
COMMISSIONED OFFICERS WITH MORE THAN 4 YEARS ACTIVE SERVICE AS ENLISTED MEMBERS
O-3E	507,057	523,616	539,205	554,070	567,656	580,211	591,970	602,411	611,778	620,284	627,442
O-2E	429,070	443,354	456,539	468,889	480,643	491,260	500,993	510,071	517,989	524,981	531,265
O-1E	363,016	375,104	386,220	396,631	406,579	415,525	423,975	431,411	438,317	444,197	449,285
WARRANT OFFICERS
W-5	533,978	551,463	589,394	605,494	638,355	652,642	693,664	705,989	717,050	726,825	735,298
W-4	479,581	495,224	527,127	541,675	572,318	585,039	623,874	634,902	644,795	653,768	661,333
W-3	421,854	435,710	464,859	477,592	489,448	500,410	528,411	537,675	546,222	553,549	560,118
W-2	378,558	390,938	418,964	430,386	441,021	450,851	459,867	468,054	475,402	481,662	487,298
W-1	351,360	362,819	373,605	383,972	393,371	402,056	410,017	417,486	423,962	429,679	434,858
ENLISTED MEMBERS
E-9	398,261	411,164	445,352	457,229	486,477	496,957	535,012	543,968	551,930	559,139	565,139
E-8	348,955	360,271	392,710	403,210	431,144	440,496	477,733	485,728	493,070	499,296	504,652
E-7	307,822	317,949	349,280	358,495	385,276	393,735	429,716	437,036	443,553	449,275	454,209
E-6	269,684	278,306	286,636	294,136	301,322	307,676	313,695	318,886	323,730	327,763	331,450
E-5	228,823	236,252	243,206	249,680	255,667	261,164	266,165	270,671	274,680	278,199	281,230
E-4	184,421	190,180	195,828	201,088	205,954	210,423	214,492	218,160	221,192	224,067	226,547
E-3	157,997	163,394	168,191	172,656	176,786	180,576	184,025	187,131	189,894	192,318	194,406
E-2	133,043	137,680	141,870	145,517	149,139	152,221	155,263	157,772	160,230	162,397	164,051
E-1	119,043	122,948	126,604	130,009	132,906	135,805	138,445	140,825	142,946	144,180	146,418

NOTE: As a result of certain provisions for advancement on the retired list or under the "Tower Amendment" some individuals would receive amounts differing from those shown above. Figures shown assume that active service and pay service are equal. Military retired pay reflects pay and pay cap increases prior to and including January 1, 1996. Active duty basic pay cap of $9016.80 per month levels out retired pay in upper grades. P.L. 102-484 granted DoD a Temporary Early Retirement Authority (TERA) for selected active duty members with as few as 15 years of service. Their retired pay is subject to reduction factors for service less than 20 years. (See following page) The FY94 Defense Authorization Act extended TERA through September 30, 1999. Assumes entry age 23 for commissioned officers and warrant officers and entry age 20 for enlisted members. Based on military specific actuarial tables, the lump sum equivalent is the amount of money required to be on hand at the time of retirement to pay a lifetime annuity to the retiree. The annuity would increase with inflation annually such that the real interest rate would be 2.75%. Warning: These figures should not be used in property settlements.